HITLER'S AMERICAN FRIENDS

ALSO BY BRADLEY W. HART

George Pitt-Rivers and the Nazis
The Global 1920s: Politics, Economics and Society (with Richard Carr)

HITLER'S AMERICAN FRIENDS

THE THIRD REICH'S · · · · · · · · · ·
· · · · · · · · · SUPPORTERS · · · · · ·
· · · · · · · IN THE UNITED STATES · · · · · ·

BRADLEY W. HART

THOMAS DUNNE BOOKS ≈ ST. MARTIN'S PRESS   NEW YORK

THOMAS DUNNE BOOKS
An imprint of St. Martin's Press

www.thomasdunnebooks.com
www.stmartins.com

Designed by Steven Seighman

The Library of Congress Cataloging-in-Publication Data is available upon request.

ISBN 978-1-250-14895-7 (hardcover)
ISBN 978-1-250-14896-4 (ebook)

Our books may be purchased in bulk for promotional, educational, or business use. Please contact your local bookseller or the Macmillan Corporate and Premium Sales Department at 1-800-221-7945, extension 5442, or by email at MacmillanSpecialMarkets@macmillan.com.

First Edition: October 2018

10 9 8 7 6 5 4 3 2 1

CONTENTS

HITLER'S AMERICAN FRIENDS

INTRODUCTION

On the evening of September 11, 1941, one of America's most famous men took to a stage in Des Moines, Iowa, to discuss the national security issue that was on everyone's mind. Exactly six decades later the date of Lindbergh's speech would be associated with a far different type of threat, but on this night the famed aviator—the first man to fly solo across the Atlantic Ocean, *Time* magazine's first Man of the Year, and once estimated to be the most photographed man in the world—was discussing the war in Europe. The United States was not yet involved in the conflict and, if Lindbergh and his fellow members of the America First Committee had their way, it never would be.

"Lucky Lindy" had been traveling the country for months arguing against American intervention in the war, making the case that the country's geographic separation from Europe and Asia, and its two bordering oceans, were sufficient protection from foreign attack. The United States should prepare for defense, not offense, Lindbergh and his associates believed; and if the country could establish a ring of air and naval bases around its perimeter, it would become an impenetrable fortress. Providing aid to Britain—the last Western European country still fighting the Germans—would simply detract from building up the country's defenses. This was the standard isolationist position before Pearl Harbor: let the Europeans fight their own conflicts and make sure America was sufficiently prepared to stay out of them.[1]

This fateful Iowa evening, however, Lindbergh deviated from the standard script. Perhaps he was full of confidence from becoming the America First

Committee's most popular circuit speaker, receiving so many invitations to towns and cities across the country that there was simply no way he could accept all of them. No doubt he was partially inspired by the Roosevelt administration's recently passed Lend-Lease policy, which had made it through Congress earlier in the year and allowed the president to provide military vehicles, aircraft, and munitions to the ailing Allies. Whatever the exact alignment of reasons and circumstances, Lindbergh chose that night to unveil his own interpretation of American foreign policy. The consequences would haunt him for the rest of his life.

In past speeches, Lindbergh had referred broadly to unnamed "powerful elements" that were seeking to draw the United States into the war, but he left the details up to the listeners' imagination. Tonight, before a crowd of more than seven thousand, he decided to reveal exactly whom he believed was behind the alleged push to war. There were, he told the crowd, three groups that had conspired to draw the country into the conflict: "the British, the Jewish, and the Roosevelt administration." Together, he continued, these groups had executed a plan to draw the country into war gradually by building up its military and then manufacturing a series of "incidents" to "force us into the actual conflict." Britain, he continued, might be able to hold out against the German onslaught. Yet even if it did, there was no hope of invading Europe and liberating France. Under normal circumstances the British government would have made peace with the Germans long ago but was merely holding out to make the United States responsible for the war "financially, as well as militarily."[2] President Franklin D. Roosevelt was simply playing into the hands of the perfidious British.

The bulk of Lindbergh's ire, however, was reserved for the second group he mentioned: the Jews. It was understandable that Jewish Americans sought war against Germany, he claimed, because, "The persecution they suffered in Germany would be sufficient to make bitter enemies of any race." However, "the Jewish groups in this country" should realize that in the event of war "they will be among the first to feel its consequences." Jews themselves, he concluded, presented a unique danger to the country because of their "large ownership and influence in our motion pictures, our press, our radio and our government." Despite the alleged machinations of these groups, Lindbergh reserved hope that they might cease their efforts to push the United States toward war. If that could be managed, he continued, "I believe there will be little danger of our involvement."[3]

Lindbergh's speech was covered by major papers and carried on page 2 of the *New York Times* the following morning. It quickly sparked a firestorm. Was Lindbergh blaming Jews for the outbreak of the war in Europe? Was he claiming that Jews were in control of the Roosevelt administration? These seemed very much like the same claims being made by Adolf Hitler and his fellow Nazis in Berlin. The comparison did not go overlooked. White House press secretary Stephen Early remarked that there was a "striking similarity" between Lindbergh's speech and recent "outpourings from Berlin." New York City mayor Fiorello La Guardia was less sparing in his condemnation, calling the remarks "a carbon copy of a Nazi paper."[4] Jewish groups denounced the slurs and called on Lindbergh to retract the comments, similarly evoking comparisons to the anti-Semitism of the Nazis.[5]

The outrage spanned the mainstream political spectrum. Roosevelt's past and future Republican rivals for the presidency both denounced the remarks. His 1940 opponent, Wendell Willkie, proclaimed himself shocked by Lindbergh's bigotry. "If the American people permit race prejudice to arrive at this critical moment, they little deserve to preserve democracy," Willkie remarked.[6] Roosevelt's future opponent in 1944, Thomas Dewey, similarly told a Republican Party picnic that Lindbergh had committed "an inexcusable abuse of the right of freedom of speech. . . . When the religion or race of any individual or group is made a part of the discussion of domestic or foreign policy, that is a challenge to our freedoms," he continued.[7]

Faced with growing pressure from all corners, the America First Committee's leaders—who had not reviewed Lindbergh's speech prior to delivery—were forced to put out a statement asserting that the organization was not anti-Semitic and blaming the interventionists (those who sought to take the United States into the war or, at a minimum, provide additional aid to the Allies) for inserting "the race issue" into the "discussion of war or peace." The attacks on Lindbergh, they claimed, were simply a distraction from bigger issues.[8] This halfhearted explanation did little to calm the controversy, with the *New York Times* noting in an editorial that the Committee had not actually disowned Lindbergh's sentiments about Jewish Americans, and "By not disowning them it associates itself with them. . . . What is being attacked is the tolerance and brotherhood without which our liberties will not survive. What is being exposed to derision and contempt is Americanism itself."[9]

Behind the scenes, however, the Committee was seeing a grassroots outpouring of support that very much contradicted the stories being seen by readers of the *Times*. In the Committee's mail room, at least 85 percent of the letters being received were supportive of Lindbergh, in part because of the anti-Semitic undertones of his speech. Some messages were so extreme in their racist language that the Committee did not see fit to even respond, but others came from regional leaders of their own organization and other paid-up members. Lindbergh was clearly far from being the only America First member to harbor such views about who was really responsible for the war.

The emerging controversy between the "respectable" voices within the America First Committee's leadership who saw the need to denounce Lindbergh, and the rank-and-file membership, was symptomatic of the wider divisions in the United States before Pearl Harbor. Lindbergh was just one of a wide range of figures who argued positions ranging from isolationism to the establishment of closer relations with Nazi Germany and, in the most extreme cases, the adoption of Nazi policies in the United States. These groups and individuals often did not get along with one another: it was supposedly forbidden for a member of the German American Bund—the nation's largest and most prominent Nazi-emulating mass organization—to join the America First Committee, or so the America Firsters claimed.[10] Yet these organizations were working toward many of the same goals whether they were aware of it or not. The America First Committee' goal was arguing to keep the United States from entering the war in Europe, an objective perfectly in line with the intentions of the German government and, in fact, the Bund itself. The German embassy in Washington, DC, for its part, instructed one of its agents to support and promote America First because it was "the best thing you can do for our cause".[11] Whether they intended to do so or not—or were even aware of it—the leaders of America First had become an important asset to Hitler's government.

The German government was far from wrong in its belief that the United States might be potentially kept out of the war in Europe. There were even some indicators that Americans, however unlikely it might seem, might even be receptive to National Socialism itself. In June 1938, Gallup polled Americans on their views of the respective merits of fascism and communism, asking them which "you think is worse." While nearly half of respondents offered no answer, 32 percent thought communism was the worse ideology. Only 23 percent saw fascism as more destructive. Seven months later, Gallup asked Americans, "If you *had* to choose between Fascism and Communism, which would you choose?" Around half again offered no answer, but among those who did, fascism and communism tied at 26 percent each.[12] Though this result was a major decline from March 1937, when a full 45 percent of respondents who had recently read about politics willingly chose fascism as their answer (with just 29 percent responding with communism), a level of comfort with the concept of fascism endured.[13] The United States was not at risk of an imminent fascist takeover in the late 1930s, but there was certainly fertile terrain in which dictatorship might be able to take root.

More important was American public opinion related to the war itself. Intervention versus isolationism was the most potent political issue from late 1939 until Pearl Harbor, dividing friends and families against one another in a way that would not again be seen until the Vietnam War era. The isolationists, led by Lindbergh and some of the country's leading congressmen, argued that America had no business getting involved in the war. Any form of intervention, they argued, would inevitably result in young men dying on faraway battlefields and financial ruin at home.

President Roosevelt and his administration led the interventionist side, arguing that Americans could not afford to sit the war out, lest the Germans and Japanese become unstoppably powerful and a direct threat to the United States. This became more than an academic argument when France fell to the Nazis in the summer of 1940 and Britain was left to face the Nazi onslaught alone. With London being bombed nightly and the British Expeditionary Force barely making it out of Dunkirk, there was no guarantee that Britain would not become the next Nazi-occupied country. If Britain were to fall, would America be next? No one knew. In August 1940, Gallup asked Americans if they thought Hitler would invade the United States if Britain fell under Nazi jackboots. Opinion was evenly split, with 42 percent believing the Nazis would invade the United States and 45 percent disagreeing.[14]

Public opinion was equally split on what the United States should actually do under these circumstances. In 1940, the British ambassador to the United States, Lord Lothian, told a friend in London that American public opinion was "95% against Hitler and 95% against being drawn into the war, but as the fear complex dies away, thinking Americans are beginning at last to ask themselves seriously about their own future if the Allies don't win the war."[15] This assessment was not far off the mark. A year before Pearl Harbor, 79 percent of Americans said they wanted their country to send supplies and equipment to Britain, but only 11 percent wanted the US military to actually help defend the country.[16] Most Americans believed sending aid would be beneficial to their own interests: in January 1941, 57 percent of respondents told Gallup sending aid to the British would help keep the United States out of the war.[17] "U.S. is still extremely friendly to the Allies and vehemently against both Hitler and Stalin, but they will not abandon neutrality until their own vital interests are affected in some obvious way," Lothian presciently wrote in January 1940.[18]

Favorable polling numbers were certainly good news for the British, but London was also aware that maintaining favorable American public opinion was a delicate task. In February 1941, a *Fortune* magazine survey reported that a full 33 percent of respondents believed the most prominent advocates of sending aid to Britain were propagandists, not patriotic Americans (a plurality of 48 percent disagreed and thought they were patriots).[19] The skepticism toward Britain evident in findings such as this meant the country's spokespeople had to be very careful not to push their case too hard, lest their American advocates lose credibility. Accordingly, the British Foreign Office issued a general prohibition on any form of public relations activity in the United States before the outbreak of war, "on account of the great sensitiveness of America to any suggestions of propaganda," as one senior government minister put it in 1939.[20] American public opinion was simply too important to risk on such a potentially amateurish endeavor. "The average Briton seems to think that what is needed in the U.S. is a flood of British speakers sent over to tell the United States what it ought to do," Lothian reported in mid-1940. "That, of course, you will understand, is both futile and harmful."[21] Nothing could build favorable American opinion, he continued, "except events. . . . The public does not pay much attention to publicists and Ambassadors," he concluded, "because it prefers wishful thinking, and if a foreigner does too much he is dismissed as a foreign propagandist and the American public is warned not to pay any attention to what he says."[22]

The Germans, for their part, had much simpler objectives. Hitler's government was not seeking aid from the United States. The entire goal of Nazi propaganda was to encourage apathy and confusion by sowing discord, discrediting the British, and turning Americans against one another. There was no positive case for action that needed to be built; on the contrary, the Germans were hoping to dissuade the United States government from any action at all. Nazi propagandists could therefore be ham-handed, aggressive, and contradictory in their approaches. As will be seen, this even meant *not* actively helping some of the key figures who were pushing pro-German views, out of fear that it might inadvertently harm their credibility. The entire German objective was to sow enough confusion and discord that the American people would grow weary and simply want to check out of the world events.

The Nazis and their supporters jumped on this task with enthusiasm. Washington newspaper correspondent David Lawrence reported in 1940 that the city was full of Nazi propaganda that had been "planted here and there in those academic circles, isolationist quarters or political precincts where almost any argument opposing the President's policy would be seized upon as valid." The Nazis "know their America," Lawrence concluded, and had been successful in influencing "certain members of Congress and certain individuals of prominence outside of Congress."[23] The Nazi propaganda apparatus in the United States was designed to influence Americans through four simple methods, he wrote:

1. Blame the last war on England. Make it a war of profit and trade, and above all scoff at the idea that it was a war to save democracy.
2. Smear the British as much as possible. . . . Make it appear that the England wants to drag America into the war.
3. Cast doubt on the integrity of newspapers and newspaper men who favor the Allied cause.
4. If the Administration starts thinking of national defense, call the president a war monger. Find out who his advisers are. Start attacks along religious and racial lines. . . . Keep the people of the United States fighting amongst themselves, and play to the keep-out-of-war sentiments of the people by painting the horrors of war.[24]

This was therefore a classic disinformation campaign full of the "fake news" and other distortions a new generation of Americans would again encounter in the 2016 presidential election. In the place of stories suggesting that President Barack Obama was secretly a Muslim from Kenya, Americans in 1940 were told that Franklin Roosevelt was secretly Jewish and had changed his name from "Rosen-feld." Rumors about dangerous communists infiltrating the United States in groups of European refugees ("Refu-Jews Go Back" was the title of a far-right song of the era) would be replaced with alarmist rhetoric about Syrians decades later.[25] Cries against the "liberal" and "left-wing" media were common to both eras. Even in the pre–social media era, combating these types of rumors and false narratives was just as difficult. Lothian bemoaned in 1940 that London was not giving him adequate funds "which would enable me to handle these matters more promptly."[26] The Democratic Party's social media experts might well have made the same complaint in 2016.

While the German disinformation campaign had fairly straightforward objectives, there were sophisticated dynamics playing out at the same time. The Nazis were actually more successful than they expected or intended when it came to inspiring Americans to adopt their views. After Hitler's ascent to the German chancellorship in 1933, the American groups examined in the pages to come began to spring up spontaneously around the country. Few, if any, received official support from the German government. Some became so embarrassing they were explicitly denounced by the German embassy. Others were deliberately kept at an arm's length, either because their leaders were disreputable or because the Nazis believed they could actually be more effective if left to their own devices.

Between the German government's disinformation campaign and the groups that voluntarily aligned themselves with Hitler, Nazism had tentacles that touched every American community to some extent. Thousands of people joined groups like the German American Bund and the Silver Legion, marching down American streets in Nazi-esque uniforms, sending their children to Nazi summer camps, and heiling their leaders. Supporters of celebrity radio host Father Coughlin's Christian Front roughed up Jews on subway platforms and discouraged Americans from shopping at Jewish-owned stores. In the marbled corridors of Washington, DC, a German agent ran an ingenious operation to disseminate shocking quantities of isolationist and pro-German propaganda at taxpayer expense. This twentieth-century version of spam email showed up unsolicited in millions of mailboxes around the country. Business leaders found themselves courted by Nazi envoys who promised huge profits in the Reich if they could only convince Roosevelt to keep out of the war. Students at American universities were caught in the middle of academic freedom battles as anti-Nazi faculty were forced off campus and pro-Nazi groups spread hateful propaganda. Most sinisterly, some Americans were enticed by German military intelligence to offer their country's secrets to the Reich. There was even a bold plot by Nazi agents and their American friends to meddle in the presidential election of 1940. Nazism's corrupting influence could not be avoided. "The American fascists are most easily recognized by their deliberate perversion of truth and fact," Vice President Henry A. Wallace wrote in 1944. "Their newspapers and propaganda carefully cultivate every fissure of disunity, every crack in the common front against fascism. They use every opportunity to impugn democracy. . . . Their final objective toward which all their deceit is directed is to capture political power so that, using the power of the state and the power of the market simultaneously, they may keep the common man in eternal subjection."[27]

Given how far Nazism managed to spread on its own in the United States, it was fortunate that the Germans were not more adept at pressing their advantages. The Nazi propaganda and spy network on Capitol Hill was never used to its full potential, and the ultimate political prize—defeating Franklin Roosevelt in the 1940 election—was never really within grasp. Pro-German organizations often ended up fighting one another for members, money, and newspaper coverage. The German government could never fully decide whether to embrace its self-proclaimed American friends or whether it should denounce them as a threat to German-American relations. Berlin ended up trying both approaches at different times, confusing the situation further. Much-needed money was funneled to some of Hitler's friends through the German intelligence and propaganda network, but rarely in sufficient quantities to influence major events.

The main reason for this failure was the fact that Hitler and his inner circle actually knew little about the United States and seem to have cared even less. In the early days of the Reich, Hitler's circle of advisers included Ernst "Putzi" Hanfstaengl, a half-German, half-American Harvard graduate who had once been in the young Franklin Roosevelt's social circle.[28] Hanfstaengl moved to Germany and became a confidant of Hitler before the 1923 Beer Hall Putsch, giving him a front-row seat for the Führer's eventual rise to power. He later recounted that Hitler was obsessed with European military history but had almost no sense of why the United States was an important player on the world stage. "I never really succeeded in bringing home the importance of America as an integral factor in European politics [to Hitler]," Hanfstaengl wrote. The result was that Hitler's perception of the United States was "wildly superficial." "He wanted to hear all about the skyscrapers and was fascinated by details of technical progress, but failed utterly to draw logical conclusions from the information," Hanfstaengl wrote. The only American Hitler admired was industrialist Henry Ford, "not so much as an industrial wonder-worker but rather as a reputed anti-Semite and a possible source of funds." He also expressed an interest in the Ku Klux Klan as "a political movement similar to his own, with which it might be possible to make some pact, and I was never able to put its relative importance in proper perspective for him."[29]

Not only did Hitler fail to understand the geopolitical significance of the United States, he was downright dismissive toward the country on racial grounds.

Over a wartime dinner in January 1942 he predicted that America's racial diversity would be its downfall:

> *I don't see much future for the Americans. In my view, it's a decayed country. And they have their racial problem, and the problem of social inequalities. Those were what caused the downfall of Rome, and yet Rome was a solid edifice that stood for something. Moreover, the Romans were inspired by great ideas. . . . my feelings against Americanism are feelings of hatred and deep repugnance. I feel myself more akin to any European country, no matter which. Everything about the behaviour of American society reveals that it's half Judaised, and the other half negrified. How can one expect a State like that to hold together—a State where 80 per cent of the revenue is drained away for the public purse—a country where everything is built on the dollar?*[30]

Hitler's American friends might have thought they were doing the Führer's bidding by trying to establish their own version of Nazism, but Hitler himself had little hope in the idea. His only personal design on the United States for the time being was to keep it from entering the war. While his followers in the country had plans of their own, this essential fact explains why the Nazis did not exploit their network of supporters in the United States more aggressively. Even Germany's most effective spymaster in the United States, embassy first secretary Heribert von Strempel, was only sent to Washington because he spoke both English and Spanish and had prior experience working in South America. His superiors in Berlin were plainly more interested in their operations in Latin America than the potential to subvert the United States. Subsequently, 90 percent of the information Strempel reported back to Berlin was merely culled from American newspapers and just 10 percent from his Capitol Hill agent, though, as will be seen, there is little doubt that more could have been obtained from this source.[31]

None of this is to say, however, that Hitler's American friends failed to make a significant impact. Until 1941, the threat of fascist subversion was very real. Even if Hitler himself believed that the United States was inevitably doomed, this did not stop his supporters from trying to "save" it by advocating their own form of dictatorship. Tellingly, few if any American Nazis ever argued that National Socialism should simply be imposed on the United States, as if the German army had conquered Washington and imposed a new regime by force. Even the most hardcore domestic Nazis agreed that their ideology should be adjusted to fit American sensibilities and conditions. This search for a "secret recipe" of Nazism and Americanism that could thrive in the United States became the main preoccupation of the groups discussed in the pages to come. American flags and swastikas were therefore carried through the streets side by side, and giant portraits of George Washington hung at pro-Nazi rallies. The ultimate fear for US national security officials was that the pro-Hitler right would unite and become an actual "fifth column"—a group of traitors who helped turn the country over the Nazis, as had been seen in France and Norway.

The most important missing ingredient in this recipe, of course, was an American Hitler who could unite the factions into a single movement. Numerous candidates thought themselves worthy of becoming the Führer and made their respective bids for power. Indeed, nearly every major figure discussed in the coming chapters was viewed as a potential Hitler at one point or another. All of them failed. Yet even the midst of these competing bids, knowledgeable observers kept a single name in their minds, believing there was only one man who could have the fame, charisma, and instant network of supporters to join the far right into a single movement. That man was Charles Lindbergh. For a few brief months before Pearl Harbor, Lindbergh became the de facto leader of a broad right-wing coalition, operating under the banner of America First, that included nearly all of Hitler's American friends alongside more moderate conservatives and even some liberals. More menacingly, this group's apparent respectability made it a political force to be reckoned with. America First was the culmination of years of Nazi disinformation and propaganda, coupled with the extremism of home-grown fascism. Whether Lindbergh was actually aware he was occupying this position is uncertain, but there is no doubt that many of his supporters viewed him as the perfect American Führer.

For its part, the US government was remarkably slow to respond to the threat posed by Hitler's American friends and emulators. In fact, for much of the critical 1940–1941 period British intelligence was better informed, and clearer-eyed, about the activities and intentions of the American radical right than even the FBI. Recently declassified files at the UK National Archives reveal that the British Foreign Office and intelligence services kept close tabs on almost every anti-interventionist and pro-German group in the United States. The British embassy in Washington was so well informed about German plots that its officials turned over evidence to American counterparts who often had no idea what was going on under their noses. British intelligence operations in the

United States were extensive and well-provisioned. In the years before the war, the British maintained a Secret Intelligence Service (MI6) station in New York City. In June 1938, this was foolishly shut down out of concern that its activities might lead to a diplomatic incident with the US. The British hoped the shutdown would generate goodwill from the US government and lead to a closer relationship with the FBI. However, little progress resulted and the British were now simply blind to what was taking place in the United States. As the war unfolded, it became clear to MI6 chief Sir Stewart Menzies that he would quickly have to reactivate intelligence operations in the United States.[32]

In June 1940, Canadian-born British intelligence officer William Stephenson arrived in New York City. On paper, Stephenson was taking up the role of passport control officer, and would mainly be involved with issuing visas and other bureaucratic tasks. In reality, this was the usual diplomatic cover held by the MI6 New York station leader. Stephenson's real mission was to secretly conduct intelligence and propaganda operations in the United States while avoiding diplomatic incidents. He set up an office on two floors of a Rockefeller Center building under the name of a front company and began recruiting agents. British Security Coordination (BSC), as his operation was known, became massively successful in gathering intelligence from German and Italian embassies in the United States, unraveling German plots and disseminating pro-British narratives to the American public through a network of sympathetic journalists and even a commercial radio station.

Among Stephenson's stable of journalists was Broadway gossip columnist and radio personality Walter Winchell, one of the most popular and influential commentators in the country. Winchell was increasingly in favor of US intervention in the war and as a result he became a friendly conduit for the British. Through a third-party conduit, Democratic Party attorney Ernest Cuneo, the White House fed Winchell key stories supporting Roosevelt's stance on the need for American intervention. Stephenson separately convinced Cuneo to feed Winchell British propaganda and intelligence about German operations in the United States. In some cases, this included information that had not previously been provided to the FBI. Winchell therefore not only became a propaganda tool for the British government and Roosevelt, but also an important intelligence source for the FBI.[33]

Ironically, the FBI's blindness to the domestic Nazi threat was partially a deliberate choice. Throughout the 1920s the bureau was focused on organized crime, bootlegging, and communist subversion. Wiretapping, a key tool for counterintelligence investigators, was forbidden by President Calvin Coolidge's administration after a series of scandals, severely curtailing agents' ability to monitor suspects. The Roosevelt administration eventually increased the FBI's powers and resources and directly requested an investigation into pro-Nazi groups in 1934, but under legendary director J. Edgar Hoover, the bureau's focus remained firmly on the communist threat. The FBI was not even formally placed in charge of US counterintelligence operations until 1939, and even then only conducted such investigations on request from the president or attorney general.[34] Stephenson quickly found Hoover to be a mercurial partner, though the director expressed interest in intelligence sharing with BSC and secretly cleared the arrangement with the White House.[35]

Despite his arrangement with Stephenson, Hoover's personal obsession with communism continued to influence the bureau's investigations. In February 1940, FBI agents arrested former members of the left-wing Abraham Lincoln Brigade who had traveled to Spain and fought Francisco Franco's troops in the Spanish civil war years before. Even though the conflict had already ended, the former fighters were accused of illegally recruiting other Americans to join the conflict back in 1937. All this looked particularly silly in light of the war currently being fought, and led to a public outcry against the FBI's tactics and priorities.[36] To its credit, the FBI was generally receptive when BSC provided evidence that helped the bureau unravel a German plot and take public credit for it, but Hoover soon became concerned that Stephenson's operation was becoming a dangerous nuisance. In spring 1941, the FBI director declared war on BSC. He told Assistant Secretary of State Adolf Berle, one of the Roosevelt administration's counterespionage experts, that BSC was "probably in violation of our espionage acts" and demanded the administration let him shut it down.[37]

Stephenson had a powerful patron of his own by this time, however. In July 1940, Secretary of the Navy Frank Knox had dispatched Colonel William "Wild Bill" Donovan to Britain as part of a fact-finding expedition related to the progress of the war. Donovan was already a living legend. He had earned his distinctive nickname as a soldier fighting Pancho Villa. He was then sent to the Western Front of World War I, where he earned the Congressional Medal of Honor. He returned to civilian life to serve as assistant attorney general in the Coolidge administration, giving him credibility with both Republicans and Democrats.[38] During his wartime visit to the United Kingdom, Donovan met Prime Minister Winston Churchill, the king, and other leading political figures. He returned to the United States convinced that Britain could survive the

German onslaught, and that there should be close coordination between US and British intelligence to make victory more likely. In July 1941, Roosevelt agreed and created the Office of the Coordination of Information (COI) with Donovan as its head. COI was essentially the American counterpart of BSC, designed to not only detect enemy plots but also conduct proactive propaganda operations and even sabotage. Donovan and Stephenson quickly became close collaborators in the fight against Germany in the United States and overseas.

Hoover's campaign to shut down BSC eventually culminated in the passage of a congressional bill that would have severely restricted the work of British agents. Donovan convinced Roosevelt to veto it. A watered-down version specifically excluding the British from its restrictions was eventually signed in its place.[39] Donovan's liaison with BSC would have far-reaching consequences. In 1942 the COI would be split into two divisions, one of which became the Office of Strategic Services (OSS), an eventual forerunner of the Central Intelligence Agency. Donovan would be the first director of OSS and later recalled that Stephenson "taught us all we ever knew about foreign intelligence."[40]

Beyond Hoover and Donovan, the other main figure behind the US government's efforts to detect and neutralize Hitler's American allies was controversial in his own right. In 1938, Texas congressman Martin Dies Jr. became chairman of the newly created House Committee on Un-American Activities. The Dies Committee, as it was commonly known, was tasked with unmasking subversive plots wherever they could be found. Dies was a conservative Democrat who had turned gradually against the New Deal and became a constant thorn in the president's side. Most of Dies's focus was on communist subversion of labor unions, making him one of the precursors of postwar McCarthyism. His critics were numerous. "There is little evidence in this man's public career to indicate that he either understands or believes in American democracy," author William Gellermann wrote of Dies in 1944. "On the contrary, the evidence indicates that he is a spearhead of a native American reaction."[41]

Dies answered his detractors by proclaiming that his only interest was "Americanism." "As I have expressed many times, I am just as much opposed to Nazism and Fascism as I am to Communism," Dies told a skeptical correspondent in 1938. "All of these 'isms' constitute a different form of dictatorship and I am sure you are just as much opposed to Communism as you are Nazism."[42] He viewed communism and fascism as two sides of the same coin. "I regard Communism to be as dangerous to the liberties of the people as Fascism," he wrote in 1938. "In fact the lawlessness and violence inspired by Communism in Italy and Germany gave the Dictators an opportunity to seize control of the government. Communism is the forerunner of Fascism."[43]

Dies's personal views aside, American public opinion was split on whether the cigar-chomping Texan should prioritize communist or fascist subversion in his investigations. A Gallup poll in February 1939 found that 23 percent of respondents thought the Dies Committee should focus on "Nazi activities in this country," 30 percent on "war propaganda," and 17 percent on the communist threat. A full 32 percent failed to answer the question.[44] Without a clear mandate from the voting public it was unclear where Dies should focus his efforts. Regardless, Dies dramatically announced in August 1939 that his Committee had discovered that "there are nearly 5,000,000 enemies within our borders. 5,000,000 people living among us, who do not believe in the American way of government."[45] If true, a threat of this magnitude demanded drastic action.

Typical treatment for a Dies Committee witness included being subpoenaed to appear in Washington and then being extensively questioned under oath. Additional witnesses were then brought forward to present their evidence, which would often contradict previous testimony and, in some cases, open the door for perjury charges against others who had testified. While few of the organizations considered in these pages were brought down directly by the Dies Committee, their leaders' testimony often brought questionable activities to public attention. Historians have occasionally referred these investigations as the "Brown Scare," drawing a comparison to the Red Scare targeting communists. While there was certainly some element of public hysteria at play in the hunt for Nazi subversion, there was also no doubt that some of the organizations investigated by Dies were a threat to national security. While far from an ideal champion of democratic values and civil liberties, Dies's efforts did help protect the country against powerful forces that wished it ill.

At the same time, the limits of this form of investigation should be acknowledged. The Dies Committee could dominate the headlines and potentially expose all sorts of damaging information, but unless witnesses perjured themselves—which did occasionally happen—there were rarely criminal charges that immediately resulted. Most of Hitler's American friends were instead brought down by three forms of illegal activity. The first was financial mismanagement. Just as bloodthirsty mob boss Al Capone was eventually sent to prison for lying on his tax returns, several prominent Nazi sympathizers ended up in prison for embezzlement, fraud, and other financial shenanigans. Their demands of absolute and unquestioning loyalty from their followers made financial crimes easy to pull off.

The second legal mechanism for putting Hitler's agents out of business was the Foreign Agents Registration Act (FARA). This legislation was passed in 1938—it is no coincidence that it was passed the same year the Dies Committee was established—and required agents working for "foreign principals" to declare their activities to the government. In other words, anyone spreading propaganda to the American people on behalf of a foreign government had to make their actions known to federal officials. The monetary aspect was key: if an agent received money from a foreign government to support their activities they were required to make a FARA filing. Several of Hitler's most useful American agents were ultimately tripped up by this requirement and ended up in prison for failing to properly reveal their activities.

FARA remains in place to the present day and returned to the headlines after the 2016 election when it was revealed that President Donald J. Trump's national security advisor, Michael Flynn, initially failed to make a FARA filing related to work he had done for a company linked to the Turkish government. Former Trump campaign manager Paul Manafort faced similar allegations related to his advocacy for various foreign clients and was indicted in 2017 on a raft of charges that included failing to properly register under FARA.[46] At least one legal commentator remarked that the Manafort indictment "gave bite to a toothless law." As will be seen, FARA's teeth similarly proved to be very sharp indeed for some of Hitler's American friends.[47]

The third crime committed by Hitler's American friends was outright espionage. This was the most serious crime of the three and carried stiff prison sentences for those convicted. Most Nazi espionage cases involved the spy rings examined in this book's final section. Many convicted Nazi spies were American citizens whose motivations ranged from money to sex, and even sometimes boredom. As will be seen, the Nazi spy network in the United States was extensive and effective, though many of the stolen technical secrets proved to be of limited use to the German military. Making up for its earlier complacency, the FBI became very adept at breaking up Nazi spy rings and managed to put the entire German intelligence network in the country out of commission by late 1941. Hitler then launched a wild last-ditch gamble to spread terror in the United States that ended in one of the most sensational espionage cases in American history.

These were not abstract, faraway events for Americans. They were very real threats to the American way of life and, ultimately, the US government. Had

Hitler's American friends been successful, the US would never have entered World War II, Britain would have fallen under Nazi occupation and, ultimately, a version of National Socialism would have taken root in the United States. To a very real extent, the United States only escaped this fate through an uneasy combination of wise statesmanship and sheer luck—as will be seen, a constellation of events never aligned in a way that opened the door to defeating Roosevelt or seizing control of the government. Ultimately, the glue that held Hitler's American friends together as a broad group was anti-Semitism. Nearly all the individuals considered in these pages harbored a deep-seated hatred toward their own country's Jewish community and had little or no sympathy for the plight of Jews in Europe. Anti-Semitic views, especially conspiracy theories about supposed Jewish control of the government and the financial sector, often served as a precursor to deeper involvement in extremist groups. This dynamic was true with individuals as prominent as Lindbergh and far more average citizens alike. The leaders of extremist groups knew this themselves and propagated anti-Semitic conspiracy theories as a key recruiting tactic. Anti-Semitism was effectively the entry point to becoming one of Hitler's American friends for the vast majority of those who traveled that path.

This book argues that the threats posed by the American pro-Nazi movement were far greater than we remember today. In addition, events only turned out the way they ultimately did due to a combination of luck and the astute responses of a few key players in the US government. As will be seen, credit must be given to the courageous journalists and law enforcement officials who risked life and limb to expose plots against the United States. Similarly, while some politicians arguably disgraced themselves in this period, others rose to do the right thing under difficult circumstances by denying Hitler's friends the political connections they so desperately craved. In an era in which Americans have once again seen swastikas carried alongside American flags in Charlottesville, Virginia, and other communities, the lessons learned from the first defeat of Hitler's American friends should once again be remembered.

What follows is a story of differing degrees of Nazi sympathy, and of some ebb and flow in levels of support for an American Reich. Yet what also emerges is the sheer geographic spread of such advocates. From upstate New York to San Francisco, and from Washington State to U-boats unloading German saboteurs and explosives in Florida, these forces spanned most of the contiguous United States. This was truly a nationwide "Plot against America" rather than a regional flash in the pan. In some ways, this made cooperation between the various groups supporting Hitler both costly and difficult. But even by very conservative estimates there were over a hundred thousand Americans prepared to affiliate with the types of bodies discussed here, close to a million prepared to vote for a long-shot third-party presidential candidate espousing a pro-Hitler platform, and over ten million we could classify as "Hitler's friends in waiting" in one form or another. This was a big deal.

The first chapter of this book examines the most high-profile group with ostensibly pro-Nazi views in the mid-1930s: the German American Bund. Founded in 1936 as a combination cultural organization and political action group, dozens of Bund chapters emerged around the country and enjoyed an estimated initial following of more than one hundred thousand people, and perhaps double that number at its peak. Its armed wing brawled with communists and union members in cities across the country and, in 1939, it was responsible for a near riot in New York City. Millions of Americans saw newsreels of Bund members goose-stepping, giving stiff-armed salutes, and greeting their leaders with "Heil Hitler." Even more menacingly, the Bund also became known for running summer camps for kids that included Nazi salutes and weapons training.

Chapter 2, The Silver Legion and the Chief, examines another radically pro-Nazi group, but one with decidedly stranger preoccupations than the Bund. This was the Silver Legion, a lesser-known but no less racist organization. Founded by Hollywood screenwriter-turned-mystic William Dudley Pelley, the Silver Shirt movement set up chapters around the country and attired its members in striking uniforms reminiscent of Mussolini and Hitler. Through a bizarre combination of Nazi ideology and claims that he was directly communicating with Jesus, Pelley built a national following and began arming his followers in preparation for civil war.

Chapter 3 changes tack to explore a movement that would be considered part of the "religious right" today. Throughout the 1930s, religion underwent a significant change in American life, serving as a bastion of solace for many people who had lost everything in the Depression. The invention and proliferation of radio presented religious leaders with access to regional or even national audiences for the first time, giving them massive pulpits. Detroit priest Father Charles Coughlin would become the best-known national figure to use the new medium of radio, reaching an audience numbering in the millions. Coughlin initially used his program to preach on a combination of the Scriptures and economic issues, and he initially supported Roosevelt. Yet by the mid-1930s he began turning toward classic anti-Semitism and, from there, clear Nazi sympathies. He was not the only religious leader to do so: similarly, Gerald Burton Winrod, a Kansas minister who prided himself on opposing all forms of "modernism," turned to radio to spread his message in the early 1930s. Both men increasingly turned from the spiritual toward the political realm, with Winrod making a serious run for the Senate in 1938. Coughlin subsequently established the Christian Front, a radical group of his followers who embraced violence and referred to themselves as "Coughlin's brownshirts." Religion and politics thus went hand-in-hand for Hitler's American friends, with devastating consequences.

Chapter 4, The Senators, turns from the radio sets in American living rooms to the corridors of power in Washington, DC, where the political battle over intervention and isolationism was playing out on a day-by-day basis. Into this turbulent milieu stepped George Sylvester Viereck, a former propaganda agent during World War I who was again on the payroll of the German government. Viereck's task was to build as much support for the anti-interventionist position as possible in Washington and to this end he quickly built himself an extensive network of sympathetic congressmen and senators. He soon established an impressive operation within the corridors of power that would disseminate propaganda directly to millions of Americans and—even more insidiously—present it as the thoughts and words of their elected officials. Viereck's activities, and the reports he filed with his Berlin overseers, quickly made him one of the Reich's most valuable agents in the United States.

The fifth chapter, The Businessmen, examines interactions between America's corporate community and the Third Reich. American businesses, heavily invested in Germany when Hitler took power, had a vested interest in the regime's success. Major brands including General Motors, Ford, and Coca-Cola maintained German branches of their firms throughout the Nazi era. More sinisterly, the Nazis soon realized that these American investments could be held hostage and used to pressure Roosevelt. As war approached, Nazi envoys approached prominent business leaders and encouraged them to advocate nonintervention. Chillingly, one American businessman even embarked on an ambitious scheme to inject German money into the 1940 presidential election and defeat Roosevelt. His nefarious plans would ultimately be thwarted by the incompetence of his associates.

Chapter 6, The Students, turns to examine a demographic group the Nazis and their American friends were particularly eager to reach: the young. Specifically targeting college students (in a period in which only about 5 percent of the population had a bachelor's degree) the Third Reich and its supporters established a variety of programs and groups to interest students in the events taking place in Germany. The most direct of these efforts could be found in the study-abroad programs many universities offered their students, as they do today. It was seen as natural at the time that Germany remained a possible destination for students to visit, especially given the high reputation the country's universities had enjoyed in the past. As the political situation in the Reich changed, however, US universities responded in differing ways, with some curtailing their involvement with German universities and others continuing it. These decisions would have a profound impact on how their wider campus communities responded to Nazism as war approached.

Chapter 7, America First!, explores the final moment of truth for Hitler's American friends, the founding of the America First Committee. As will be seen, this organization was essentially an amalgamation of all the groups considered in the previous chapters. Its chairman, General Robert E. Wood, was an executive for Sears, Roebuck and company and brought a number of leading business leaders into the organization. These men were rich and some were famous, but none could approach the fame of the America Firsters' best asset: Charles Lindbergh. Throughout 1940 and 1941 the famed aviator traveled the country arguing against the prospect of intervention in the unfolding European war. Lindbergh's views of the conflict had been undoubtedly colored by his various trips to Nazi Germany in the mid-1930s and, as will be shown, he was viewed by the British as effectively a Nazi agent. Despite the vocal protestations of its leaders to the contrary, the America First movement became one of Hitler's key American friends.

The final chapter, The Spies, explores a group of individuals whose significance to the Reich was based on their names remaining completely outside the public eye. These were, of course, Hitler's intelligence and espionage agents. From the mid-1930s onward the Germans escalated their efforts to obtain information about American defense preparations and weaponry. The Nazi intelligence network was widespread and focused largely around its consulates in major cities around the country. The FBI kept a close eye on the activities of known German agents but it was naturally impossible to be aware of everyone who might pose a risk to national security. The Germans were therefore able to gather a great deal of intelligence about the United States, though much of it turned out to be low-value. This section also explores the activities of two high-profile spies whose loyalties were less easy to pin down. Captain Fritz Wiedemann, Hitler's former commanding officer in the First World War, found himself appointed consul general in San Francisco and subsequently ran a spy network that extended all the way to South America. He was joined there by his erstwhile mistress, former Hitler confidant Princess Stephanie von Hohenlohe. The American press and the FBI assumed that both of them were high-profile German agents, which they were. Everything was not what it appeared, however. They were also both looking to help secure an early end to the war and, to that end, tried to make back-channel overtures to the Allies. The two people Americans assumed were Hitler's highest-profile friends were in fact the opposite.

Collectively, these sections provide a wide-ranging view of the pro-Nazi movement in the prewar United States. Some aspects had been built and sponsored by the German government while others, such as the German American Bund, were actually seen as unhelpful by the Reich's leaders. However, whether Hitler would have embraced their friendship or not, they all purported to be his friends and represented themselves as such in the public eye. The darkest underbellies of American society were at the heart of all this: anti-Semitism, religious bigotry, and greed were the fundamental forces that drew these groups together. With the American economy in dire straits, businessmen fearing the potential rise of communism, and disenfranchised voters looking for a political solution to their woes, the climate was potentially right for the rise of fascism. There had already been some indications that antidemocratic politicians were on the rise. The most prominent example had been Louisiana governor and senator Huey Long, who ruled his state with an iron fist from 1928 until his assassination in 1935. Analogies between Long's meteoric climb and the simultaneous rise of European dictatorships were widely discussed at the time.[48]

Throughout this book, I have told the story of Hitler's American friends using a wide range of underutilized and sometimes even forgotten sources. From archives in Liberty, Texas, and North Newton, Kansas, to the Hoover Institution Library & Archives and the UK National Archives in London, I have deliberately drawn upon material ignored or overlooked by past historians when possible. My intention is to tell this story from the perspective of the people who lived and experienced it in a variety of ways. I have drawn upon official American sources, particularly FBI files, when necessary, but I have relied more heavily on the papers of individuals who were firsthand participants in the events described. My hope is that this approach not only sheds important new light on Hitler's allies but also gives a sense of how unstable and frightening this period was for the American people during one of the most uncertain periods in US history.

The culminating moment for Hitler's American friends came in the 1940–1941 period, when anti-intervention sentiment reached its peak simultaneously with the power of the far right. Bund members marched through American streets giving Nazi salutes. Silver Shirts armed themselves in preparation for war. "Father Coughlin's brownshirts" beat up Jews. Senators made wild allegations about the president becoming a dictator. Nazi agents tried to convince American businessmen to oppose and defeat Roosevelt. In the background, the figure of Charles Lindbergh loomed—the man the far right had chosen as their leader, though he himself was ignorant of the fact. It was a violent and uncertain atmosphere unlike any the country would experience again until the unrest of 1968. It seemed and appeared that everything was in play, and potentially everything was at stake.

In 1972, political scientist Bruce M. Russett argued that in "cold-blooded realist terms, Nazism as an ideology was almost certainly less dangerous to the United States than is Communism. Marxism-Leninism has a worldwide appeal; Nazism lacks much palatability to non-Aryan tastes."[49] Russett may well have been correct about the threat posed by communism, but the appeal of Nazism and fascism was far greater than he and most Americans have recognized. In the end, Hitler's American friends were not only often representatives of the nation's worst qualities but also showed how many of their countrymen could be lured into supporting a reprehensible regime even as its violent nature was increasingly becoming clear and war loomed on the horizon.

Looking back from the first decades of a new century that has already seen its share of bloodshed—though thankfully far less than the equivalent decades of the twentieth century—it is worth remembering how easy it can be for an ideology based in hatred to spread widely. Appeals to fear and prejudice are powerful things. Hitler's American friends were successful for a time because they seemed to provide an alternative set of answers to those being offered by the political establishment. In the end, those answers would be discredited and rejected by the vast majority, but this was never guaranteed to be the case. If nothing else, the example posed by Hitler's friends should remind us that the maintenance of a free, liberal, and democratic society requires diligence and active confrontation with antidemocratic ideas that threaten the very system that allows them to be discussed in the first place. Hitler's friends would go down to unequivocal defeat, yet, for a brief period, it appeared that the American flag and the swastika might well end up flying side by side.

1

THE BUND

The 1937 Fourth of July celebration in Yaphank, Long Island, had many elements of a typical Independence Day gala. It was a warm day and families sat at picnic tables under the leafy trees while the adults swigged beer and sang traditional songs. As the day wore on and the alcohol took effect, there was dancing and more carousing before a fireworks display concluded the evening.

Yet this was far from a typical patriotic celebration of American history. Many of the thousands in attendance were in uniform, but not the olive-green uniform of the US Army. There were speeches by local dignitaries, but these were focused less on a celebration of the Declaration of Independence than a series of homages to prominent foreign leaders. "Heil Hitler" and "Heil Mussolini" were the standard greetings of the day. A huge swastika adorned the stage, which one speaker told the crowd represented "Aryan groups in all countries," including the United States. More than three hundred men in silver-gray shirts with black ties and Sam Browne belts that passed over their right shoulders, and others in black shirts, goose-stepped past the stage and saluted their leaders with extended right arms. These storm troopers "are not a military organization," the crowd was assured by one of the afternoon's keynote speakers. He continued by predicting dark days ahead: "It would be ridiculous to believe they are drilling to take over America. . . . Trouble is coming to America soon and these men will be ready to fight for real American ideals against the homeless, Godless minority that is seeking to take us away from true Americanism."[1]

This was the Fourth of the July celebrated in the style of the German

American Bund, the country's leading organization for German sympathizers and Nazi imitators. Over the course of the 1930s, the Bund would go from being the butt of jokes nationwide to one of the government's top domestic security threats. At the same time, the outrageous behavior of the Bund's leadership would lead the German government itself to disavow it and eventually even ban German citizens from joining its ranks. By the outbreak of World War II, the Bund had largely been broken under the weight of its own corruption and a string of government prosecutions. While the Bund was home to Hitler's most visible American friends, they were in many ways his least effective allies in the country.

The downfall of the Bund would be largely brought about by one of the men attending the 1937 Fourth of July celebration. He was wearing the uniform of the German American Bund—a Hitler-style shirt and tie with the Sam Browne belt—with his hair and moustache shaped to imitate the Führer's personal styling.[2] For all appearances he would have cut the profile of an avid Hitler admirer and, to his comrades in the Bund, he was exactly this. Over the course of the past few months, Hellmut Oberwinder had managed to gain the trust of the Bund's leadership and has even been dispatched on a series of secret missions to make contact with Bund cells across the country.

In reality, there was no Hellmut Oberwinder, at least as his fellow Bund members knew him. The man going by that name in 1937 was actually John C. Metcalfe, a German-born reporter for the Chicago *Daily Times* who had painstakingly established a false identity over the course of months to infiltrate the Bund and gain the trust of its leadership. (Hellmut Oberwinder was in fact his German birth name, which he changed after moving to the United States in 1914).[3] By late 1937, just months after traveling twenty thousand miles on a series of fact-finding trips on behalf of the Bund's leadership, Metcalfe and two other reporters—one of whom was his brother, a former FBI agent who simultaneously infiltrated a Chicago-based Nazi group—published a series of articles that blew the lid off the Bund's operation and revealed the extent of its intentions to the American people. Congress would subsequently appoint Metcalfe as a special investigator for Martin Dies's House Committee on Un-American Activities. In the course of the coming years he would personally expose a range of plots by Hitler's American friends across the country. Metcalfe quickly accomplished more than any other single individual working to unravel the threat posed by Nazi sympathizers to US national security.

Metcalfe's dramatic successes infiltrating the Bund and the wider American

Nazi movement partially stemmed from the fact that, as a relatively recent German immigrant to the country, he was part of the exact demographic from which many of these organizations were seeking to recruit. In 1910, the United States had more than 8.2 million residents who had either been born in Germany or had German-born parents. Many spoke German as their primary language. In a country of just 92 million people, this made the German-American bloc a major demographic force. Before World War I there were numerous German-language newspapers across the country and a wide range of German cultural and heritage organizations that catered to the growing German-speaking community.[4]

America's 1917 entry in the war changed all this quickly. Though the overwhelming majority of German Americans were demonstrably loyal to the United States, the wider community quickly found itself on the receiving end of xenophobic abuse fanned by press accounts of German atrocities in Europe and on the high seas. The most aggressive attempts to counter this narrative and support the German cause (by propaganda agents including George Sylvester Viereck, discussed later) backfired and led to more prejudice. Alarmist reports about German espionage attempts in the United States led to further outrage, and in 1917 President Woodrow Wilson ordered all German noncitizens over the age of fourteen to register with the government as a preemptive measure. This helped foster a febrile atmosphere. On April 5, 1918, a German coal miner in Illinois was lynched by an angry mob and, in the ensuing trial, none of the accused killers were actually convicted. While this death was the only one immediately attributable to the national panic, its effect on the wider German-American community was profound.[5] German-language newspapers began to disappear, and many German-American families decided that rapid integration into American society and the English language was the surest way to protect themselves from another outbreak of violence.

The arrival of peace in 1919 had another profound effect on this dynamic. Between 1919 and 1933, more than four hundred thousand German immigrants would arrive on American shores, in large part because postwar Germany was in the midst of economic collapse. Unlike the German Americans who had come before and now mostly decided to adopt an American identity, a portion of these new migrants saw themselves as temporary expatriates fleeing economic and political turmoil. Many did not expect to stay in the United States for long and some even saw themselves as right-wing political refugees fleeing the vagaries of the newly established and liberal Weimar Republic. The German American

Bund's membership would largely be drawn from these more recent immigrants.[6]

German politics was changing rapidly in the 1930s, and German Americans took a keen interest in the events taking place there. In 1933, Hitler was appointed chancellor by President Paul von Hindenburg following an indecisive parliamentary election. Hitler had been a controversial political figure for more than a decade. In 1923 he had led an unsuccessful coup called the Beer Hall Putsch against the government of Bavaria. The uprising ended in bloodshed and Hitler was sent to prison for his role in the plot. While there, he penned the autobiographical *Mein Kampf*, an account of his past political activities that contained a strong dose of anti-Semitism. After being released from prison in late 1924, Hitler returned to the political fray as leader of the nascent National Socialist Party. The party's vote share would never be massive, and under his leadership it won just 37 percent of the national vote in July 1932. This was nowhere near a majority, but it positioned Hitler to take on a key role in the next government. Conservative politicians believed they could control the Austrian former soldier who, for all his impressive rhetorical skills, lacked many of the social graces that were expected of traditional politicians. Hitler quickly took advantage of events, accepted their support, and outwitted them.

Following the burning of the Reichstag in a terrorist arson attack a month after he took office, Hitler began to consolidate power for the Nazi Party. An Enabling Act was passed allowing Hitler to effectively govern without parliamentary oversight. Civil liberties swiftly disappeared and all opposition parties were banned. Opponents of the Nazi Party found themselves in concentration camps. In August 1934 Hindenburg died, leaving the presidency vacant. Rather than take on the role himself, Hitler simply assumed Hindenburg's power and created a new position for himself: Führer (leader). Most semblances of German democracy ceased to exist in under two years.

Hitler's rapid rise was watched closely around the world. "He [Hitler] has a blank check from nearly twenty million Germans to rule the Fatherland however he wills," Hungarian-American journalist Emil Lengyel wrote in April 1933. "Hitler is thus Germany's dictator by the right of the electorate. The bad boy of Germany, the boy the neighbors fear, is on his own."[7] German Americans were split over these developments. In Brooklyn, one of the largest German-American organizations issued a strong denunciation of Hitler's anti-Semitism in June 1933.[8] Others were more eager to support Hitler's new government. In December 1933, a crowd of twenty thousand cheered Hitler's name at a

Madison Square Garden meeting of the Steuben Society, a prominent German heritage organization. German ambassador to the United States Hans Luther encouraged the crowd to "study the truth about Germany and not be satisfied with incomplete reports whose correctness is so often contradicted and inherently questionable."[9] As in Germany, there was clearly substantial, though far from unanimous, support for the country's new leader among the expat community.

The first group with clear affinities for Nazism to emerge in the German-American community was called the National Socialist Teutonia Association. Founded in Detroit in 1924, the association was openly supportive of the nascent National Socialist movement. Some members had even been part of the Nazi Party before the Beer Hall Putsch and had fled to America to avoid prison time. Association members sent much-needed funds to the struggling Nazi Party in addition to publishing a local newspaper. Its leaders were all young men who had recently immigrated to the United States and shared aspects of Hitler's anti-Semitic outlook. Some would eventually return to Germany and receive rewards for their financial contributions to the Nazi Party at this critical phase in its existence. However, the goal of the Teutonia Association was not to build a branch of the Nazi Party in the United States but to provide a temporary home for exiled Nazis. Most expected to eventually return to Germany and continue their struggle there. If they could gain new recruits among their fellow recent immigrants, all the better, but the notion of trying to build a mass movement among the wider German-American community was far from the primary aim.[10]

The biggest problem for Teutonia was that it was far from the only Nazi show in town. While it remained a powerful force in the Detroit area, there were other Nazi Party members living in exile elsewhere, most notably New York City. In 1931, an organization of these members wrote to the Nazi Party's foreign section in Hamburg and suggested that they be commissioned to form an official Nazi branch in New York City. The leader of the foreign section agreed to the proposal, effectively cutting Teutonia out of the official party apparatus and creating a new "official" Nazi organization called Gauleitung-USA (District Headquarters USA, or Gau-USA for short). For the next several years, rival Nazi groups verbally sniped at one another claiming to be the most authentic, with the press giving increasing column space to the conflict as Hitler's profile grew. Teutonia's leadership eventually declared the organization defunct and joined Gau-USA, but this proved to be only a temporary solution.[11] Following Hitler's ascent to power in 1933, the German Nazi Party decided that its public image in the United States needed improvement and founded a completely new organization, the Friends of Germany, to spread propaganda and build support for the new government.

Farcically, the leaders of Gau-USA refused to acknowledge the legitimacy of the new organization and still claimed themselves to be the true embodiment of American Nazism. At the same time, dissenters within the group broke away to found their own organizations. The American press had a field day as a ridiculous internecine conflict unfolded, hardly giving the German embassy the propaganda coup for which it had hoped. Fed up with the entire situation, the Nazi Party's leaders in Berlin eventually threw up their hands and ordered everyone to shut down their groups immediately. The American branch of National Socialism was causing far more problems than it was solving.

The solution was clearly to be found in applying more discipline and structure to the American Nazi movement's many disparate pieces. In mid-1933, a former member of Teutonia, Heinz Spanknöbel, obtained party permission to form a new organization that would include both German Americans and German nationals living in the United States under one umbrella group called Friends of the New Germany. Unlike Gau-USA, this new group would include all factions of the American Nazi movement and avoid the infighting that had plagued its previous incarnations. More menacingly, Spanknöbel took a page from Hitler's own playbook and set up an armed wing of the organization—called the Ordnungsdienst or OD—which had previously been part of Teutonia and was modeled on the Nazi Party's violent brown-shirted Sturmabteilung (SA). In the event of a threat to Spanknöbel's leadership or the wider organization, the OD was trained to respond with force.[12]

Between 1933 and 1935, Friends of the New Germany recruited a membership of about five thousand. This made it a small but potent force—similar to the six thousand members the American Communist Party had in 1932. The group published two newspapers in the New York area and soon opened branches in five other cities including Detroit and Chicago.[13] Despite these successes, Spanknöbel himself quickly turned out to be exactly the loose cannon that the Nazi Party had tried to prevent from tarnishing its name in the United States. In 1933, he attempted to intimidate the owners of a major German-language daily paper in New York City into accepting him as the legitimate voice of the German government, only to be thrown out of their offices. Later that year the OD painted swastikas on the doors of Manhattan synagogues. A subsequent anti-Semitic rally in New Jersey ended in a brawl between the OD and protestors in the audience. The press once again had a field day, and dark memories of the hysteria over German espionage and subversion in World War I began to resurface in the German-American community.

The German government ordered Spanknöbel to stop attracting attention to himself. He simply ignored the instructions coming from Berlin and the controversy continued. Alarmed by the group's growing profile and violent tendencies, the chairman of the House Committee on Immigration and Naturalization requested Spanknöbel's deportation on the grounds that he had failed to properly register as an agent operating on behalf of a foreign government. Spanknöbel skipped town and left the country before he could be apprehended by federal authorities.[14] Congressional hearings soon resulted and, in 1935, the German government once again threw up its hands and ordered all German nationals to resign their membership in the organization or face having their German citizenship revoked. Friends of the New Germany had not only failed to improve Nazism's reputation in the United States but had in fact become a major liability for the German government. The Friends were only the precursor of what was to come, however. In late March 1936, Friends of the New Germany was officially declared defunct, and was absorbed into a new group: German American Bund (*Amerikadeutscher Volksbund* in German, which appeared above its English name on its official letterhead) at a national convention in Buffalo, New York. The new organization would be partially headquartered on East Eighty-Fifth Street in in the Yorkville Section of New York City, not far from Central Park and the Metropolitan Museum of Art.

The German American Bund's leader was Fritz Julius Kuhn, the group's former Midwest division leader. Kuhn's background was typical for those who were attracted to the German-American far right of the 1930s. Born in Munich in 1896, Kuhn served in the First World War as a machine gunner and won the Iron Cross. After the war he joined a right-wing militia and brawled with communists on the streets of Munich. In 1921 he joined the National Socialist Party and enrolled at the University of Munich to study chemical engineering. In 1923 he left Germany to take a job in Mexico. He would later claim to have been present for the Beer Hall Putsch and said he was forced to flee in its aftermath to avoid criminal changes, but there is no evidence that this was actually the case. More likely, Kuhn moved for the same economic reasons that compelled many young men to leave Germany in the 1920s, when the country was in financial turmoil.[15]

Kuhn moved to the United States at the age of thirty-one and settled in the

Detroit area, putting him at the hotbed of pro-Nazi sentiment in the United States. One of his first employers included the Ford Motor Company, from which he was reportedly fired for practicing speeches on company time. (After Kuhn became nationally notorious, Ford officials denied any long-term connection to him and allegedly changed his employee card to suggest that he had quit at an earlier date).[16] From there he worked a variety of jobs while gradually pursing his political career. Kuhn had not rushed to join the Teutonia organization after arriving in Detroit, but, perhaps inspired by Hitler's recent rise to power, he joined Friends of the New Germany in mid-1933. His past experience in the Nazi Party and fanatical loyalty to Hitler ensured a swift rise, along with his powerful oratorical skills—at least when speaking German—and organizational prowess. By 1935 he had risen to the position of midwestern *Gauleiter* (district leader) in the organization. Simultaneously embracing his new American identity, at least on paper, he was naturalized as an American citizen in 1934.[17]

Kuhn's personal appearance and speaking style would become the source of much mockery in the years to come. He spoke English with a thick German accent and tried to imitate Hitler's erratic hand gestures and passionate body language when addressing a crowd. Lacking the Führer's charisma, he merely looked ridiculous and tripped over his English words. On the other hand, it is possible to detect some of the appeal that charmed many in the Bund. He was five feet, eleven inches tall and weighed more than 200 pounds, making him an easy figure to spot onstage. He wore glasses, giving him a somewhat scholarly appearance similar that of SS head Heinrich Himmler. His military background gave him the gait of a warrior. He was often photographed in Bund uniform wearing his Iron Cross and military decorations, consciously evoking the humiliation that many German Americans felt the fatherland had suffered at the end of World War I.[18] Despite his rather bumbling image as a public orator to non-German-speaking Americans, Kuhn managed to cut a larger-than-life, playboy profile in the press. He was often seen at New York City nightclubs listening to jazz (despite his frequent denunciations of the music as "Negroid") with a progression of beautiful mistresses, including a former Miss America.[19] Like many demagogues throughout history, Kuhn realized that his image as a glamorous celebrity was just as important, if not more so, than his image as the putative American Führer.

Most dangerously, Kuhn would soon try to combine this memorable persona with a new ideological concoction of Nazism and loyalty to the United

States. Bund rallies would see the American flag carried side by side with the new German national flag bearing the swastika. All the standard imagery of Nazi Germany and fascist Italy—goose-stepping troops in jackboots, straight-armed salutes, and swastikas—were now being associated with symbols of the United States and Americanism itself. The Bund's slogan, often repeated in its proclamations and on its letterhead, was "Free America," by which it would increasingly mean an America free from Jewish influence.[20]

The Bund's most well-publicized events were similarly inundated with the language of Americanism. Its most infamous event—a 1939 mass rally at Madison Square Garden that would be steeped in violence—was officially termed a "Pro American Rally" with "George Washington Birthday Exercises." A description of the event proclaimed that "The Bund is opposed to all isms in American public life, INCUDING NAZISM AND FASCISM, regarding these political systems as affairs of the people who live under them (supported, as they are, by upeard [sic] of 95 per cent of the electors in nationwide plebiscites), but impracticable and inexpedient innovations in the American system of government." At the same time, the Bund left little question as to what it did stand for, and it had some remarkable similarities to Nazism: "The Bund opposes Zionism as an infectious disease gnawing at the core of American political, social and economic life, covering an ever-widening field of activities, which have already developed a power of American life which cannot be shaken off as long as Jews controll [sic] the press, the radio, the screen and the stage."[21] Rather than importing Nazism to the United States directly, Kuhn's entire strategy was to combine the essence of Americanism with a new and insidious version of National Socialism.

Organizationally, the Bund modeled itself on the structures that underpinned its predecessors. Kuhn retained the OD as the organization's uniformed security force. Its members carried nightsticks and other legal weapons that could easily be used with lethal effect. OD members underwent extensive training at Bund camps and marched in formation down American streets across the country in their distinctive uniforms, giving the stiff-armed salute. This training was not just for show, and there is little doubt that its members prevented Kuhn from being harmed or even assassinated on a number of occasions when Bund events ended in violence (often precipitated by the OD itself). It is difficult to know how many men were in the OD in the course of its existence, but Kuhn estimated that it had about five thousand uniformed members at any given time—certainly not a huge military force, but enough trained and armed fighters to cause serious local unrest. Membership was open to all Bund men over the age of eighteen.[22]

The most significant organizational principle of the Bund was the *Führerprinzip* (Führer principle). Derived from the structure of the Nazi Party, this principle stated that the will of the Führer (Hitler, or in this case, Kuhn) could never be questioned and should be seen as overriding all other considerations, including the law. In Germany, this meant that Hitler's personal whims were seen as more important than precedent, law, or the opinion of others. The Führer could, by definition, never be incorrect in his views or pronouncements and they should therefore be followed without question. The ultimate responsibility of the Nazi Party or Bund member was to demonstrate absolute loyalty to the dictates of the leader. As will be seen, Kuhn would eventually abuse this principle to subsidize his larger-than-life image.

Beneath Kuhn and his fellow national officers, the Bund's presence around the country was organized into three regions, each called a *Gau* (district)—the East, Midwest, and West. A *Gauleiter* (district leader) was placed in charge of each. Nearly every major city had a local branch that reported to their respective regional center and, ultimately, to Kuhn's national headquarters. By 1939, Kuhn reported that every state in the country except Louisiana had at least some measure of Bund presence, with more than a hundred local units in total.[23] These seemed like impressive numbers, but actual membership figures are more difficult to pin down. In line with its ideological orientation, applying for Bund membership meant an applicant had to state they were "of Aryan descent, free from Jewish or Colored Blood" and pay both registration fees and monthly dues, making the possible membership base small to begin with. There were also two levels of affiliation: full membership, which entitled the bearer to take part in all Bund activities; and sympathizer membership, which allowed the holder to attend meetings with the permission of their local unit leader only.[24] Membership cost $9 a year (about $160 today) and was paid in monthly installments.[25] People presumably floated between these statuses over the course of the Bund's existence, while others joined for a period and then resigned as the political situation changed. In 1939 Kuhn estimated in an internal report that there were more than 8,000 full members in the Bund (an almost impossibly low figure if there were truly 100 functional local units). He later testified that the number was closer to 20,000 with about 100,000 sympathizers. The Justice Department believed the number to be smaller than either of Kuhn's estimates, but one German government official would later outlandishly claim that Kuhn had 50,000 members at the peak of his popularity. Given how many Bund documents were later destroyed, and the fact that the membership application allowed for the use of pseudonyms, historians have barely done better determining numbers. Estimates have ranged from Kuhn's figure of 10,000 or fewer to an upper end of 30,000 or so, with many more sympathizers.[26]

Given how many local units existed at the peak of the Bund's power, it is likely that Kuhn himself did not know the true number of members and sympathizers. Extensive card catalogs of members were supposedly kept at the local level but it is unclear how regularly local leaders reported updates to the national organization. Taking the most generous estimates of 30,000 members and around 100,000 sympathizers, in a country of 132 million people this meant a mere 0.001 percent of the population was involved with the Bund. By way of comparison, Oswald Mosley's similarly unsuccessful British Union of Fascists peaked at 40,000 members in a UK population of around 46 million. Given the volume of votes for Conservative members of Parliament who barely concealed their admiration for Hitler, British fascist sympathizers probably ran into the hundreds of thousands in a country that was much smaller than the United States.

Yet despite its seemingly limited support base, the Bund was punching well above its actual weight in the public eye. It was hardly comforting that in early 1921, a mere twelve years before taking power, the Nazi Party had just 2,000 members before exploding to ten times that number by the end of the following year in a country less than half the size of the United States.[27] The Bund was arguably further along in building its membership base than the Nazis had been just a few years before Hitler became chancellor. Who was to say that under the right circumstances Kuhn could not pull off a similar feat? The fact that membership in the Bund required one to be of Aryan background was a major restriction on its potential as a mass party (particularly given an African American population of more than twelve million, along with millions of others with European backgrounds considered to be non-Aryan, such as the Irish). Yet it was conceivable that this difficulty might be overcome if the Bund could form alliances with similarly minded groups that appealed to Americans of different ethnic backgrounds and identities. The prospect of a broad far-right front forming was not beyond the realm of possibility, especially as Kuhn had moved beyond his predecessors' obsession with spreading German propaganda at the expense of building an American version of Nazism. Indeed, there was some evidence that local Bund chapters were already seeking alliances with other far-right groups including the Ku Klux Klan and the Silver Legion, discussed later. A broad right-wing front, especially if it joined forces with Hitler's other American friends and their money, might well be in a position to make a bid for power. Kuhn had become the first candidate for the potential position of American Führer.

The Bund's aggressive use of youth camps did little to calm the growing concerns about Kuhn's intentions. The use of such camps was adopted directly from the Nazi Party's playbook. After Hitler's rise to power, German young people of both genders were regularly indoctrinated through compulsory membership in the Hitler Youth and the League of German Girls, in which they were taught both Nazi ideology and war-related skills. Similarly, the Bund's Youth Division was established nationwide and held Nazi-themed summer camps in at least fifteen locations around the country—Kuhn himself purported to be unclear on the actual number—mostly in the New York area, upper Midwest, and California. According to the Youth Division's leader, most of the parents who sent their children to Bund summer camp were German immigrants who had migrated to the country after the First World War.[28] The Bund's campers wore uniforms similar to those of the OD, including the iconic Sam Browne belts; marched in formation; learned German; and were tutored in the fundamental principles of National Socialism. As undercover reporter John C. Metcalfe would testify to the Dies Committee, the main orientation of the camps was instilling the four Hs: Health, Hitler, Heils, and Hatred. "American boys and girls sing hymns to Der Fuehrer and to the Vaterland they never have seen," Metcalfe told the Committee. "Their youthful feet goose-step in a march of racial and religious hatred. The minds and souls of these 'babes in the woods' are a fertile field for the propaganda of the Bund."[29]

The exact number of children who took part in the Bund summer camps remains unknown, but two camps for which records do exist appear to have had enrollments of 200 and 400, respectively, in the summer of 1937.[30] Using these figures, and assuming an average enrollment of 300 children in a maximum of twenty-four camps, yields a figure of about 7,200 children nationwide who may have been in Bund camps each summer of their existence. This number would fit well with a total Bund membership of about four times that figure. The most promising young people from the camps were occasionally sent to Germany to continue their training in the Hitler Youth.[31]

Regardless of how many children were actually enrolled in the Bund's camps, it was understandably worrying for many Americans to have an organization

modeled on the Hitler Youth drilling children to goose-step and to salute
ler. The ideology of the camps themselves was not the strangest outcome of the
Bund's activities on this front, however. Since housing hundreds of children for
the summer required extensive facilities, Kuhn and his lieutenants created a
series of puppet corporations that ostensibly owned the campgrounds and were
responsible for the construction and maintenance of facilities. Kuhn himself was
often the titular head of these corporations, but on paper they were separate
entities—a legal issue that would soon be used in the government's assault on
the Bund.[32]

The most famous of these legal fictions was called the German American
Settlement League and was formed to develop a facility called Camp Siegfried
in Yaphank, Long Island. Joining the league required an applicant to be a
member of the Bund, ensuring that all members had met Kuhn's rigid racial
requirements. Unlike most of the other entities that owned the Bund camps,
however, the league was a membership corporation rather than a business,
meaning that its two hundred or so members were effectively its owners.[33]
Because Siegfried was the closest facility for New York City Bund members,
it developed into a showpiece that hosted major events and rallies. The camp
soon included a small community of homes and other facilities. Adolf Hitler
Street was a major thoroughfare, and other streets were similarly named for
Nazi bigwigs. Guests from Germany were frequently hosted at Siegfried, and
during the summer the OD trained there with rifles and other firearms. Promising members of the Youth Division from all over the country were also sent
to Siegfried to further their education and training, making it effectively the
center of Bund training operations nationwide.[34] Major celebrations, such as
the Fourth of July celebrations that began this chapter, could attract tens of
thousands of people from New York City to Siegfried's leafy surroundings.

Camp Siegfried would have an odd afterlife after the Bund's official demise.
Because it was legally a separate entity and a membership corporation, the German American Settlement League was able to retain possession of Yaphank after
World War II. The land was held collectively, but the individual houses could
be sold by their respective owners. Over the years, the original residents moved
away or died. However, the corporation's bylaws were never changed, meaning
that anyone purchasing a home still had to meet Bund racial requirements and
be of Aryan descent. A corporate board of existing homeowners was required
to sign off that all new buyers met the racial qualifications to purchase the property. This strange state of affairs continued mostly unchallenged until 2015,

when a couple hoping to sell their home sued the league for practicing discrimination and violating the Fair Housing Act. The following year, the Settlement League agreed to finally change its policies.[35] Decades after its demise, one of the Bund's final legacies had been erased.

By mid-1936 Kuhn had established the basic structures of the Bund and solidified his own power at the top of the pyramid. The only thing missing, the official endorsement of the German government, was obviously in question given the difficulties of its predecessor groups. Kuhn's solution was clever. The Olympic Games were heading to Berlin in 1936, and Hitler would be making a large number of appearances with foreign delegations and other VIPs as part of the festivities. With the world's press focused on the Reich and the Nazis eager to make a good impression on the international stage, it would be difficult for Hitler to refuse a meeting with a delegation of enthusiastic overseas Germans like the Bund. The gambit paid off. Hitler agreed to meet with a Bund delegation and accepted a book listing the names of Bund members who had contributed to the German Winter Relief program, a poverty relief charity the government was promoting as an easy way for Germans abroad to help the fatherland. Hitler shook hands with each of the Bund members present for the meeting and muttered a bromide to Kuhn along the lines of "Go back and carry on your fight."[36]

Kuhn returned to the United States with the apparent endorsement of the Führer and photographs documenting their meeting. In reality, Hitler had given him no such approval and had only minimal interest in the Bund. Even the fact that Hitler had met the Bund members meant almost nothing: He had many such meetings, particularly during the Olympics, and they generally progressed in the same way with the usual receiving line of handshakes, photographs, and some vaguely supportive remarks being uttered by Hitler before he was shuttled away to his next engagement. In some cases, Hitler was apparently unaware of whom he was actually meeting until an aide whispered to him each person's name as the hand-shaking began.[37] In Kuhn's instance he was probably aware of his guest's identity, but it was hardly a striking endorsement for the Führer to effectively tell him to "keep up the good work."[38] Kuhn was aware that Hitler's reception was less than a glowing endorsement. This fact did not dissuade him from trying to capitalize on it, however. He began to exaggerate the trip in speeches, describing personal meetings with grandees including Hermann Göring and propaganda minister Joseph Goebbels. The German embassy in Washington began receiving questions from American politicians and the press about the depth of Kuhn's connections to the Reich government, but had no idea how to answer. Berlin quickly assured its diplomats that Kuhn was simply lying, and that the Bund had no real link to the Nazi Party.[39]

Regardless, Kuhn had secured the domestic propaganda coup he sought. Accounts and photographs of the meeting were widely reproduced in Bund propaganda, and it seemed fully plausible that Kuhn had received the Führer's endorsement to set up an American version of the Nazi Party. This perception would ultimately be part of the Bund's downfall, but for now it suited Kuhn to be seen as Hitler's closest American friend. He quickly put his plans into overdrive. In October 1936 Kuhn issued a "Bund Command" endorsing Republican candidate Alf Landon for president over Franklin Roosevelt because of the latter's "preference for the Jewish element and his placing of many Jews in public office." Landon, on the other hand, was desirable because "it can absolutely be assumed that under his administration more favorable commercial relations with Germany would be effected. . . . For if we want to help Germany there is no better way than in an economic way."[40]

The following day, Kuhn issued a proclamation accepting German citizens into a branch of the Bund. This directly contravened the guidelines established by the German embassy toward Friends of the New Germany. Now the Bund would contain both American citizens and German nationals.[41] In 1937, Kuhn established new uniform guidelines for the OD ("black long trousers without cuffs—black shoes. Steel gray shirt with breast pockets, long black tie. Shark gray uniform jacket . . . The present arm-band, black cap with the Bund insignia . . . black belt with shoulder strap") and standards for public speaking ("The German American Bund is an American organization and has no official connection with Germany and receives no monies. . . . President Roosevelt is not to be attacked personally in any speech"). As was standard, most of these proclamations ended with a rousing "Sieg Heil!"[42] Kuhn had rapidly solidified his power and now intended to turn the Bund into a well-functioning and disciplined organization.

For its part, the German government was becoming concerned that Kuhn's larger-than-life persona and tendency to go rogue might prove more of a liability than a benefit. As the former press officer at the German embassy in Washington testified after the war, the German Foreign Office's policy was to avoid any activity that might unnecessarily endanger relations with the United States or, at worst, provide a pretext for war. While the Bund had received some financial support from the foreign section of the Nazi Party in the past, the German ambassador recommended in 1938 that Kuhn be cut off completely. Embassy officials were subsequently banned from having any contact with Kuhn or the Bund, though this was violated by the German consul in New York City.[43]

The other worrying aspect of the Bund was its decentralized nature. In such a large country there was simply no way for Kuhn to be aware of what was taking place in local chapters in areas as far-flung as California or Texas. Several Bund commands were issued to demand that local leaders file reports with the national office about local opinion, membership numbers, and other issues, but these were often ignored.[44] More significantly, this meant that Kuhn and the national leadership could not necessarily police the activities of local leaders. In 1938, for instance, four local groups failed to send Winter Relief funds in the proper manner, leading to a rebuke from Kuhn. Time and time again he had to insist that his orders be carried out precisely and without delay.[45] John C. Metcalfe would soon discover that local Bund leaders simply found it easy to ignore the mandates coming out of New York. Some units failed to abide by Kuhn's uniform regulations, while others failed to charge required membership fees (or simply skimmed the money away before it was reported to Kuhn's office). Despite Kuhn's thirst for power, controlling a far-flung network of local chapters would prove almost impossible.

By 1937, Kuhn's high public profile and the publicity surrounding his visit to the Third Reich was attracting substantial public concern around the United States. Kuhn's uniformed OD storm troopers and youth cohorts giving him stiff-armed salutes were obviously reminiscent of Nazi Germany and fascist Italy. Rallies featuring the swastika next to the American flag understandably struck many Americans as an affront. Where would this all lead? Was Kuhn preparing to launch a coup? Would he unleash his storm troopers and youth followers in a rampage of anti-Semitic violence as had been seen in Germany? There had already been some low-level violence at Bund rallies, usually between members of the OD and protestors who exchanged harsh words and then used their fists to settle the matter.[46] Plus, what exactly was going on in the Bund's youth camps?

These were all valid questions. On the other hand, though, there was little that could legally be done to stop Kuhn at this point. Germany and the United States were not at war. There was no law against displaying the swastika, wearing a uniform, and saying "Heil Hitler." Officially, the OD was not an armed paramilitary group but a security detail that carried legal weapons and received firearms training. There was also no law against this, and Kuhn even denied that there were any guns involved despite extensive testimony to the contrary. The government had no direct evidence that the violence seen at Bund rallies had been planned. In some cases, the OD members involved might have even been able to argue they were acting in self-defense when they fought protestors. At the end of the day, it could be argued that Bund members were simply exercising their First and Second Amendment rights. Indeed, an FBI investigation in late 1937 concluded that there was no evidence Kuhn or the Bund had broken any federal laws and there were therefore no grounds upon which anyone could be indicted for criminal wrongdoing.[47] Suspicion that Kuhn was up to no good was simply not enough to shut down the putative American Führer. Far more evidence would be needed.

The Bund had an important vulnerability on this front: It was remarkably easy to infiltrate. This was in part because obtaining membership was fairly straightforward. A prospective infiltrator had to simply agree to various political statements, meet the racial requirements of admission, have a plausible false identity that did not arouse suspicion, and possess some knowledge of the German language. This is certainly not to say that spying on the Bund was without significant risk. There was often bold talk at Bund chapter meetings about what should be done to newspaper reporters who wrote negative or incriminating stories about the organization. Without doubt, anyone caught in such a position would have been in serious peril. The most famous infiltrator—John C. Metcalfe—received numerous death threats after his subterfuge was revealed, and later had his car riddled with machine-gun bullets in an ambush. He narrowly managed to escape unharmed.[48]

The Los Angeles chapter of the Bund was among the first to find itself under pressure from infiltrators and informants. In 1936, a group of Hollywood bigwigs including screenwriter Donald Ogden Stewart (writer of the Oscar-winning *Philadelphia Story*), German director Fritz Lang (*Metropolis*, *M*), and exiled German politician Prince Hubertus zu Löwenstein formed a group called the Hollywood Anti-Nazi League. Their goal was to combat the growing influence of National Socialism and fascism in the movie industry. They were assisted in this effort by Otto Katz, a communist agent who had been raising money for anti-Nazi causes for a year, making the Anti-Nazi League essentially a communist front.[49] Most of the league's efforts were directed at building anti-Nazi sentiment through radio broadcasts and publications, but it also arranged protests at Bund rallies and other events. Loaded with cash from Katz and its rich patrons, the league opened its own intelligence network to keep tabs on the local far right. From 1936 until its dissolution in 1939, the league had investigators attending many of the Bund's meetings and events to file detailed reports on everything that was said. Their colleagues sat outside and recorded the license plates of every car parked in the vicinity of the meeting, and then cross-referenced the plates to discover the name and address of their owners. The league was effectively building a database of every Bund member and sympathizer in the LA area.[50]

What the league's investigators found was worrying. The LA chapter of the Bund—run out of a building called the Deutsches Haus on Fifteenth Street and headed by Herman Max Schwinn, the Bund's West Coast *Gauleiter*—was loaded with anti-Semites who were unsparing in their hatred for both Jews and the league itself. One meeting attended by hundreds that was branded with the slogan "America First" quickly descended, in the words of one informant, into "the vilest Hitleristic attack on all American ideals that Los Angeles has ever seen or heard" and included a rabid attack on Jewish film and radio star Eddie Cantor. Bund threats against Cantor eventually became so extreme that the league considered taking legal action to protect him and his family.[51] Allegations of Jewish control over the film industry were commonplace at these gatherings, and speakers "expressed the Bund's determination to rid the picture industry of them."[52] Impressively, the league even managed to infiltrate local Bund youth meetings, which included the usual anti-Semitic rhetoric followed by "an obscure routine of clapping hands, heiling Hitler, and shooting an invisible enemy." One such meeting was so heavy-handed in its rhetoric that the League's informant reported that "At this point I became nauseated and was glad I had had a few beers to see me through."[53]

The need for alcohol aside, the league's investigators amassed a remarkable amount of information about the LA Bund's activities. Yet the usefulness of these accounts to law enforcement was put in question because of the source reporting them. As it turned out, the league itself was under government investigation, and in August 1938 Congressman Martin Dies Jr. denounced it by name as a communist front in a national radio broadcast. Ironically, one of the telegrams of support Dies received afterward was from *Gauleiter* Schwinn, who offered to provide corroboration for the allegations about the league's communist ties from the Bund's own sources.[54] The league was seen as simply too questionable to be taken seriously.

The evidence Dies needed to start exposing the Bund finally began to emerge thanks to "Hellmut Oberwinder." Joining the Bund in March 1937, "Oberwinder" became a member of the OD and gained Kuhn's trust remarkably quickly. After having been a member for just a few months and rising through the ranks, Kuhn selected him as his personal representative to visit Bund chapters around the country and report back on the state of their activities and membership. As we know, "Oberwinder" was really John C. Metcalfe, a Chicago newspaper reporter and a former FBI informant. Metcalfe's plan was fraught with risk, and he was told that the bureau would disavow him in the event that he was discovered or harmed in the course of his subterfuge. In 1935 he had managed to secure an invitation to the Nazi Party's annual Nuremberg Rally but was dissuaded from going by FBI contacts who told him they could not guarantee his safety.[55] Now Metcalfe had embarked on an infiltration mission that was at least as dangerous.

Traveling around the country with Kuhn's blessing, Metcalfe obtained access to the highest levels of the Bund and recorded his experiences in a series of compelling journal entries. Along the way he sent regular telegrams to his brother James, a fellow newspaper reporter, signed with the pseudonym "Henry Hayes." What he uncovered was eye-opening. In Los Angeles, Metcalfe was told that Bund members had engaged in fistfights with communists on the streets of the city and won "moral victories" against overwhelming odds (perhaps suggesting that the physical outcome for the Bundists was less glorious). Industrialist Henry Ford was a local hero, "especially because of his anti-Semitic and anti-C.I.O. [anti-union] feelings." In addition, the California branch of the Bund was in close touch with the local Ku Klux Klan and the fascist Gold Shirt movement in Mexico, which supposedly had a membership of one hundred thousand to two hundred thousand and was "getting set for a revolution." (In fact the Gold Shirt movement had long since been all but wiped out by the Mexican government and its leader exiled to Texas, which understandably rankled many Americans. Remnants of the group would be responsible for a small uprising in 1938.)[56]

In contrast, Metcalfe discovered in Texas that the local Bund chapter disregarded nearly everything Kuhn commanded, including his uniform rules and the requirement to charge membership dues. While the local Bund chapter was essentially just a social club, he found the local residents held some worrying views: "People laugh at the Nazi threat in U.S. that they hear and read about. . . . However, their ears leap at the very mention of communism. . . . So, they laugh at the Nazis, they fear the communists and, without my mentioning it, despise the Jews. The anti-Semitic feeling is strong and they have a set idea that communism means Jewish dictatorship in America."[57]

Metcalfe found similar circumstances across the Midwest and East. Some Bund chapters were barely active and had small numbers of members, while others were more militant in their views and disciplined in their logistics. Nearly all the Bund leaders and most of the members were openly anti-Semitic and hardly shy in their praise for Hitler. In St. Louis, Metcalfe was told the local police were the Bund's "best friends" because many were of Irish and German descent and "they hate the Communists as much as we do." In Washington, DC, he was told conspiratorially that someday "Washington will be our Deutscher capital," though everyone he met assiduously denied that there was a local Bund chapter there. In Cleveland, he met a grizzled German war veteran who showed him the rubber hose he had used to beat Jews on the streets of his home country. Similarly shown a ten-inch knife the owner kept for protection against "Communists," Metcalfe feared that the experienced brawler had discovered his true identity and made a swift break for the door. "I think you better find a good hideout for me (a good one) when the yarn breaks," he told a collaborator. "I'd hate to meet that guy . . . after dark."[58]

The frightening veteran had not uncovered Metcalfe's plans, however. Returning to New York, he reported his findings directly to Kuhn. The would-be American Führer now began asking for Metcalfe's advice on how to proceed with his plans to expand the Bund's national appeal. He was particularly incensed by Metcalfe's report that some units had not purchased uniforms and disregarded his authority.[59] The man who saw himself as the American Hitler was not even in control of his own organization. The fact that Kuhn was having this conversation with an infiltrator hardly spoke to the strength and effectiveness of his leadership either.

The tables now turned abruptly on Kuhn. In early September 1937, Metcalfe and his collaborators published the first of a series of sensational articles in the Chicago *Daily Times* focusing on the OD and suggesting that it was a paramilitary force preparing to overthrow the government. The articles immediately sparked a national controversy. Kuhn was embarrassed by the revelations and tried to deny everything. The German embassy was outraged by the damage he had potentially done to relations with the United States. A German consul was forced to comment that "The idea that any one is attempting to form a Nazi army in America is ridiculous" and assured the *New York Times* that the revelations were greeted with "mixed amusement and irritation" in Berlin. One unnamed government official tried to poke fun at the claims, chortling to a reporter, "We would be flattered. Imagine Germany—already alleged to be preparing vast conquests in Europe—considered to be powerful enough by some people to be plotting quite incidentally to seize control also of the United States—perhaps in [its] spare time."[60]

Berlin was not laughing behind the scenes. Kuhn had already exaggerated his connections with Hitler and been the source of embarrassment in the past. Now he had been exposed as a national security threat to the United States. What damage would he do next? Something had to be done, and quickly. The obvious solution was for the German government to deal with the Bund as it had dealt with its embarrassing predecessors: By threatening the German citizens who took part in its activities. In February 1938, a group of German government officials agreed on exactly this plan. The German ambassador duly informed the US secretary of state that German citizens would no longer be permitted to be members of the Bund, just as they had been forbidden to join Friends of the New Germany in its final days.

Kuhn was outraged and decided not to go down quietly. He sailed to Germany immediately to meet directly with Hitler. In a major affront, the Führer declined the invitation and sent his personal adjutant Fritz Wiedemann—a figure who would himself soon feature as one of Hitler's key friends in the United States—to the meeting instead. Wiedemann told Kuhn that the decision was final and the German government expected him to abide by all US laws in the future. Kuhn slunk back to New York in disgrace. He had simply become too much of a liability for the Germans to tolerate any further. Behind the scenes, German consuls around the United States began quietly advising their citizens to get out of the Bund before there were more serious consequences for them. Membership numbers started to drop.[61]

Kuhn had one final trick up his sleeve—large-scale provocation. With the Bund's coffers rapidly draining, Kuhn decided to seize the maximum platform for himself in a desperate attempt to change the narrative. He hired Madison Square Garden for a celebration of George Washington's birthday in February 1939 and obtained the permits for a mass demonstration. This was an obvious provocation to New Yorkers of many backgrounds, and there were calls for the event to be banned. New York mayor Fiorello La Guardia was personally anti-Nazi and gambled that the Bund would make itself look ridiculous through its antics. The British Foreign Office reported that La Guardia had described the meeting as "an exhibition of 'international cooties'" that he "believed in exposing . . . to the sunlight instead of keeping them bottled up."[62] Letting the Bund into the sunlight would prove to be a fateful decision, but the event was allowed to go forward.

The Bund swiftly sold a massive twenty-two thousand tickets for what would be its last major hurrah. The event was an outrageous spectacle from the start, with three thousand uniformed OD men marching into the venue carrying American flags next to German flags bearing swastikas. Nearly two thousand New York City police officers guarded the venue from an estimated hundred thousand angry protestors. A massive full-length portrait of Washington stood behind the stage, flanked by American and German flags. Fights broke out on the floor of the hall between protestors and Bund members. During Kuhn's culminating speech, a Jewish hotel worker, Isadore Greenbaum, tried to rush the stage. Uniformed OD members tackled him and dragged him offstage, ripping off much of his clothing in the process. He had to be rescued by police officers who carried him out above their heads, and was later booked on disorderly conduct charges.[63]

The press went wild. "All the trappings of the spectacular mass assemblies familiar to Nazi Germany adorned the occasion," the *Los Angeles Times* reported. "Storm troopers strode the aisles. Military bands blared martial airs and German folk songs. . . . Arms snapped out in the Nazi salute."[64] If anything, Kuhn was flattered by the comparison. The putative American Führer had gotten the publicity he sought and was back on the newspaper front pages. Ironically, however, it would be the Madison Square Garden rally that would rapidly doom the Bund.

Mayor La Guardia was outraged by the violence that had taken place in his city and ordered an investigation into the Bund's financial records. In May 1939, the Bund's headquarters in the Yorkville neighborhood of New York City was raided and its financial records seized. Investigators soon found what they were looking for. The Bund's books revealed that more than $14,000 (about $250,000 in 2018) raised from the Madison Square Garden rally was effectively unaccounted for. Kuhn was arrested and accused of embezzlement. At nearly the same time, Kuhn was subpoenaed by the Dies Committee. He complied with the subpoena but gave away little in his testimony. The Bund's fate would soon be sealed by outside forces, however. The Committee was outraged shortly after to hear the testimony of a nineteen-year-old former Youth Division member who testified she had been sent to Germany by the Bund to indoctrinate her with Nazi ideas. She went on to allege that that Kuhn's youth camps were rife with homosexuality.[65]

Dies had other information to use against the Bund as well. Following his reporting coup, Metcalfe had been hired by the Dies Committee as its first full-time investigator. As he testified in 1938 (in his OD uniform, for maximum effect), in his view the "Nazi movement in the United States" had three main goals:

1. The establishment of a vast spy net
2. A powerful sabotage machine
3. A German minority with the present group [the German American Bund] as a nucleus and to encompass as many German Americans as possible[66]

The Bund was therefore at the center of Nazi plans for the United States. This prediction would prove to be prescient, and one that understandably worried the Dies Committee's members.

Meanwhile, the noose of public opinion was also tightening quickly for Kuhn. In April 1939, just months after the Madison Square Garden rally, the Bund was subjected to mass ridicule on the silver screen when Warner Brothers released the sensationalist film *Confessions of a Nazi Spy*. The film was presented in the style of newsreels and focused on a dangerous German spy ring based in an organization of uniform-wearing, heiling Nazi sympathizers. The Bund comparisons were obvious. It ended with a Nazi character explaining how America could be conquered through a clever use of propaganda "ridiculing democracy" and increasing "racial prejudice."[67] It was a mediocre film, but a major turning point for Hollywood. As historian Francis MacDonnell has written, it was "the first film to specifically identify and attack Hitler's regime" in a period when most studios were still trying to play nice with the German government for business purposes.[68] *Confessions* was such a brutal repudiation of this practice that it prompted the German ambassador to file a formal complaint with the State Department.[69]

Making such a heavy-handed film was risky for Warner Brothers. FBI director J. Edgar Hoover was worried the publicity surrounding its release would increase the public's concern about German spying. He eventually filed a formal complaint about the studio's use of FBI badges in the film without proper permission.[70] The Bund sued for libel. More than a dozen countries banned its release, and during the war German troops confiscated prints they found in occupied Europe. Isolationist congressmen called for an investigation, and even

President Roosevelt declined a private viewing from studio executives. The film made only modest profits in the United States and was widely considered to be a flop (though it did well overseas and seems to have ultimately pulled a profit). During congressional hearings about the film, Warner Brothers executives confirmed that Metcalfe's reporting had been the partial inspiration for the film. The message studio executives took from the experience, however, was that in 1939 the American public was simply not interested in films about Nazis and wars.[71]

Kuhn's eventual trial was even more of a spectacle than the Dies Committee hearings or the furor surrounding *Confessions of a Nazi Spy*. At least some of the missing money from the Madison Square Garden rally, it emerged, had been spent on his mistresses, including more than $700 (about $12,000 in 2018) in long-distance telephone charges and $66 on an unspecified "doctor's bill" for the former Miss America. To Kuhn's embarrassment, his love letters to one of the women were introduced into evidence. In several he referred to himself by the pet name "Fritzi." The man who had once styled himself as America's Hitler had been revealed to be an embezzling adulterer with a penchant for silly nicknames.[72] Kuhn was convicted in December 1939 and was formally expelled from the Bund by his successor, Gerhard Wilhelm Kunze, the following day. The prospective American Führer now sat in Sing Sing prison.

The Bund quickly spiraled into the abyss. Local chapters disbanded or merged with other groups. A number of states, including its former stronghold of California, banned it as a subversive group. Kuhn's legal battles were not over, however, and neither were those of the other Bund leaders. In November 1941, Kunze abruptly announced his resignation as Bund leader and secretly fled to Mexico. Evidently, he had been pursuing an extracurricular career as a spy for German military intelligence and, sensing that things were heating up, decided to make his exit while he still could. As will be seen, he was not the only Nazi spy to be found in the German American Bund's ranks. Kunze's successor, George Froboese, had been the leader of the Bund's Milwaukee branch and was left with the unenviable task of being Bund national leader when Germany declared war on the United States.[73] His end would be grim. In June 1942, Froboese was subpoenaed to appear before a federal grand jury investigating the Bund in New York. Leaving from Milwaukee, Froboese stepped off the train in the town of Waterloo, Indiana, and evidently decided he could go no further. He walked around the small railway station into the darkness in front of the train and lay down with his neck on the track. The disembarking locomotive decapitated him instantly. His headless body lay there for hours before being discovered by the conductor of a stopping train. FBI agents responding to the scene found a copy of the grand jury subpoena in his coat pocket. More salaciously, a local newspaper reported one of his hands was found "in a position that one official said looked almost like a 'heil Hitler!' salute."[74] The Bund essentially died on the railway tracks with him that night.

The German American Bund was, without doubt, the most prominent organization of Hitler's American friends before the outbreak of World War II. For Hitler, it was always like a cloying friend who seeks attention but with whom it is simply too embarrassing to be seen in public. The Nazis rightly realized the potential damage that Kuhn and his followers would inevitably do to relations with the US government. It was simply not worth risking a war to assuage his huge ego. "The Bund never made much headway in this country," Deputy Attorney General Oetje John Rogge, the US government's leading expert on Nazi subversion, later wrote. "Most Americans of German descent were not in sympathy with the Nazi regime, which was the source of considerable disappointment to the Nazis in Germany in the early years of the Third Reich."[75]

Rogge was correct, but at the same time it is undeniable that thousands of Americans saw Kuhn as a major political leader and, potentially, a future Führer. Metcalfe's surveillance diaries are replete with conversations with average Bund members and nonmembers alike who believed that the United States should seek closer relations with Germany, escalate its battle with communism, and adopt anti-Semitic legislation. Even an official membership of thirty thousand demonstrates the appeal that the symbols of National Socialism and fascism had for a sizable number of people. Some of them were willing to wear uniforms, "heil" their leaders, and send their children to Nazi-themed summer camps. The Bund was not so much an artificial creation of a charismatic demagogue and his inner circle but an organization that had intrinsic appeal for a substantial number of people. Kuhn was simply the voice that emerged to articulate the views many of them already held, as Metcalfe found in his travels.

In the end, the Bund was a miserable failure, destroyed by the vanity of its charismatic leader. Hitler and his government never placed much stock in Kuhn and ultimately disowned him. For the millions of Americans who saw newsreels of OD members marching in uniform and Kuhn delivering stemwinders to a crowd of heiling Bundists, it was the epitome of what a fascist regime might look like in the United States. It was not an image most Americans enjoyed seeing. For that reason, Kuhn and the German American Bund were ultimately

Hitler's most visible friends in the United States, but also the ones he liked the least. As J. Edgar Hoover's FBI and Congressman Martin Dies would soon discover, however, the Bund was by no means the most dangerous—or bizarre—group claiming Hitler's mantle before the war. With Kuhn's spectacular downfall, his rivals for the title of American Führer would only increase their efforts to claim the potential crown.

2

THE SILVER LEGION AND THE CHIEF

In January 1939, a crowd of three hundred packed the Swedish Hall in downtown Seattle to attend an evening event thrown by the "League of American Patriots." That was the name of the organization that reserved the venue, at least. The main speaker that night certainly thought of himself as a patriot. He was Roy Zachary, the national field marshal of the Silver Legion based in Asheville, North Carolina. He was as fiery and unsparing as usual in his speech. "We are fighting people who have no ethics whatever; will let nothing stand between them and their goal," he told the audience. "Matter of conscience doesn't matter; they are taught 'anything goes.'" At some point in the near future, Americans would have to "rise and stop these forces."

Who were these insidious enemies? The Jews. "Jews came to America, got control of credit and finance; they control the nation thereby," Zachary charged. "They have control of industry, distribution, education and politics—what more do you want?" All business men in "the East" were Jewish, he continued, and the Jews "have a monopoly on moving pictures and radio." The Russian Revolution was one example of the Jewish plot in action, he claimed, as was the Great Depression. What was Zachary's proposed solution to all this? "Our battle cry will be echoed from the stars," he said. "Our battle cry is for Christianity and the Constitution. Our objective is to rid America of subversive influences that would destroy the constitution of our forefathers." Exactly how this was to be accomplished was left unsaid, but the meeting closed with the speakers encouraging the audience to return for a German American Bund event at a later date.[1]

Zachary's rousing rhetoric that evening—a surveillance agent who infiltrated the event noted he was "an exceptionally good speaker and a pleasant personality"—was the typical fodder of the organization he represented. As one of the Silver Legion's leading members, Zachary traveled the country making speeches of exactly the sort he made in Seattle that night, calling on Americans to join a movement that he and his fellow Silver Shirts claimed would free the nation from the shackles of Jewish and communist oppression. They were at least moderately successful in gathering supporters. At one time the Silver Shirts had nearly the same number of members as the German American Bund and a national network of local chapters. Founded by eccentric mystic, former Hollywood screenwriter, and failed novelist William Dudley Pelley, the Silver Shirts became one of the nation's leading national security threats in the mid-1930s. Unlike the German American Bund, Pelley and his fellow leaders were open about their desire to establish a fascist government in the United States. Pelley himself would even run for president on that platform. While never coming close to actually achieving national political power, the Silver Shirts represented perhaps the most direct effort to emulate Hitler's Nazi Party in the United States.

Even more disturbing to the US government, however, was the fact that Pelley and the Silver Shirts were adept at making alliances with similarly minded groups at the local level, even as their leaders clashed over money and personal differences. Pelley was irascible, controlling and, in the minds of many, a complete madman, but his local organizers proved far more capable and managed to strike meaningful alliances with several local German American Bund and Ku Klux Klan chapters. The Klan was a particularly fertile recruiting ground for Pelley, and several of his trusted lieutenants were current or former Klan organizers as well. Unlike the Bund, Pelley deliberately structured the legion as a "Christian" and "Aryan" organization. Most of his members were Protestant. These demographics made overlaps and affinities with the anti-Catholic Klan inevitable. As will be seen, he would eventually claim there were Silver Legion chapters in anywhere between twenty-two and forty states, with a membership of around fifteen thousand at its 1934 peak and many more sympathizers. Given the difficulties estimating exact membership for either group, it can be assumed that the Silver Shirts probably had fewer members than the German American Bund, but probably not by a huge amount. Both groups had an ill-defined number of hangers-on who probably numbered around one hundred thousand each, with some crossover between the two (and they reached their peaks at different times).[2] These were not insubstantial organizations, par ticularly since many of their followers were militant and, as will be seen, armed. Despite his reputation as a madman, Pelley certainly had the chance to make a bid for the title of American Führer if he could bridge the divide between the far-right factions.

There were some indications that Pelley might be able to accomplish this. The German government was more intrigued by Pelley's organization than it was by the German American Bund, particularly after its conflict with Fritz Kuhn. In 1937, the head of the World Service—the Nazi Party's international propaganda organization—prepared a memorandum for Hitler in which he described Pelley as one of the "national men" in the United States and someone who could be counted on to support the German cause. Nazi ideologues drew on Pelley's writings in their own anti-American propaganda, often for distribution through its propaganda networks in the United States, and referred to him as "one of the first native Fascists" in the country.[3] A Dies Committee report published in early 1940 referred to the Silver Legion as "probably the largest, best financed and best publicized" of the groups directly emulating Hitler and the Nazi Party.[4]

The biggest difference between the Silver Legion and the Bund, beyond the former's religious orientation, was that the Bund was fundamentally more than one man's quixotic venture. Certainly, the fall of Fritz Kuhn put the final nail in its coffin, but the Bund had also been born out the pro-Nazi organizations of the 1920s and Friends of the New Germany. Bund members were unified by their shared cultural heritage, and while the ideological orientation of the Bund was never really in question, there was at least an additional aspect to membership that theoretically superseded politics. The Silver Shirts had no such fallback beyond a general adherence to "Christianity." It was fundamentally a cult of personality rotating around Pelley and the divine prophesies he claimed to be delivering. This divine inspiration, as will be seen, supposedly led to Nazism.

Founding the Silver Legion was in many ways a strange apogee for Pelley's career. He was born in Massachusetts in 1890 as the son of a Methodist pastor. A voracious reader and writer, the young Pelley began publishing his own journal in 1909. Many of his early writings focused on the role of religion in society, and he came to the view that Christianity would need to reform itself to remain relevant in the modern world. A few years later he turned to fiction, writing tales about the West (which he had never visited) and starting a career in journalism. In 1918, with World War I still raging, he embarked on an ill-timed reporting assignment on Methodist missions in China and India with his young wife. They were soon stranded in Japan.[5]

The strange decision to travel during a world war would soon present an opportunity for Pelley. In mid-1918, President Woodrow Wilson ordered thousands of American troops into Siberia to fight Bolshevik forces in the ongoing Russian civil war. The YMCA pledged to provide humanitarian assistance to these troops, and one of their primary volunteer recruiting grounds was Japan. Pelley signed up and soon found himself traversing across the Siberian wilderness. Along the way he filed reports for the Associated Press. His experience in war—particularly a war between communists and anti-communists—would have a profound effect on his later views. Pelley would later claim that in Siberia he first discovered the peril posed by Jews, particularly through their alleged links to communism. As was the case for so many who turned to the anti-Semitic right in the 1930s, the Russian Revolution was the catalyst for the development of Pelley's views on both communism and Jews.

In the meantime, however, Pelley's career as a writer seemed to be moving along swimmingly. In 1921 he sold one of his stories to a movie studio and, after splitting with his wife, joined the production team in New Jersey. Infatuated by the film industry and the prospect of living in California, Pelley moved to Hollywood and began a career that would see him write or assist with nearly two dozen movie scripts and net him a small fortune of more than $100,000 (the equivalent of nearly $1.5 million in 2018). As a young and recently divorced man with a good income, Hollywood had no shortage of fun opportunities. Pelley later admitted that he spent many of his years in the film industry enjoying the pleasures and sins of the flesh that came with wealth and growing fame.[6] Amidst all this fun, however, Pelley seems to have had a sort of midlife crisis, and abruptly decided in 1927 that his life had gone off the rails. His personal anti-Semitism had been heightened by interactions with Hollywood movie bosses, and he believed that the Jewish conspiracy he saw everywhere had now targeted him personally. He also dabbled unsuccessfully in the Los Angeles real estate business, heightening his sense of personal victimization. Frustrated by Hollywood despite its pleasures and evidently filled with guilt about his own indulgence, Pelley purchased a house in the mountain community of Altadena and retreated from the film industry. It was here that he would purport to have a spiritual experience that changed his life.

Pelley would later claim that as he lay in bed on the evening of May 28,

1928, he experienced a vision of being whisked away through a "bluish mist." He regained consciousness lying on a marble slab next to two men who began to reveal the secrets of the universe. Among these was the revelation that death was only temporary and that all human beings are reincarnated to proceed up a ladder to higher existence. Even more important, Pelley reported, the men told him that he would receive additional revelations in the future. Claiming himself to have been "reborn," Pelley declared that when he woke up the next morning his physical appearance had changed, lines had disappeared from his face, and he appeared more relaxed. The "Great Release," as Pelley called it, put his life on a new course. Over the next several years he experimented with aspects of spiritualism including automatic writing and clairvoyant mediums, all of whom unsurprisingly told him that his experiences had been genuine glimpses into the spiritual realm.

In 1929, Pelley moved to New York and began to publish accounts of his experiences. Inspired by his stories about the divine and convinced that he could offer the secrets of the universe, a small group of readers began consulting him for spiritual guidance, and his influence grew.[7] Pelley's career as a spiritual guide to humanity's biggest questions had begun. Ever the salesman, Pelley soon turned his spiritual awakening into material success, publishing a spiritualist journal that he claimed had more than ten thousand subscribers. It offered personal lessons in how to grow personal wealth and cure various ailments through spiritual means. Ninety percent of his followers were women, some of whom gave him vast sums of money to assist with their needs. In 1931, Pelley founded his own publishing company, called the Galahad Press, and opened a small college in Asheville, North Carolina, to spread his teachings.[8]

This seems like a very strange career move for a successful, albeit frustrated, Hollywood writer to make from an early-twenty-first-century perspective. It was less unusual at the time. Millions of Americans were interested in spiritualism, and it was particularly popular in Hollywood (First Lady Nancy Reagan, herself a product of Hollywood in a somewhat later period, would become infamous for consulting an astrologer for advice on aspects of her husband's presidency). Critically, Pelley tried to reconcile his spiritualist teachings with Christianity, claiming he been able to contact Jesus through his spiritualist methods. He declared Jesus was the greatest spirit of all that could be contacted, and that their conversations had revealed the truth about Christianity. The clergy, Pelley proclaimed, had long suppressed the idea of rebirth that he was now touting because it did not suit their earthly interests. Because he was the first to discover this fact, Pelley concluded, he was now able to receive messages directly from Jesus.[9]

Pelley would later claim to have received a critical message from his spiritual sources in mid-1929. The world would soon be plunged into economic turmoil, Pelley learned, and the entire political and social system would undergo major change. In the midst of this chaos, Pelley was to create a "Christian Militia" to save the United States, triggered when a new leader—a "certain young house-painter"—came to power in Germany.[10] This "prophesy" was fulfilled in late January 1933 when Adolf Hitler became chancellor of Germany. Pelley kept up his side of the bargain by announcing the creation of the Silver Legion. The legion was intended to be a paramilitary organization that, according to Pelley, would bring about a spiritual and political renewal of the United States. He quickly turned his Asheville operations toward supporting the legion and claimed that Jesus himself had once again been in touch to endorse its creation. To complete the transition, Pelley now bestowed a new title on himself: the Chief.

Membership in the Silver Legion was open to any person, male or female, over the age of eighteen, except for African Americans and Jews. Unlike the German American Bund, fees were low and eventually disappeared entirely. The legion's anthem was the *Battle Hymn of the Republic* and its regulation uniform consisted of a silver shirt, tie, blue trousers, and a standard cap. A giant red L appeared on the breast of each shirt, over the heart, and supposedly symbolized "Love, Loyalty, and Liberation." The legion's flag was a white banner with a similar L on it.[11] Outfitted so distinctly, the Silver Shirts were instantly recognizable wherever they went. Pelley himself sported a stylish goatee that turned gradually gray over the course of the decade, and maintained well-coiffed hair that gave him a sense of Hollywood glamour. Outfitted in his own legion uniform, the Chief cut a compelling public profile that was less outrageous than the one cultivated by Fritz Kuhn but equally charismatic and inspiring to his supporters.

The legion was administratively run on the same model as the Bund. The Chief was at the top of the hierarchy and, even more undemocratically than the Bund, never had to face an election. The *Führerprinzip* applied, meaning Pelley's word must always be obeyed. Alongside the Chief was a general staff, elected for ten-year terms, and variety of other officials with pretentious titles including quartermaster, sheriff, and censor. State chapters were headed by a commander who reported to the national organization. Local chapters included a chaplain and other officials who managed finances and records. The paramilitary wing of the organization was called the Silver Rangers and was divided into cadres of one hundred armed fighters. Their weapon of choice was a scourge whip based on the one Jesus had supposedly used to drive money changers from the temple in the Gospels. Like the Bund's nightsticks, this was a legal weapon that could potentially be used with lethal effect.[12]

Pelley's stated goal was to bring about a "Christian Commonwealth" in the United States. This governmental system would not be fascist, communist, capitalist, or presumably fit any other known political model. Instead it would be based on a system of "Christian economics" that he himself had devised. As an American Jewish Committee report on Pelley noted, this system was based in "a curious sort of mysticism, compounded of astrology, mythology, and spiritualism."[13] All property would be held by the government, and every qualified citizen would be a stockholder in the state. All citizens would receive a guaranteed basic income of at least $1,000 per year, paid out as dividends on their "shares." More stock in the state, and therefore income, could be acquired only through meritorious action. No property or money could be inherited between generations and only white citizens would be allowed to own stock. African Americans would be reduced to slavery to provide a supply of cheap physical labor, and Jews would be excluded entirely.[14]

Unsurprisingly, Pelley believed that the main obstacle to establishing this system was the Jews. In his future government, he proclaimed, there would be a "Secretary of Jewry" who would be responsible for dealing with the Jewish population by restricting them to a single city per state and closely monitoring their activities. This was necessary because there was a vast and international Jewish conspiracy responsible for every negative influence and event in world history, he claimed. In Pelley's mind, Jews controlled most current media, politicians, and financial systems. Their main vehicle for sowing unrest presently was communism. A Silver Legion training document entitled *The Reds Are Upon Us* emphasized that "only an insignificant fraction of the real Communist work being carried on in America is openly and shamelessly stamped with the insignia of Communism." The vast majority of communist plots were "camouflaged" behind a variety of covers that were seemingly innocuous. The training continued by asking recruits to guess how many communists there were in the United States (the "correct" answer being 22 million, which Pelley reached by counting every person "under the control of his rabbi") and the number of rabbis (allegedly

2 million). Needless to say, these numbers were vastly exaggerated. In reality, most demographers put the actual number of Jews in the United States as being somewhere around 3 percent of the overall population, or around 4.5 million people in the 1930s (Pelley claimed that this number should be multiplied by five because "Jews reckon population only by males who have reached their majority" and failed to count anyone else, ignoring the fact that the official number had come from the US Census Bureau).[15]

Regardless, aspiring Silver Shirts were told that "We are not against the Jews as a people, but because they are slaves and serfs beneath the control of their rabbinate. And that rabbinate wants to see Communism come in and close all Christian churches."[16] As the American Jewish Committee summarized it:

> One cannot always be certain of what Pelley favors, but one is seldom left in doubt as to what Pelley opposes, and he opposes many things. The Jews, of course, are his chief objects of hatred. To Pelley, the Jews are the root of all evil. Whenever he is against anything, it is because Jews are connected with it, and if he can't find Jews, he creates them. Thus, his chief objection to Communism is its alleged Jewishness.[17]

Pelley intended for the Silver Legion to defeat this vast alleged conspiracy.

Despite Pelley's outlandish and pretentious ideas, the Silver Legion was surprisingly successful in recruiting members. Much like the Bund, the decentralized nature of the Silver Legion makes finding exact membership figures difficult. Pelley claimed to have 50,000 followers a few months after launching the organization, but later revised this and claimed to have attracted 25,000 members and three times as many sympathizers at the peak of his popularity. Historians have generally suggested that the numbers were somewhat smaller, with the most widely cited estimate being 15,000 members at its peak.[18] As with the Bund, the fact that members would have joined and left the organization as the political situation changed made it nearly impossible for Pelley or anyone else to know the true number of active members at any given time. Regardless, even 15,000 would have made the legion a formidable presence in its local strongholds. Demographically, most legion members appear to have come from British and German backgrounds and were either working or middle class. About 15 percent were engaged in professional, white-collar careers. The medical profession seems to have been particularly well represented, perhaps reflecting the Chief's appeal to whites who were inclined to believe their social status was under attack from the minority groups Pelley loudly denounced. Membership numbers were largest in the upper Midwest and the far West, especially Washington State and California.[19]

It would indeed be the West where Pelley focused the bulk of his efforts. The Nazis themselves recognized that the West and South were the regions most likely to be sympathetic to their propaganda due to their respective racial tensions (between whites and African Americans in the South; and Asians, especially the Chinese, in the West).[20] Washington State would become Pelley's biggest stronghold. One estimate has placed Washington membership at around 1,600 people, primarily in the Seattle area. In a state of about 1.6 million people in the mid-1930s, this suggests that the legion membership was around 0.001 percent of the overall population, which, as already seen, was also the exact approximation of Bund membership and sympathizers in the total US population.[21] Uniformed Silver Shirts would soon become a regular sight on the streets of Seattle.

As the Chief's membership began to grow, however, so did his legal difficulties. These stemmed in part from his past career as a spiritual leader. Back in 1932, Pelley devised a scheme to sell shares in the Galahad Press to his readers to generate cash for its operations. He then advertised those shares for sale in his own publication. After the founding of the legion, Pelley started moving funds between various accounts to support his activities, including some money that had been received as donations from well-wishers and cash raised from the sale of the shares. However, this financial chicanery left the press bankrupt. In early 1934, Pelley ordered an associate to burn the press records, and declared bankruptcy. This, however, meant he had defrauded the shareholders by effectively looting the company. Pelley was duly indicted in North Carolina on a range of charges and many of his personal records were seized. The resulting legal battles would drag on for years, but, unlike the Bund's Fritz Kuhn, this would be far from the end of Pelley's career as one of Hitler's American friends.[22]

Pelley was subsequently arrested, convicted, and released on parole. He blamed the legal woes on the Jews and renewed his activities with the legion in late 1935. Membership numbers in the organization had fallen as Pelley's legal problems unfolded, and several of his close associates broke away to form their own splinter factions. Always the showman, Pelley knew that a big comeback would require dramatic action. He did so by announcing that the Silver Legion was getting into politics at the highest levels by seeking the presidency. Claiming to have received a divine message predicting another economic crisis, Pelley announced the formation of the Christian Party with himself as its head. As such, Pelley would be its presidential candidate in the upcoming 1936 election. The party's platform was a carbon copy of Pelley's other teachings, including the heavily anti-Semitic aspects. In the course of the campaign he vowed to prevent Jews from owning most property and pledged to enact his economic plans. He had already denounced the president as a secret Jew, accusing him of concealing the fact that his actual family name was "Rosenfeld." Now he claimed the president's Republican opponent, Alf Landon, was conspiring against the Christian Party by having his staff hold events in the same towns Pelley was visiting to draw away his crowds.[23] This was all conspiratorial and outlandish, but it was also vintage Pelley rhetoric.

Pelley's openly anti-Semitic and mystical platform gained him little support, particularly when his predicted economic crisis failed to materialize. Despite a national speaking tour he only managed to make it onto the ballot in Washington State. He garnered fewer than two thousand votes there in November. This result humiliatingly put him behind both the Socialist and Communist candidates on the ballot.[24] As left-wing journalist Gustavus Myers noted acidly, "The scattered vote cast for the Christian Party was so altogether negligible that almanac compilers of election returns did not take the trouble to give it notice."[25] The entire campaign had really only been a ploy to put Pelley back in the national spotlight, however. After the 1936 defeat his followers began to take a more active role in the political organization he had built. In the course of his work in Washington, Pelley met Roy Zachary, the anti-Semitic demagogue with whom this chapter began. Zachary was a former clerical worker who owned a Seattle restaurant and became enamored with Pelley's supposed connection to the divine. He quickly became the Chief's chief political organizer in the state, selecting the slate of other Christian Party candidates (all of whom would lose) for a wide range of federal and state offices. Following the defeat, Pelley chose Zachary to be his nationwide second-in-command. In this new role, Zachary began traveling the country on Pelley's behalf, ending his career as a restaurateur but gradually rebuilding the organization's membership.[26]

Zachary's importance to the Silver Legion lay in not only his personal dynamism as a speaker and his organizational skills, but also in the fact that he quickly proved able to make connections with Hitler's other American friends. The Bund had long shied away from any kind of alliance with Pelley in part because its leaders saw him as a dangerous madman. Fritz Kuhn told the Dies Committee that he had only met Pelley on one occasion in 1936 and "never cooperated with the Silver Shirts at all."[27] The Bund might be interested in an alliance with the legion, Kuhn continued, if it "would have a good organization," but he professed that he did not "care for them at all."[28] Most of Hitler's other American friends saw Pelley as a "lone wolf" who was not only uncontrollable but would demand "dictatorial powers" in the event that they cooperated with him.[29]

Pelley's lieutenants were a different story, however. Surveillance reports filed by John C. Metcalfe and Hollywood Anti-Nazi League investigators record the presence of Silver Shirts at Bund meetings up and down the West Coast. Even if Pelley himself was an undesirable ally, his supporters were welcomed with seemingly open arms. In Los Angeles, Metcalfe was told that the local legion leaders would drop into the Bund headquarters, the Deutsches Haus, on a periodic basis and conceal their identities from all but a handful of key officers. The Bund leaders there were "constantly in touch with them and [worked] together." The LA Silver Shirt headquarters—"ironically enough" located next to a federal naturalization bureau—had shut down entirely by the time he arrived, but Metcalfe found the organization to still be "quite active." The aims of the Silver Shirts and the Bund, one Kuhn lieutenant told him, "are very similar in many ways," and there was therefore a natural affinity between the groups.[30]

Pelley did try to build some of these alliances himself. One of his more bizarre ploys involved an effort to convert Native Americans to the Silver Shirt cause. Pelley's sudden interest in Native Americans stemmed from a supposed divine realization that the Bureau of Indian Affairs had been taken over by Bolsheviks. Native Americans were therefore natural allies for his political movement because they too were supposedly victims of the Jewish conspiracy Pelley saw everywhere. Among the many problems with this eccentric plan was the fact that Pelley did not actually know many Native Americans. His efforts to reach out by referring to himself as "Chief Pelley of the Tribe of Silver" and writing articles in prose that could have been lifted from the stock characters of Hollywood Westerns gained few supporters.[31] One Native American ally Pelley did manage to recruit was a mixed-race Portland attorney named Elwood A. Towner who soon took on a bizarre role. Adopting the "Indian title" of Chief Red Cloud, Towner began attending legion and Bund meetings up and down the West Coast and drew sizable crowds as he wore a stereotypical feather headdress and clothing covered in swastikas.[32]

Towner's primary mission was to recruit Native Americans into the legion, but most of his appearances were before Bund and legion audiences and focused on providing a bogus Native American backstory for Nazism. Once described by a Hollywood Anti-Nazi League investigator as the "Charlie McCarthy of the Bundsmen" and their "spiritual symbol," a typical appearance involved the fake chief speaking in broken English about how "the coming of the German to these shores was glowingly prophesied." The Jews, he claimed, were also prophesied and "were the traditional Aryan enemies, the gold worshippers who would corrupt the Aryan Indians and put them in concentration camps." Native Americans "from Alaska to Tierra del Fuego" had been taught to "blame the Jews for their generally pitiful conditions" and were ready to accept "the Nazi doctrines of violence, rebellion and race-hatred." He usually concluded this bizarre tale by claiming the swastika and the Nazi salute both originated in Native American culture. "Our people admire Hitler for this reason that he adopted for his symbol the swastika," Towner told a Los Angeles Bund gathering. "It means prosperity, good luck, and Christian government. . . . Hitler also adopted our salute [Gave salute and audience cheered and responded] which means 'Peace be unto you—advance friend.'" This bizarre reading of history was generally greeted with applause and heils at Bund and Silver Legion meetings, but apparently did little to actually recruit Native Americans.[33]

As Pelley's fame grew, the German embassy in Washington, DC, was becoming increasingly skeptical of his activities. First Secretary Heribert von Strempel later recalled he believed it would be unwise for German officials to receive Pelley in any official capacity because he was so openly anti-Semitic and potentially a loose cannon (regardless, embassy staff may still have funneled Pelley some money through back channels).[34] The embassy's caution was understandable. As his public profile increased, Pelley became more and more delusional. In late 1937, he instructed associates in Washington State to begin outreach to "key Japs" in the area who might support the legion financially. Pelley's reasoning was that the Japanese community feared the potential of war breaking out and would therefore be willing to back the legion. There was supposedly a deeper backstory too. When he was seventeen, Pelley now claimed, he had been sitting in church when he suddenly heard a disembodied voice say, "When you grow up you are to be the instrument for stopping a great war between your country and Japan." Pelley now believed that his task was to "minimize the troubles between the two countries as destiny may serve me with the opportunity."[35]

There is little evidence the Japanese-American community was at all interested in Pelley, but this attempted outreach demonstrates the extent of his ambitions. In 1938, Pelley laid out his future plans directly in a manual entitled "A Million Silvershirts by 1939." The pamphlet called upon state organizers to sign up one hundred new members *per day*, a significant increase from the prevailing average of five.[36] Faced with this impossible quota, legion organizers tried to increase their appeal by arguing that they were not anti-Semitic and were part of a patriotic, Christian organization. "The only reason we make open opposition to the Jews is because they are the ones . . . who support communism which is atheism and are out to destroy Christianity," a Washington State organizer wrote to a critic in 1938. He continued, "We are not Jew haters as reported, we are only against their system. . . . I do not hate a single Jew, but I do feel sorry for them. I do not hate a single person on this earth including all Jews."[37]

As the legion's stature increased and its tone seemingly moderated, it became more difficult for the US government to ignore its activities. Roosevelt himself saw Pelley as a serious annoyance if not an outright threat. In 1938, the president asked the Department of Justice whether it would be possible to sue Pelley for libel. This ill-conceived plan came to nothing, but the following year Roosevelt asked Attorney General Frank Murphy the same question after Pelley accused him of embezzling money intended for a disabled children's charity. Murphy wisely advised the president that he would almost certainly be called to testify in any trial, which would put him under oath and at Pelley's mercy. Roosevelt sensibly decided that this was a bad idea.[38] Public fury against the legion was growing at the same time. In 1938, Roy Zachary was "run out of town" in Sharon, Pennsylvania, when dozens of World War I veterans attacked a Silver Shirt meeting, smashing windows and beating up at least two participants. As the violence unfolded, Zachary ran to his car "with a dozen veterans on his heels" and hightailed it across the Ohio state line.[39]

Congressman Martin Dies Jr. had far more of an opportunity to deal with Pelley than the president or mobs of angry veterans. The public's growing impatience with the legion mirrored the growing distrust of the Bund, giving Dies a political motivation to go after Pelley. The Chief had also long been openly flouting the law as well. At one point he was reported to be accompanied by a "personal bodyguard" of forty uniformed Silver Shirts who carried pistols in shoulder holsters and dared local law enforcement to "do anything about it."[40] In 1938, Zachary told a Milwaukee reporter that he was advising all Silver Shirts to have sawed-off shotguns and two thousand rounds of ammunition at home, "for the protection of what Mr. Zachary terms 'white Christian America.'"[41]

All this suggested that Pelley was planning a significant escalation in his ac-tivities beyond rhetoric.

With his work on the Bund wrapping up, Dies turned his Committee's at-tention to the legion in 1939. He was immediately faced with an odd and trou-bling development. Early in the year, the Committee received an application for employment as an undercover agent from a man named Frasier S. Gardner, who had strangely been attending all of the Committee's open hearings as a member of the public. At nearly the same time Gardner applied for the posi-tion, "a local attorney active in anti-radical work" sent the Committee a letter claiming that Gardner had offered to sell him information about the witnesses scheduled to appear in later hearings before the list became public knowledge. Exactly how this information was obtained is unclear, but it suggests Gardner must have had a source inside the Committee. Subsequent investigation revealed that Gardner was in fact an employee of Pelley's Skyland Press. The obvious implication Dies drew was that Pelley was attempting to infiltrate his Commit-tee.[42]

Dies resolved to expose the plot by letting Gardner hang himself rhetori-cally. Calling Gardner to testify on the pretense that he was being background-checked for employment, the Committee put him under oath and asked whether he had any connection with organizations the Committee was investigating. Gardner replied that he did not. With this denial duly recorded, the Commit-tee adjourned into open session and called Gardner as a witness to confront him with telegrams its investigators had obtained that had seemingly been sent from Pelley to Gardner. Gardner's testimony quickly changed from the claim that he had "nothing to do with Pelley" to the admission that they had met several times and finally the revelation that they had talked on the phone on several occasions about "reports that refugees were brought into this country in violation of the law." Through it all, however, he denied that he had been paid directly by Pelley and insisted that he had simply been an employee of the press. No one was impressed, and Gardner ended up going to prison for perjury. Dies described the case as being of a "specially grave nature" and warned that other organ-izations might well try to infiltrate his Committee as well.[43]

Had Pelley tried to infiltrate the Dies Committee? There is no direct proof he did, but it is easy to see why Dies would be concerned by the Gardner case. There was only one way to find out the truth: subpoena Pelley. The summons was issued in August 1939. However, in a decision that one biographer has un-derstatedly described as "truly poor," Pelley decided to go on the run instead of testifying. Traveling across the country and undoubtedly being aided by Silver Legion local chapters, he openly mocked federal investigators in published articles describing his adventures. Adding insult to injury, Pelley then sued the entire Dies Committee for an astonishing $3.15 million for defamation after Committee members publicly described him as a "racketeer."[44] The suit was filed by Pelley's attorneys and lacked even an affidavit from him, which would have been difficult to justify having since he was technically missing. The case came to nothing and was eventually dropped, but it served to keep Pelley's name in the press just as the outbreak of war in Europe was dominating the headlines.[45]

The net was still closing quickly around the Chief. In October, a judge in North Carolina ordered Pelley to appear for a parole hearing. As with the Dies subpoena, he ignored the summons. This opened the door to a full investigation of his activities in the state. The Silver Legion's national headquarters was soon ransacked and its records seized.[46] Pelley's flair for the Hollywood-esque once again came to the fore. In January 1940, as war raged in Europe and the debate over American intervention heated up on Capitol Hill, Democratic congressman Frank E. Hook of Michigan—a liberal Roosevelt ally—introduced shocking letters on the floor of Congress that were purportedly between his colleague Dies and Pelley himself. The explosive correspondence supposedly revealed a secret alliance between the Silver Shirts and the Dies Committee chairman, though the letters were oddly signed "Pelly" rather than the correct spelling of the Chief's name. If true, this was a massive revelation, and it shook Washington to the core. Liberals who believed Dies was targeting unions and the left rather than the real fascist threat rejoiced at the thought of bringing down their archnemesis. Unfortunately for them, the letters were quickly shown to be forgeries, and within weeks the Committee had elicited a confession from the forger responsible (a disgruntled former employee of the Dies Committee, it emerged).[47] In a strange move, Hook still refused to retract the letters or apologize until the Department of Justice conducted its own investigation. The House tied itself into knots for days debating the issue and requesting more information, derailing consideration of a major agriculture bill.[48]

As the controversy boiled, Pelley decided at this moment to travel to Washington unannounced and stroll into the Dies Committee offices. As the *New York Times* put it, this caused the "sensation of the day" across the Beltway. The Committee was caught completely off guard. Dies himself was sick with a cold and did not attend the hearings. Pelley was questioned under oath about the letters, which he (truthfully) denied writing. He further rejected claims he had links to

Nazi Germany. Oddly, he spent much of the time praising the Committee's work rooting out communists, telling reporters when he first surfaced in Washington that he was there to give "Martin Dies a clean bill of health; I admire the work he's done." Whether this was intentionally ironic, given Dies's illness that week, went unexamined.[49] The most bizarre moment came when Pelley told the Committee that he would be willing to disband the entire Silver Legion if the Committee members were willing to take up the mantle of hunting down the communist menace in the United States. It was a strange offer, and the Committee was unimpressed.

Slipping out of Washington to escape extradition to North Carolina, Pelley fled to Indiana and struck up an alliance with the local Ku Klux Klan. He remained there for months and, in the meantime, was sentenced in absentia to two to three years in a North Carolina prison for parole violations. He still refused to return to face the music.[50] Meanwhile, the Dies Committee's hearings continued in Washington. In April 1940, a female government agent named Dorothy Waring testified that she had infiltrated the legion in 1934 at the behest of the Dickstein Committee, an investigatory precursor to the Dies Committee. Waring's cover had been to work as a secretary for another right-wing organization, "The Order of '76," and establish herself within similar groups by presenting the image of being a wealthy potential donor. In that capacity she met Pelley, who visited her in her Park Avenue apartment "in full uniform," carrying two pistols, including a German Luger, and tailed by bodyguards. After dismissing the guards, he allegedly bragged to her that he intended to "be dictator of the United States" and would "put into effect the Hitler program" after overthrowing the government.[51] It was explosive testimony.

The Silver Legion's days were numbered. With his legal troubles mounting, the last thing Pelley needed now was being accused of plotting to overthrow the government. His bizarre offer to disband the group if the Dies Committee continued its work opened a face-saving way out of some troubles. Writing from Indiana to his supporters in Washington State, Pelley acknowledged that "the rancor against us is significantly increased." The situation had become increasingly perilous, he continued, because "Never have I exerted more influence in this nation that [sic] I find I do at present—and not only in this nation but abroad as well. . . . Never had I less money. Never was I personally in more danger." However, he argued that Dies and the America First Committee, discussed later, were the true inheritors of the legion's legacy:

> *Unbeknown, certainly unsuspected, Silvershirts have been responsible for much of the constructive side of the work of the Dies Committee— exposing the alien menace to America—they have been active in the formation of the American First. . . . they have veelated their hands in the stupendous mail that has reached the White House and Capitol Hill, retraining our mercurial politicians from plunging into war. . . . They have actually stood up on platforms and introduced Martin Dies to audiences when the gentleman no more suspected who was sponsoring him than he expected to be named as President of the Nazi Reichstag. . . . All this is no alibi for a seeming hiatus in bold action in the present. It is merely a reminder that we can take no small satisfaction out of the influence we have wielded, and still wield, to hold American upon even keel.[52]*

Whether any of this was true or not, Pelley used the Dies Committee as his excuse for shutting down the legion. In late 1940, Pelley announced that because Dies was still doing his work, he would uphold his side of the bargain and shut down the Silver Legion completely. The Chief resigned. A few of his followers, especially on the West Coast, continued to meet in secret or joined forces with surviving Bund chapters, but the glory days of the legion were long past.

The Dies Committee excuse was merely a smokescreen.[53] Practically speaking, Pelley had little choice but to retreat from open political activity at this point. In October 1941, he surrendered to North Carolina authorities and was released on bond. In January, he was sentenced to two to three years for his violation of the 1934 parole.[54] Pelley appealed, and the case dragged on. The Chief was not yet finished, however. Following his old playbook, he attempted to reinvent himself yet again and began publishing two new journals. One of these was called *The Galilean* and was theoretically focused only on religious matters. It quickly generated a subscriber base of more than three thousand. After Pearl Harbor, Pelley interpreted religious matters to include the war effort, and published a number of articles accusing Roosevelt of having tempted the Japanese into war. The Pearl Harbor attack itself was one aspect of "divine justice punishment," he foolishly wrote.[55] The Roosevelt administration was not entertained. When a single copy of *The Galilean* was discovered in a soldier's duffle bag, Pelley was indicted for sedition under the Espionage Act of 1917 along with several of his associates and arrested in April 1942. He would spend the rest of the war fighting a series of protracted legal battles that would see him in court alongside a number of Hitler's other American friends.

What was the true impact of William Dudley Pelley and his Silver Legion? Certainly, he never came close to achieving the Christian Commonwealth or corporate state that he had envisioned in the mid-1930s. A following of fifteen thousand nationwide was not huge but, like the Bund, it was substantial enough in its strongholds to cause major local concern, especially given that many members were armed. Pelley envisioned creating a mass movement to bring about a future corporate state, but what he was left with instead was a small movement of dedicated radicals who proved themselves willing to cut local alliances with the Bund, even if this was not part of Pelley's national plan. Pelley's ideas quickly outgrew the narrow confines he had established for them.

Two factors made Pelley uniquely dangerous. First, unlike the Bund he was openly anti-Semitic and used racial prejudice as a major facet of his teachings. The Christian Commonwealth was fundamentally premised on removing Jews from society and segregating them from society, with the implication of worse things to come. Similarly, he was an open admirer of Hitler and barely went through even the motions of denouncing Nazism. For this reason, the British *Manchester Guardian* referred to the Silver Legion as "the largest American fascist organization" in a 1942 article.[56] Depending on how one defined "fascist organization" this may well have been true, despite the legion being numerically smaller than some of its rival groups. Part of Pelley's personal appeal undoubtedly lay in his personal charisma and personal presence, which he had cultivated as a Hollywood screenwriter. The 1920s were a key period in entertainment history, with the move from silent film to the talkies that required producers to rethink the way their plots and characters were seen and understood by the audience. Pelley would have been faced with these lessons on a daily basis during his time in the studio system. It is easy to see the echoes of a Hollywood mentality in the way Pelley designed the legion uniform (the giant L leaving no question as to what organization was being represented) and his own flair for dramatic action (barnstorming the country to run for president, and turning up unannounced at the Dies Committee office at the moment his presence would attract maximum attention).

These were the actions of a man who was entirely aware of what would impact his audience the most. In addition, the fact that Pelley had run a religious movement that very much resembled a cult before launching the legion stands as another testimony to his potential appeal. The American Jewish Committee noted that he had a remarkable penchant for pivoting to issues he knew an audience would support, including attacks on Catholics, Christian Scientists, and Greeks at different times, in addition to his standard attacks on the Jews. This ability to "attack every organization, group, or development which was in any way open to misrepresentation and abuse" was the key to his success and the danger he presented, as the organization reported at the time:

> *It is little wonder then that in spite of his repeated failures, Pelley has always managed to obtain some sort of following. There is always a sufficient number of discontented, unemployed human misfits, there are always enough fanatics of either a religious or political variety ready to accept demagogues of the Pelley type as their saviors.*[57]

Pelley was effectively a blank slate upon which a wide range of complaints could be written and seemingly explained.

Like the Bund, the Silver Legion was ultimately a failure, destroyed by the vanity of its leader and the improprieties that had stemmed primarily from ego and personal ambition. In the middle years of the 1930s, however, it was a growing organization that commanded a nationwide presence and was a force to be reckoned with in its strongholds. Its potential for greater success would have lain in the striking of alliances with the Bund and other groups, but these were precluded at the national level by Pelley's personal quest for power. The story was much different at the local level, where Bund–Silver Shirt cooperation was a reality.

With a higher degree of personal discipline, Pelley might well have become the leader around which the far right could coalesce. With his ideological flexibility, flair for the dramatic, and ability to harness religious language (even in his own unique way), Pelley could have been formidable. As it turned out, he was merely a flash in the pan who ended up being exposed as an unscrupulous fraudster.

Pelley would not be the only one of Hitler's American friends to use the language of religion to push his followers toward a political extremism, nor was he the only political extremist to use the lessons of entertainment and mass media to spread his message. Indeed, Pelley's star would soon be dramatically outshone by friends of the Führer who managed to combine religion with the power of mass media to build even more substantial followings.

THE RELIGIOUS RIGHT

On the Sunday afternoon of November 20, 1938, millions of Americans tuned their radio sets to one of the country's most popular weekend programs. The sounds of a church organ and a choir followed. Soon a familiar and sonorous voice came to the airwaves. It was that of Detroit priest Father Charles E. Coughlin, one of the country's most popular and controversial media figures. For years Coughlin had courted controversy with increasingly political statements and criticism of the Roosevelt administration. Today's address would be his most provocative public utterance yet.[1]

Coughlin quickly launched into a startling defense of Nazi Germany's policies toward the country's Jewish population, which had culminated in the recent violence of the Kristallnacht pogrom that left nearly a hundred people dead and shopwindows smashed across the Reich. Claiming to oppose persecution against all religions, Coughlin insisted that Nazism was merely a natural response to the threat posed by communism. Picking up a Nazi publication, Coughlin listed twenty-four Jews he claimed had been integrally involved in the Russian Revolution. "I speak these words, holding no brief for Germany or for Nazism," he said. "Simply as a student of history, endeavoring to analyze the reasons for the growth of the idea in the minds of the Nazi party that Communism and Judaism are too closely woven for the national health of Germany, do I make these references."[2] Nazi violence against Jews was therefore the result of "the fact that the Jews through their native ability have risen to such high places in radio, press and finance." The Jews might be a minority in

Germany, Coughlin continued, "but a closely woven minority in their racial tendencies; a powerful minority in their influence; an aggressive minority which has carried their sons to the pinnacle of success in journalism, radio and finance." He went on to blame Jewish bankers for financing the Russian Revolution, naming the financial firm Kuhn, Loeb & Co. as a specific offender. He concluded by supporting President Roosevelt's recent decision to withdraw the American ambassador from Berlin to protest recent anti-Semitic violence, but added, "If we are sincere we'll call all ambassadors and ministers from communist countries."[3]

By now, Coughlin was used to the controversy his fiery radio speeches generated. He often managed to use such storms to raise money. Yet the obvious affinity between his remarks in November 1938 and Nazi ideology generated the largest conflagration yet. New York station WMCA, which had surreptitiously managed to obtain an advance copy of the speech, programmed an immediate follow-up broadcast by the director of the Non-Sectarian Anti-Nazi League. A cascade of angry calls and telegrams poured into Detroit station WJR. The chancellor of the Roman Catholic diocese of Detroit was quoted in the press the next day saying "Coughlin spoke for himself, not for the church." Detroit Jewish leaders were outraged, with one denouncing Coughlin's address as "one of the most vicious talks that I have listened to in a long time."[4] There was soon a backlash against the backlash, however. When WMCA announced that it would no longer carry Coughlin's program due to the "religious and racial hatred and dissension" he was stirring, two thousand Coughlin supporters descended on the station to demand his reinstatement. For months afterward, protestors carrying pro-Coughlin and occasionally anti-Semitic slogans showed up at the station doors on Sunday afternoons to keep up the pressure.[5]

Coughlin was in many ways a pioneer in American mass communication history. For years he had used increasing fame to build one of the first multifaceted media empires. Through the emerging technology of radio, he quickly built a following of supporters who not only tuned into his program on a regular basis but were willing to support their belief in the "Radio Priest" with real-world action. Coughlin expanded into publishing a newspaper, *Social Justice*, with a circulation of more than two hundred thousand in 1940, though he claimed it to be closer to one million.[6] In many ways, Coughlin established the model for the indignant, belligerent, no-holds-barred talk show hosts that hit the airwaves in every American city in the late twentieth century. Glenn Beck's rants during the Barack Obama years about cabals of shadowy global elites, later illustrated with chalkboard flowcharts on his Fox News television program, could have been pulled directly from Coughlin's playbook. Yet Coughlin himself was far more successful than any of his future emulators. A December 1938 Gallup poll found that a full 22 percent of Americans reported listening to Coughlin's radio program in the previous month. A majority of those said they had listened to him two times or more in that period. This figure translates into an estimated monthly audience of nearly twenty-nine million listeners, with nearly fifteen million listening more than once a month.[7] These are astonishing numbers, especially given that Coughlin's broadcasts that year were only carried by forty-six independent stations, with no network backing, on the East Coast. No stations west of Kansas or in the South carried his program.[8] Historians have estimated that his audience was the largest in the world and far surpassed that of every major radio star of the era, and was possibly the largest of all time.[9] By comparison, the most successful talk show host of later years, Rush Limbaugh, commanded a peak audience of more than twenty million in the 1990s. Limbaugh loudly proclaimed himself to have "talent on loan from God," but his religious predecessor would have had a better claim to a divinely delivered audience.[10]

What made Coughlin's voice uniquely resonant for millions of Americans was fundamentally his religious message. He was, after all, an ordained and practicing priest who had instant credibility with Catholic listeners. Much of his popularity lay with Irish and German immigrants on the East Coast who had been badly hurt by the Depression. He referred to himself as "your spokesman" and presented himself as standing up for the common man against vested interests ranging from international banks to the Roosevelt administration. Coughlin's radio talks were "flowery, emotional, and misleading," historian David H. Bennett has written. "He knew all the tricks of the propagandist, from name calling to glittering generality."[11] Propagandist or not, by 1938 Coughlin had convinced millions of Americans that he understood their problems as no one else could and was giving them a voice.

For all his appeal and success, however, Coughlin's influence was intrinsically limited by several factors. First, he was a Catholic priest in a country where serious anti-Catholic sentiment still existed. While the shared experience of anti-Catholic prejudice no doubt heightened his appeal among his Catholic listeners, those outside the fold had a harder time accepting the word of a priest—or worse. Coughlin himself had crosses burned on his lawn by local Ku Klux Klan members when he first arrived in Michigan.[12] His audience undoubtedly included Protestants, but the influence of any Catholic on the national level would have an upper limit. Second, Coughlin was not originally American at all, having been born in the Canadian province of Ontario. This might have been trivial for his radio listeners, but it made him constitutionally ineligible for the presidency. This would become a major issue in 1936.

These limitations also meant that no matter how popular he became, Coughlin would always face rivals peddling similar messages. Throughout the 1930s, a series of demagogic leaders rose to national prominence with religiously based, anti-Roosevelt messages of economic equality and, later, nonintervention in the European war. Dynamic Kansas minister Gerald B. Winrod ingratiated himself to midwestern Protestants and then took his message nationwide with a series of lectures and radio broadcasts. By the late 1930s he joined Coughlin in defending Nazi Germany and denouncing the Jews. Winrod no doubt hoped to position himself as a Protestant Coughlin, but fell short in his ambitions. Crowding the stage further was Gerald L. K. Smith, a veteran political organizer who worked closely with Louisiana demagogue Huey Long and then took his show on the road after Long was assassinated in 1935. Smith's message had been honed and battle tested in the Louisiana swamps. Like Long, he was a populist firebrand who railed against economic and political elites while simultaneously denouncing communism and throwing in a mixture of anti-Semitism and old-time religion. He was such a fiery and charismatic speaker that he would overshadow even Coughlin during public appearances.[13]

What these men shared was not only rhetorical style but similar messages. All three promised radical economic change. They identified similar, if not identical, causes of the Great Depression: economic elites, politicians, and Jews (ironically, both Coughlin and Smith were heavily influenced by Henry Ford, arguably the most important economic elite in the country but himself a well-known anti-Semite). Each became a staunch opponent of Roosevelt and, similarly, all three fell into becoming a friend of the Third Reich. By 1941, each man had voiced admiration for the New Germany and expressed support for Hitler's anti-Semitic worldview. There is evidence that the German government in turn recognized the potential significance of these religious demagogues in shaping American public opinion.

What made these men uniquely resonant for many Americans was their use of religion. The United States of the 1930s was still a deeply religious nation, though denominational affiliation and participation in churches dropped significantly during the Great Depression. Hearing pro-Hitler sentiments seemingly supported by quotations from the New Testament had a powerful influence on many of the faithful, who responded by opening their pocketbooks and donating their hard-earned cash to the cause. Hitler's friends thus used the deepseated religious devotion of Americans to further their political aims and spread anti-Semitic prejudice and pro-Nazi views at a critical moment in the country's history.

Much like the modern-day "religious right," Coughlin and his associates were not content to exercise their authority in the spiritual realm alone. The Radio Priest was political from nearly his first day on the airwaves and directly entered politics during the 1936 presidential election. Winrod ran for the US Senate as a Republican in his home state of Kansas on a platform that was widely denounced as having more in common with the Nazi Party than the GOP. Smith was fundamentally a political organizer who used religious rhetoric to frame his messages. Ironically, with the possible exception of Hitler's agent on Capitol Hill, the Führer's religious friends were the most directly active in American electoral politics. The US government was slow to realize the unique threat they posed to national security, but once the danger became clear it responded with overwhelming force. The ultimate fear was that the Coughlin, Winrod, and Smith factions might manage to unite their forces and join with the German American Bund or, later, America First to create a broad far-right coalition that would include demagogic leaders with fanatical followers and an armed paramilitary wing. As with the Bund and its fellow far-right groups, however, a combination of egos and philosophical differences prevented such an alliance from forming. The United States government would never have to face the full threat these groups might have been able to pose.[14] Of the three men, Coughlin was the most likely candidate to fit the bill of future American Führer. He made a major push toward political power that was only derailed by his own missteps and, ultimately, the church hierarchy.

Charles Edward Coughlin was born in Hamilton, Ontario, to working-class parents of Irish ancestry in 1891. The young Coughlin was raised as a devout Catholic and entered the seminary in Toronto. He was seen as an outstanding student. After a few years teaching in Catholic schools and colleges, Coughlin was sent to the Detroit diocese. In 1926, Bishop Michael Gallagher, who would become the most important figure in Coughlin's career, decided to establish a shrine in the suburb of Royal Oak, then about a dozen miles north of the city. There were only a few Catholic families in the area, and the anti-Catholic Klan was prominent. Local KKK members welcomed Coughlin and his new church, the Shrine of the Little Flower, by burning a cross on its front lawn two weeks after it opened.[15]

Coughlin decided the best response was to make the shrine glamorous and exciting for the public. He convinced a sympathetic local baseball scout to bring some big-name players to the shrine to increase its public profile. Impressively, the scout not only delivered appearances by Detroit Tigers players but also set up visits by New York Yankees stars, including Babe Ruth, the following summer. Thousands turned out to see the Yankees legends, who collected money from starstruck visitors at the door. Coughlin netted $10,000 from the stunt and, more important, established a public profile as a celebrity man of the cloth. A 1928 story in the *Detroit Free Press* published during the World Series referred to Coughlin as "a rabid baseball fan himself and a close personal friend of Babe Ruth, Harry Heilman[n] and other famous players."[16] (Ruth and his Yankees swept the Series that year, making Coughlin's alleged friendship with the Bambino all the more impressive).

Coughlin's big break came in September 1926 when he sat down for a meeting with the station manager of Detroit radio station WJR. The priest's initial pitch was for a religious program that would raise awareness of his church and help combat Klan prejudice. The station manager agreed to give him the time for free, but Coughlin insisted on paying for it. Bishop Gallagher gave his own blessing to the idea. The Radio Priest's first broadcast was on October 17, 1926, just days before his thirty-fifth birthday. He was an immediate hit. As one sympathetic biographer has written, "His voice registered well over the radio and his enunciation was unusually pleasing. First there was a musical program and then he spoke. He was a knockout, 'radio-ically' speaking."[17] This was the same basic format Coughlin would use throughout his radio career, and his on-air presence would only improve with practice.

Visitors from all over the country—and later the world—began converging on the Shrine of the Little Flower to see Coughlin preach in person. His weekly congregation steadily grew. So too did the donations, which soon came pouring in through the mail from all over the country and even overseas as his fame spread. Coughlin hired an army of female clerks to deal with all the correspondence and the money flowing into his coffers. To give his followers a sense of identity and encourage their continued support, Coughlin created the Radio League of the Little Flower. Membership cost $1 a year (about $15 in 2018 terms), putting it within reach for all but the most impoverished listeners.[18] All the proceeds were considered charitable contributions and were therefore tax free under federal law.[19] By 1928, Coughlin was meeting with New York architects to plan the construction of a grand new church in Royal Oak, including a huge tower with a crucifix emblazoned on each side that would include his personal office.[20] It would become the center of his national radio empire.

Coughlin now expanded his radio presence in part to help raise the cash needed to build this monumental edifice. He bought time on stations in Cincinnati and Chicago, augmenting his weekly reach dramatically. The timing was impeccable. In late 1929 the stock market crashed, plunging the country into the Great Depression. Coughlin's popularity had always lain with the poor and the working classes of the country's big cities. These groups quickly felt the brunt of the downturn as jobs disappeared, savings accounts vanished, and homes were lost to foreclosure in astronomical numbers. The Radio Priest suddenly found himself not only providing spiritual council to his audience but also voicing and shaping their political responses to the turmoil. In early 1930, Coughlin changed tactics to move away from biblical teachings and focus on denouncing "socialism, communism, and kindred fallacious social and economic theories."[21] It was a fateful decision. In fall 1930, Coughlin negotiated an agreement with the CBS radio network to put him on sixteen stations across the country. This gave him a potential weekly audience of forty million. Coughlin's political views were now heard nationwide. The level of fan mail arriving in Royal Oak skyrocketed, as did donations. Coughlin had gone from being an obscure Michigan priest to becoming a household name across the country in under five years.

This was a dangerous road to be walking in the early 1930s, however. Loudly denouncing socialism and communism could attract a radio audience and donations, but it increasingly drew Coughlin into the purely political realm. In early 1931 Coughlin planned to use his time on CBS to denounce the Treaty of Versailles that had ended World War I, and the "international bankers" supposedly profiting from it. This was a commonly understood code for Jews. CBS got wind of the plan in advance and asked Coughlin to tone down the remarks, and he accordingly offered to focus on a completely different topic entirely. When Sunday afternoon came around, however, CBS executives tuned in to hear Coughlin denouncing their own network for their attempted intervention. Over the weeks to come, Coughlin attacked the "bankers" repeatedly. This was an act of astounding arrogance that understandably upset the network's leaders. CBS announced that it would be pulling the plug on Coughlin at the end of the current season, with no chance of renewal. Coughlin then approached rival network NBC, but its leaders similarly refused to let him to buy time.[22]

This might have been the end for Coughlin's radio career had it not been for Bishop Gallagher. Rather than order the priest into silence or ask him to tone down his rhetoric, Gallagher encouraged him to find an alternative outlet to spread his views. Coughlin subsequently pieced together a plan to buy time on eleven stations. This eventually grew to twenty-seven across the nation. The expensive arrangement cost him $14,000 a week (nearly $300,000 in 2018 dollars), all of which was covered by donations from listeners.[23] Coughlin was now free from the content restrictions imposed by CBS. His voice would continue to be heard across the country as long as individual stations would allow him to purchase time. In 1931, Coughlin used his newfound freedom to level direct attacks on President Herbert Hoover. Coughlin argued that Hoover's plans to alleviate the Depression were inadequate and inhumane, no doubt echoing the sentiments of millions. The following year, Coughlin met Democratic nominee Franklin Roosevelt personally and endorsed him at the Democratic National Convention. In January 1933, President-elect Roosevelt met with Coughlin again. The priest reportedly offered advice for Roosevelt's upcoming inaugural address, much of which was probably ignored.[24]

It was perhaps inevitable under these circumstances that Coughlin would turn his personal interest and radio program to an extended discussion of economics. After all, his endorsement of Roosevelt had been based on the hope for new policies to combat unemployment. "It is Roosevelt or ruin," he told anyone who would listen during the campaign.[25] Once in office, the new president's policies quickly disabused the priest of any hope that radical economic measures were on the horizon. Coughlin argued that the president should quickly begin minting money and back it with a combination of gold and silver. This would in turn create rapid inflation that Coughlin believed would eliminate debt, reduce employment, and improve agricultural output. (Similar policies were advocated by British fascist leader Oswald Mosley and American fascist intellectual Lawrence Dennis, discussed later.)[26]

The notion of dramatically inflating the dollar flew in the face of economic orthodoxy and was swiftly rejected by banking leaders and the Treasury Department. Stung by the administration's rejection of his ideas, Coughlin began to harden his views toward Roosevelt and the bankers he increasingly believed were pulling the president's strings. The administration did not take this criticism lying down. In 1934 the Treasury Department dramatically revealed that Coughlin's secretary personally owned 500,000 ounces of silver, making her the largest individual silver holder in Michigan. It later emerged that the Radio

League of the Little Flower had partially funded this huge purchase. Any increase in the price of silver by using it to mint coinage would thus have resulted in a massive profit for Coughlin's church and his associates.[27]

Angered by Roosevelt's rejection of his ideas, Coughlin now threw his lot directly into the political ring. In late 1934 he announced the foundation of the National Union for Social Justice, an interfaith political organization designed to bring social change while resisting communism and socialism. He drafted a sixteen-point manifesto that called for the nationalization of public resources and abolition of the Federal Reserve. He later laid out a plan calling for the government to make massive investment in roads, dam-building, and reforestation efforts. This was in effect a much larger and more radical version of the economic recovery plans the Roosevelt administration itself was proposing.[28] One important difference, however, was that Coughlin believed this all might be achieved quickly if the interference of bankers could be circumvented. The country's financial establishment, he increasingly believed, was standing in the way of recovery for the average American. Late in the year, Coughlin took this message further and shocked listeners by telling them that there was little hope for the future of capitalism and democracy in the United States. The only chance to avoid falling into communism or fascism, he told them, was through adopting his social justice platform.[29]

This was a radical move. Coughlin was now effectively calling for the US government to be replaced with a new regime of his own design that would take radical steps to end the Depression. The analogues with Hitler's economic policies were obvious. Since taking power in 1933, the Nazis had poured huge amounts of money into military spending and infrastructure projects (along with reintroducing military conscription for men). The result was that by mid-1936 unemployment had all but disappeared in the Third Reich.[30] In March 1935 the former head of the National Recovery Administration, General Hugh S. Johnson, made the Hitler-Coughlin comparison in searing terms on national radio. "Someone sent me a parallel of what both you and Adolf Hitler proposed and preached and they are as alike as peas in a pod," Johnson told Coughlin. "As a foreign-born you could not be president but you could become a Reichsführer—just as the Austrian Adolf became a dictator of Germany."[31]

These barbs did little to staunch public support for Coughlin. National Union for Social Justice meetings attracted thousands of supporters. Branches sprung up across the country. By late 1935, Coughlin claimed to have more than 8.5 million supporters signed on to his sixteen-point agenda. Months later he announced that another 5 million people had joined the National Union. Historian David H. Bennett has estimated the organization's membership at "well over one million" but lower than Coughlin's estimates.[32] However many people actually signed up for membership, the priest's influence was undeniable. A 1936 Gallup poll found that a full 7 percent of Americans—around 9 million people—would be more likely to vote for a political candidate simply because Coughlin had offered an endorsement (20 percent said they would be less likely).[33] This was substantial influence to wield for a man who had never held political office. "He has become dangerously important," a biographer wrote in 1935. "He has become a mob leader and all such leaders are sources of worry to the more sedate and conservative minds of a people. . . . Sober economists may scoff at the anti-capitalist, anti-banking, anti–international league views of Father Coughlin, but they cannot laugh off easily the acceptance by millions of his home-spun doctrines, political, economic and social."[34]

Coughlin now sailed directly into the headwinds of national politics. He was far from the only voice promising radical economic and social change. In Louisiana, Governor (later senator) Huey Long had become a national figure by promising to "share the wealth" and give every American $5,000 a year. Long's populist slogan was "Every man a king," and he was widely seen as a potential rival to Roosevelt in the 1936 election. By late 1934 there were dark whisperings in Washington that he and Coughlin were planning to strike some kind of pact to combine their movements. It was not to be. Long's career was dramatically ended by an assassin's bullets on the steps of the Louisiana State Capitol in September 1935, but his message and tactics lived on.[35]

Long's most prominent successor was Gerald Lyman Kenneth Smith, a former midwestern preacher who moved to Louisiana and turned his attention to politics during the Depression. Smith was an outstanding speaker who could reputedly hold congregations and audiences in rapt attention.[36] He gradually fell in with Long's organization and became "the apostle who converted masses to Longism," in the words of one historian.[37] Long was regarded as a very good public speaker; Smith was seen as outstanding and frequently overshadowed his boss. After Long's assassination, Smith delivered a moving graveside eulogy before making a power grab for "the reins of the Long empire," as the FBI put it. He was unsuccessful and forced out of Louisiana by rival claimants to Long's crown.[38] Smith then took his show on the road, traveling the country to heap scorn on Roosevelt and dub the First Lady "that female Rasputin." He eventually began working with Francis E. Townsend, a retired physician who had built a national following by pledging to pay out large monthly pensions to the elderly on the condition that every penny had to be spent in the following month. This economic stimulus would supposedly end the Depression and net huge tax revenues for the government at the same time.[39]

The "Townsend Plan" was clearly outlandish, but the idea of extending old-age pensions and generating economic stimulus sat well with Coughlin's wider political program. Townsend and Coughlin agreed to an alliance in late 1935 to create an anti-Roosevelt, anti–Wall Street political coalition. Months later, a Coughlin representative approached Smith and asked him to join the combined movement. Smith agreed, hoping to use the opportunity to further his own political career and potentially even launch his own bid for the presidency.[40] Critically, he agreed to appear and speak at the national convention of the Union Party, a new political organization Coughlin would shortly be launching to put his agenda in the national spotlight. Coughlin believed that by combining his supporters with Townsend's and Smith's factions he would be able to influence up to twenty million votes in the 1936 presidential election.[41] It would not be enough to win the presidency outright, but it would make Coughlin one of the biggest power brokers in the country.

Coughlin accordingly launched the Union Party in summer 1936. Its platform was nearly identical to that of the National Union for Social Justice, though Coughlin toned down some of the more socialist-sounding proposals. The new party faced two immediate and crippling challenges. The first was finding a viable presidential candidate to stand in the election that was just months away. Coughlin's birth in Canada made him ineligible for the office. He also would have faced an uphill climb as a Catholic, especially in states with heavy Klan influence.[42] Asserting control of the party with a dictatorial fist, Coughlin decreed that its nominee would be North Dakota congressman William Lemke. Coughlin liked the Republican because he had introduced a radical agricultural relief bill that called for the Farm Credit Administration to buy up the mortgages of foreclosed farms and reissue the debt at much lower rates.[43] The Roosevelt administration viewed the proposal as dangerous economic meddling and ensured its defeat in Congress. The embittered Lemke now threw his hat in with Coughlin and Townsend. No one seems to have believed that the Union Party could actually win the election outright, but by combining their forces its leaders hoped they might be able to ensure Roosevelt's defeat or even deadlock the Electoral College and send the election to the House of Representatives. Even if victory in 1936 was out of reach, there was still 1940 to think about too.[44]

These rosy predictions would prove naive, largely because of the second prob-lem the Union Party's leaders encountered. This was the inevitable clash of personalities and egos within its leadership. Coughlin and Smith were the first to fall out. Weeks before the Union Party's national convention, both men ad-dressed a gathering of Townsend's followers in an effort to enlist their support. Smith spoke first, pulling out a Bible and unleashing a tirade of vitriol while he flailed both arms wildly in the air. The crowd was thrilled and vocally cheered his applause lines. "The lunatic fringe is about to take over the government," Smith proclaimed proudly.[45]

Coughlin addressed the gathering the next day. Following Smith was an un-enviable task for even the best public speaker, and even at his personal best Coughlin was more effective behind a microphone than in front of a live audi-ence. His speech fell flat. Two weeks later, both men spoke again at the Union Party convention (in an odd twist, one of the invitees was Congressman Martin Dies Jr., whom Coughlin offered to endorse at the convention. It does not appear Dies accepted.).[46] Smith whipped the crowd into a frenzy, stripped down to his shirt sleeves and, with sweat pouring down his face, viciously denounced the Roosevelt administration as "a slimy group of men culled from the pink campuses of America with a friendly gaze fixed on Russia." The crowd roared its approval.[47] Coughlin's speech could once again hardly hold a candle in com-parison. Outdone at his own event, Coughlin vowed he would never again appear on the same stage of Smith.[48]

The wider country viewed these developments with a mixture of incredulity and concern. Left-wing columnist Dorothy Thompson condemned the Union Party as proto-fascist. "Lemke, Coughlin and Smith attack the moneyed interests of Wall Street, the gold standard, and the 'reactionaries, Socialists, Communists, and radicals,' but they reserve their greatest vituperation for advanced liber-alism which they lump with socialism," Thompson wrote. "So did Mr. Hitler."[49] In October 1936, Smith fully embraced the label of antidemocrat by announc-ing that the Union Party was no longer sufficiently radical for his tastes. He proclaimed that he now intended to directly seize control of the country by unspecified means. He was expelled from the Union Party and assaulted days later in New Orleans by unknown attackers. He began to hint publicly that there was an assassination plot against him, evoking the specter of Long's death years before.[50] An FBI informant reported that Smith was simply "an extreme egoist and is definitely out to benefit himself only" who would "give public speeches in favor of any group which will support him financially." Another reported that

Smith was "very fond of liquor" and "aspired to be a dictator . . . he admires Hitler's cause and has made the statement that when he gets in power, he will set up a system of storm troopers in the United States to take care of the Jews."[51] Whatever chances the Union Party might have had evaporated with Smith's antics. Roosevelt won reelection easily. His Republican opponent, Alf Landon, received just 36 percent of the vote and won two states. Lemke received 892,000 votes and carried no states. Coughlin was devastated and wept in his church office as the results came in. In the following days, he disbanded the Union Party and announced he would no longer broadcast his ideas to a seemingly ungrateful nation.[52] Privately, he blamed Smith for the loss and denounced him as a "viper" and a "leech."[53]

Perhaps unsurprisingly, Coughlin's radio silence would be short-lived. On January 1, 1937, he put out a New Year's Day message stating that he was willing to resume his program if there was public demand. Weeks later his protector and patron, Bishop Gallagher, died. Gallagher's dying wish was reportedly that Coughlin should resume his broadcasts. The priest accordingly did so, but a new dynamic had emerged in the church hierarchy. Gallagher's successor, Bishop Edward Mooney, was far less sympathetic to Coughlin's activities and saw it necessary to denounce him in print when the broadcasts resumed. Coughlin continued to publish his more outspoken views in *Social Justice*, but even that was becoming tricky. Coughlin's audience was changing at the same time. His listeners before 1936 included disaffected Protestants and even some Jews who were attracted to his economic populism. Many of these listeners tuned out after the Union Party fiasco, leaving him with primarily Catholic audiences on the East Coast and in the upper Midwest.[54]

Coughlin also faced increasing competition from imitators who realized that his message could be used to build similar and equally fanatical followings. The most prominent of these emulators would be Gerald Burton Winrod, a pale imitation of Coughlin who would nonetheless make a name for himself as one of Hitler's top American fans. Coughlin and Winrod were similar in many ways. Both were men of the cloth who used the language of religion to build their support. Both took a direct interest in politics and sought political power. By the late 1930s, both were using anti-Semitism to further their political agendas. At the same time, Winrod was in many ways everything Coughlin was not. Unlike the Detroit priest, Winrod was an entirely self-educated fundamentalist Protestant who built his following in America's rural heartland. This made him both a potential ally to Coughlin and a rival simultaneously.

The similarities were obvious to thoughtful observers. Winrod started out with a purely religious message, but "Suddenly he achieved an interest in politics and started after the new deal with somewhat the same appeal as that adopted by Father Coughlin in his latter period," as one Kansas newspaper put it in 1938.[55]

Winrod was born in 1900 as the son of a hard-drinking Wichita saloon owner. The elder Winrod—piously named John Wesley Winrod—had been compelled to flee his native Missouri after a drunken brawl and settled in Kansas. He calmed down slightly when he married in 1899 but still enjoyed carousing. The Wichita saloon he tended was so notorious that it reputedly became the first establishment targeted by militant temperance campaigner Carrie Nation, who joined her followers in kneeling to pray before smashing up the venue with hatchets. The experience was evidently enough for Winrod to abandon not only selling alcohol but also his own consumption habits. He turned to religion instead.[56]

A decade later, the young Gerald's mother was stricken by cancer and underwent a crude double mastectomy. Facing almost certain death in the era before antibiotics and modern chemotherapy, she soon developed a severe morphine addiction and became increasingly withdrawn from the world. Their lives changed one evening as her now devout husband prayed over her and, he claimed, some form of divine intervention occurred, whereupon she was cured of both her drug addiction and her cancer instantly. Whatever the truth of the story, the elder Winrod committed his life to the ministry a few years later, and his son would harbor a lifelong suspicion of doctors. Now convinced that divine intervention was the only way to be healed, the family refused to even have medicine in their home, let alone consult physicians.[57]

Gerald soon demonstrated an even stronger religious devotion than his parents. He left school as a teenager to become a traveling minister and was wildly successful as a public speaker. By twenty-one he was reportedly being sought after by churches all over the Midwest, but decided to settle back in Wichita. In 1925, he assembled a group of fellow fundamentalist ministers to form Defenders of the Christian Faith, a group composed of ministers and congregations who saw themselves engaged in a war against "evolution, atheism, intemperance, and that theological monstrosity so terribly misnamed modernism."[58] The organization's official newspaper, the *Defender*, would become the platform for Winrod's ideas. Crowds at his sermons began to swell, and his trademark look—a well-groomed moustache, balding head, and dark suit—made him instantly recognizable. His powerful diatribes in favor of Prohibition and against the theory of evolution made him a regional celebrity. By 1932, more than sixty thousand people had purchased subscriptions to the *Defender*, and Winrod had expanded to publishing short books.[59]

Like Coughlin, Winrod began to dabble in politics as the Great Depression unfolded. At some point he stumbled across the *Protocols of the Learned Elders of Zion*, one of the most notorious anti-Semitic conspiracy theories of all time. The *Protocols* purported to reveal the existence of an international Jewish plot to control finance and politics by spreading discord throughout the Gentile world. Its American fans included Henry Ford, who subsidized mass distribution of the text. Like many anti-Semites, Winrod now believed the text had predicted the Depression and revealed that Jews were responsible for it. While Coughlin had only dabbled with this message before 1936 in his rants about bankers, Winrod embraced it head-on. For the Kansas preacher, Roosevelt's failure to smash up the international banks became proof of his connections to the Jewish conspiracy. The New Deal was also a Jewish plot. Winrod soon established a second publication—the *Revealer*—that was loaded with purely political commentary and "revealing" Jewish machinations.[60]

Winrod's discovery of the *Protocols* started him down the road to becoming one of Hitler's key American friends. By the mid-1930s he was expressing admiration for the Führer in print and proclaimed that the Nazi regime was protecting Christian churches from Jewish and communist threats. In 1935, Winrod traveled to Germany for a three-month stay and met representatives of the German government that included Nazi ideologue and propaganda publisher Julius Streicher. The trip was arranged in part by a Nazi agent in the United States who recognized Winrod's potential to help the German cause.[61] Returning to the United States, Winrod embarked on a nationwide speaking tour to talk up Hitler's government. The Führer was, Winrod claimed, "a leader . . . law-abiding, living quietly in a Christian way that not even his enemies can find fault with. . . . He is a true man's man, and the worst that can be said of him is when he sets himself about a task he does it most thoroughly and conscientiously." Germany, he continued, "is today the best country in Europe."[62] Months later, Winrod favorably compared Hitler to Reformation leader Martin Luther.[63] Both the *Defender* and the *Revealer* soon took on a heavily anti-communist, pro-German slant. *Defender* circulation soared to more than one hundred thousand by 1937. States with the highest number of subscribers included California, Pennsylvania, and Illinois, illustrating Winrod's nationwide appeal.[64] This was still about half of Coughlin's *Social Justice* following, but Winrod's increasingly pro-Nazi remarks were quickly gaining him a national following.

Winrod was far from shy about his connections to the Third Reich. He frequently received Nazi propaganda material and published translated versions of Nazi propaganda. In return, the German press began quoting Winrod as a leading American anti-Semite. One German newspaper went so far as to brand him "The American Streicher."[65] Relishing his newfound fame, Winrod started to plan how he could translate this success into political power. First, though, he would have to solidify his status with the Germans to ensure their continued support. The most obvious obstacle was that Winrod himself did not speak German. To overcome this hurdle, he quietly secured the services of John J. Kroeker, an anti-Semitic Kansas Mennonite who spoke fluent German in addition to Russian and several other languages. Kroeker was a refugee from the czarist empire who had fled the Russian civil war through Berlin in 1920. His personal obsession with the Third Reich would eventually lead him to abandon his family in Kansas and return to Hitler's Germany.[66] In mid-1937, Kroeker began contributing articles to the *Defender* under the pen name John Jacob.[67] Much of his work was oriented toward exposing the "Jewish" origins of communist revolutions using secret "sources."[68] Kroeker thus provided Winrod with critical material to support his growing anti-Semitic campaign.

As Coughlin's political movement temporarily crashed and burned after the 1936 election, Winrod saw an opportunity to pick up the pieces for his own benefit. One of Kansas's two Senate seats was coming up for reelection in 1938. It was held by weak incumbent Democrat George McGill, who was expected to lose as the state was swinging to the GOP (at the time of writing, no Democrat has been elected senator in Kansas since McGill). Winrod's plan was to secure the Republican nomination and ride the GOP electoral wave into the Senate. From there, he would have almost certainly been eyeing the presidency in 1940 or 1944. It was not a bad plan, and Winrod initially seemed to have the upper hand in the campaign.

Pulling another card from Coughlin's playbook, Winrod now developed a regional radio presence to spread his political message. He regularly bought time and appeared on WIBW (Topeka) and KCKN (Kansas City), among other stations. In March 1938, Winrod delivered a series of strident radio addresses denouncing the country's economic system in his usual conspiratorial language ("Perhaps you have thought the United States Congress controls the Nation's money. This most decidedly is not the case"). He denounced Roosevelt for criticizing Italy, Japan, and Germany without attacking the Soviet Union equally. Opposition to fascism and supposed support for communism, he warned, meant that "Every conceivable attempt will be made, in coming months, to pull us into another holocaust. . . . 'War never pays.'"[69] By the time the election rolled around, Winrod was addressing voters over the radio twice a day. Crowds flocked to his speeches and rallies as he barnstormed around the state.[70]

Winrod also showed political shrewdness by moderating his anti-Semitism on the campaign trail, though his comments about groups exerting secret control over the economy were a dog whistle for anti-Semites.[71] Yet his past views and statements still caught up with him. In 1937, a longtime opponent, Reverend Leon M. Birkhead of Kansas City, Missouri, founded a group called Friends of Democracy to fight fascist influence and quickly made Winrod one of his primary targets. By 1938, Birkhead and his allies were publicly accusing Winrod of being a Nazi sympathizer and receiving campaign funds from Germany. Birkhead even claimed to have personally seen Winrod's name on a list of Americans expected to help the Nazis in the event of war during a visit to Germany.[72]

The unfolding political fiasco in Kansas soon gained the attention of Washington's power brokers. With the August GOP primary approaching, Roosevelt made a personal inquiry into the race. Writing to Progressive leader and Kansas newspaper editor William Allen White, Roosevelt asked whether it was true that Winrod "is openly a fascist and in addition to that is showing KKK tendencies."[73] Proclaiming himself to have been "afraid of Winrod for several years," White reported that the preacher had been "selling Jew-baiting literature" and had "all the money he needs for the radio, which is expensive." In addition, "He speaks well, either on the radio or to an audience, and is a strapping, handsome, smooth-talking man much like a medicine vendor or a soap-peddler." Barring a dramatic intervention from within the Republican Party, White predicted, "he will win in the primary" and probably end up in the Senate.[74]

The national media now got wind of the "Nazi" who might end up in Washington. References to Winrod running on a "straight Fascist ticket" started to show up in newspapers around the country.[75] In early July, the *Chicago Times* headlined a story about Winrod by describing him as an "arch-fascist" and lamented that Republican leaders had not intervened in the race.[76] The *New York Times* described Winrod as an "authentic voice" of "religious, racial and social bigotry" and called for his defeat in the hope that it would "discourage Winrodism from coast to coast."[77] By election day, the *Times* was reporting that

Winrod had been branded as the "Kansas Nazi."[78] Pressure began mounting on GOP leaders to do something. Weeks after the press frenzy began, Republican National Committee chairman John D. Hamilton, a former Kansan himself, denounced Winrod in an open letter to supporters. A Winrod victory, he wrote, would encourage "intolerance" in Kansas that was reminiscent of the Ku Klux Klan's heyday in the 1920s. "We have all been shocked by the manifestations of intolerance growing in the world elsewhere and should be more than shocked at its appearance on our very doorstep and therefore doubly vigilant," he wrote. If this was not enough, he concluded, "May I ask them to consider the possible disastrous effects which his nomination would have upon the entire State and local Republican tickets in November."[79]

The Kansas GOP now found the political will to unite against Winrod. Mainstream Republicans convinced former governor Clyde Reed to enter the race, and coalesced around his candidacy. He went on to win the primary and the general election handily. Winrod received a mere fifty-three thousand votes in the primary, putting him in humiliating third place. The *Times* reported that the six counties he won (out of 105 total) "were centers of Ku Klux Klan activities when the Klan made an unsuccessful effort to gain dominance in this State [in the 1920s]."[80] Winrod blamed the defeat on "an organized conspiracy, a dastardly program of persecution and falsehood, engineered by the very interests which are now carrying us toward war."[81] In other words, he thought the Jews were responsible.

Winrod's bid for the Senate was the closest any of Hitler's American friends would come to a direct electoral mandate. Without the intervention of the Kansas GOP, it is likely he would have won the primary and potentially gone on to win the seat. This was far further than the machinations of the German American Bund or the Silver Legion had ever propelled their chosen candidates. It also gave Winrod national notoriety. In November, the Kansan was scheduled to give a series of sermons at evangelist Aimee Semple McPherson's famous Angelus Temple in Los Angeles. The announcement of his visit to California was greeted not with the adulatory crowds he had found in the past but instead with protests and threats of violence. The Hollywood Anti-Nazi League contacted McPherson directly to protest the appearance of an "advocate of Fascist dictatorship." Bomb threats were phoned to the temple on the day of Winrod's first appearance but failed to deter the 4,500 attendees who turned up for the event. "I know that I am not a Nazi," he told the crowd. "I know that I have never received a single dollar from Germany." No doubt to the relief of many, Winrod announced shortly after that he was canceling his remaining sermons at the temple, and quietly slunk out of California.[82]

By mid-1938, anti-Semitism was increasing across the country, no doubt fanned in part by the antics of Winrod, Smith and their fellow travelers. A *Fortune* poll in August 1938 found that 32 percent of respondents believed there was growing hostility toward Jews.[83] In March 1939, that number had grown to 45 percent in a nationwide Gallup poll.[84] Four months later, a full 32 percent of Americans told *Fortune* that the government should take steps to "Prevent Jews from getting too much power in the business world" and 10 percent said Jews should be deported outright "to some new homeland as fast as it can be done without inhumanity." This latter number meant roughly thirteen million Americans believed Jews should be removed from the United States.[85] Always the showman, Father Coughlin decided to jump directly on this bandwagon of prejudice. In early 1938, he launched a new series of broadcasts in which he leveled attacks on Wall Street bankers and other targets who all had Jewish last names. *Social Justice* began publishing excerpts from the *Protocols* and translated speeches by Nazi propaganda minister Joseph Goebbels. Coughlin was now modeling his actions on Winrod's activities.[86]

Things only grew darker from there. In January 1938, Coughlin announced the formation of two new political organizations to spread his message. The first, called the Million League, fell flat almost immediately. The second, the Christian Front, would soon make Coughlin even more notorious. The Front was organized into local chapters and was tasked with fighting the spread of communism and the "insidious enemy" in the United States. Jews were excluded from membership, and local chapters began organizing "buy Christian only" campaigns to intimidate the patrons of Jewish shops. Members began arming themselves, and practiced shooting at gun ranges and sports clubs. Christian Front followers became known for beating up Jews on the streets of American cities and proclaimed themselves to be "Father Coughlin's brownshirts." In April 1939, hundreds of people attacked newsboys selling *Social Justice* on the streets of New York, leading to a brawl with Christian Front thugs who came to their aid. Whispers began to spread around the city that Irish-American Catholics in the New York City Police Department were deliberately letting the violence unfold and refused to take action against the Christian Front. Coughlin himself remained silent as the violence grew, but continued to voice general support for the organization.[87] Critics began acidly referring to his church, the Shrine of the Little Flower, as the Shrine of the Little Führer.[88]

Predictably, Coughlin's relationship with the Nazis only grew stronger as a result of these developments. The anti-Semitic rag *Der Stürmer* praised Coughlin as one of the only Americans with the courage "to speak his conviction that National Socialism is right."[89] German foreign minister Joachim von Ribbentrop reportedly asked a Coughlin aide in 1939 to "Give my regards to Father Coughlin. I have a high regard for him." Other Nazi officials later reported that Coughlin was discussed "with extraordinary frequency" in the Foreign Ministry.[90] The priest even attained popularity with the German public. An American student studying in the Reich later recalled a beer hall patron remarking that Coughlin "would make a good pope" following the death of Pius XI in 1939. The young American and his friends quickly dropped the subject rather than risk a barroom brawl.[91]

Despite his growing popularity in both the United States and the Reich, the German embassy in Washington deliberately kept Coughlin at arm's length. As former embassy first secretary and spymaster Heribert von Strempel told postwar interrogators, "I was very much against the Embassy having any relation with Father Coughlin, because such relations would have been used to smear him in order to destroy his integrity. I believed he would be more effective to be left alone."[92] There was some evidence of collusion, however. Nazi propaganda agent George Sylvester Viereck, discussed later, contributed several pieces to *Social Justice* and met Coughlin in New York.[93] The priest was effectively doing business directly with the Third Reich, though both sides were careful to keep their arrangement quiet.

Winrod had been once again overshadowed by Coughlin after the creation of the Christian Front. Still commanding a substantial audience, however, the Kansas preacher tried to mobilize his followers in a similar direction. In early 1939 he tasked John Kroeker with researching and preparing articles exploring "the question of Jewish influence on Germany's religious developments."[94] Sensing the direction wider events were taking, Kroeker began to push Winrod to take a stand not just in favor of Germany, but also against US intervention in a future war. He told Winrod the *Defender* should be used to soften American feelings toward Germany in an effort to subvert a future war effort. "If you'll raise the flag against bloodshed now, and high, you'll launch the greatest battle you ever did," Kroeker told Winrod in April 1939. "It's a battle for Christ's kingdom, even if we do talk mostly about lives, wives, and money." The benefit of a dedicated peace effort, he continued, might not be felt until a conflict actually began: "*If* we are late, the campaign will considerably *shorten* the war because people will enter it with doubts in the backs of their minds. . . . If we warn the people before a war is on, the struggle for control at home, afterwards, will be half won!"[95] The materials Kroeker proposed using included *Mein Kampf* and information provided directly by the office of Ernst Bohle, the British-born head of the Foreign Organization of the Nazi Party.[96]

This arguably subversive piece would never be written. The following month, Kroeker told Winrod that he was going to Germany on a "scholarship" provided by the Association for German Cultural Relations Abroad. This was theoretically a cultural education organization that helped Germans abroad reconnect with their heritage. In reality, it was a recruiting mechanism for potential spies who could be returned to their home countries.[97] The Reich had clearly identified Kroeker as a potential agent they could return to the United States at a future date.[98] Kroeker quietly left Kansas for the Reich, where he would remain until the end of the war. Winrod seems to have hardly missed the departure of his collaborator and continued to push the antiwar, pro-German line. When war broke out in September 1939, Winrod encouraged prayer from his followers and warned of "sinister agencies" and a "Hidden Hand" that was trying to "pull us into the European holocaust."[99]

Coughlin and Winrod now both turned their attention to encouraging American nonintervention in the European war. Coughlin argued that the war was a clash of competing capitalist interests, not a fight to save Europe from the barbarism of Nazi domination. He praised Hitler openly and attacked Roosevelt.[100] Winrod's message was similar. Less than a month before Pearl Harbor, he was still arguing that the European war was raging because "a reaction has developed in the old world, against Jewish Communism and Jewish Capitalism. International Jewry is in a state of great perplexity. And it so happens that we have an Administration at Washington, which is pro-Communist, and Jewish-dominated."[101] The war, he claimed, was therefore the fault of Europe's Jews and communists, and the United States should play no role.

Coughlin and Winrod were both becoming increasingly difficult for the US government to ignore. Martin Dies Jr. was roundly criticized by a fellow congressman in 1942 for not having called Coughlin or Winrod to testify. Dies retorted that it was too dangerous to subpoena clergy because if they refused to testify, they would be held in contempt and "from all over the country there would have arisen an outcry denouncing us as being against certain religions." Instead, Dies claimed that his Committee had gathered information on Winrod and Coughlin "using other methods."[102] There was an element of truth to this: As it turned out, the Dies Committee had quietly dispatched investigators to Kansas during the 1938 Senate campaign. Winrod himself was interviewed and refused to answer questions except through his attorney. The investigation did reveal a number of interesting facts, however. A Wichita bank president reported that the KKK was backing Winrod behind the scenes. This was potentially interesting, but not the investigators' main focus. Their primary objective was to establish whether Winrod was receiving large donations that could be traced to Germany. They uncovered nothing particularly suspicious in this regard, and discovered that local opposition to Winrod was greater than had been assumed. A local radio station manager even told the detectives that he was personally opposed to Winrod's politics, but felt he had no choice but to sell him airtime because there was no legal way to prevent him from doing so. The manager had received so much negative mail from irate listeners that he was considering using static interference to make the broadcasts unlistenable.[103] While this investigation turned up little, Winrod was certainly on the government's radar, and, unlike Coughlin, his legal troubles would only grow. In 1940, a book entitled *The Fifth Column Is Here* listed Winrod by name as one of the Americans working to "break down our psychological defenses against Hitler and Mussolini."[104] Winrod's days of freedom were numbered.

Coughlin was also on the government's radar but was taking careful steps to cover his tracks. Christian Front violence was spreading, and in July 1939 Coughlin told listeners that he was "neither the organizer nor the sponsor of the Christian Front; and moreover, that it is not becoming for me to identify myself with this organization or any other organization."[105] This was a clever rhetorical dodge, but it fooled no one since Coughlin had founded the group. Ill-advisedly, Coughlin now began appearing at German American Bund meetings while paperboys distributed copies of *Social Justice* outside the venues.[106] The priest was forced to deny rumors in the press that the Christian Front and the Bund—then in the midst of its final collapse—would soon be merging.[107] In January 1940, this delicate situation boiled over. On January 7, Coughlin delivered a radio speech in which he questioned whether democracy was actually a worse political system than dictatorship, because democracy "has failed so long to function advantageously for the nation." In his mind, dictatorship would presumably do better.[108]

Less than a week later, FBI agents led personally by Director J. Edgar Hoover launched raids to arrest eighteen members of the Christian Front's Brooklyn chapter. Press reports the next day revealed that the men had allegedly been planning "the overthrow of the Government of the United States," as the *New York Times* front page put it. It was a startling plot. Most of the men had served in the armed forces or the New York National Guard and therefore had experience with weapons. Over the past few months they had managed to acquire explosives, a dozen Springfield rifles, thousands of rounds of ammunition, and other small arms. Hoover dramatically announced to the press that the men had been planning to blow up bridges, seize power plants and telephone networks, and then take control of the Federal Reserve gold supply. "Plans were discussed . . . for the wholesale sabotage and blowing up of all these institutions so that a dictatorship could be set up here, similar to the Hitler dictatorship in Germany, seizing the reins of government in this country as Hitler did in Germany," Hoover told stunned reporters. "Their scheme was to spread a reign of terrorism so that the authorities would become thoroughly demoralized." The group also aimed for "the eradication of the Jews of the United States," he added. "The fantastic notion of a program of such size being carried out by eighteen men with twelve rifles and eighteen bombs—in a city with 18,000 well-equipped police and several regiments of United States Army regulars handy—was apparently no part of their thought," the *Times* remarked.[109]

Regardless of how outlandish the plan may have been, the revelation sent shock waves around the country. Left-wing critics jumped on the discovery as proof that Coughlin was a national security threat. "The terrible danger of the arrests . . . is not so much the disclosal [*sic*] that Coughlin's followers are caching rifles and cordite, but that millions of unemployed, millions of those on starvation wages, millions of desperate youth who see nothing but a hopeless blank future under capitalism . . . will turn to Father Coughlin as the only one who offers them a way out," Trotskyite leader Joseph Hansen told his followers.[110] Coughlin himself quickly disavowed the plotters, unconvincingly claiming that he had advocated "a Christian front" rather than "the 'specific' Christian Front involved in the conspiracy charges."[111] Embarrassingly, it only took reporters a few days to find articles in past issues of *Social Justice* praising the plot leader by name.[112]

Worried a larger plot might exist, US Attorney General Robert H. Jackson believed the government should make an example of the Christian Fronters. He dispatched one of the government's top investigators, Assistant Attorney General O. John Rogge, to oversee the inquiries and eventual prosecutions. Rogge, who went by his first initial and middle name, was well on his way to becoming a Justice Department legend. After graduating from Harvard Law School at twenty-one, he was appointed head of the department's criminal division. In that role he was responsible for breaking up the remains of Huey Long's political machine in Louisiana after its leader's assassination. Among the men Rogge sent to prison on corruption charges was Governor Richard W. Leche, Long's direct successor.[113] Rogge now turned his considerable talents to investigating Hitler's American friends, and the Christian Front would be only his first target among many.[114] Coughlin now made the situation even worse with a serious misstep. On January 21, he made a broadcast supporting the accused men, saying that as a fellow Christian he had no choice but to support them "until they are released or convicted."[115] He now branded himself a "friend of the accused" who was willing to "take my stand beside the Christian Fronters."[116]

The eventual trial of the "Brooklyn Boys," as the press dubbed the Christian Front plotters, was a circus. The prosecution case relied heavily on the testimony of an FBI informant who had infiltrated the gang and recorded key conversations on the inside of his shirt sleeves, along with some audio recordings.[117] The Boys' defense attorney, a former Brooklyn judge, portrayed the prosecution as an attack on Catholicism. He claimed the recorded conversations were merely a form of youthful bragging, not a serious plot. A friendly crowd cheered the defendants as they entered the courtroom each day. The entire proceeding ended in disaster for the government. Three defendants were released early through lack of evidence and another, bizarrely, committed suicide, apparently distraught that if convicted he might not be able to travel to Europe and fight for Hitler. After forty-seven hours of deliberations, the jury returned a verdict of not guilty against nine defendants, and a mistrial against the other five.[118]

Coughlin was overjoyed, but the victory was short-lived. The Catholic Church was increasingly worried about the impact of his activities, and the death of Bishop Gallagher had robbed Coughlin of his key supporter in the church hierarchy. Now the knives were coming out for him in earnest. In late 1938 Coughlin's superior, Bishop Mooney, warned Coughlin that his activities might be in violation of Vatican regulations.[119] Despite the increasing pressure, Coughlin kept broadcasting throughout the 1939–1940 season ending in May of that year. He simultaneously kept feeling out the limits of Mooney's tolerance with inflammatory *Social Justice* articles. The archbishop was not pleased, and resolved to keep Coughlin from engaging in politics as he had in 1936.

In late 1940 it was rumored in the press that Coughlin might attempt to intervene in the upcoming presidential election by returning to the airwaves. Mooney quickly outmaneuvered him by demanding that Coughlin submit his radio scripts in advance to a church board for possible censorship. Mooney had already used this power to prevent Coughlin from delivering an anti-Semitic diatribe in February 1940, and now he threatened the priest with official church sanctions if he submitted undesirable scripts. At the same time, Coughlin's radio stations were balking under public pressure to drop his program due to its controversial content. Faced with pressure from both the public and the church, Coughlin had little choice but to abandon his broadcasting plans. *Social Justice* would henceforth be his only public voice.[120]

The US government now stepped in on this front. In March 1941, *Social Justice* was banned on military bases as a potentially subversive publication. It was a sensible move. Even the bombing of Pearl Harbor in December of that year did not change the Coughlinite party line, which now vocally blamed Roosevelt and the Jews for precipitating the attack.[121] Winrod took a similar stance in his own writings. "There would be no brutal Nazism today, had it not been for savage Communism, shackled upon the nations by Jewish Money Power," he wrote in early 1942.[122] The last straw for the government came in early 1942, when State Department official Adolf A. Berle requested a full FBI investigation of *Social Justice*. The inquiry quickly turned to whether Coughlin was giving aid and comfort to the enemies of the United States. In March 1942, Coughlin had foolishly declared in a *Social Justice* article that the war had been caused by "the race of Jews" rather than German aggression.[123] The following month, the postmaster general suspended the distribution of *Social Justice* on the grounds that it might harm military morale. Coughlin was not technically the publisher of the newspaper and therefore could not face criminal sanctions, but he quickly offered to testify before a grand jury if distribution of the newspaper resumed. Creating a martyr of Coughlin and potentially alienating millions of Catholics was seen as too great a risk in the middle of a war, so the government declined the offer.[124] Still, *Social Justice* and Coughlin were finished. Mooney sent Coughlin a letter of rebuke for violating his past promises to abstain from politics. The Radio Priest dropped out of the public eye and resumed his career as a parish priest, though there were dark rumors about his past activities and future plans that would follow him for the rest of his life.[125]

Coughlin's forced silencing by Mooney and the US government likely saved him from a worse fate. Since May 1941, a federal grand jury had been quietly investigating Hitler's American friends to determine the scope of their activities and ambitions. Coughlin's departure from the political scene, and his status as a Catholic priest, insulated him from what was to come, but Winrod was less fortunate. In early 1942, the Dies Committee concluded that Winrod had been among the men who were intended to be part of a "'united Fascist movement' which never got going," and the claim was widely reported in the press.[126] In July, the grand jury issued indictments against twenty-eight people believed to be seditious and seeking to "interfere with, impair and influence the loyalty, morale and discipline" of American servicemen. Winrod's name was first on the indictment list.[127] He turned himself in to federal authorities four days later. Rather than be arrested at home, the Kansas preacher paid his own train fare to Washington. The legal proceedings against him would last until well after the end of the war.

While Coughlin and Winrod had captured the bulk of the public's attention, Gerald L. K. Smith was quietly biding his time. Chastened by his break with Coughlin and Townsend, he founded a group called the Committee of One Million to oppose Roosevelt and the New Deal. His fiery rhetoric as he traveled the country increasingly focused on the threat of communism and labor unions. He personally met Henry Ford in 1937 and claimed the industrialist convinced him that the real threat to the United States came from Jews. Smith's rhetoric now turned heavily anti-Semitic.[128] In 1939 he moved to Detroit to be closer to the business donors who now were bankrolling his operations, allegedly including Ford. By 1941 he had made the move to nonintervention campaigning, adopting the America First label in addition to his usual anti-Roosevelt politicking.[129] The following year he announced a run for the US Senate in Michigan on the Republican ticket. His campaign platform was "the Bible and America First," and he openly called for his supporters to back Father Coughlin's ideas. The Republican Party eventually united to bury him in the GOP primary, as it had with Winrod. Smith then foolishly decided to run as a write-in candidate, and received a few thousand votes in the general election. The fiasco was a major blow to his political prestige, but unlike Coughlin and Winrod, Smith would survive to became a major player in the postwar far right.[130] For now, however, all three demagogues were out of business.

Hitler's religious friends had been particularly effective at communicating with America's most disaffected citizens. While groups like the Bund and the Silver Legion were based on shared cultural heritage and bizarre mysticism, Coughlin, Winrod, and Smith rooted their messages in old-time religion and the suffering millions of Americans experienced in the Depression. Polls consistently found that Coughlin's supporters were largely drawn from the urban poor in the Northeast and the upper Midwest.[131] The priest's message of radical economic leveling and political revolution naturally appealed to people who had lost everything and were seemingly being left behind by the government's relief measures. Similarly, Winrod's supporters were mostly farmers and rural Americans who had likewise been devastated. Winrod was essentially the Protestant repackaging of Coughlin's message with an added element of homespun midwestern appeal.[132] Smith was an amalgamation of both messages. His experience with Huey Long gave him unparalleled insight into how to connect with rural audiences, but he could make the transition to urban settings as well. As the most powerful speaker of the three, Smith had the best potential to make the move into mainstream politics after the war.

All three men turned to Nazi sympathies for similar reasons. Winrod thought Hitler was a Christian bulwark against Jewish communism. Coughlin believed there was an international Jewish conspiracy running the banks and the Roosevelt administration. Smith shared both views and developed a seething hatred of the president. Remarkably, Winrod and Coughlin proved to be the most politically successful of Hitler's American friends. Coughlin was a force to be reckoned with in 1936 and after, though his star was tarnished by the disastrous Lemke presidential campaign. Winrod would have likely ended up in the US Senate if the Kansas Republican Party had not united against him. The United States narrowly escaped having a Nazi sympathizer elected to high office due to a combination of luck and the consciences of key power brokers in the Republican party. In the search for an American Führer, both Coughlin and Winrod had their moment in the sun, only to be brought down by their inability to work together; and, ultimately, by the diligence of the US government.

Regardless of their failure to achieve power, Hitler's religious friends held a special influence over millions of Americans. There are few forces more powerful than religion, and these men used their authority to convert Americans to a prejudicial and hateful ideology. It is telling that the German government viewed these men as key propaganda assets in the United States and were reluctant to give them direct aid only because it might make them less effective in spreading pro-Nazi ideas. There were obvious consequences for these actions. Coughlin's superiors in the Catholic Church were outraged by his conduct and ensured he never again entered the political realm. He would live out his days in a strange combination of obscurity and infamy. Unshackled from church hierarchy, but also less protected, Winrod would be less fortunate. It would be left to Smith to carry the torch of Hitler's religious friends into the postwar world, and this he would do with enthusiasm.

THE SENATORS

O n June 19, 1940, Senator Ernest Lundeen of Minnesota took to the chamber floor to deliver his latest broadside against the Roosevelt administration. As the Senate's only Farmer-Labor Party member and a former ally of the president, Lundeen had made a national name for himself by viciously turning against Roosevelt's efforts to aid Great Britain and institute the draft at home. The Senator consistently proclaimed he did not want to live in an America that would sacrifice its sons for the selfish interests of European powers, especially the British Empire. Despite future events, he would not personally do so. Within three months of his speech that day, and with whispers about the senator's Nazi sympathies growing, his scattered remains would be recovered in a Virginia field. The question marks surrounding his death remain to the present day.

On that June Wednesday, Lundeen used his status as a senator to enter a stinging denunciation of Britain's ambassador to the United States, Lord Lothian, into the official *Congressional Record*. The ambassador had previously been associated with the pro-appeasement wing of the Conservative Party in his home country, and Lundeen took it upon himself to point out the contradictions between Lothian's efforts between those past views and his current effort to build political support for Britain against the Nazis. "The discrepancy between his own view [supporting appeasement] and those which, as British Ambassador he is now daily urging upon the American Government and people, cannot but recall Talleyrand's famous definition of an Ambassador's duty—'to lie for his country,'" Lundeen proclaimed. "Today Ambassador Lothian must try to persuade Americans that Hitler is a monster, nazi-ism an unmitigated evil, and the German people essentially barbarous. . . . And that, in fact, the preservation of civilization, as we have known it, requires that American might, money, and men shall be freely offered to Britain to save her from defeat in a war which Lord Lothian, before he became Ambassador, warned his countrymen to shun."

"Of the two souls in his lordly bosom," Lundeen concluded with dramatic flair, "one was evidently very friendly to Germany."[1] The addition of Senator Lundeen's speech in the *Congressional Record* went almost unnoticed among the other business of the Senate that day. Comparatively speaking, it was not even one of his most provocative public statements. Six months earlier, Lundeen had called for Bermuda and other British colonies in the Caribbean to be transferred to the United States—or even seized by force—to help pay off the country's World War I debts. Months later, he demanded that the Roosevelt administration keep trading with the German government "neutrally" and declared himself to be an opponent of the "new-fangled internationalism" in the Senate.[2]

But Lundeen's action that day was notable for another reason. The senator from Minnesota had a secret that was known to only a few of his fellow lawmakers and staffers. As it turned out, large sections of Lundeen's best-known and widely publicized speeches and articles had not been written by him or even a member of his staff. They had, in fact, been at least partially written by a professional propagandist on the payroll of the German embassy and tasked with eroding support for American intervention in Europe. Senator Lundeen's powerful and often eloquent rhetoric was coming more or less directly from Berlin through a Nazi agent on Capitol Hill.

He was far from the only member of Congress to undertake such subterfuge. From the late 1930s until Pearl Harbor, the German embassy operated an ingenious propaganda operation that used more than two dozen US senators and representatives to disseminate pro-German and anti-British invective to millions of Americans. A congressional office in a House office building became the center of this insidious plot. Sacks of printed material and preprinted envelopes arrived by the day and sat in their closet to await distribution across the country. Nearby, the congressional aide responsible for this aspect of the operation took phone calls directly from the German agent who set up the scheme. It was like a scene from a Hollywood espionage thriller, yet it was all playing for real in the halls of Congress. Even worse, many of the elected officials involved were aware of what was taking place. They willingly became accomplices of Hitler's most effective propaganda agent in the United States.

At the center of this vast network of misinformation and propaganda sat a single mastermind: George Sylvester Viereck. Little remembered today, Viereck was once one of the most hated and feared men in the United States. The left-wing New York tabloid *PM* referred to him memorably as "Hitler's No. 1 Benedict Arnold," and he would be the first person subpoenaed to appear before Congressman Martin Dies's House Committee on Un-American Activities in 1938, affording him a subversive status roughly equal to the FBI's "Public Enemy Number 1."[3] Even the attention of the press and the government failed to dissuade Viereck from his mission to build American support for Nazi Germany and, above all else, keep the United States out of Hitler's war in Europe. He was, without a doubt, the Nazis' most effective tool for recruiting new American friends in the vaulted corridors of Washington, DC. Through it all, he made regular intelligence reports to Berlin and became the single most important source of US political intelligence for the Third Reich.

Viereck was no newcomer to shady propaganda operations. Born in 1884 in Munich, Viereck's father was rumored to be an illegitimate son of the Kaiser and a famous actress. Regardless of his true parentage, the elder Viereck embarked on a literary career and migrated to the United States in 1896. There young George began a literary career of his own, working for a journal edited by his father and writing poetry. In 1910 he published a book entitled *The Confessions of a Barbarian* in which he argued for the merits of German culture. Special attention was reserved for critiquing the women of various European backgrounds and recounting his sexual conquests. Former president Theodore Roosevelt was among the book's fans and invited Viereck to meet and discuss ways to build German-American understanding. At the president's encouragement, Viereck launched a short-lived journal exploring the subject.[4]

With the outbreak of World War I, Viereck took a predictably pro-German stance and argued that Germany had been tricked into war by the nefarious British and the French. Launching a new publication called the *Fatherland*, Viereck and his collaborators vocally argued the German perspective on the unfolding conflict and encouraging Americans to remain neutral.[5] However, as the American public would soon learn, these activities were not based purely in the spirit of peacemaking. Suspicious of Viereck's German connections, the Wilson administration had placed him under surveillance. In late July, agents intercepted a briefcase full of documents that included propaganda plans and other materials from the German government. Even more damningly, the documents included letters to and from Viereck discussing the best way to conceal payments being made from Germany to the *Fatherland*. Rather than keep the investigation confidential, Treasury Secretary William McAdoo leaked the documents to the New York *World*, which subsequently published a multipart series on the subject. Since the United States was not yet at war with Germany, no prosecutions resulted and Viereck continued his work unhindered. At the same time, there was no doubt about the source of the material he was peddling to the American public.[6]

Viereck's tone barely changed even after the United States entered the war in 1917. In a preview of his later tactics, Viereck launched a publishing company to disseminate anti-British and pro-German tracts. He then employed traveling salesmen to hawk the propaganda to consumers across the country.[7] The American public, now in the grip of a growing anti-German frenzy, responded less tolerantly than the government had. Viereck was expelled from his athletic club in New York and the Poetry Society of America. Leaving New York to hide out with his father-in-law and family, an angry mob chased him back to the city. In June 1917, his office was raided under the Espionage Act, and he was hauled before a congressional committee to answer a battery of allegations related to the money he had taken from the German embassy. However, given that the Sedition and Espionage Acts were not in effect when he had received the money, there was no way the government could charge him with violating them. Under questioning, Viereck openly admitted that he had burned his correspondence with the German government when the United States entered the war. He claimed this was purely for his own emotional release, but it also conveniently carried the benefit of destroying most of the relevant evidence.[8] Viereck had temporarily skated past any criminal consequences for his actions.

After the war, Viereck continued his pro-German agitation unabated. He campaigned against the Treaty of Versailles and denounced it as unfair to Germany. In the mid-1920s he was given a column in William Randolph Hearst's newspaper chain and penned articles about events taking place in Europe.[9] In 1923 he met Hitler and was "dazzled," claiming that he was the rightful heir to the spirit of Germany and the man to save the country from Bolshevism.[10] Inspired by Hitler's promise, Viereck established new connections with the German consulate in New York and urged its officials to launch a propaganda operation to improve Americans' perception of Nazism. In 1933, he arranged a contract with the German Tourist Information office and a public relations firm to publicize vacations in the country. The following year he was put in touch directly with the Foreign Ministry in Berlin. Viereck was quickly setting himself up to become Germany's leading propagandist and one of the Reich's most effective agents in the United States.

His timing in all this was impeccable. By the late 1930s, the British and German governments were effectively waging a war for American public opinion, with both sides knowing that the United States would play an essential role in a second war. These propaganda battles would, paradoxically, have to be carefully planned outside the public eye but simultaneously be fought on the widest possible stage. The Germans would soon base their operations around Viereck's operation and their consulates around the country. Influencing congressmen, senators, and other elected officials was essential to this strategy, which had three major goals:

1. Convince the American public that the Allies, especially Great Britain, were doomed in the event of war, primarily through spreading rumors and disinformation in the press.
2. Ensure the American public remained opposed to the notion of entering a war in Europe under any circumstances, by pressing public officials to support neutrality and disparaging the Roosevelt administration.
3. Ensure continuing trade between the United States and Germany both before and during a war.[11]

Nearly all aspects of German propaganda in the United States would be directed toward these goals, and Viereck's Capitol Hill activities were seen as essential to its success. Traveling to Berlin on one of his regular visits in late 1938, Viereck was given the task of running a large-scale anti-British propaganda campaign in the United States. Given his past experience, German officials believed he would be able to operate without arousing American suspicions or causing an international incident—and, indeed, Viereck would soon demonstrate his aptitude for circumspection.[12] To complete the arrangement, Viereck was hired by the German Library of Information—a propaganda operation based in Manhattan tasked with placing favorable stories in the American press—as a writer doing "special editorial work." Invoking his status as an American citizen, his official letter of acceptance told his German handlers that "I can think of no more important task from the point of view of fair play and the maintenance of peace between your country and mine than to present to the American public a picture unblurred by anti-German propaganda of the great conflict now unhappily waging in Europe."[13]

Viereck's plan was twofold. First, he would publish as much as possible under his own name or in publications he controlled, much as he had done during World War I. Some of these pieces would be written by him, but others would simply be translations of other propaganda publications being produced in Berlin. More insidiously, Viereck acutely realized the importance of influencing elite opinion on Capitol Hill. Perhaps reminded of his own failure to sway the Wilson administration, the second part of his plan involved lobbying lawmakers directly. For these services, he would be paid a monthly salary and be given money to further projects approved by the embassy. In total, Viereck would receive somewhere between $70,000 and $120,000 (about $1.2 million to $2.1 million in 2018) to support his activities, mostly in untraceable cash.[14]

Viereck's key contact and paymaster was Heribert von Strempel, first secretary of the German embassy in Washington. Strempel was the central casting image of a German diplomat and spy. Newspapers described him as "tall and handsome" with a fashionable dueling scar across his cheek.[15] He became known for attending wild parties and was seen with a progression of beautiful women, including the then-four-time-married heiress Merry Fahrney (her most recent husband had been Oleg Cassini, First Lady Jackie Kennedy's future fashion designer, and she would go on to have four more husbands after him). Rumor had it she rejected Strempel's effort to become husband number five after he encouraged her to embroider gold swastikas on her gowns.[16] His personal foibles aside, there is no doubt that Strempel was an effective diplomat and spymaster for Hitler. His career had begun with a posting in Paris followed by Chile, where he was promoted to chargé d'affaires. He was recalled in 1934 over suspicions about his loyalties because he had not joined the Nazi Party. He then spent a few years in the press section of the Foreign Office before being sent to Washington as first secretary in late 1938.[17] Strempel was only appointed to the post because he was fluent in both Spanish and English and there were no other suitable candidates available.[18] He would soon prove his worth to the Reich.

Strempel's mission in Washington was twofold. First, he was supposed to make contact with Latin American diplomats who might be friendly to the Reich. To this end he quickly struck up social relationships with counterparts from Argentina, Brazil, and Chile, though nothing significant resulted.

Strempel's second mission was far more successful: He was told to report to Berlin about American public opinion and "see that the German point of view was favorably presented in the American press," as American intelligence summarized it.[19] Viereck was a key part of this plan. Strempel paid Viereck any money he requested and, in exchange, Viereck handled the embassy's relationship with Washington's leading isolationist politicians. Contact with these politicians was deemed too dangerous for Strempel or his colleagues to make directly, so they used Viereck to do it through his nearly unlimited funds.[20] "I felt no need to account for any money given to him," Strempel later recalled.[21] This arrangement also gave Strempel the information he needed to make reports back to Berlin. "About 90% of his information was obtained from the press or newspapermen in Washington—the other 10% from Viereck," American intelligence concluded.[22] Strempel was running the Third Reich's most effective political intelligence and propaganda agency in the United States.

The political climate in the Washington of 1939 and 1940 could have hardly been more fertile terrain for Viereck and Strempel. Isolationist and anti-interventionist sentiment ran high, with congressmen and senators from both parties chafing at the Roosevelt administration's efforts to provide aid to the Allies. In 1937, the administration managed to convince Congress to amend the Neutrality Act to allow the president to sell war materials to European countries in the event of war. This "cash-and-carry" clause lapsed in 1939, but Roosevelt convinced Congress to renew it after the German invasion of Poland. Following his reelection in 1940, Roosevelt campaigned to abandon this system entirely by championing a "Lend-Lease" policy that allowed military equipment to be "loaned" to the Allies without payment upfront. Each of these victories only came after vicious congressional debate between the isolationist and interventionist factions. This was the unstable political climate Viereck and Strempel hoped to subvert for their own purposes.

Viereck's plan was in motion well before the 1940 election. His first approach was to Ernest Lundeen, who had entered the Senate in 1937. The senator was a well-established antiwar politician and there were already whispers that his sympathies might also lie in the Reich's direction. First entering the House of Representatives in 1917, Lundeen carried the distinction of being among a handful of congressmen who voted against the US declaration of war that year. After the armistice, he became an outspoken opponent of the League of Nations and traveled the country to denounce Woodrow Wilson's plans. These stances were so unpopular that during a congressional trip to the Western Front he was humiliatingly denied permission to visit American troops in the field. Returning home, he was once forced to flee from a Minnesota town in a locked refrigerator car when an angry mob protested one of his anti-League speeches. Faced with mounting criticism, Lundeen lost his seat after just one term. He eventually made a political comeback and was reelected to the House in 1932. Four years later he made it into the Senate after the Farmer-Labor party's nominee died.[23] It was a meteoric rise. Lundeen was passionately antiwar, undeniably isolationist if not pro-German and, above all, defiantly rebellious.[24] As Viereck told him, Lundeen now had "the Senate of the United States as a forum and the world as an audience." It was the ideal platform for Nazi propaganda.[25]

Lundeen quickly proved to be more than helpful to the German cause. Viereck inundated him with copies of his own books and back issues of the *Fatherland* for a "World War Library" the senator was assembling in his office. By June 1937, the men were "collaborating" on an article denouncing the Roosevelt administration's "secret agreements" with the British and French.[26] In reality, it was not so much a collaboration as a ghostwriting arrangement. Viereck provided the research background and most of the actual writing; while Lundeen made a few revisions, approved the finished product, and took a cut of the royalties (which Lundeen, who was in such dire financial straits that he allegedly forced his staffers to kick back part of their salaries to him, was particularly eager to collect).[27] The senator's name was the only one that showed up in the byline.[28] By the end of 1937, Viereck was writing speeches for Lundeen to deliver on national radio, and the "secret agreements" piece had been bought by a Hearst paper. No doubt sensing the power he was wielding over his powerful ally, Viereck told Lundeen bluntly that "I think in the long run you will find collaboration with me, especially if we can regularize it, more profitable both politically and financially than anything that you yourself can do, loaded down as you are with work."[29] This was quite the offer, coming as it did from a man who had been a known German propagandist during the First World War.

Viereck's connection to Lundeen would pay major dividends to both men. By early 1938, Viereck was not only penning speeches and articles appearing under Lundeen's byline but had also introduced himself in the corridors of Congress. His circle of contacts now included Republican congressman Hamilton Fish III of New York, a leading isolationist who often supported Lundeen's statements opposing intervention in Europe. In the Senate, his contacts came to include Burton K. Wheeler, Democratic senator from Montana; and Senator Rush Holt, Democrat from West Virginia, both leading isolationists (Holt lost his seat in 1940, preventing him from playing a major role in the Viereck plot). Wheeler would later become closely involved with Charles Lindbergh in the America First movement. Federal prosecutors eventually identified more than twenty members of Congress Viereck managed to influence or manipulate in the course of his Capitol Hill campaign.[30]

From this impressive list, Lundeen and Fish proved most eager to collaborate with Viereck. Boldly, Viereck set up shop in Lundeen's office, dictating sections of his speeches and openly calling his contacts at the German embassy on office phones to obtain new material. He was effectively dictating German propaganda directly onto the floor of the US Senate. As will be seen, Fish and the congressional staff he employed would soon take on a key role in Viereck's propaganda operation as well. Thanks to the deep level of access he had gained to the inner workings of the American government, Viereck began filing weekly intelligence reports directly to Hans-Heinrich Dieckhoff, the former German ambassador to the United States who had returned to Berlin in 1938. The German Foreign Ministry quickly dubbed their Capitol Hill spy the Reich's "most valuable liaison agent" for his ability to not only influence American lawmakers but also relay valuable information back to Berlin.[31]

These increasingly aggressive activities were starting to attract less welcome attention in Washington, however. Back in 1934, Viereck had been called to testify before the McCormack-Dickstein Committee, the precursor to the Dies Committee. At the time, Viereck admitted that he had traveled to Germany the previous year to secure funding for the German Tourist Information Office. Was the American political situation discussed in these Berlin meetings, Committee members inquired. "Undoubtedly. The topic could not be escaped," Viereck replied, dodging the more pertinent question of whether those discussions had actually been directed at how to influence American politics.[32] At the same time, Viereck maintained, all his activities were not actually propaganda on behalf on the Third Reich but rather a genuine and legal effort to convince Americans that Hitler's Germany was not their enemy. The Committee was hardly convinced, but, much as during World War I, there was little they could legally do to stop Viereck.

In mid-1938, Viereck was summoned to appear before the Dies Committee. Viereck purported to be annoyed by the summons, telling Fish that he had "nothing to conceal and [I] have never been engaged in any un-American activities. I was against our entrance into the World War, but so were many other good Americans, and most people agree with me today."[33] There was little to worry about at this point, however. Much like the McCormack-Dickstein Committee, the Dies Committee could do little more than question Viereck about the nature of his activities, but in the absence of evidence of criminal wrongdoing there was again nothing that could legally be done to stop him.

Viereck now faced a complication in his plans, however. In June 1938, Congress passed the Foreign Agents Registration Act (FARA). This legislation required anyone acting as an "agent of a foreign principal" (in other words, anyone working to advance the interests of a foreign country, at that country's direction) in a public relations or publicity capacity to register with the State Department. The intention was to unmask propagandists operating exactly on Viereck's model. Returning from an October 1939 visit to Berlin, Viereck had little choice but to register himself under the law. Given the government's knowledge of his activities, he would have been thrown in jail immediately if he had failed to comply. At the same time, he could hardly broadcast the fact that he was taking money from the German embassy to influence American congressmen. Instead, he contrived a clever workaround. Securing himself a nominal affiliation with a Munich-based newspaper, Viereck registered himself as the paper's American correspondent and, simultaneously, as an employee of the German Library of Information (as it turned out, his official contract was dated the day after his initial registration as a journalist). Through this clever maneuver, Viereck could plausibly claim that he had adhered to the letter of the law—he was a registered foreign agent, and had provided copies of his contracts to the State Department indicating that he was drawing upon German funds—without revealing anywhere near the extent of his activities. It was an ingenious legal dodge he would soon be grateful for having devised.[34]

The 1939 outbreak of war quickly put Viereck's plans into full swing. Lundeen and Fish were firmly entrenched in his propaganda apparatus, and dozens of other congressmen were seemingly friendly to his anti-interventionist and anti-British message. Lundeen personally requested a list of every reference to the United States in Hitler's *Mein Kampf,* no doubt to argue that the Führer had no designs on North America. Viereck was only too happy to oblige, passing him a series of extended passages from the book and extending the senator and his wife a personal invitation to stay at his home in New York during their next visit to the city.[35]

This was all undoubtedly pleasing to Viereck's superiors, but it was nowhere near as broad an audience as the Germans needed to reach. Viereck had secured a base of power in Washington, but now he intended to use his influence on a much larger scale. Armed with his unlimited funds from the embassy, Viereck purchased a German-American-owned publishing house in New Jersey called Flanders Hall that would become an important aspect of his mission. As Strempel described it, the Flanders Hall operation was simple:

> *The manuscripts of certain books came from the Foreign Office in Berlin in the diplomatic pouch or otherwise, and then went to the German Library of Information. Viereck selected from those manuscripts those which he thought might criticize and unmask British propaganda and egoistic British foreign policy, and which could easily be sold in the United States.*[36]

Flanders Hall publications looked and felt cheap, carrying a standard brown cover and a simple nameplate. The content was almost always anti-British and isolationist, directly in line with Nazi propaganda goals. One publication, crudely translated from the original German and bearing a false byline, was a vicious indictment of British policy in India, while other texts criticized Britain's policies toward Ireland.[37] One of Lundeen's speeches criticizing Lord Lothian found its way into print this way (combined with a foreword by Viereck, writing under a pseudonym), as did an account of the outbreak of the war that held the British exclusively responsible. Republican congressman Stephen A. Day of Illinois published one of his own works with the press, heavily influenced if not ghostwritten by Viereck himself.[38]

For each book published by Flanders Hall, the German embassy advanced Viereck whatever amount of money he requested to publish it, in "lump sums of 5 or 10 thousand dollars," as Strempel put it.[39] If the book did well, Viereck pocketed the profits and kept the German subsidy. Most of the books were profitable, Strempel recalled, Lundeen's book on Lord Lothian exceptionally so. Books about Ireland also did well, no doubt because they sold well in the Irish-American community.[40] Advertisements for Flanders Hall tracts ran in a wide range of newspapers including the *New York Times*, heightening their legitimacy and assuredly boosting their sales. Flanders Hall swiftly became the predominant publishing platform for Nazi propaganda in the United States, reaching a large audience and simultaneously boosting Viereck's coffers. He also received assistance in this venture from William Griffin, the virulently anti-British publisher of the *New York Enquirer*. Griffin was a diehard isolationist who had once sued Prime Minister Winston Churchill for libel in a spat over Britain's First World War debt to the United States.[41] According to Strempel,

Griffin ran large ads for Viereck in the *Enquirer* and personally sold copies of Flanders Hall books to Irish-American groups. He had been given these books for free and pocketed the profits, providing him a direct financial benefit from Viereck's activities. "Viereck and Griffin were working—how do you say it— hand in glove," Strempel told his postwar interrogators.[42]

The final phase of Viereck's plan relied on combining his various operations into a single propaganda campaign. By early 1940 he had launched an ingenious scheme to distribute his anti-British and anti-interventionist propaganda for free—at least free for him. Under prevailing precedent and federal law, congressmen and senators were able to obtain official reprints of speeches from the official *Congressional Record* at a heavily reduced cost for distribution to their constituents, interested third parties, or merely their own records. The bulk of the cost was borne by taxpayers. Further, it was (and is) possible to insert large portions of text into the *Record* without the actual words being spoken on the floor of the House or Senate, effectively allowing any member to insert statements for the historical record with minimal oversight. This was the method that Lundeen had used to insert many of his most virulently anti-British sentiments into the official record without having to actually face his fellow senators on the floor of the upper house.

Members of Congress also enjoyed (and still enjoy) another important privilege called franking. Dating back to precedents established in the British Parliament, franking allows federal officials, including members of Congress, to send official mail for free. The original intent was to allow elected officials to correspond with their constituents without suffering a financial penalty, but over the decades it had been subjected to a variety of abuses and subsequent reforms. By the late nineteenth century congressmen and senators had lost most of their franking privileges. Mailing out copies of the *Congressional Record*, however, was explicitly protected on the notion that citizens should be able to receive copies of congressional proceedings for free.

Viereck and his congressional allies soon saw the potential to use this system to their advantage. Lundeen, Fish, and Republican congressman Jacob Thorkelson of Montana devised a plan in which they would deliver speeches on the chamber floor (or simply insert the speech into the *Congressional Record* appendix) and then order huge numbers of official copies from the congressional printing office. One of Lundeen's secretaries would later testify that she personally arranged for one hundred thousand copies of a speech to be delivered to Fish's office on Viereck's request. The German agent then made arrangements for the copies' distribution, using the senator's office phone and with him stand-ing nearby.[43] On another occasion, Viereck requested an astonishing six to seven *million* copies of a speech from isolationist Republican Senator Gerald P. Nye, who showed better judgment than some of his colleagues by refusing the request. Viereck then simply acquired a smaller number of copies through one of his front organizations.[44]

The genius of this plan was not in the acquisition of the *Congressional Record* offprints, nor in the fact that Viereck was effectively writing the speeches being printed. It was in the distribution. One of Fish's secretaries, George Hill, managed to acquire huge numbers of unaddressed franked envelopes from a variety of congressional offices, sometimes with the permission of the congress-men but other times unwittingly.[45] These were as good as gold for Viereck, who now had the ability to mail out unlimited amounts of propaganda for free and with the legitimacy of a congressional return address on the envelope. Hill ar-ranged for the huge stacks of mail to be sent out quietly by requesting trucks to arrive directly at the office where it was being held. It was a clever and almost undetectable scheme. Hamilton Fish's mail room in the Cannon House Office Building—Room 1424—was reputedly stuffed with bags of unaddressed en-velopes and speeches.[46] The cover letter included with one such speech by Fish asked the recipient to pressure their own member of Congress to support isola-tionist legislation and help keep America out of the war. Further copies of the speech, the letter concluded, "are available for distribution to interested indi-viduals and groups, already inserted in franked, postage free envelopes which will require only addressing and mailing. Requests to me [Fish] will receive prompt permission."[47]

Between his activities with Flanders Hall, the congressional franking scheme, and his growing power on Capitol Hill, Viereck had easily proven his worth to Berlin. In addition to congressional speeches, Viereck also authorized the mail-ing of more than a million postcards mocking Roosevelt and urging support for isolationism. Many such cards were sent out using Wheeler's congressional frank, despite being seen by Strempel as being a "cheap type of propaganda." Viereck required permission from no one to proceed and simply went ahead with the mailings.[48] In addition, Viereck began acquiring lists of addresses belong-ing to Americans who had expressed sympathy for isolationist views, or belonged to prominent anti-intervention groups, in an effort to better target his mailings.

By late 1940, millions of Americans had received unsolicited mailings from a German propaganda agent carrying the return address of prominent congressmen from across the country. The Flanders Hall press was pumping out anti-British and anti-interventionist tracts as quickly as they could be produced, some of which were selling large numbers of copies. The profits from these, combined with the money Viereck could command at a moment's notice from the German embassy, gave him the ability to instantly finance nearly any propaganda he desired. A 1941 report from the Office of Naval Intelligence in San Diego to the FBI referred to him as "the paymaster" behind a wide range of propaganda efforts, including, it was eventually suspected, Charles Lindbergh and the America First Committee.[49]

Viereck's work with Lundeen also continued apace. From their surviving correspondence, it is clear that Viereck viewed the senator as his most important ally in the Capitol. He was certainly the most receptive to Viereck's message and the most willing to use his speeches. By August 1940, the two men were collaboratively working on a major speech focusing on "German-American contributions to our national life." This was intended to be a major campaign address touching on the merits of German culture generally and, possibly, including praise for Hitler himself. Viereck undoubtedly looked forward to printing and distributing it on a mass scale. The initial draft manuscript of background information ran at more than one hundred pages and included contributions of several of Viereck's "collaborators," probably from the German embassy. Lundeen intended to deliver the first version during a Labor Day event in Minnesota. Viereck duly provided a finished copy for him on August 30.[50]

The afternoon of August 31 was a tumultuous one in Washington. The weather seemed to suit the political atmosphere as a tremendous thunderstorm gradually made its way across Virginia toward the capital. A Douglas DC-3 operated by Pennsylvania Central Airlines sat on the tarmac of Washington Airport waiting for conditions to clear. Its destination was Pittsburgh, but most of the twenty-one passengers on board, including Lundeen, were planning to transfer to other flights from there. After a twenty-six-minute weather delay the flight took off to the northwest, climbing to six thousand feet and passing near the town of Leesburg before nearing the foothills of the Blue Ridge Mountains. Then it flew directly into the blinding storm the plane had been delayed to avoid.

What happened next was never fully established to anyone's satisfaction. Witnesses on the ground claimed to hear an explosion. Federal investigators would discount this possibility and conclude that the aircraft was most likely struck by lightning. Whatever the exact cause, at around 3:40 p.m. the plane plunged into an open field near Lovettsville, Virginia, at full throttle, killing Lundeen, its other twenty passengers, and four crewmembers instantly. The impact was so destructive that the plane's engines were buried fifteen feet in the ground. The victims' bodies were scattered over a twenty-five-acre area, and first responders to the grim scene were unable to determine how many fatalities they were looking at. It was the nation's worst commercial air disaster to date.[51] The FBI agents sent from Washington who finally identified Lundeen's body found the copy of Viereck's speech in his coat pocket, ready to be delivered at the end of a journey the senator would never complete.[52]

The nation was shocked, and Lundeen's death dominated the headlines. It was only a matter of days before rumors began to spread. It soon emerged that the dead included two FBI employees, a stenographer named Margaret Turner and a newly appointed special agent named Joseph Pesci. Were Pesci and Turner trailing Lundeen? Was one of the country's best-known isolationist senators under federal investigation? And—to be even more conspiratorial—was there perhaps something sinister about Lundeen's death? Full answers are still unclear decades later. At the time, both Attorney General Robert Jackson and FBI director Hoover argued that the presence of the FBI employees was pure coincidence. "No inquiry into the affairs of Senator Lundeen has ever been instituted or contemplated, either by the Federal Bureau of Investigation or by any other agency of the Department of Justice, and any statement or report to the contrary is untrue," Jackson told Lundeen's widow in the months after the crash.[53] A subsequent investigation into the crash led by Senator Pat McCarran of Nevada met with a similar denial from the FBI.

Declassified bureau files suggest a different story. A 1942 FBI report concerning the publication of a "tell-all" book discussing the Lundeen-Viereck connection noted that all the information contained in the publication had "come to the attention of the Bureau previously" and that there was little to be learned from its revelations. Whether Lundeen himself was actually under direct investigation is unclear, but there is no doubt that the FBI was keeping a close eye on Viereck by this point.[54]

Regardless of whether Lundeen had been the subject of FBI investigation, his dramatic death marked the beginning of the end for Viereck's scheme. Just two weeks before the crash, the New York newspaper *PM* had published an exposé on Viereck that referred to him as "Benedict Arnold" and linked him to the German Library of Information. More dangerously, however, it briefly referred to the *Congressional Record* plan, though not to Lundeen by name. Writing to Lundeen, Viereck assured him the article was merely a "witch-hunt" and a "curious mix of falsehood."[55] The truth could only remain concealed for so long, however. After the crash other reporters jumped on the story, fueled by increasing speculation about Lundeen's death. The Viereck connection was quickly discovered, as was the appearance of Lundeen at events attended by members of the German government and other officials. A press frenzy began. By October, columnist and radio commentator Walter Winchell had jumped on the bandwagon and suggested in his column that Lundeen had been under investigation at the time of his death.[56]

Tactlessly writing to Lundeen's widow Norma just weeks after the crash, Viereck begged to be given the chance to "discuss ways and means of meeting these outrageous attacks upon Ernest." He received no reply for months.[57] In reality, Norma Lundeen was facing an onslaught of her own. In the midst of her mourning, she was appalled by the revelations being made about her husband's involvement with Viereck and the German embassy. More conspiratorially, she began to receive letters suggesting that the senator had been assassinated. "Stranger things have happened to still a 'voice crying in the wilderness,'" one such letter read. "*British* fifth columns are here, too."[58] There was, of course, no proof for this claim, but there was increasing evidence that the senator had cultivated a circle of questionable associates. Norma Lundeen refused to back down, however, and made it her mission to defend her late husband's reputation. Talking to the NBC Blue Network in May 1941, she claimed that the senator had an "imperishable record of true Americanism." The suggestion that Viereck had written her husband's speeches was "a deliberate falsehood—designed to mislead . . . He was fully capable of writing his own—and he wrote his own." At the end of the day, she said, "He knew but one patriotism and that was for America."[59] Norma Lundeen's defense of her husband's memory was perhaps understandable, but it was also based in falsehoods. She must have known that Viereck had written her husband's speeches because—as later emerged in court—she asked his staff to remove all the letters between the men from his office archive and place them in her possession after he died.[60] This was a deeply suspicious act for a woman who supposedly had nothing to hide.

Viereck's days as a propagandist were numbered. While he had been able to bat away the Dies Committee and evade the FBI so far, he was less successful escaping British intelligence. The critical flaw in his plan surrounded the reports he was filing with Berlin. Like most German agents in North America, his usual technique was to mail these to German intelligence contacts at prearranged addresses in Europe (usually in neutral countries, to evade suspicion). As army intelligence discovered after the war:

> *The reports contained clippings from American papers and articles, the opinions of citizens in Capitol Hill, interspersed with "inside tips" on future Presidential policy, what notables had been received at the White House, and notes on industrial development and production bottlenecks. Only the latter items were of value.*[61]

Valuable or not, the Germans had an agent on Capitol Hill who was feeding them information. Ironically, it would not be the FBI that took the lead in shutting this threat down, but William Stephenson's British Security Coordination agents. This fact was a long-concealed secret of wartime intelligence operations. Key files opened at the UK National Archives in 2013 prove conclusively that BSC agents were not only aware of Viereck's scheme before the FBI, but also took critical action to shut it down.

As it turns out, the British first detected Viereck's activities in early 1940 when they discovered that Americans on the mailing list of a publication called *Facts in Review* were also receiving isolationist speeches reprinted from the *Congressional Record* mailed with the congressional frank. *Facts in Review* was a Nazi propaganda rag published by the German Library of Information— Viereck's nominal employer. British agents verified the connection by inserting fake names and addresses into the library's mailing list. Before long, those names began receiving isolationist propaganda without specifically requesting it. There was clearly a link between the German Library and whoever was mailing the material from the halls of Congress. "The volume of this mail and the frequency of it soon made it clear that there must . . . be some guiding genius directing the distribution, planning the insertion of the propaganda into the *Congressional Record* so that it could later be mailed out in franked envelopes, arranging for the 'dummying' of the various mailing pieces, and planning to get the pieces ordered and distributed to all those people and organizations who finally addressed and mailed the franked envelopes," a secret British intelligence report concluded in 1941. The genius behind it was, of course, Viereck.[62]

British agents on Capitol Hill quickly determined the broad outline of his plan. "Without any doubt George Hill, Hamilton Fish's second male secretary, is the purchasing agent and the guiding control of the franking 'racket' in the

United States," they reported. "George Sylvester Viereck is the 'big shot' who remains in the background."[63] The weak link in the scheme was obviously Hill. The British soon placed "a very capable feminine operator" to extract information from the divorced Hill (as the British discovered, he was known for having "many girls" in the Washington area and for spending opulently to impress them). The British operative quickly convinced Hill to give her a full account of the franking scheme using methods that remained unspecified in the official report. From there, British agents discovered Hill was personally embezzling some of the money he received from Viereck and intended to "retire at an early age" from his earnings.[64] The British had all they needed to make a move on Viereck. BSC agents leaked Hill's involvement in the scheme to the Washington press, causing a minor scandal. "Most of the stories printed in the newspapers about this particular case have only been partially true as we only gave them sufficient [information] to drag Hill's name before the public and the appropriate Washington authorities," they told London.[65] Through these strategic leaks, the British dropped the scheme on the laps of both the FBI and federal prosecutors.

The British had another source of secret information about Viereck's activities as well, and it was even more sensitive than BSC's Capitol Hill intelligence network. After the outbreak of war, British intelligence began directing ships carrying mail intended for Europe to a secret censorship facility in Bermuda, where the mailbags were offloaded and their contents inspected. Mail deemed sensitive or likely to reveal military secrets was inspected and censored while less threatening mail was allowed to continue to its destination, but the contents of anything interesting were noted and sent on to London. This was obviously a very delicate and secretive operation given that it meant interfering with the private mail of American citizens.

From at least mid-1941, if not before, the British intercepted Viereck's reports to his handlers in Berlin and sent summaries of their contents to both London and the FBI. While it would have been possible to cut off Viereck's connection to the Reich by intercepting the letters, MI6 advised that the reports should be allowed to reach their destination uncensored so they could continually gather intelligence from them.[66] Viereck was allowed to continue sending information he thought was going directly to Berlin while in reality he was handing British intelligence the means to unravel his wider plot.

Both Viereck and Hill soon found themselves in dire legal straits. In September 1941, a Washington grand jury opened an investigation into Nazi propaganda activity and subpoenaed Viereck to appear. But, just as in World War I, could he actually be indicted? Had a crime been committed? It was not illegal to disseminate propaganda, and it could easily be argued that Viereck had simply been exercising his First Amendment rights. There was no evidence that he had passed on classified material to the German government, nor had he attempted to subvert the US military. He had also registered with the State Department under FARA, as required.

On the other hand, had he registered properly and complied with the *spirit* of FARA? His official FARA declaration listed him as a journalist and author, but he had not reported his other activities related to the Flanders Hall press. Were these not also actions being taken to further the interests of a foreign government? This omission provided the government the legal opening it needed. In October 1941, Viereck was indicted on five counts related to his failure to report the Flanders Hall operation, his use of false names on publications, and his activities with the *Congressional Record* on his FARA declaration. None of these activities had been properly revealed, the government argued.

Viereck was arrested and released on bond. For the rest of the war he would be embroiled in a complicated legal battle that would eventually find its way to the Supreme Court.[67] One of the key witnesses against him would be the British censorship examiner who intercepted his reports to Germany. The examiner, it turned out, held the only direct evidence of his contact with the Nazi government.[68] Hitler's most effective propagandist in the United States had finally been put out of business. A few weeks later George Hill, the congressional staffer who had proved so useful, was called before the grand jury himself. Asked directly if he knew Viereck and other key figures in the plot, Hill answered that he did not. He was immediately indicted for perjury.[69] He ended up being sentenced to between two and six years behind bars.[70] With his arrest, Viereck's operation on Capitol Hill was effectively shut down.

What had Viereck been able to accomplish? Certainly, he was able to disseminate a huge amount of pro-German and anti-British propaganda to the American public. Yet there is little evidence he convinced a large number of people to view the Third Reich positively. Instead, Viereck's value lay in his ability to manipulate political elites. His relationship with Lundeen, Fish, Wheeler, and other isolationists on Capitol Hill undoubtedly steeled their resolve in opposing the Roosevelt administration and gave them a larger platform for spreading isolationism. Opinion polls showing a majority of Americans opposing entry into the war were no doubt to some extent influenced by the "respectable" voices in Washington endorsing and pushing these views. In addition, Viereck's reports to his superiors at the German embassy and in Berlin offered valuable firsthand information about what was taking place within the corridors of power in Washington.

There would be stark consequences for the congressman who helped Viereck achieve these aims. Many would further tarnish their names by becoming involved with the America First Committee after his arrest. This was far from the extent of the Nazis' involvement with American politics. Heribert von Strempel was not just the paymaster for Viereck; he was also responsible for another aspect of the German government's plans against the United States. This would involve convincing American businessmen to not only oppose Franklin Roosevelt but directly attack his 1940 reelection campaign. Strempel would soon end up helping one of Hitler's key American friends in a bold attempt to unseat the president.

THE BUSINESSMEN

I n mid-1933, a midwestern oilman found himself sitting in the opulent director's suite of the Reichsbank in Berlin to make a peculiar business pitch. Around the table were a dozen German bankers and bureaucrats, few if any of whom were impressed with the proposals of the visiting American. If Germany wanted to do business with American oil companies, most thought, why were the representatives of Standard Oil not sitting in front of them? The powerful president of the Reichsbank, Hjalmar Schacht, was among the skeptics. This on its own should have doomed the scheme to immediate rejection.

But the American had a supporter even more powerful than Germany's leading financiers. As he began his pitch, a door abruptly opened to reveal the uniformed figure of the Führer himself. Muttering a few words of approval, Hitler disappeared as quickly as he had come. The short visit was enough. At the end of the meeting, no opposition to the plan could be found among the Reichsbank's directors.[1] This momentous meeting would mark the beginning of an international plot that would eventually ensnare a Boston bank, the Mexican government, and one of America's most prominent labor union leaders in a daring plan to unseat President Franklin D. Roosevelt at the behest of the Nazi government. The machinations begun that day were deemed so serious that O. John Rogge, the American investigator who examined the plot after the war, deemed it the "single biggest scheme" hatched by the Nazis in the United States, even exceeding George Sylvester Viereck's Capitol Hill machinations.[2] It would ultimately center around a cleverly planned but ham-handed attempt by a hostile foreign power to influence a US presidential election.

The American businessman sitting in the Reichsbank that day was William Rhodes Davis, an Alabama-born oil speculator who had already made and lost several fortunes by the start of the Great Depression.[3] A shadowy figure with a constant chip on his shoulder against the "international combine" of Big Oil companies he believed were plotting to keep him down, Davis's biographer has compared him to the main villain in the 1989 film *Indiana Jones and the Last Crusade*.[4] In the film, unscrupulous American businessman Walter Donovan tricks Jones into becoming part of a Nazi plot to find the Holy Grail, only to ultimately be outwitted himself and meet a grisly end. There would be no such outwitting of the real-life Davis, though his own end would be nearly as premature.

The plot centered around Davis was certainly serious and over the course of the coming years would not only bring Nazi money into American politics but also provide the Reich with nearly 1 million barrels of badly needed oil. Rather than as a character from an Indiana Jones film, Davis might more accurately be seen as a prototypical James Bond villain, sitting at the middle of an extensive web of deceit while maintaining an impeccable wardrobe and lavish lifestyle designed to impress and entice allies and enemies alike. The eventual intervention of British intelligence in the Davis case only furthers the comparison.

Putting aside the more sinister aspects of Davis's plot, however, he was far from being the only foreign businessman who engaged with the Third Reich. Before 1939, a wide range of American corporate executives showed little reluctance in doing business with Hitler's government. Many American corporations were heavily invested in Germany and had little option but to cooperate with the new regime, or face serious losses. The 1920s had been an era of rapid globalization, particularly by American firms that used their prosperity to acquire imperiled European rivals. Until the 1929 stock market crash, this looked like a winning strategy, particularly for American companies looking to tap an underdeveloped German market. A prominent example could be found in the auto industry. A 1929 press report estimated that there were only 1.2 million automobiles on the road in Germany, while 23 million were operating in the United States. German automakers like Mercedes produced excellent luxury cars, it continued, but no company produced "a good, serviceable, and cheap car for the average man." The German market, seen as "one of the most promising in the world at the moment," would soon entice both General Motors and Ford.[5]

Other firms were tempted by similar opportunities. International Business Machines (IBM) would soon have a European division, as would the Coca-Cola corporation.[6] One of the world's most powerful corporations, Standard Oil, entered a business relationship with German firm I.G. Farben in 1929 that resulted in Standard taking a 25 percent share in the latter's gasoline business.[7] In addition, Standard and I.G. Farben entered a patent-sharing agreement that ended up giving Farben the ability to boost its octane levels and supply the Luftwaffe with more effective fuel.[8] American corporations ended up with an estimated $300 million invested in German corporate branches and manufacturing facilities when Hitler rose to power in 1933. This was far too much capital for American corporate bosses to simply walk away from when political conditions changed. Many of America's corporate leaders were therefore more or less being held economic hostage by the German government from the first day of Hitler's reign.[9]

There was therefore a clear incentive for American corporate leaders to behave as if they were Hitler's friends, whether they agreed with his politics or not. As will be seen, some of these figures would later become leaders in the noninterventionist America First movement. Corporate opposition to the Roosevelt administration was also nothing new by the late 1930s. Roosevelt's efforts to pull the country out the Great Depression were greeted by accusations from Wall Street that he was alternatively borrowing from the fascist or communist playbooks, despite those same critics being less vocal when Roosevelt had dramatically intervened to save the American banking system in the first weeks of his presidency.[10]

There were dark rumors about where corporate America's hatred of Roosevelt might lead. In late 1934, Marine Corps General Smedley Butler was called to testify before Congress and told a hair-raising story. Butler claimed that earlier in the year he had been approached by a shadowy group of American Legion members who wanted to enlist his support for a plot to overthrow Roosevelt and replace him with a fascist-military dictatorship. The outlandish scheme was supposedly backed by a list of prominent bankers and industrialists who were discontented with the president's policies. According to Butler, the plotters wanted him to lead a half-million-man army of veterans to march on Washington to pressure Roosevelt into resigning or becoming the figurehead of a fascist government. The plotters had supposedly already raised $3 million to support

Butler's army, and were said to be willing to spend a hundred times that amount if necessary. If true, money of this scale could only have come from America's most powerful banks and corporations.[11]

Butler claimed he had been appalled by the scheme and played the plotters for time while he contacted FBI director J. Edgar Hoover. Rumors of the conspiracy were soon circulating around Washington, and Butler was called to testify before Congress along with several of the alleged connivers.[12] The story broke explosively in the nation's newspapers, the editorial pages of which responded with a mixture of alarm and incredulity. "The old saying that where there's some smoke there must be some fire may apply in this case but the details revealed to date seem too preposterous to give much credence to the story," the Wisconsin Rapids *Daily Tribune* told readers.[13] "New York doesn't know whether to laugh or get mad about Smedley Butler's story of a Wall Street–engineered Fascist putsch. . . . General Butler has never been known to shun the front page," nationally syndicated reporter James McMullin wrote, before suggesting that Butler should take some tips on the "beauty of silence" from famously mute comedian Harpo Marx.[14] "What can we believe?" the *New York Times* asked simply.[15]

The official congressional report on the matter was less skeptical, concluding that some kind of plot likely existed and might have been set into motion without Butler's intervention. In the end, however, there were no prosecutions, and Roosevelt himself appears to have wanted the matter to simply go away. Historians have debated ever since how serious the "Business Plot" really was, with most concluding that some kind of scheme probably existed but did not get far past the planning stages. Serious or not, novelist Sinclair Lewis used it as a partial inspiration for his 1935 novel *It Can't Happen Here*.[16]

Regardless of whether a shady cabal had actually tried to overthrow the government, there was no doubt that prevailing business opinion was staunchly anti-Roosevelt. The president's diplomatic recognition of the Soviet Union in November 1933, which both Democratic and Republican administrations had refused to do since the Russian Revolution, scandalized right-wing opinion.[17] A tradition of business support for fascism dated back to Mussolini's ascension to power in Italy and was well established by the time Hitler appeared on the scene a decade later. "With few exceptions, the dominant voices of business responded to Fascism with hearty enthusiasm," historian John P. Diggins has written about the Italian case.[18] Similar sentiments about Hitler were easily found as well. "There are those who consider Hitler a fool or a madman," the

business-minded *Barron's* editorialized in 1936, "but whether in his own capacity or under the guidance of advisers, he sees the necessity of forming a strong,
and ever-stronger, Central European front facing eastward—a defensive cordon
against Bolshevism, for the protection of the capitalist system and the rights of
private property."[19] Hitler might not be the ideal capitalist leader (he was, after
all, an avowed "National Socialist") but at least he was not a communist. O. John
Rogge later described this position as the argument that "You can do business
with Hitler."[20] There were some hints the American people were sympathetic
to this view too. A July 1940 *Fortune* poll asked respondents if, in the event
Hitler won the war in Europe, the United States should "Find some way of
continuing our old European commercial business with Hitler's new Europe" or
alternatively "make every effort to develop business only with countries not
under Hitler's control." A plurality (44 percent) declared themselves in favor of
continued business ties, while 40 percent said the United States should only
do business with countries not under German control.[21] The prospect of doing
business with Hitler was therefore hardly abhorrent to many Americans.

Many of America's corporate leaders seem to have quickly embraced this very
notion. As already noted, some thought they had little choice but to comply
with the German government's diktats to protect their investments. The automobile industry presented perhaps the most prominent examples of American
corporations simply becoming too deeply mired in the Third Reich to easily ex-
tricate themselves. In March 1929, both General Motors and Ford made
attempts to purchase Opel, the largest automaker outside the United States.[22]
GM's Alfred P. Sloan outmaneuvered Ford by acquiring 80 percent of Opel
stock for a sizable $33.3 million, making the German company GM's largest
foreign holding. The prospect of using Opel's manufacturing facilities to produce a low-cost automobile initially seemed shrewd, yet by the early years of
the Depression GM was losing money in Germany. The natural solution was to
make a swift exit from the German market, but in 1931 the government imposed capital controls to prevent companies from taking money out of the country. GM was trapped.[23] Smarting from its loss in the Opel bid, Ford opened a
subsidiary in the German city of Cologne—Ford-Werke-AG—which soon became the only foreign Ford plant allowed to produce powerful V-8 engines.[24]
As with GM's Opel facilities, Ford's plant would soon deliver dividends for
Hitler's government.

A similar story could be found with the most iconic American brand: Coca-
Cola. In the heady year of 1929, an American expat named Ray Rivington Pow-

ers began bottling Coca-Cola in Germany and quickly found a market for more than one hundred thousand cases of the soft drink. Powers was a colorful character and a great promoter, but was less talented when it came to running a business. The withdrawal of a German partner left his operation in financial jeopardy, resulting in the corporation dividing German Coca-Cola between the official company, Coca-Cola GmbH, and a second company that would control bottling and be run by Powers.[25] Coca-Cola GmbH fell under the control of Max Keith, a German former bookkeeper with a dictatorial manner who was occasionally compared by subordinates to the führer and harbored a fanatical love of the brand. As one historian has recounted, for Keith the slogan to follow was not the Nazi "Deutschland über Alles" but "Coca-Cola über Alles." By 1934, Keith had launched an aggressive advertising campaign to promote his beverage in restaurants and cafes that traditionally served only beer. The effort was so successful that Keith was able to open a new plant in Frankfurt and a series of warehouses to hold the finished product. By 1936, more than a million cases of Coca-Cola were being sold in the Third Reich, making it one of the country's favorite beverages.[26]

Entanglements of this kind gave many of America's leading corporations a vested interest in the success of the Third Reich from its earliest days onward. Many executives soon found that it was definitely possible to do business in the Reich as long as they played their cards right. As the German economy began to bounce back and even thrive in the early 1930s, corporate profits followed. The autobahn system stimulated the automobile industry not just for consumer vehicles but also trucks. One of Hitler's first acts in 1933 was slashing taxes on automobile purchases. Opel sales doubled in the first year of Hitler's reign alone.[27] Coca-Cola sales followed suit, as thirsty and tired workers turned to a caffeine-laced beverage that was safer to drink on the job than beer.[28] IBM tabulators kept track of the economic growth—and the German population itself—using punch cards that could be used to quickly and easily count at previously unthinkable speeds.[29] Hitler seemed to have delivered remarkable economic prosperity at a time when the rest of the world was still mired in the doldrums.

The situation was not completely rosy, however. The German government's economic policies still prevented profits from leaving the country without complicated machinations. It was possible to convert small quantities of German marks to dollars, but it meant accepting a deliberately extortionate exchange rate. The intent was to spur continued investment in the Reich. Its effect was to sharply reduce the actual profits American corporations could reap from their

holdings. Many foreign firms doing business in Germany simply let their profits pile up in accounts when they had no further need to invest. Some, including GM, would eventually manage to recoup some of their profits after the war.[30]

There were political dangers associated with doing business in the Reich as
well. Nazi ideology was expressly German-centric and took a dim view of
foreign-owned businesses, especially those that might be owned or run by Jews.
Opel, for one, changed its management structure to bring in German directors
who became the public face of the company. Its bosses also added several Nazi
Party "old fighters"—members of the party who had joined before Hitler obtained power, serving as testimony of their commitment to the cause—to increase its standing with the regime.[31] Opel then arranged its factories according
to Nazi ideological dictates and sacked most of its Jewish employees (though,
to their credit, executives occasionally tried to find the victims of Nazi racism
alternative jobs at GM's holdings outside Germany).[32] GM's general manager
of overseas operations, Graeme Howard, reported to his superiors in 1936 that
Hitler enjoyed nearly universal support among the German population and that
it would be foolish to antagonize the Nazis in any way. Howard, whose father
was a Stanford professor, had lived in Berlin and Heidelberg and would shortly
become one of the most vocal advocates of doing business with Hitler.[33]

Coca-Cola faced similar challenges. The 1936 Berlin Olympics provided a
sizable sales boost, but later that year new government restrictions imperiled its
ability to import the American-made concentrate that served as the base for its
drink. Executives were forced to negotiate behind the scenes with Luftwaffe
chief Hermann Göring to ensure that needed supplies of syrup could be brought
into the country.[34] That same year, a Nazi industrialist who hoped to launch a
German rival to the American beverage was foolishly invited to tour a New York
bottling plant. During the visit he snatched several bottle tops bearing the Star
of David to demonstrate the drink's kosher credentials to Jewish customers. He
subsequently distributed thousands of posters in Germany showing the caps and
claiming the company was owned by Jews. Coca-Cola GmbH managed to
survive the subsequent sales drop, and the following year Göring was photographed sipping a Coke at an event in Düsseldorf. Rumor had it that even the
famously health-obsessed Führer himself enjoyed an occasional tipple.[35]

American corporate leaders were thus very aware of the vagaries of doing
business in the Reich. Many decided that it was simply impossible to exit the
country, or that the money to be made was too substantial to leave on the table.
Nazi policies offered some intriguing opportunities as well. Hitler's tax cut on

automobiles was followed by a speech in 1934 in which the Führer announced a national effort to produce a small and affordable car that could be purchased by five million Germans making average incomes. The idea of owning a "People's Automobile"—or *Volkswagen*—became so sensationally popular among the German public that the government had to warn that it would take "months if not a few years before such a thing is possible."[36]

This was exactly the opportunity GM had been looking for when it purchased Opel. In 1934, Opel was already offering the cheapest car in the country, so it would have made sense for Hitler to choose the company to produce his People's Automobile. GM executives began making plans to convince the government to give Opel exclusive rights to the Volkswagen. They were outmaneuvered by engineer Ferdinand Porsche, who successfully networked his way through the Nazi bureaucracy and into the Führer's affections. Stinging from the loss, Opel pivoted to manufacturing trucks that became the German army's favorite form of mechanized transportation. As the country rearmed, Opel's profits soared.[37] GM executives could only hope they would someday be able to repatriate the substantial profits building up in their German accounts that were, for the moment, untouchable. The same was true for Ford-Werke, which quickly moved into second place in German truck production. Revenues quadrupled for Ford-Werke between 1934 and 1938, but as with GM the money was essentially inaccessible outside Germany.[38]

It was not just profit motives and business opportunities that drove American corporate bosses into the arms of the Nazis. Some were motivated by genuine affinities for Nazism. The most prominent example was Henry Ford, arguably America's most famous businessman. Ford's engineering and business prowess were beyond doubt, but there had always been indications that his personal views might be less admirable. During World War I, Ford adopted the view that the conflict had been the product of an international plot by Jewish bankers.[39] Anti-Semitic slurs soon became a common aspect of his vocabulary, and in the early 1920s he owned a newspaper called the *Dearborn Independent* that transformed into a viciously anti-Semitic mouthpiece. The automaker also began personally distributing huge numbers of the anti-Semitic tract *The Protocols of the Learned Elders of Zion*. He was eventually forced to apologize for these activities after losing a libel suit brought by a Jewish agricultural leader whom the *Independent* had accused of plotting to corner the international wheat market. Privately, however, Ford's views were unchanged. Like so many of Hitler's American friends, by the mid-1930s Ford was blaming "financiers and money lenders" for both the New Deal and the prospect of another world war. Rumors circulated in the late 1930s that he was secretly funding the German American Bund, though those claims were never conclusively proven.[40] One of his many admirers was Hitler himself, who once indicated his desire to help "Heinrich Ford" become "the leader of the growing Fascist movement in America."[41]

The mutual admiration between Ford and Hitler had a real impact on the company's German production facilities. By 1938, Ford's Dearborn office was making arrangements to secretly supply truck parts to its Cologne plant to meet the German government's demand for military vehicles. These had to be officially built in Germany, so Ford simply provided prebuilt components that could be quickly combined to produce working vehicles. In June 1938, the German military requested more than 3,100 trucks from Ford for use in the future occupation of Czechoslovakia. The vehicles were quickly assembled in the dead of night at the Cologne factory after being shipped in pieces from the United States.[42] On July 30, the German consul in Cleveland pinned the Grand Cross of the German Eagle on Ford's chest in honor of his seventy-fifth birthday and his services to the automotive industry, though his specific contributions to the German truck industry went unmentioned. As will be seen, this was a major honor and the same medal that would be controversially awarded to Charles Lindbergh later that year. Jewish comedian Eddie Cantor, one of the most outspoken anti-Nazi activists in the country, denounced Ford's acceptance of the award in no uncertain terms. "I doubt the Americanism of that great industrialist, Henry Ford, for accepting that citation from Hitler," Cantor told a Jewish women's group. "I think he is foolish to permit the world's greatest gangster to give him a citation. I question the Americanism and the Christianity of Mr. Ford."[43] The leaders of Jewish War Veterans of the United States similarly called on Ford to return the award, calling it "an endorsement of the cruel, barbarous inhuman action and policies of the Nazi regime."[44]

Regardless of the exact reasons for their involvement in the Reich, American businessmen were deeply enmeshed in the German economy by the start of World War II. Economic historian Adam Tooze has estimated that Standard Oil had the most to lose in the German economy through its almost $65 million stake in the petroleum industry and its agreements with I.G. Farben. GM's stake in Opel was the second largest and valued at more than $50 million, while Ford's interests were worth around $8.5 million. Other American corporations including Woolworth's and the Singer sewing machine company held assets worth around $20 million each.[45] The prospect of war with Germany therefore presented a very direct financial risk to some of America's leading corporations. As war approached, the Nazi government began using this fact to its own advantage.

This was where William Rhodes Davis and his strange plot entered the picture. Davis was far from being a leading American executive, but he would play the most direct American role in the Third Reich. Born in Alabama in 1889, Davis worked as a driller in the Oklahoma oil fields but soon found his real talent as a promoter and salesman. In 1913 he set up an oil and gas company and made a small fortune, only to lose it all through subsequent investments. After serving in World War I he went back to the oil fields and became a wildcatter. A lawsuit by jilted investors cleaned Davis out a second time in 1924, after which he moved to Europe and began promoting oil properties for the British-Mexican Petroleum Company. The following year he resigned and set up an oil pipeline business in Arkansas, only to be blocked in his efforts by Standard Oil. Another colorful effort, this time to enter the Peruvian oil market, subsequently failed, and at the start of the Great Depression Davis was dead broke but thirsty to get back to living the high life.[46]

Davis saw his opportunity when Hitler gained power. Correctly assuming that the new chancellor's ambitions would require huge amounts of oil that the Reich lacked, Davis concocted a plan. He first formed a new oil company with the deceptively bland title of the Foreign Oil Company, Inc., and secured financing from the Bank of Boston. He then set out exploring several oil fields in Mexico and Nicaragua, all of which were unsuccessful. His true stroke of genius came when he traveled to Germany and acquired a Hamburg oil storage company called Eurotank that was in dire financial straits, and began converting it into a full-fledged oil refinery. The plan was to import crude oil from somewhere in Latin America, refine it in Hamburg, and sell it at a profit to the German government or other European customers. This scheme would obviously require the support and financial backing of the German government, which Davis managed to secure in the Reichsbank that fateful day in 1933. By 1934, the plan was a go. Davis hired Winkler-Koch Engineering of Kansas to build the actual refinery (Winkler-Koch was headed by Fred Koch, the father of present-day billionaire activists David and Charles Koch). The refinery was completed the following year and became the third-largest refinery in the Reich.[47] In 1936, the German navy signed an agreement to purchase fuel oil from Davis, giving him a guaranteed source of income and putting him back on the road to the high life.[48]

Davis now had an unusual problem, however. He had the capacity to refine huge amounts of crude oil, but no reliable source to fill his tanks. Initially, Davis simply bought crude oil from his archnemesis Big Oil rivals, but as he became more prominent they started to raise prices and squeeze his profit margins.[49] Davis looked again to the oil fields of Mexico to solve his problem. Having had purchased in 1934 a majority stake in a Mexican oil company, he now devised a complicated barter plan that would allow him to get money out of Germany by trading it for other goods that could then be sold elsewhere. This plan required the involvement of the US government, however, because one of the things being traded was cheap surplus cotton being held in federal warehouses. To secure the assistance of the Roosevelt administration for his scheme, Davis turned to the time-honored tradition of campaign contributions. In the 1936 election cycle, Davis donated a substantial $175,000 (about $3 million in today's money) to the Democratic Party. Most of the cash paid for radio programming and the rest went to key Senate races. The generous contribution not only gained Davis an autographed photograph of Franklin Roosevelt, but also access to the Oval Office.[50]

Davis now put his plan into action and asked the Roosevelt administration to set up a meeting with Mexican officials, including President Lázaro Cárdenas, to nail down the details of his plan. The Mexican government agreed to its side of the deal, but Roosevelt got cold feet when he realized the United States would be indirectly doing business with the Nazis. The US government pulled out and Davis lost access to the cotton.[51] To complicate matters further, the left-wing Cárdenas government abruptly began nationalizing foreign-owned oil fields as part of a populist campaign to punish companies that were supposedly exploiting the country's workers.[52]

Davis shrewdly saw a second chance to close the deal. He now struck a backroom agreement with the Mexican government to purchase oil from the nationalized fields at below-market prices. This was an exceptionally clever move, because following nationalization Shell and Standard Oil launched a worldwide boycott of Mexican oil, making it difficult for the government to sell the crude anywhere. Davis had both tankers and a refinery, and he could provide Mexico a guaranteed market for its oil even if he was paying less than the market value. The deal was too good to pass up for everyone involved, and Davis made a profit every step of the way.[53]

The plan was extraordinarily successful. By August 1938, Davis reported he had shipped nearly 1 million barrels of Mexican oil to the Eurotank refinery.[54] In mid-1940 it was rumored in Washington that he had shipped at least 8 million, and perhaps as many as 30 million, barrels of oil out of Mexico, the majority of which had ended up in Germany.[55] Historians have estimated that about 30 percent of the Reich's total oil supply in 1938–1939 was provided by Davis, making him an essential player in the Nazi economy and a very rich man at the same time.[56]

This was where Davis's plot took another strange twist. In the course of negotiating the Mexican oil deal, Davis had called upon the help of John L. Lewis, the powerful head of the four-million-member strong Congress of Industrial Organizations (CIO) and a celebrity in the international labor movement.[57] Lewis was close friends with leaders of Mexican labor and supported Cárdenas's nationalization campaign. For reasons that remain opaque to the present day, he agreed to help Davis secure the necessary agreement with Cárdenas, and intervened on his behalf with the Mexican government. Questioned later by author and activist Saul Alinsky about the relationship, Lewis cited Davis's support for the Democratic Party and quipped that "If William Rhodes Davis was good enough for Roosevelt, he was good enough for me. That, of course, would be a false answer. The fact that a person was good enough for Franklin Delano Roosevelt really was not an exalted criterion."[58]

As this remark indicates, Lewis was no friend of the Roosevelt administration despite his left-wing union credentials. Lewis and the president had long disdained each other in private, with Lewis believing Roosevelt to be dishonest and disloyal to labor. Roosevelt reciprocated and thought Lewis was a demagogue and a grandstander. These personal feelings aside, the men maintained an awkward show of public friendship through the 1936 election to avoid a political split that could only benefit the Republicans.[59] The fragile arrangement collapsed almost immediately after the election. As tensions grew with Germany, Lewis began to fear the impact a war would have on organized labor. Rumors that the administration was already convening secret war planning meetings that included prominent businessmen but no labor representatives hardened his views further.[60] After Hitler's invasion of Poland made war in Europe a reality, Lewis found himself in the noninterventionist camp. He would soon transition from being a critic of Roosevelt's domestic policies to one of the most outspoken antiwar activists in the country, and strike a strange alliance with both corporate interests and Nazi Germany in a stunning attempt to destroy the president.

Around this same time, the Nazis themselves realized that their connections with American businessmen offered one of their best chances to tie the Roosevelt administration's hands on foreign policy. The most obvious opportunity lay with Davis, who had been living the high life off his questionable oil deal for years and would almost certainly do anything to keep the cash flowing. Indeed, the war quickly caused him major problems and the cash spigot began to run dry. A British navy blockade of German ports prevented Davis from docking his ships in Hamburg, meaning he could not offload his Mexican crude. The logical alternative was to ship the oil to Italian ports instead and transport it from there, but the British soon figured out the scheme and ended it.[61]

Now fighting an actual war, the German military needed the oil more than ever before, and Davis was unwilling to let another fortune slip through his fingers. Desperate to save his imperiled business, he now launched an outrageous scheme to personally make peace in Europe. Just two weeks after the invasion of Poland, Davis asked Lewis to call the White House and request a meeting for him with the president. Lewis did as he asked, and Roosevelt accepted the appointment but only on the condition that Assistant Secretary of State Adolf Berle, an expert on counterintelligence, be present.[62] In the meantime, Davis used his contacts in Berlin to extract a vague pledge from Hermann Göring that Germany would be willing to negotiate peace if Roosevelt would act as a neutral arbiter, and insinuating that the Luftwaffe head would even be willing to overthrow Hitler and seize power himself to accept the deal. Davis offered to travel to Rome in late September to meet secretly with German and Italian officials who would start the wheels of the peace plan in motion. All he needed to put this audacious peace plan in motion was a green light from the president.[63]

Undoubtedly chagrined by the outlandishness of Davis's proposal—and the idea that a shady oilman would think himself capable of stopping a major war—Roosevelt and Berle listened politely in the meeting. The president committed to nothing and told Davis that "naturally any information as to the situation would be interesting; but pointed out that until some proposal reached him through some government, he could not take any position."[64] After Davis left the room, Berle remarked that he believed Davis to be "almost a Nazi agent."[65] He recommended the oilman be placed under FBI surveillance, which, if anything, seems to have been rather late to be taking such a basic step. Berle subsequently reported to Roosevelt directly about the outcome of the surveillance operation, which would naturally include Davis's contacts with Lewis.[66]

Davis made the trip to Italy and traveled to Berlin from there. Meeting with

Göring in the Air Ministry, and presumably giving copious Nazi salutes in the process, Davis recounted his conversation with Roosevelt but wove in his own alternative facts at the same time. He suggested that the president was generally sympathetic to the idea of reforming or even overturning the Treaty of Versailles, and might even be willing to extend Germany a generous loan if it ended the war. Understandably surprised by this news, Göring stated that these positions were not far from the "views of Mr. Hitler and his government." A subsequent conversation turned to the possible role that Lewis might play in the negotiations. Davis assured the German delegation that he and Lewis were close friends and on the same page when it came to the peace plan. In turn, Göring assured Davis that if Roosevelt agreed to mediate peace, Germany would consider agreeing to the creation of a reconstituted Polish state and a restored Czechoslovakian government. It seemed like a good deal. Davis departed the meeting believing he held the keys to world peace in his back pocket.[67]

The plan quickly fell apart when the oilman returned to Washington. He and Lewis both contacted the president, but Roosevelt declined their request to meet. The president and his advisers were sensibly skeptical about both the proposal and the messenger carrying it. Instead, Davis was granted a meeting with Berle, to whom he subsequently lied about his activities in Germany and the details of his meeting with Göring. Berle presented a somewhat exaggerated version of this evidence to the president, who was outraged and refused to have anything more to do with Davis. Even a direct intercession by his old ally Lewis fell upon deaf ears. The peace plan had completely collapsed in just days.[68]

Davis, unwilling to give up his efforts to stop the war, now launched an even more audacious plan. If Roosevelt could not be counted on to make peace, Davis reasoned, then the president would have to be replaced. With the election of 1940 approaching, this was an effort the Germans were eager to support. Back in Berlin, Davis had taken the ultimate step to becoming one of Hitler's leading American friends by agreeing to become an agent of German military intelligence (the Abwehr).[69] He was assigned the agent designation C-80 and, interestingly, Lewis was registered as agent C-80/L, meaning he was considered a sub-agent of Davis. Whether Lewis ever knew the Germans considered him to be an agent working on their behalf is unknown, but the registration itself was telling.[70]

During his meeting with Göring, Davis had already begun to lay the groundwork for his bold contingency plan. He asked Göring for millions of dollars to influence the American election in favor of any candidate running against

Roosevelt from either political party. After the war, Heribert von Strempel—the same paymaster who was funding George Sylvester Viereck's operations in Washington, DC—told interrogators that Davis requested and received $5 million (a stunning $87 million in 2018) for this task. Total expenditure in the 1940 election by both political parties has been estimated at $21 million, mostly on the Republican side. If Davis's money had been fully used as intended, it could have made a major impact on the race.[71] In his own postwar interrogation, Göring chortled at the sum. "If a serious representative . . . approached me and told me that he could influence the Presidential election so that they elected a President who was favorably inclined toward Germany," he replied, "for such a purpose I would have spent $100 million to $150 million." (The notoriously corrupt Göring also remarked that he once considered hanging a sign in his office establishing $10 million as the minimum amount of "business transacted here").[72] Göring's bluster aside, $5 million was apparently allocated for the plot and made available to Davis from the German embassy.[73] But who was the candidate who could defeat Roosevelt? Davis told his Nazi connections he had the perfect candidate already: John L. Lewis. The oilman was even willing to put in some of his own money to further the plot and, presumably, help cover the source of the German money he would be drawing from. In exchange for all this, Davis asked to be appointed secretary of state in the future Lewis administration.[74]

With Davis's plan moving forward, the Nazis simultaneously focused on mobilizing the American business community to push for an end to the war. In this effort they found a host of willing allies. American businessmen with holdings in Germany had a vested financial interest in making peace, especially with the Royal Air Force starting to bomb German factories that might soon include their own. Remarkably, even after the war's start American corporate bosses tried to maintain a sense of normalcy in relations with their German divisions. Ford's Dearborn office continued to communicate with its Cologne factory, and even sent new equipment to the plant in 1941 to boost production for the German military.[75] In 1938, Ford-Werke was responsible for producing a full 48 percent of German 2- to 3-ton trucks. One estimate at the end of the war suggested that 15 to 20 percent of *all* vehicles used by the German army were built by Ford. Profits in the Cologne plant soared.[76]

The situation was somewhat different at General Motors's Opel subsidiary. In 1939, Opel—and the GM home office—agreed to a request from Göring's Air Ministry to begin producing aircraft parts based on American technology. This was seen as a political concession that would allow Opel to continue its profitable automobile operations on the side.[77] The ministry then appropriated Opel's factory in Rüsselsheim to produce parts for Junkers JU-88 bombers that could not be produced in sufficient quantities by their parent company. Opel vehicle production fell substantially and, in 1940, was shut down completely.[78] In the words of historian Henry Ashby Turner Jr., by late 1940 Opel's Rüsselsheim plant was "producing parts for the Junkers bombers heavily used in raining death and destruction on London and other British cities during the air attacks of the Battle of Britain."[79] GM executives remained apprised of the activities at Rüsselsheim until at least June 1940, at which time the home office lost contact with the now-all-German managers there.[80]

The US government was understandably concerned about the military assistance the Germans were receiving from these American investments. In November 1939, reports emerged that the government estimated the value of American holdings in Germany at $300 million ($5.2 billion in 2018), nearly all of which were now feeding the German war machine. "Eventually, the situation may lead to the formation of an administration policy against the future establishment of American factories abroad," the Associated Press reported.[81] For American corporate leaders, the prospect of the United States entering the war was simply an unacceptable business risk with this amount of capital on the line. Even those without extensive holdings in Germany were worried about the changes war would bring. U.S. Steel president Tom Moses, for instance, told John L. Lewis in 1939 that a European-wide war would end up opening the entire continent to communism. Making peace as quickly as possible was therefore essential.[82]

Others had more direct interests in peace. Aware of the risks to Opel, GM bosses were especially vocal in their efforts to convince American politicians and the public that it was still possible to "do business with Hitler." President of GM Overseas Operations James D. Mooney set up a dinner meeting with Göring in October 1939 (just weeks after Göring had met with Davis) and tried to sound out the Air Ministry boss on the peace terms Germany would accept. Göring told him roughly the same thing he had told Davis. Mooney then tried to convince US ambassador to France William Bullitt that this was an unmissable opportunity. Bullitt declined to pass the message along to the French government.

Mooney refused to give up and now tried to convince the British Foreign Office to take the offer. British diplomats were unsure what to make of this bungling interference in international affairs. The country's ambassador to the United States, Lord Lothian, cabled London to warn that Mooney had been "completely got at by the Germans," might be "quite off his head," and that GM was "much embarrassed by his behavior."[83] Mooney was again un-fazed and requested a personal audience with Roosevelt in early 1940. A strange episode followed in which Roosevelt apparently sent Mooney back to talk to Hitler directly about the prospects of peace. Mooney did so and extracted more vague commitments from the Germans, only to find that Roosevelt was no longer interested in what he had to say when he got back to Washington. Mooney then went public with the story, writing a piece in the *Saturday Evening Post* claiming that the United States was lurching toward an avoidable war under Roosevelt. The White House was not amused. Left-wing New York tabloid *PM* went on the offensive and labeled Mooney a treacherous "Benedict Arnold." Mooney was soon under FBI investigation.[84]

Undeterred, in March 1941 Mooney personally sponsored (going out of his way to distance GM from the effort) an exhibition at the Department of Commerce entitled "Econorama." The displays Mooney paid for were designed to demonstrate the supposed superiority of the Nazi economic system, and were accompanied by narration from a slick-talking young speaker. Major themes included the argument that the United States should curtail domestic spending and embark on a massive defense spending program similar to the one undertaken by the Nazis. Appalled by what he was hearing, one visiting Federal Reserve economist asked the speaker, "If you like the Nazis so much, why don't you bring Hitler over here?" There was apparently no reply.[85] Mooney's emerging reputation as a Nazi sympathizer was hardly helped by the publicity that followed this effort.

Mooney's GM deputy, Graeme Howard, was no less outspoken in opposing potential American involvement in the war. In 1940, Howard published a short book entitled *America and a New World Order* that became an isolationist rallying cry. One postwar investigator quipped that the book "might just as well have been titled *You Can Do Business with Hitler*." This assessment was not far from the mark.[86] According to Howard, the United States should increase its military budget and enforce the Monroe Doctrine in the Western Hemisphere to keep European powers out of American affairs. Eventually, the United States, Canada, Mexico, Cuba, the Central American states, and "the two northern states of South America" should be combined into a single American federation to increase economic efficiency and build an impenetrable military deterrent.[87] In the meantime, the United States should "keep out of foreign wars";

reestablish "satisfactory relations with all countries," including Germany and Japan; and serve as an impartial arbiter to end the war.[88] By enacting this program, Howard concluded, a "better America" and a "better world" would be achieved.[89]

Howard's book was an obvious restatement of the isolationist position of the period combined with a strong dose of appeasement. Critics predictably pounced. "He [Howard] explains that the 'meaning of the word appeasement is "conciliation" and "concession," a quality essential to all life,'" *The Philadelphia Inquirer*'s book reviewer told readers in October 1940. "Sounds plausible, doesn't it? Just as plausible as it sounded to England and France in 1938."[90] Historian Charles Higham has described Howard as an "outright fascist" who was under constant FBI surveillance and believed in creating a "United States of Fascism in which General Motors would no doubt play a prominent part."[91]

The machinations of GM executives were merely a dangerous sideshow to the main act pursued by Davis and Lewis, however. Increasingly intoxicated by the idea of unseating Roosevelt, Berlin decided to take direct action to mobilize its business contacts in the United States. In April 1940, Foreign Minister Joachim von Ribbentrop enlisted Gerhardt Alois Westrick, a prominent attorney who had helped secure American loans to Germany after World War I, to join these efforts. Back in the 1920s Westrick had served as legal adviser to the German divisions of Coca-Cola, General Motors, and Woolworth's, among other companies.[92] There was no doubt that he enjoyed extensive connections to the American business community.

Renting a palatial hotel suite in the Waldorf-Astoria in New York City and a house in Westchester County, Westrick undertook a blundering effort to charm American corporate leaders. As Heribert von Strempel recalled, Westrick's mission was to "use his personal relations with influential American business men that they should engage in propaganda to keep America out of the war and that if Hitler would win the war in Europe, it would be of great benefit for American economics in general and to their business in particular."[93] In essence, Westrick was there to convince American corporations that a German victory would help their bottom lines. In June 1940, he hosted a party at the Waldorf-Astoria to celebrate the fall of France. Among the attendees was GM's James D. Mooney. Westrick subsequently reported to Ribbentrop that "reliable" American friends had assured him they would soon be pushing Roosevelt to appoint a new ambassador to Berlin, change ambassadors in London, and suspend arms shipments to Britain.[94] To sweeten any potential deal, Westrick was authorized to offer help to American businessmen "through unfreezing their blocked credits in Germany," thus giving them access to their profits in the country.[95] This was outright bribery.

Appealing to corporate pocketbooks was a clever plan, but it soon went awry. The presence of a high-rolling German envoy charming the business community quickly attracted the attention of reporters who began following Westrick's every move. Local police and the FBI kept an eye on the vehicles entering and leaving his driveway. Reporters staked out his house and interviewed both his wife and his live-in secretary at the Waldorf-Astoria, Baroness Irmingard von Wagenheim. The press latched on to Wagenheim particularly—reputedly a relative of Nazi foreign minister Joachim von Ribbentrop by marriage—and printed her photo next to stories about Westrick. One reporter working for the Hearst-owned International News Service condescendingly described her as "attractive rather than beautiful. She could pass for any nondescript little New York stenographer."[96] Facing this level of publicity, Westrick simply gave up on his efforts and left the country for Japan in late 1940. As Strempel recalled, a major reason for the failure was the exposure of his links to American businessmen by "[Walter] Winchell and other American newspapers."[97] The German Chargé d'Affaires in Washington similarly reported to Berlin that Westrick had to go because his American business contacts "are so compromised before the public that they have found themselves compelled to sever these relations."[98] Public association with the Nazis was now becoming too great a liability for American businessmen.

With Westrick out of the picture and US corporate leaders increasingly running for cover whenever the Reich was mentioned, Davis ended up standing almost alone in his plot to unseat Roosevelt. By mid-1940, things were not going well on this front either. Davis's key assumption had been that he could convince either Lewis or someone else to run for the vacant Democratic nomination if Roosevelt did not seek an unprecedented third term in office. His first choice after Lewis was Burton K. Wheeler, the isolationist Montana senator who would shortly be drawn into the Viereck franking scandal.[99] Wheeler was an implausible candidate for a variety of reasons, but not least because he had virtually no support in the national Democratic Party. A March 1940 poll found that just 2 percent of Democratic-leaning voters preferred Wheeler for the presidency (a full 57 percent preferred Roosevelt).[100] Similarly, Lewis's poll numbers were nowhere near where they would need to be for a presidential run. An April 1940 *Fortune* poll showed that just 33 percent of Americans believed Lewis had been "on the whole helpful to labor," while 45 percent thought he had harmed his own movement.[101] As a labor leader, this should have been his greatest strength with the public.

The German government inadvertently harmed Davis's plan further. As the oilman bumbled in his efforts to find a viable candidate to take on Roosevelt, Göring dispatched a German agent who had worked with him previously, Joachim Hertslet, to help run the plot. This proved a major mistake, as one of Hertslet's first acts was to take control of the $5 million stashed at the German embassy. Hertslet now demanded to approve all of Davis's expenditures in advance. More damagingly, his appearance in the United States also tipped off the FBI to the direct German involvement with Davis's activities. Agents began keeping a close eye on both men. Foolishly, Lewis then agreed to meet Hertslet and Davis in person to discuss the possibility of a presidential run. This attempt at subterfuge gave the FBI yet another opportunity to gather intelligence on Davis's plan.[102]

Everything began to fall apart in May 1940 when Roosevelt announced that he would seek an unprecedented third term in office. Neither Wheeler nor Lewis had any real chance of beating Roosevelt, so the Democratic nomination was immediately put out of reach for Davis. Interestingly, Davis seems to have had few if any connections in the Republican Party and, regardless, he was a well-known Democratic Party donor who would have little credibility crossing the aisle. Both Lewis and Wheeler subsequently appeared at the Republican National Convention to denounce Roosevelt, and German agents managed to pay off a Republican congressman to insert a plank in the party platform opposing involvement in the war.[103] Lewis then, bizarrely, tried to convince GOP delegates to give the nomination to former president Herbert Hoover, another non-interventionist but also no friend to organized labor. This effort fell completely flat and the convention nominated Wendell Willkie, an internationalist and former Democrat who had only recently joined the GOP. It was a catastrophic defeat for the isolationists and for Davis.[104]

Lewis and Davis had only one option left: Support Willkie and hope he could beat Roosevelt. This was not a completely outlandish idea. Polling the week before the election had the president beating Willkie by a narrow 52 to 48 percent margin. This was a substantial lead, but one that might be overcome in the final days of the campaign.[105] Davis made substantial personal donations to the Republican campaign, though he apparently ended up spending less than half of the money stashed in the German embassy.[106]

Just days before the election, Lewis dramatically tried to turn the tables on Roosevelt. In a nationwide radio address on October 25, Lewis directly denounced Roosevelt in strident language and endorsed Willkie. Reelecting Roosevelt, he told the nation, would mean "war and dictatorship." It would also, he said, be a personal insult. To up the stakes, he promised to resign as head of the CIO if Roosevelt won.[107] It was a stunning moment for the American labor movement. More than twenty-five million Americans heard the address and, as Saul Alinsky put it, "Union men and women wept with bitter disappointment at this break between their two idols."[108] What those men and women could not have known was that the $55,000 used to pay for the national radio hookup of Lewis's speech had come from a Nazi agent in the form of Davis.[109]

Lewis's speech made no discernable impact on the final result. Roosevelt crushed Willkie to win nearly 55 percent of the popular vote and 84 percent of the electoral college. Polling had substantially overestimated Willkie's support. Humiliated, Lewis dutifully resigned as head of the CIO. Davis attempted to continue his efforts to end the war, but by now the US government had amassed plenty of evidence that he was up to no good. In January 1941 he applied for a passport to visit Europe and was denied. Months later he was still telling associates that Germany would win the war and Roosevelt would be discredited.[110] By now it was Davis who was discredited, however. There was increasing clamor in Congress for a full investigation into his activities, and pro-intervention congressmen began linking their isolationist rivals to Davis's schemes. Wheeler was publicly accused of being "in the confidence of one William Rhodes Davis" by a fellow senator during a debate over Lend-Lease, and was forced to deny any connection to the oilman.[111] The growing pressure did not deter Davis himself, however. In July 1941 he made a radio address for the America First Committee denouncing Roosevelt's Lend-Lease proposal and calling for continued nonintervention in the war.[112] He would not be the only American business leader to do so, as will be seen.

Following Roosevelt's reelection, Hitler's corporate friends gradually retreated into the background. Some became involved in America First while others increasingly focused on their business affairs. After Pearl Harbor, most put on a newly patriotic face, denying that their sympathies had ever lain with Hitler and proclaiming their unyielding support for the war effort. James D. Mooney was commissioned as a navy lieutenant commander, though he was still occasionally criticized in the press for his previous activities.[113] Graeme Howard entered military service and ended up in the postwar economics division that was tasked with uncovering the role of German business in wartime atrocities. This was a bizarre role for a man who had been so outspoken about his pro-German views, and his past activities would soon come back to haunt him.[114] Mooney, Howard, and their GM colleagues lost touch with the Opel leadership shortly after the war's beginning, but profits continued to pile up in the division's German accounts. After the war GM would manage to reap the rewards of the Third Reich's genocidal war effort.[115]

Similarly, Coca-Cola GmbH would survive the war and even reap profits. The company sold 4.5 million cases of the caffeinated beverage in 1939 alone.[116] When war broke out, the British blockade of German ports meant the sugary concentrate the drink required could no longer be easily imported.[117] The head of Coca-Cola GmbH, Max Keith, realized survival meant coming up with a new product. His chemists devised a new fruit-flavored drink created from the by-products of other food industries, including cheese making and apple cider pressing, that still had the caffeine that made Coke popular with German workers. The beverage received an exemption from wartime sugar rationing in 1941 and began selling well. Coca-Cola became generally unavailable that same year and the new drink—Fanta—caught on as a replacement.[118] Coca-Cola remained a fond memory for many Germans, however. One entertaining story holds that a group of German POWs arriving in New Jersey late in the war were astounded to see Coca-Cola advertising in the United States because they assumed the product was authentically German and only existed in their homeland.[119]

Of the American corporations doing business in the Reich, Ford's leadership engaged in arguably the most questionable conduct of all. The company's elderly founder, Henry Ford, remained personally infatuated with Nazism throughout the war. By at least one account, he continued to make personal birthday gifts to the Führer until it was no longer possible to do so. His son, Edsel, opted to continue operations in France after the country fell to Germany occupation. A Ford plant near Paris began turning out aircraft engines, military trucks, and other vehicles for the German military, just as it had done in Cologne. Remarkably, Edsel kept up his contacts with the occupation French government for much of the war. In May 1942 the French plant was bombed by the British, and Edsel expressed relief that the pictures shown in American newspapers had not identified it as a Ford-owned property.[120] Ford's secret remained safe and the profits continued to pile up. Production resumed at the plant following repairs and, as with Opel, much of the Ford operation soon began profiting from forced labor.[121]

One American businessman who did not ultimately profit from his involvement with the Third Reich was the man who had been closest to its leadership: William Rhodes Davis. Just weeks after delivering his 1941 radio address calling for continued isolationism, Davis was staying in a Houston hotel when he suddenly became ill. Before a doctor could arrive, Davis fell to the ground and died on the spot. He was just fifty-two and considered to be in good health. The official verdict was that he had died of a sudden heart attack. Rumors started to spread that he had been poisoned, but the FBI discouraged further investigation into the circumstances of his death.[122] His body was quickly cremated and no funeral was held. News of his death was carried in newspapers across the country, which referred to him both as a "well-known oil man" and a "reputed Nazi peace agent." "From one skirmish after another with the powerful enemies he had made, this remarkable man emerged with his head bloody but unbowed," his Associated Press obituary concluded.[123] The full extent of his involvement with the Germans was still far from known.

In a strange postscript to an already strange life, Davis's story did not end there. His substantial estate was soon mired in legal battles that lasted years. In 1971, espionage historian William Stevenson reported seeing a British intelligence document noting that Davis was still attempting to find a way to export oil from Mexico to the Reich when he died. "The swiftest way to put a stop to this scheme was to remove Davis from the scene," the document allegedly concluded.[124] The clear implication was that Davis's untimely death was in fact an assassination by an American government agency or, much more likely, British intelligence. Stevenson provided no citation for his claim and the document he cites has never been found by other historians. Davis's only biographer rejects this claim on the basis that the deceased had already suffered from a blood clot, indicating a possible heart problem, and that neither the US government nor British intelligence had a real motive or opportunity to poison him at the time.[125]

Given the wider context of Davis's involvement with Hitler's American friends and the German embassy, it seems unlikely that either government would risk the fallout from assassinating so prominent a figure. Furthermore, keeping Davis alive might have produced a wealth of counterintelligence information, especially if he could be convinced to change sides and use his connections to unmask German agents. Davis was, if nothing else, a political survivor who had made and lost several fortunes already. The US government would have had a great deal of leverage to secure his cooperation by threatening his hard-won but questionable fortune. On the other hand, it remains possible that the British in particular feared the future machinations of Hitler's most important American business friend, and took a dramatic step to ensure his early departure from history. Either way, Davis did not live to enjoy the ill-gotten fortune he had worked so hard to obtain or see the defeat of the country he had worked to support. At the same time, the Third Reich lost one of its key supporters at a moment when it could least afford it. It would be left to Hitler's other American friends to pick up the pieces of their German holdings and face the consequences of their actions after the war's end. As it turned out, the most quintessentially American brands—Ford, Coca-Cola, General Motors—had all successfully done business with Hitler, at least for a time.

THE STUDENTS

I n October 1933, the Hoover War Library at Stanford University unveiled an exhibit of books that had recently been placed on the official censorship list by Nazi officials. The display included works by some of the most notable names in the literary world—Ernest Hemingway, Thomas Mann, and Erich Maria Remarque were all represented—and the *Stanford Daily* noted that it had attracted "considerable attention" since being set up. Political science professor Edwin A. Cottrell explained that the censorship was "useless" because recent book burnings in the country had only destroyed a few thousand copies and was "merely a gesture."[1] Earlier in the year, the *Daily*'s editors had facetiously condemned the "over-zealous" mass burning of books as "the work of German freshmen, or junior college transfers, if there are such individuals in the German school system."[2]

Such public condemnations did little to temper the university community's general enthusiasm for German culture and the country itself. Throughout the 1930s, Stanford maintained an active German club, put on German-language plays, and sent its students to study at German universities.[3] One such student wrote just months before the outbreak of war in Europe that his counterparts from the United States could "help greatly clarify the international differences of opinion through their conversation and writing. Things can be explained as they really are. . . . Friendship, not hate, between two peoples may be an idealistic, but not impossible contribution to peace."[4] This was a noble ideal, and for many American university administrators there seemed to be good reasons for sending students to study at German institutions. A number of German universities had, after all, been considered world-leading, at least until they expelled their Jewish faculty members at the behest of the Nazis. There was no obvious reason to shut down the German club that encouraged learning a foreign language (one that, after all, would be critical if there were another war with Germany) or to stop producing German plays. Perhaps conflict could indeed be avoided by building international connections between young people.

The reality of the German university system was far different than what its American defenders believed, however. Just a few years after Hitler seized power, German universities were almost completely imbued with Nazi ideology. American students studying at the great instructions of Heidelberg and Göttingen were fed a steady diet of Nazi propaganda, stiff-armed salutes, and anti-Semitism. Some American young people undoubtedly chose to study there out of genuine academic interest or to master the German language. Others were seemingly ideologically attracted to Nazism and spent their time studying the words of Hitler more than the words of Goethe. Every student who spent time in Nazi Germany certainly did not count themselves among Hitler's American friends, but the German study-abroad experience in the 1930s exerted untold influence on thousands of young Americans.

In turn, American universities did little to curtail the influence of pro-German speakers on campus. Throughout the decade, German exchange students, some of whom were Nazi Party members and were likely operating as propaganda agents, and other speakers were given mostly unchallenged platforms on university campuses. American universities therefore offered the German government a remarkable level of establishment legitimacy in the United States, even after the violently anti-Semitic nature of the regime had become clear. Just as Hitler's corporate friends had showed little reluctance doing business with Reich, his friends in academia maintained their own relationships with the Reich.

Both the Nazis and the US government were aware of the propaganda potential provided by American universities. Testifying before the Dies Committee, John C. Metcalfe argued that the German government had a particular interest in American students. "The purpose of the 'exchange students' to universities has long been to foster good will and peace among the nations. . . . The result is greater understanding," Metcalfe testified. "But this worthwhile aim has been neglected in the exchange of German students for American. Now American students are being indoctrinated with the aims of fascism in Germany both abroad and at home to the detriment of democratic institutions in America."[5]

The Bund's youth camps were a key part of this indoctrination, he continued, but the Nazis were making efforts to indoctrinate older American students as well.

Some of this rhetoric served as the intellectual precursor of 1950s McCarthyism, when the fear of communist infiltration led to repression of academic freedom and free speech rights in American universities and elsewhere. Yet, as in those later years, there was some element of truth in these claims. The Nazis did indeed benefit from a dedicated propaganda network within the American academic establishment. Historian Stephen Norwood has expertly documented the extent to which American university administrations systematically appeased the Nazis throughout the decade, often over the vocal objections of faculty members and their own students.[6] Academic freedom was heavily curtailed by administrators, who in this period generally only allowed professors latitude to freely speak on their areas of expertise. This meant faculty members could effectively be fired for commenting on anything beyond their immediate field of study. Students were, by extension, presumed to have no scholarly expertise and were given even fewer rights.[7] As Norwood notes, this set the stage for the "most sustained free-speech fight until the 1960s" as both students and faculty faced administrative sanctions.[8]

Around the country, students and faculty alike increasingly became embroiled in unfolding international tensions as the 1930s progressed. Most often, it was the vocally anti-Nazi professors, some of whom were themselves Jewish refugees from Nazi oppression, who faced the brunt of administrative repression. At one point it was even rumored that the German consul general in New Orleans was offering cash to universities that dismissed anti-Nazi professors.[9] The same was much less often the case for openly pro-Nazi professors unless student or public pressure demanded action. There were apparently no sanctions leveled, for instance, when University of Idaho mechanical engineering department head Henry Gauss traveled to a controversial Göttingen University celebration in 1937, declared himself to be the representative of "American universities west of the Mississippi" despite having no official remit to do so, and then gave "the Hitler salute to the rector." He remained department head until 1952, and a building on campus bears his name today.[10] Faculty members and administrators could have made a major impact by denouncing the open prejudice of Nazism and protecting dissenting voices. Too often, they let their students down by failing to do so.

Occasionally, student pressure demanded a response from administrators.

In 1939, University of California, Los Angeles, students rose to the defense of Germanic languages professor Rolf Hoffman when he found himself embroiled in controversy. The German-born Hoffman had reputedly made it known he "did not think so much of the goose-stepping" among his pro-Nazi colleagues within the department, and consequently they "made it so unpleasant for him that he offered his resignation." Ironically, Hoffman had previously been accused of being pro-Nazi after the student-run *California Daily Bruin* published an interview in which he recounted a lengthy trip to Germany, described seeing Hitler in a Munich wine shop, and bizarrely described the Führer's "light skin and baby blue eyes . . . He seemed like a jovial human being. His laughter came heartily from the inside—like anyone."[11]

Evidently his views toward Hitler had changed and he now found himself in trouble with his colleagues, one of whom was reported to "return with great solemnity a 'Heil Hitler' salute derisively directed at him on the campus by a student."[12] Given the large German American Bund and Silver Shirt presence in Southern California, the presence of Nazi sympathizers on the UCLA campus was perhaps not a great shock. Faced with a hostile work environment, Hoffman offered his resignation, only to then change his mind and try to retract it. University administrators refused to reconsider the case and insisted that Hoffman had properly resigned. Hoffman hired an attorney and the story made it into the national press with dark rumors that "the move to oust Dr. Hoffman was initiated by Nazis in Germany" (the university firmly denied this allegation).[13]

Outraged by Hoffman's ouster, the student editors of the *Bruin* contacted the university president on his behalf, leading to hearings and Hoffman's negotiated exit, with a severance package, from the university. The university president denied that politics had played any role in the case, but a student committee vocally claimed to have uncovered evidence of never-revealed unethical behavior in the German department. The *Bruin* praised the student body's involvement in championing Hoffman's cause as "the first step in the evolution of true academic democracy."[14] It was a small victory given that Hoffman still lost his job, but it was at least something in an era that was often devoid of such successes.

These campus conflicts were directly fed by the surprising degree to which American universities and faculty members remained willing to send their students to study in the Third Reich, even after the anti-Semitic and violent nature of Nazism were clear. There were, of course, still some legitimate reasons to sponsor student study at German institutions. Before 1933, German universities were among the best in the world and boasted an impressive number of Nobel Prize winners. German remained a popular language to study in American universities, with an estimated sixty-seven thousand students nationwide taking courses in the 1933–1934 academic year. While many students were reported to have merely "scientific" interest in the language—German was an international language of scientific publication and seen as essential for aspiring researchers and physicians—a sizable number were simply learning it out of personal interest.[15] Studying in a German-speaking country would be essential for any student wanting to become fluent. As a result, German universities and language institutes offered short-term summer courses for students wanting to improve their language skills, most of which also included courses along the lines of "studies concerning contemporary Germany" that were undoubtedly ideological.[16] In the overall scheme of things, this was probably fairly innocuous: Summer language students were only in the country for a month or two, and some of them were already practicing doctors or teachers who probably had well-formed political views and were less vulnerable to propaganda.

The experience of longer-term students at German universities was far different. Elite American universities had a long tradition of sending students to foreign countries, usually in Europe, for a junior year overseas that was designed to broaden their horizons before graduation. Pre-Nazi Germany had been a popular destination before 1933 not only because of the quality of its universities but also because of its avant-garde reputation and the sheer amount of fun on offer. Students in late 1920s Berlin encountered the cultural scene immortalized in the 1972 Liza Minnelli film *Cabaret*, full of freely available booze, sex, and drugs. American educationists W. H. Cowley and Willard Waller argued in 1935 that German beer halls "flourished as informal educational agencies of considerable value" similar to "coca cola [*sic*] sipping in the campus hangout to the tune of jazz" in the United States.[17]

Perhaps, but for American students used to living under Prohibition at home, at least until its repeal in 1933, the beer hall had certain other benefits as well. So too did access to the hard-drinking and often Nazi-leaning dueling fraternities that existed in every German university town and included nearly half the male student population in 1933.[18] No doubt equally exciting for American men were the seventeen thousand German women enrolled at universities in 1933 when many of their home universities were still gender segregated.[19] A Berlin University graduate student studying at Stanford in 1932 sang the praises of the "German fraulein, flaxen-haired and buxom" who would not hesitate to join a male companion on a weekend trip without a chaperone. World War I, he continued, had done away with "false modesty" and made German women "free."[20]

This all abruptly changed when Hitler took power. The Nazis swiftly began to pull German universities under their control at all levels. The right to appoint the highest position in the university, the rector, was taken from faculty members and centralized by the government. Hiring, firing, and transferring faculty members became the responsibility of rectors and government officials, with no faculty consultation. Just as all Germans were expected to follow the dictates of the Führer, all members of the university were expected to abide by the decisions of the rector. The main rival to the rector's power came not from faculty members but the Nazi Students' League, a national union of students with branches at every university. Members were given a seat on every faculty senate in the country and vocally denounced professors who failed to toe the Nazi Party line. Hundreds of faculty members were driven from their posts, including leading academics who were expelled for being Jewish. This latter group included a host of current and future Nobel Prize winners. Their replacements were chosen for political reliability rather than academic accomplishments.[21] Academic freedom all but ceased to exist in Germany in a matter of months.

The government's changes to student life were even more dramatic. Male students were encouraged to join the *Sturmabteilung (SA)* and spent so much time in paramilitary training that academic standards began to fall. Dueling fraternities and other organizations were gradually banned as the party began to fear their potential as an alternative organization commanding student loyalties.[22] The truth was that Hitler and his lieutenants cared little for higher education at all, and were far more interested in preparing young men to serve the Reich militarily. In early 1934, the number of students entering university was capped at just 15,000 nationwide, meaning that the vast majority of secondary school students would not find a place. By 1939, fewer than 41,000 students would be enrolled at German universities from a high of more than 100,000 before Hitler's assumption of power.[23] The number of women in higher education declined even more precipitously: In 1934, legislation restricted the number of spots for female students to just 10 percent of the number reserved for men, or a mere 1,500 nationwide. Just 6,000 were still enrolled in 1939.[24] Women were expected to focus on childbearing and home life, not higher education and careers.

Education in the Third Reich was thus a combination of Nazi ideological

indoctrination and whatever legitimate scholarship managed to survive the regime's oppressive measures. Those who managed to get spots at universities were
still expected to take part in rigorous physical service, leaving little time or en-
ergy for studies. Professors were likewise required to take part in labor service
before being appointed and were required to have clean political records.[25] Many
faculty members already in their posts retreated into a narrow field of special-
ization or technocratic administrative functions to avoid politics. While only a
small minority of PhD dissertations completed under the Third Reich demonstrated obvious Nazi ideological themes, producing research openly contrary
to the interests of the party was inviting trouble.[26] As prominent American
historian Charles Beard summarized it in 1936, "Turned in upon themselves,
nourishing deep resentments and lashed to fury by a militant system of
education, the German people are conditioned for that day when Hitler, his
technicians, and the army, are ready and are reasonably sure of the prospects of
success in a sudden and devastating attack, East or West."[27]

All this was designed to push Germany's young people to view themselves
first and foremost as warriors for the Reich rather than as aspiring professionals
or intellectuals. As education minister Bernhard Rust put it in a 1936 speech,
"The great body of German youth have torn themselves free from the overpow-
ering influence of a culture not their own; they have turned again toward the
life of manly discipline and glorified once more the spirit that leads one to sacrifice his own good for the good of all. In so doing they have found their eyes
opened and they know themselves closely akin to the heroic youth of ancient
Sparta."[28] The "old of idea of learning," he concluded, "is gone." Education
would now prepare the country to "release its vital spiritual forces and fulfill its
historic destiny."[29]

American students in the Reich could therefore expect to encounter a combination of direct indoctrination through compulsory Nazi salutes, marches,
and the labor service of their fellow students, even if they were exempted from
the more onerous of these by their nationality. Open discussion of politics, unless
obviously supportive of the regime, was dangerous if not out of the question.
Escape from official ideology might be possible in the classrooms of professors
who carefully resisted the inclusion of propaganda themes, but was impossible
in the wider confines of German society and the university environment. US
Foreign Service officer Cyrus Follmer, who served in the Berlin embassy from
1935 to 1940, later recalled American students being "propagandized to the utmost
by special societies which practically swept them off their feet by showering

them with conveniences, showing off the beauty, the cleanliness, and the impressive marble edifices of Germany." The effect, Follmer told the FBI, was that the young Americans "'ate it up' and became imbued with the superiorities of Germany."[30]

On many US campuses, there seems to have been little if any concern about the conditions students would encounter in the country. The prestigious all-women Seven Sisters colleges continued to send dozens of students to the country through their Junior Year Abroad program. Many were sent to Munich, the birthplace of the Nazi movement. When Vassar College's student newspaper questioned whether it was suitable to send students into such a climate, a German department professor commented that no student was forced to accept the opportunity if they did not want to.[31] With a few minor disruptions in periods of international tension or outbreaks of violence in Germany, many study-abroad programs functioned more or less normally until the war.[32] In 1937, the professor in charge of Mount Holyoke's exchange program reported to the university president that the exchange was becoming *more* popular as time went on.[33]

Similarly, Stanford University continued to send its students to Germany and host German exchange students in turn.[34] German instructor Stanley L. Sharp continued to take students on summertime tours of Europe that included a tour through Germany. Highlights of the group's 1937 trip included a visit to the Zeppelin construction facility in Friedrichshafen and the famous Hofbräuhaus in Munich, where the students led drinkers in the Stanford fight song "Come Join the Band."[35]

No doubt many exchange students and summer visitors were simply taking advantage of the opportunity to travel in Europe and improve their language skills. In retrospect, they would be among the last Americans to see Europe prior to the destruction of World War II. For some, however, travel to Germany had ideological as well as touristic objectives. In 1933, American writer and magazine editor Malcolm Letts attended a summer session at Heidelberg University. Letts had served in the US Navy during World War I and, now in his mid thirties, leapt at the chance to "fulfill a boyhood desire" and "see history in the making in the country of his former enemy."[36]

Letts immediately found Germany to be full of "patriotic fervor," with the average person walking with "a spring in their step" reminiscent of marching SA men who were "seen everywhere throughout the country, singing with an enthusiasm that was contagious."[37] Letts admitted feeling conflicted about giving the Hitler salute as a foreigner, but compromised by doing so when he was walking with Germans but not doing so when he was on the streets alone. Despite widespread press reports about incidents of anti-Semitic violence, he claimed, there was no "outward evidences of them," and "no one had even heard of these alleged persecutions we read so much of in our American press."[38]

Much of Letts's account described nights of heavy drinking and pursuing women, followed by daytime lectures and weekends of exploring the German countryside. Ultimately, he concluded, Nazism was nothing like how it had been presented in the American press:

> Who are the Nazis? The Nazis are the people with whom I broke bread; with whom I swam; the ones who sat around me at the concerts in the castle courtyard; the students in the University; the musicians and waiters in the cafes; the policemen on their beats; the citizens who raised their steins in the bierstube with a friendly "Zum Woll" [Cheers]; the tobacconist who sold me my daily cigars; the mailman riding his motorcycle; the white-bearded man on the bicycle; the porter who carried my bags; in fact, the German people are the Nazis.[39]

The ubiquitous German use of "Heil Hitler," he continued, "impressed me with their sincerity and unanimity of purpose."[40]

The following year, Canada-based physiologist E. W. H. Cruickshank published an account of his visit to an international student conference that had taken place in Bavaria around the same time of Letts's visit. Despite some elements of "unreasonable" anti-Semitism, Cruickshank reported that the "freedom of speech permitted was remarkable" and included discussion "on subjects as far apart as Fascism and extreme Communism." At the same time, "It was clear that the Germans were eagerly endeavouring to place in as fair a light as possible the whole purpose of the new Government. It was also clear that many Scottish and English, Italian and French students were just as eager to put the whole Nazi system under the withering fire of a searching criticism." A similar level of intellectual freedom, he continued, "has been allowed exchange students at certain German universities."[41]

Accounts such as these served to normalize Nazism in the American popular imagination and academic circles. The claim that Nazism might contain some anti-Semitic elements, but was also open to intellectual critique, was at best naive. The suggestion that Nazi students were so eager to defend their new government in part because of the withering criticisms of foreigners gave their arguments an unwarranted intellectual legitimacy at the same time their government was expelling Jewish academics. As a result of these semisympathetic accounts from respectable academics and commentators, Nazi ideology began to exert a corrupting influence on American university campuses. There were also soon dark rumors that the Nazis had more direct plans for America's students.

In 1934, left-wing muckraker John L. Spivak published a salacious exposé entitled *Plotting America's Pogroms* that purported to expose Nazi plots in the United States. Based on a series of articles originally published in the radical newspaper the *New Masses*, its seventh chapter was dedicated to exposing the "Hate the Jew Campaign in the Colleges." The allegations contained in it were explosive. After Hitler's rise to power, Spivak claimed, the German government set in motion a plan to spread Nazism and anti-Semitism in American universities. German exchange students would play one role in the plot, but the real threat lay in the use of domestic fifth columnists:

> *What the vast majority of students and professors do not know is that in our universities and colleges there is a secret anti-semitic [sic] organization directed by German exchange students to carry on pro-Hitler propaganda and develop the "Hate-the-Jew" creed for the sake of "pure Aryan culture." Working with this secret organization are Nazi agents who came here ostensibly to study, and one hundred percent Americans in the "patriotic" organizations which are distributing anti-semitic propaganda in cooperation with secret Hitler agents in the United States.[42]*

Spivak claimed one such "patriotic" organization, called the Paul Reveres, specialized in "espionage and propaganda" in American schools and universities. Most of its impact was felt in the greater New York area and centered around cells based at New York University, the City College of New York, and Columbia University. Spivak even named the alleged Nazi "contact man" at Columbia as Pelham St. George Bissell III, the son of a prominent New York judge, and claimed his efforts were being assisted by Professor Thomas Alexander, dean of the experimental New College for the Education of Teachers.[43] These Nazi-backed groups, he claimed, were responsible for the development of "open race hatred" on American university campuses. More insidiously, the Germans had also corrupted a substantial number of university professors and other educators by offering them free trips across the Atlantic and giving them tours of the country in which they were "filled with Nazi propaganda and many of them came back to deliver enthusiastic lectures about the fine conditions in Germany, especially the way the Jews are treated over there."[44]

The Paul Reveres were founded by Elizabeth Dilling, one of the most viciously anti-communist and anti-Roosevelt demagogues of the decade. In 1934, she published *The Red Network*, a salacious tract purporting to reveal the existence of a vast communist conspiracy in the United States. Among the "Reds" listed were Roosevelt and New York mayor Fiorello La Guardia.[45] Dilling's main associate in the Paul Reveres was Edwin Hadley, a World War I veteran and businessman. He similarly published a series of anti-communist books in the 1930s before founding the Paul Reveres.[46] Unlike Dilling, however, Hadley insisted that it be "kept strictly a gentile organization."[47] Dilling was viciously anti-communist but not particularly anti-Semitic, and resigned from her own organization. The Paul Reveres would become the primary anti-Semitic group on American university campuses. Branches sprung up on campuses across the country, though they often remained underground to avoid public criticism. Regardless, Dilling would continue her opposition to Roosevelt and end up indicted for sedition.

Spivak's articles and book caused a predictable sensation. Alexander and Bissell both denied the allegations, though the latter admitted to having attended meetings that included anti-Semitic discussions.[48] The university briefly investigated Alexander, who had arranged for a delegation of Columbia students to visit Germany the summer after Hitler's ascension. No action was taken, and he continued to act as a conduit for students who wanted to study in Nazi Germany. In 1936, he would be among three faculty members to organize a student trip to the Berlin Olympics.[49] Spivak's claims were undoubtedly overstated. There was little evidence to support his broad claim that a vast conspiracy of German exchange students were plotting against their host country, or that the Paul Reveres were recruiting a network of saboteurs and propagandists. At the same time, there were some elements of truth. Anti-Semitism was indeed on the rise across the country, especially on college campuses. Harvard had already limited the number of Jewish students it admitted, in part because administrators feared an influx of refugees. Other universities followed suit, often fearing a backlash from donors if they admitted too many Jews or refugees.[50]

At the same time, pro-German voices were consistently given public platforms on American college campuses throughout the decade. In late 1938, for instance, one of the approximately seventy remaining German exchange students in the United States addressed a crowd at Stanford to defend his country's foreign policy (Stanford was host to four of the seventy exchange students, highlighting the closeness of connections between the university and Germany). Hitler sought only the return of Germany's prewar colonies, the student claimed, and any suggestion to the contrary was propaganda from "American newspapers." To ensure peace, he advised Americans to visit Germany or "obtain true information about my country, which is a land of peace and work and no more unemployment."[51] The following year, Stanford's American Student Union hosted a debate between another German exchange student, Adolf Bode, and the daughter of a refugee professor. The event was designed to present a "complete and objective" discussion about Nazism but evidently became a platform for Bode to defend Hitler's government.[52] Bode's name was later discovered by the US Army on a captured list of active Nazi Party members who returned to the country shortly before the war, suggesting that his presence at Stanford may have involved more than just academic pursuits.[53]

Spivak was also correct that the universities based in the New York area were particularly imbued with anti-Semitism and Nazi influence. Columbia was the most prominent example. Self-proclaimed American fascist Lawrence Dennis was invited to speak at the university throughout the decade and made numerous appearances before student groups.[54] Dennis was a somewhat bizarre figure and unapologetic in his support for fascism. He also concealed a secret throughout his life: he was half African American and had "passed" as white for most of his life.[55] As a child, he had been a celebrated "Negro" preacher who traveled the world giving prodigious sermons before the age of 10.[56] Realizing that being identified as African American would have major consequences for him in the Jim Crow South, Dennis decided to change his identity. Carefully concealing the color of his mother's skin, he attended an elite prep school before getting into Harvard and obtaining a position in the State Department.[57]

After leaving government employment Dennis became an investment banker and worked on Wall Street until the crash.[58] Around the same time, he became obsessed with Mussolini and began praising fascism in rousing public speeches no doubt influenced by his past career as a preacher. With his undeniable intellect and powerful stage presence, Lawrence soon became the intellectual face of American fascism, publicly heiling Hitler when he appeared on movie theater screens but also writing sophisticated tracts criticizing the American capitalist system and predicting the rise of a Hitler figure in the United States.[59] In

1936 he attended the Nuremberg Rally and, after returning to the United States, began meeting with George Sylvester Viereck and his embassy paymaster Heribert von Strempel. Dennis increasingly appeared to be acting as a Nazi agent.[60] He became a frequent visitor to the German embassy in Washington and bragged about his chats with Nazi bigwigs including Goebbels and Göring.[61]

Following George Sylvester Viereck's playbook, Dennis launched a newsletter called *Weekly Foreign Letter* focusing on foreign affairs and economics. It was closely read at the German embassy, and Berlin suggested that he might be able to launch a larger publication to further Nazi aims among American intellectuals and business leaders. "Berlin insisted that, America being a country of business affairs of great importance and their leaders being politically influential we should publish magazines which would deal with international economic problems," Strempel recalled after the war.[62] Dennis would be their chosen man to take on this task. "Dennis' [*sic*] opinion was that it is very important to explain to leaders of business and finance the economical consequences of the second world war and to commence regularly on international events in order to demonstrate where the real economical interests of the United States were at stake," Strempel remembered.[63] Viereck himself forwarded German money to Dennis to subsidize such a publication, though the project never actually made it to print.

In 1936, Dennis published a hefty volume entitled *The Coming American Fascism*. As the title suggests, it argued that the American political and financial systems, especially Wall Street speculation, had become unworkable and should be replaced with a version of European fascism that would solve the country's ills and avert "a bitter class war."[64] Dennis predicted that this would take place in the next five years. The book was taken seriously in the American academic community. University of Wisconsin, Madison, economist John R. Commons—certainly no fascist himself—called the book "the leading theory of American fascism" and praised Dennis's analysis of business cycles and investment banking. The "popular indications in America," Commons continued, "are that the prospects are better for fascism than for communism."[65]

Dennis's support for fascism did not go unnoticed among the students he was repeatedly invited to address. The *Columbia Daily Spectator* denounced him as a fascist and "one of America's more artful sophists."[66] Yet despite his obvious connections to the Third Reich, he remained on the university speaking circuit and used his platform to argue for fascist revolution in the United States.

The German-American Bund became known for its large-scale rallies and demonstrations in which the swastika appeared next to the American flag and other patriotic symbols, as seen in this October 30, 1939, parade on East Eighty-sixth St. in New York City. (*LC-USZ62-117148,* New York World-Telegram and Sun Newspaper *Photograph Collection: Library of Congress*)

Cigar-chomping Texas Democrat Rep. Martin Dies Jr. became a Capitol Hill celebrity for his strident pursuit of both fascists and communists in the years before World War II. Despite doing much to shut down the Bund and the Silver Legion, Dies's main obsession lay with uncovering alleged communist subversion. (*LC-H22-D-8425, Harris & Ewing Collection: Library of Congress*)

Rep. Martin Dies Jr's star witness was John C. Metcalfe, a former Chicago journalist who infiltrated the Bund at its highest levels. Metcalfe caused a sensation by testifying in open session and giving the congressman a Nazi salute in front of the cameras before taking the stand on August 12, 1938. (*LC-H22-D-4398, Harris & Ewing Collection: Library of Congress*)

Veteran political organizer and firebrand Gerald L. K. Smith became known for his fierce denunciations of the Roosevelt Administration and the New Deal. His rhetoric became so extreme in the late 1930s that he alienated many of Hitler's other American friends. Nevertheless it positioned Smith to become a key figure on the far right after the war. (*LC-H2-B-10873, Harris & Ewing Collection: Library of Congress*)

Farmer-Labor Sen. Ernest Lundeen of Minnesota became one of Hitler's key friends on Capitol Hill by helping launch George Sylvester Viereck's plot to use congressional franking privilege to distribute anti-interventionist propaganda. This portrait was taken in April 1940, after the launch of the Viereck plot and just months before his untimely death. (*C-H22-D-8739, Harris & Ewing: Library of Congress*)

Republican Rep. Hamilton Fish III's office became the center of the Viereck plot when the congressman's secretary began ordering huge quantities of reprinted speeches for distribution in franked envelopes. The anti-interventionist's long political career would be destroyed by the revelation of his involvement. (*LC-H22-D-6569, Harris & Ewing Collection: Library of Congress*)

Chargé d'affaires Hans Thomsen, seen here with his wife at a White House reception, took over the German Embassy in November 1938 and oversaw the Viereck plot, the William Rhodes Davis scheme, and other influence operations in the United States. (*LC-H22-D-8014, Harris & Ewing Collection: Library of Congress*)

Famed aviator Charles Lindbergh (center) put himself in the middle of the debate over intervention in the European war in the months before Pearl Harbor. His trips to Nazi Germany and later involvement with the America First Committee made him one of Hitler's key American friends and would permanently stain his reputation. Here he is seen trying to avoid reporters while leaving the White House after a tense meeting with President Roosevelt on April 20, 1940. (*LC-H22-D-6381, Harris & Ewing Collection: Library of Congress*)

O. John Rogge's personal intensity made him a powerful opponent of Hitler's American friends both before and after World War II. His dogged investigation of American business and political ties to the Third Reich ended abruptly when he was fired for getting too close to the truth. It would be decades before the stunning report he authored would become available to the public. (*LC-H22-D- 6620, Harris & Ewing Collection: Library of Congress*)

He was embraced by the American academic establishment as an intellectual leader despite his obvious Nazi sympathies and increasing anti-Semitism. He would end up as a confidant of Charles Lindbergh and the America First movement, and on trial for sedition.

Columbia also turned out to have at least one actual German agent on its payroll. In 1928, Friedrich Ernest Auhagen arrived at Columbia as a master's student and then progressed to begin his doctorate. He simultaneously served as an instructor of German. "We thought he was a fine man, a promising young man," Auhagen's department chair recalled later.[67] By 1936, however, Auhagen's interests changed and he began "neglecting his University duties."[68] This change was undoubtedly caused by the fact that he had become a paid Nazi propaganda agent. Until his eventual arrest in 1940, Auhagen ran a "lecture bureau" called the American Fellowship Forum that was paid for by the German embassy and spread Nazi propaganda on American university campuses. He gave some speeches personally and subsidized others to do the same, including Dennis. Auhagen also sent Berlin lists of names and addresses belonging to prominent Americans so they could be bombarded by pro-Nazi and isolationist mailings from Viereck and others. Despite these efforts, the Germans were not particularly impressed with Auhagen, in part because he cut a high public profile and attracted the attention of the Dies Committee. "His behavior in the United States was stupid," Strempel told interrogators after the war. "He was not to be trusted with a political mission. He was a very unreliable man."[69] Auhagen would end up sitting out the war in prison for failing to register as a German agent under the Foreign Agents Registration Act.

Dennis and Auhagen were not Columbia's only connections to the Third Reich. As Stephen Norwood has noted, Columbia president Nicholas Murray Butler was well-known for cozying up to the German embassy and controversially invited the German ambassador, Hans Luther, to speak on campus over extensive protests.[70] Butler had previously attempted to limit the number of Jewish students at Columbia by imposing discriminatory admissions tests, though this proved difficult to accomplish in a city with such a large and well-established Jewish community.[71] Over the course of the decade, Butler was involved in the dismissal of an anti-Nazi (and Jewish) faculty member, established an Italian cultural institute that was accused of supporting fascism, and oversaw the expulsion of a student who led a protest against Nazi book burning in front of his house.[72] Butler's administration was essentially an ongoing contribution to Nazi propaganda efforts. It took him until 1938 to start denouncing the German government's anti-Semitic measures.[73]

This febrile dynamic had a real impact on Columbia's student body. While some students were vocal in their protests of the administration's pro-German policies, others were quietly supportive or even wished their campus leaders would go further in supporting the Reich. Among this latter group was Henry Miller Madden, a doctoral student studying European history at Columbia under the supervision of Carlton J. H. Hayes, future US ambassador to fascist Spain. Madden was, and would remain through his life, an enigmatic figure. As a young man growing up in the San Francisco Bay Area he maintained a network of German pen pals and developed a general affection for the country. "Germany to me has always been a land that is about as ideal as a country could be: I have a deep admiration of all things German," he told a correspondent at the age of seventeen.[74] After completing junior college he transferred to Stanford to study history, where he also mastered the German language and founded a short-lived campus nudist group. (The club abruptly shut down when itching powder was deliberately sprinkled on its usual sunbathing spot).[75]

In 1934, Madden began his doctoral studies in Manhattan. He was unimpressed with New York and bemoaned it as a "second Jerusalem" with Jews who "monopolize all the profession [sic] in New York; they control finance; they own the press; they dictate all the amusements. They are genuinely alarmed for fear that some day the Americans will follow the example of Germany and put them in their place."[76] A year later, he violently summarized his views to a friend:

> The Jews: I am developing a violent and almost uncontrollable phobia
> against them. Whenever I see one of those predatory noses, or those
> roving and leering eyes, or those slobbering lips, or those flat feet, or those
> nasal and whiny voices I tremble with rage and hatred. They are the
> oppressors. . . . Whom do I hate more than the Jews? They have oppressed
> my mother, stolen her savings from her, chained her with interest
> servitude, made a Via Dolorosa of her life. They must go![77]

As Madden's anti-Semitism grew, so did his open admiration for Hitler. "Whenever I see him in the newsreels, I do my best to drown out with my applause the Bronx cheers and hisses which usually greet his inflammatory orations," he told a German friend in 1935. "Heil Hitler! Heil Deutschland!"[78] Madden soon found colleagues at Columbia who shared his favorable views toward the Reich. Among them was William Oswald Shanahan, a fellow history PhD student who had done his undergraduate work at UCLA, another hotbed of pro-German sentiment. Shanahan soon began sending Madden letters that included doodled swastikas and closed with "Heil Hitler" or similar sentiments.[79] The two men ranted about Jews and plotted how they could best spread their views to the wider student body.

In late 1936, as student protests against the administration's seemingly pro-German stances were escalating, Shanahan warned Madden that changing circumstances required a "strategic retreat" from open anti-Semitism. "It is a retreat of front rather than of principle. . . . It is unfortunate that the only aberrations that are tolerated are those related to the radical-socialistic-Marxist-non-Aryan variety, but we must adapt ourselves to the university system as it is, sans academic freedom of mind and freedom of choice. And don't be too optimistic about converting our friends in the College." In other words, Shanahan warned him, "in the future don't shoot off your bazoo so god damn much—either in relation to the university or in relation to ideologies."[80]

Madden himself was already in Central Europe by the time his Columbia friends began feeling the heat. In summer 1936, he departed for an extended trip to Germany and Hungary, ostensibly to continue his research but seemingly to immerse himself in the atmosphere of the Reich as well. In detailed letters to his mother in California, Madden recounted his adventures traveling the Continent and highlighted his fascination with Hitler and Nazism. "Germany really appears to be prosperous—building a new subway in Berlin, new buildings, no begging on the streets, no bums and tramps as in U.S.," he told her. "And the Jews aren't hanging from the lamp-posts, either."[81] Along the way, he perfected both his German and Hungarian language skills. Returning to the United States in 1937 and dreading a return to Columbia, he took a teaching position at Stanford that would occupy him until the war. "Half of Columbia this year is *Jew*," Shanahan warned him darkly during the trip.[82]

Madden, Shanahan, and their circle of Hitler sympathizers reflected the depth of the political extremism and anti-Semitism that was virtually unchallenged on American university campuses in this critical period. The fact that Columbia's president did little to argue against Nazi racial views created an environment in which these views could go largely unchallenged. "If you're really a Fascist, Nicholas Murray Butler at Columbia will be a very interesting chap to talk with. . . ." a friend challenged Madden in 1937. "Are you a Fascist because you come from Teutonic forebears, or because you reconcile it better with the

Spirit of '76?"[83] The fact that American university leaders refused to take a stand on behalf of their Jewish students and faculty created an atmosphere in which extremism could flourish unchecked and with an aura of respectability.

As the Second World War approached, this position became increasingly untenable. Violence against German Jews was routinely reported in American newspapers, creating concern over the physical safety of students studying there. It also became increasingly difficult to give pro-German speakers a platform to spout their views while relations between the countries were plummeting. There was, however, no immediate cessation of academic relations. There were still dozens of German students studying in the United States in 1939, at least some of whom were almost certainly working for the German embassy as propaganda agents. At the same time, American students continued their visits to the Reich. In mid-1938, Lafayette College student Walter W. Williamson accepted a fellowship to study at the University of Frankfurt. Williamson intended to use the opportunity to perfect his German and vowed not to let politics "interfere with achieving my purpose."[84] This proved more easily said than done. The "Heil Hitler" greeting was expected in all contexts, and Williamson was warned that Gestapo informants were sitting in on his classes and listening in on private conversations.[85] Williamson subsequently witnessed the anti-Semitic violence of the Kristallnacht and was so appalled that he cycled to the American consulate and asked if there was any way he could help the affected Jews. He was warned that even approaching a Jewish household would result in immediate arrest and deportation.[86]

Williamson later ended up visiting Prague on the day German troops entered the city in March 1939. Sensing that the international situation was deteriorating, he decided to cut his trip short in June and return to the United States. During his goodbye party in Frankfurt, Williamson's group got into a verbal altercation with a group of Germans in a tavern. Angry that his farewell celebration was being ruined, the departing Williamson turned around in the doorway, gave a Nazi salute to the barroom, and shouted "Heil Roosevelt!" An outraged mob rushed after them and accused Williamson of shouting the more provocative "Heil Moscow!" A physical altercation followed and Williamson's face was pummeled by a German brawler. His group was eventually rescued by an elderly World War I veteran who led them out of the angry crowd and to safety. The frightened group ended up telling their story in a German police station. Fortunately for them, the officers on duty found the "Heil Roosevelt" remark hilarious and apologized for the resulting violence. Williamson left the

Reich two days later, disturbed by what he had seen and experienced in the country.[87] The war broke out just two months after his ship docked in New York.

Williamson was not the only American student still in Germany in the last days of the Reich. Stanford University still had a student at the University of Heidelberg in May 1939 who openly expressed a desire to build "mutual friendship channels" as the international situation deteriorated. (Tellingly, the fraternity scholarship committee that funded his studies had already announced that the 1940 recipient would be studying in Oslo rather than Heidelberg.)[88] Twenty-two Stanford students were in Europe when Hitler invaded Poland, including several who were still studying in the country through exchange programs. A female student on vacation with her family narrowly escaped being killed in aerial bombing, while the others quickly embarked on the treacherous ship journey home.[89] At Columbia, Madden and his circle of Germanophiles were devastated by the news from Europe. "For you and me this war will be a double tragedy—our memories of happy days in Germany, our hopes, our fears—all dashed to pieces. . . ." Shanahan wrote Madden days after Hitler's invasion of Poland. "Nothing but a complete destruction can result. . . . But the task is clear; strict neutrality. Maintenance of peace and our own task of building the national well being."[90]

Shanahan's prediction came true as previously pro-German student and faculty sentiment rapidly shifted to supporting nonintervention and America First. Yale University would become the birthplace of America First and the center of its early activities. Chapters sprung up across the country and attracted thousands of interested students and faculty. In April 1941, Columbia hosted a forum on American foreign policy that included America First speakers and was expected to attract two thousand student participants.[91] A month later, Stanford hosted a raucous debate over intervention that attracted seven hundred students and community members.[92] The debate on American college campuses now revolved less around whether Hitler's ideas had merits and more on whether the United States could avoid entering the war he had started. Just months later, Pearl Harbor and the US declaration of war meant the young men who had been sympathetic to Hitler in the 1930s now faced conscription. Madden himself attempted to find a way out of military service, at least initially. "I have been opposed to war and violence in international relations ever since I have been able to give thought to the matter. . . . I am therefore, I suppose a conscientious objector," he told an Army Medical Corps officer in 1942.[93] Madden's undeniable linguistic skills were too valuable for the military to pass up, however, and he ended up in the navy. He would go on to a successful career in both the US military and academia after the war, as would his friend Shanahan. Whether both men's anti-Semitic, pro-Hitler stances were a mere youthful indiscretion or an indicator of deeply held views remains uncertain, but both were seemingly successful in keeping them out of the public eye for the rest of their lives.

Madden and his circle of Hitler enthusiasts at Columbia provide a powerful example of how American students were influenced by wider international politics and the policies of their own universities. From 1933 to the end of the decade, American campuses provided an important platform for Hitler's American friends to spread their views to the young. University administrators systematically refused to confront the consequences of continuing to send students on study-abroad trips to Germany. An unknown number of American students— assuredly in the thousands—visited Germany on ostensibly academic visits during the decade. While for some this was merely a way to expand their language skills and intellectual horizons, it still placed them in an environment where "Heil Hitler" and unceasing anti-Semitism were omnipresent. Some, like Madden, were already sympathetic toward Germany and embarked on their studies there for at least partially ideological reasons. Others, like Williamson, had their eyes opened to the inhumanity of Nazism by their time in the Reich. "The lack of freedom in Germany troubled me greatly," he recalled decades later. "Having lived all my life in a democracy, usually I took freedom for granted. . . . Now I recognized fully how important is it not to lose it."[94] The exact proportion of students that fell into each category will never be truly known.

More significantly, however, it is undeniable that American universities provided important legitimacy for pro-German speakers and propagandists before the war. The continued presence of German exchange students, at least some of whom were probably Nazi Party members acting as foreign agents, provided a seemingly authentic voice for peace and friendship. Interviews and public appearances by German students nearly always highlighted these themes and strongly suggested that young people would be the ones to build international understanding and avoid war. It hardly needs to be said that this rhetoric directly served Hitler's foreign policy aims. Tellingly, many of those who had supported friendship with Germany earlier in the decade quickly pivoted to advocating nonintervention after 1939. "The attitude of American youth is an aspect which rightfully worries interventionist leaders," British intelligence concluded in 1941. "For years pacifist and communist propaganda had been concentrated on colleges throughout the States. The combination of communist propaganda and the isolationist influence of the wealthy (anti–New Dealers whose influence is important because most United States college subsist on contributions from the wealthy) has produced a situation in the American Universities which justifies concern."[95]

More insidiously, the notion that speakers such as Lawrence Dennis should be given high-profile platforms by universities to spread their views authoritatively was questionable at best. Certainly, these speakers should have been afforded their academic freedom and First Amendment rights, as they were. The same could be argued for the professors who attended the controversial celebrations at Göttingen and other German universities. On the other hand, American university administrators consistently denied those same rights to anti-Nazi students and faculty members. Madden and his circle at Columbia may have felt themselves to be the victims of a left-wing plot, but they still recognized that their views were shared by much of the administration, if not their fellow students. American universities essentially allowed anti-Semitic and pro-Nazi views to go virtually unchallenged on their campuses while working overtime to suppress opposing stances until public and student pressure nearly reached a breaking point late in the decade. A more courageous stand would have gone far to discredit Nazism and prejudice among the next generation of Americans. Instead, the country's intellectual leaders chose a path of engagement, legitimization, and tacit support that would carry long-term consequences.

AMERICA FIRST!

Almost exactly two years after Fritz Kuhn's German American Bund disgraced itself by explosively combining the symbols of Americanism with Nazism in Madison Square Garden, another event was held at the same venue. This time, the turnout was even larger than it had been in 1939. the *New York Times* called it a "capacity crowd" of around twenty-two thousand, with around ten thousand more listening to the proceedings on loudspeakers set up outside. They were flanked by tens of thousands of protestors and a more than thousand New York police officers sent to provide security. Some of the attendees had probably also been there for Fritz Kuhn's last big hurrah, and some pro-Nazi groups canceled their own meetings that night to encourage attendance. A New York City official hyperbolically claimed 60 percent of the attendees that night were "members of or sympathizers with the German American Bund." Members of Father Coughlin's Christian Front were in attendance as well and hawked copies of *Social Justice* on the street.[1] This was a catch-all gathering of Hitler's American friends.

The event was headlined by two of the biggest names in American politics: aviator-turned-celebrity-political-activist Charles Lindbergh and Montana senator Burton K. Wheeler, the staunch isolationist and Roosevelt opponent. Both men were given a nationwide radio audience that night that numbered in the millions, with Lindbergh's remarks broadcast live on the Mutual Broadcasting System and Wheeler being carried by NBC and CBS. Both used the platform to denounce the "war makers" they claimed were trying to drag the country into the European war, and told the audience that "America has nothing to fear from foreign invasion, provided it has the right leadership." Even if Britain were to fall under the boot of German oppression, they continued, America would be "strong and mighty enough not to worry about its defense from any invader." The crowd uproariously supported these sentiments and loudly booed every mention of the president, members of his cabinet, and the British ambassador. Wheeler told the crowd Roosevelt was being pushed into war by "jingoistic journalists and saber rattling bankers in New York." Lindbergh received a four-minute standing ovation.[2] By any definition, the event seemed to be a massive success.

This was the America First Committee at its political peak the summer before Pearl Harbor. Since its inception the previous September, America First had rapidly become the country's most vocal and best-known group seemingly articulating the concerns held by millions of Americans about the country's entry into the European war. With France defeated and occupied by German troops who made a point of parading down the iconic Champs-Élysées in Paris, American involvement was becoming more likely by the day. Or was it? If Wheeler and Lindbergh were to be believed, even if Buckingham Palace ended up flying a swastika flag it would matter little to the average New Yorker or midwestern farmer.

Why should Americans concern themselves about a conflict that was thousands of miles away, expending blood and treasure to save European empires from destroying one another? The sacrifice of young American men such a war would involve was made clear that May night in Manhattan by the appearance of the New York State chair of the Gold Star Mothers, an organization of women who had lost sons in war. The audience was told explicitly that the event's objective was to "make sure there should be no more Gold Star Mothers here." In addition, Senator Wheeler told them, the outbreak of war might lead to the emergence of "one-man government," the "end of constitutional democracy," and dictatorship at home.[3] Presented in this way, the argument was clear-cut. Who could possibly support American entry into a faraway war to save the British Empire if it would mean weeping mothers and widows, financial ruin, and dictatorship at home?

This was the essence of the America First Committee's argument and appeal. While Roosevelt was trying desperately to help save Britain from imminent defeat and prepare the United States for what he believed was inevitable entry in the conflict, the America Firsters were busy appealing to roughly the same group a future president—Richard Nixon—would memorably refer to as the "silent majority": the mass of Americans who want law and order, and otherwise to be left alone. In Nixon's era, this would mean assuring worried citizens that American pride and the nation itself could survive increasing anti-Vietnam protests, but in 1941 it meant appealing to the genuine desire held by a similar group of Americans to stay out of another distant conflict. Decades before Donald J. Trump adopted an identical slogan for his own campaign, America First represented the idea that issues beyond the country's borders were dangerous, expensive, and unworthy of American attention.

Yet there were always hints of a darker side to America First too. Among the audience that night in 1941 was Joe McWilliams, the self-proclaimed Führer of a group called the Christian Mobilizers and a favorite target of the left-wing press for his frequent statements praising Hitler. When an America First speaker told the audience McWilliams was present, much of the crowd called for him to be thrown out of the event, but at least one man was himself thrown out for audibly defending McWilliams. The Christian Mobilizer's leader was allowed to remain. Minutes later, the crowd shouted down the idea of singing "God Bless America" on the grounds that the lyrics were too "interventionist" (the fact that it had been written by a Jew, Irving Berlin, probably did little to increase its appeal too). The New York America First chapter chairman told the crowd his organization was interested in the support of "the 100,000,000 Americans who are against the war" and not "a handful of Bundists, Communists and Christian Fronters who are without number, without influence, without power and without respect in this or any other community," but it still was undeniable that the event had a fair amount of representation from those groups.[4]

The British government saw more sinister intentions in the America First movement from its earliest days onward. The America Firsters were obviously a major obstacle to the Roosevelt administration being able to provide much-needed aid to the British, and therefore William Stephenson's BSC agents realized the need to monitor its activities closely. Their reports to London must have been stomach-turning for Winston Churchill's government. A top secret dossier produced in 1941 argued that while the organization was "fundamentally American" and "conducted on American lines," it was also "the most effective weapon at the disposal of the enemy for the purpose of keeping the United States out of the war."[5] More dangerously, no matter how respectable appearances might be, "It is the raw material of American Fascism . . . the present tactics and methods of action of the movement reveal it as the American Fifth Column, sowing racial hatred and accentuating internal division. This is the effect of its activity and whether the process is conscious or unconscious is irrelevant."[6] In other words, the British believed that no matter how it might present itself, America First was fundamentally an organization of Hitler's most important American friends.

The British were in many ways right. From its inception, America First attracted an array of anti-Semites and right-wing extremists alongside seemingly respectable members of Congress and business leaders. It was, in fact, the final amalgamation of all the groups discussed in previous pages. As will be seen, America First was founded by a Yale student whose father was a corporate scion. Bundists, Silver Shirts, Coughlinites, and a bevy of other extremists rushed to join its ranks, despite the denials of America First's leaders that this was taking place. The same senators who had taken part in George Sylvester Viereck's Capitol Hill scheme now appeared on platforms around the country alongside the one man who still might have the chance to unite the far right and claim the title of American Führer: Charles Lindbergh. America's most famous aviator may well not have known how he was viewed by his most extreme supporters, but there is little doubt that he was hailed as the future American Hitler by a cross section of Americans.

America First's leadership always vehemently denied that they had any links to Hitler. Yet it was undeniable that the organization still retained a remarkable ability to attract the support of people with questionable views at best. There was a natural alliance between America First and groups such as the Bund that opposed American intervention in the war for their own reasons. There were further affinities between their stances as well. Foremost of these were strong undercurrents of anti-Semitism alongside anti-British, anti-Roosevelt, and anti–New Deal sentiment. The fact that all three of these aspects had a habit of regularly showing up in the public pronouncements of America First's leaders served to endear the group further to the subsection of Americans whose views toward Hitler were far from unfavorable. As self-proclaimed American fascist Lawrence Dennis recounted decades after the war:

> The anti-intervention or then so-called isolation [sic] cause was basically anti–New Deal. It was against America getting into the war only because the New Dealers seemed to be using American intervention in the war as essentially a New Deal strategy. The America Firsters or anti-war factors were not really pacifist or anti-war. They were anti–New Deal and that made them anti-war in that period and situation.[7]

In other words, America First had at least as much to do with opposing Roosevelt and the New Deal than the war itself.

This heavy anti-Roosevelt sentiment stemmed in part from America First's business representation. As already seen, corporate America was hostile to Roosevelt from the early days of his administration, and many firms had a vested interest in ending the war before their European investments were threatened. America First truly began in the law school classrooms of Yale University, where Robert Douglas Stuart Jr., son of the vice chairman of Quaker Oats, embarked on what British intelligence described as "an ambitious project of adolescence" in early 1940 and began holding meetings with about two dozen fellow students to discuss the deteriorating international situation.[8] With Roosevelt running for his controversial third term, the group believed that an elite group of up-and-coming attorneys who leaned Republican might well be able to affect the trajectory of national politics. Seeking to unify the isolationist right wing and "all political and social forces opposing the foreign policy of the Roosevelt Administration," Stuart officially launched America First and began courting anti-interventionist senators including Wheeler, Robert A. Taft (who would later run for the GOP presidential nomination, only to be defeated by Dwight D. Eisenhower), and Robert La Follette. Former secretary of state William Castle Jr. showed sympathies for the cause and had already been in touch with Charles Lindbergh about the prospect of launching a similar movement, but their plans had gone nowhere.[9] Now they would both be pulled under the America First umbrella.

More important than the politicians, however, was the fact that Stuart was able to recruit the support of corporate leaders with major name recognition: Jay C. Hormel, president of the meat-packing empire responsible for Spam (which would ironically become widely known for its place in the American soldier's standard diet during World War II); William Regnery, a wealthy cloth manufacturer whose son would launch a conservative publishing empire; and General Robert E. Wood, the first and only national chairman of the organization. Wood was in some ways the most distinguished and well-known of all America Firsters except Lindbergh. He had served as a solider in the Philippines and as quartermaster general during World War I before embarking on a high-flying corporate career that included positions in the powerful Panama Rail Company, the United Fruit Company, and Montgomery Ward. He also served as a deputy chairman for the Federal Reserve in Chicago. In 1939 he became the chairman of Sears, Roebuck and Company and was known as a major player in the Republican Party. Between him and Regnery, the financial stability of America First was immediately assured. In the summer of 1940 temporary offices were opened in the same building that housed the headquarters of Quaker Oats. America First was quite literally owned and operated by some of the country's most powerful corporate interests.[10]

In September 1940, America First was officially incorporated as a nonprofit organization and began its formal activities. Organizationally, it was run as a national body with local chapters. At the top of the organizational chart was a Chicago-based executive committee that included Wood, Regnery, Stuart (who served as national director and was responsible for most day-to-day operations), Hormel, and three others. Surrounding them was a wider national committee of around fifty people who were chosen for their economic power or sheer prestige. Some did very little to help the cause beyond lending their names, including Henry Ford (though he did promise "to do everything possible for us" and offered a donation, according to Lindbergh).[11] Among the most active and significant national committee members would of course be Lindbergh, who consistently refused invitations to take Wood's job; and Senator Wheeler's wife, who served as the treasurer of the Washington, DC, chapter and was, according to the British, a "forceful and dangerous woman."[12]

The heart of America First was therefore found in Chicago, where many of its elite corporate leaders were based and a substantial staff of around one hundred worked to keep operations running. The Midwest was also the natural place for such an organization to be headquartered. As British intelligence put it, Chicago was the "obvious centre of any nation-wide isolationist movement" because of "the strong concentration of Americans from German origin here . . . This area is naturally the focus of opposition to active aid to Great Britain with its ultimate danger of involving the United States."[13] The Midwest would indeed remain the America First Committee's geographical base, with two-thirds of its members located within three hundred miles of Chicago.[14]

There were many other chapters around the country as well, however. Procedurally, anyone could launch their own local chapter simply by simply writing to the Chicago headquarters. This led to the obvious problem that some chapter leaders might take their organization in undesirable directions—as Fritz Kuhn had found, to his dismay, with the Bund. Over the course of 1940 the national headquarters began promulgating rules and regulations to prevent local chapters from becoming national embarrassments. Several state chapters were even formed to keep an eye on the activities of other local leaders, and larger

groups were amalgamated from smaller ones in urban areas, including Los Angeles, to prevent the proliferation of many groups competing for the same
membership (and in the case of LA, perhaps to prevent small groups from falling under the influence of the powerful Bund–Silver Shirt alliance in the area).[15]

By Pearl Harbor, nearly every major city in the country would have a func-
tioning chapter of some description, though some areas proved more receptive
then others. The Committee had terrible difficulty organizing in much of the
South, including Georgia, Mississippi, Louisiana, and both Carolinas. One reason for this may have been the relative lack of German and Irish immigrants in
those areas, the competing influence of the Ku Klux Klan, and the fact that the
Committee was a fundamentally Republican and Northern big business undertaking while the South was heavily Democratic (it is also interesting to recall
that Louisiana was the only state in which the Silver Legion had been unable to
organize, likely because of the residual influence of the Huey Long political machine).[16] At its peak, the America First Committee probably had a total of more
than eight hundred thousand members, making it by far the largest organization
of its type in the country.[17]

British intelligence astutely, if bluntly, divided the membership of America
First into six categories, most of which also corresponded to the main factions
of Hitler's American friends:

1. Big business men in Chicago ("The most important" group)
2. Republicans and "leaders of opposition to the New Deal"
3. "The pacifism of Quakers, intellectuals, and liberal philanthropists
   (Note the university connection.)"
4. "Extreme left wing opposition" to the Roosevelt administration,
   including labor leader John L. Lewis and his daughter, who became a
   prominent leader in the organization
5. "The anti-Semitic Fascism of retired generals and ex-servicemen"
6. "Emotional Mothers"[18]

Members of America First could expect to receive a healthy dose of mailings and other promotional material, along with invitations to regular local
meetings. Those living in or near major cities might also be able to expect a visit
by one of the organization's leading figures, or even several of them.

America First's most popular speaker, by a long margin, was Lindbergh.
Lucky Lindy's speeches became so popular with America First audiences in 1941

that he would frequently receive ovations lasting for minutes. At one point national headquarters held a contest offering a Lindbergh speech to the local chapter that could recruit the most members.[19] Events featuring Lindbergh could attract crowds numbering in the tens of thousands, and British intelligence described him as "the one man who commands the support of the masses in the AF [America First] movement," though he was also "politically immature," "untrained in democratic argument," and possessing a "messianic view of politics." At the same time, his "apparent and adolescent honesty has a definite appeal."[20] Lindbergh was really the only name in America First that mattered.

In large part, this was because Lucky Lindy was the perfect celebrity spokesman. He was still regarded by many as a national hero for his daring 1927 solo flight across the Atlantic. The subsequent kidnapping and death of his son just a few years later led to one of the greatest outpourings of national sympathy and grief in American history.[21] Yet Lindbergh's path to becoming America's best-known isolationist was anything but straightforward. Following the kidnapping case and the resulting trial, Lindbergh and his family moved to England to escape the limelight. His European exile was hardly destined to be quiet and uncontroversial.

In June 1936, Lindbergh and his wife, Anne Morrow Lindbergh, received a letter from Major Truman Smith, the American military attaché in Berlin. Smith wanted to know whether the aviator would be willing to visit the country and produce a report for the United States government about recent developments in German aviation. Smith himself was a Yale graduate and an infantryman by training, making him intellectually well-qualified for his post but ill-prepared to evaluate the military implications of air power. "There's the man who could help me if he would!" Smith exclaimed to his wife, Kay, when he heard that the Lindberghs had arrived in England. Indeed, Lindbergh's fame and personal expertise seemed to make him perfect for the task at hand.[22] Smith's proposal for the visit was approved in advance by Luftwaffe head Hermann Göring, who was no doubt eager to reap the publicity benefits of a visit by the world's most famous aviator and, as has been seen, also seemed to meet every prominent American who came to town. Lindbergh accepted the invitation on the condition that press access to the event be severely restricted because "what I am most anxious to avoid is the sensational and stupid publicity which we have so frequently encountered in the past; and the difficulty and unpleasantness which invariably accompany it."[23]

The visit took place in July 1936 and included trips to airfields, aircraft factories, and research facilities. There were social functions as well, including a luncheon packed with government officials in which Lindbergh delivered a lengthy speech on the destructive potential of aerial bombardment. The speech received widespread attention, with American newspaper columnists overwhelmingly praising its sentiments. The *New York Times* used a quotation on its editorial page and reprinted the speech in its entirety starting on the front page.[24]

Lindbergh, Smith, and their wives later paid a social call to Göring. After lunch the Luftwaffe chief gave the group of Americans a tour of his art-stocked residence before introducing them to his pet lion, Augie. The excited three-foot-tall feline jumped onto Göring's lap like a house cat and started licking his face, only to abruptly become frightened when it noticed the other humans present and urinating on his immaculate white uniform. Lindbergh tactfully turned to study a painting on the wall as the scene unfolded, sparing his host additional embarrassment.[25] Göring changed clothes and continued the tour. He showed Lindbergh an impressive sword from his collection and invited the aviator to hold it. Fearing that an unflattering photo might be taken if he held such a menacing weapon, Lindbergh sensibly declined.[26]

Lucky Lindy's caution was not without reason. Despite his eagerness to avoid the press, the entire visit had become a minor sensation in the United States. The *New York Times* reported his daily movements, noting on July 26 that Lindbergh's visit to an aviation research center had taken place "almost secretly." It nonetheless managed to report most of his travel itinerary and threw in an anecdote about him signing an autograph for a famed German airman later in the day. The press, it seemed, could simply not be dissuaded from reporting on his every move.[27] Lindbergh's final major stop was a visit to the opening ceremonies of the 1936 Olympic Games in Berlin. This was not part of his original itinerary, but was added when Lindbergh "became so interested that he decided to accept the invitation of the German Government to stay for the opening day as a guest in the official box," as Kay Smith put it.[28] In the box he sat "within speaking distance" of Hitler himself but evidently did not do so. The *Times* remarked caustically that "Nobody, apparently, made any effort to introduce them. In American diplomatic quarters it was explained 'no time could be found that was convenient to both for which to arrange a meeting.'"[29] (The source of this quote was almost certainly Truman Smith, who had been hoping to arrange this exact meeting.)[30]

Lindbergh's public and private sentiments toward Germany were nearly identical following his visit. The *Times* reported that he was "intensely pleased by what he had observed in Germany" in the area of aircraft innovation.[31] Privately, he told Smith that his admiration of the country extended to "many other standpoints as well." Specifically, "The condition of the country, and the appearance of the average person whom I saw, leaves with me the impression that Hitler must have far more character and vision than I thought existed in the German leader, who has been painted in so many different ways by the accounts in America and England."[32]

As already seen, this sentiment was not unusual in the heady days of 1936. Hitler had indeed led the country to rapid economic recovery that had dwarfed the accomplishments of Roosevelt's New Deal and economic recovery efforts in most other countries. The Berlin Olympics was seen as a major propaganda coup for the German government. The Lindberghs' visit had been entirely stage-managed by Göring and his underlings, so it actually would have been more surprising if Lindbergh and his wife had *not* come away impressed. Truman Smith himself believed Lindbergh's visit had helped improve German-American relations substantially and also gave the US military new information about the Luftwaffe's development.[33]

The Lindberghs would visit Germany twice more in the coming years. Through early 1937 Lindbergh continually fed Smith information about what he believed was taking place with German aircraft production ("I would expect the Junkers factory to be producing twin-engine bombers rapidly at the present time, unless they have greatly reduced the number of their workmen") while planning his next visit.[34] In October, the Lindberghs arrived in Munich. More tours of aircraft production plants followed over the coming days, including several that were considered off-limits to most foreign visitors. Lindbergh was enthralled. "I shall not attempt to outline in this letter how greatly I was impressed with the progress of German aviation during the last year and the general conditions of the country," he told Smith.[35] By March, he told Smith that he was "almost convinced that they [the Germans] have the strongest air force in the world and that it is growing more rapidly than that of any other country. Our aviation development in the United States is still rapid but it does not seem to be holding pace with the Germans."[36]

The Munich visit was not all about work, however, and the Smiths and Lindberghs decided to take the opportunity to visit to the infamous "Degenerate Art" exhibition being held in the city. The art on display had been taken from other German museums and was chosen for its supposedly anti-German qualities. Modern art was heavily represented, as were pieces by Jewish artists. The exhibition had been strongly condemned in much of the American press and elsewhere as a heavy-handed attack on artistic expression. The Smiths and the Lindberghs disagreed. As Kay Smith remembered, "The continuous viewing of ugly distorted faces and forms, with blood and vomit spewing from them, produced a definite physical reaction. I felt nauseated." Lucky Lindy apparently felt the same way. "For the first time in my life I feel like having a drink," the famously teetotal aviator remarked after leaving the venue. Lindbergh's affinities for Nazi Germany now apparently extended beyond purely economic and technical matters. "As for me I heartily supported the name Degenerate Art which Hitler had applied to it," Kay Smith remembered.[37]

Lindbergh's final, and ultimately most important, visit to Germany would come almost exactly a year later. It took place in the immediate aftermath of the 1938 Munich crisis, when tensions over the Sudetenland region of Czechoslovakia had nearly pushed Europe into war. Lindbergh told Smith from France that "I have always felt that the Germans were too intelligent to permit war this year over Czechoslovakia, but I am greatly concerned about the possibility of a European war developing in the fairly near future." The key to averting conflict, he rather naively believed, was "getting the German problem better understood in America and Europe" and making the Germans realize that "they could accomplish more with a different attitude toward other nations."[38] Privately, Lindbergh was also pessimistic about British chances in a war against Germany. "The English have, as usual, been asleep and are in no shape for war," he confided in his journal. "They do not realize what they are confronted with. They have always before had a fleet between themselves and their enemy, and they can't realize the change aviation has made."[39] The idea that Britain was doomed would later become a driving force behind his involvement with America First.

Lindbergh arrogantly concluded that a visit to Berlin was the only appropriate response to the unfolding international circumstances. In mid-October he abruptly flew to the German capital and stayed again with the Smiths. On the evening of October 18, he attended a dinner at the American embassy that included Göring and other German dignitaries. Without warning, Göring was handed a small note and began delivering a speech. In it, he announced that the Führer had decided to award Lindbergh the Service Cross of the Order of the German Eagle in recognition of his services to aviation. This was a prestigious award—in theory, the second highest in the Reich—and was generally awarded to foreign diplomats who had assisted the Reich's interests and other notable non-Germans. It was also similar to the award that had been so contro-versially given to Henry Ford. Thinking little of the gesture and unable to under-stand Göring's speech, Lindbergh stuffed the box holding the medal into his pocket and continued socializing.[40] Later that night, Kay Smith translated the note for him and the group realized what had taken place. Anne Morrow Lind-bergh remarked immediately that the medal was an "albatross." Her husband would end up wearing it metaphorically for the rest of his life.[41]

The backlash in the United States began immediately. The *New York Times* ran the medal story on the bottom of page 1, alleging that Lindbergh had "dis-played an embarrassed smile and thanked Marshal Goering but proudly wore the decoration during the evening." (According to Kay Smith's account, Lind-bergh never actually wore the medal that night.)[42] In Britain, *Everybody's Mag-azine*, a weekly periodical with a tabloid bent, advised Lindbergh not to bother returning to the country. "And though we have no wish to be rude," the pe-riodical editors wrote, "we would feel happier if he went home."[43] Two weeks later, the *Times* reported on the front page that the Lindberghs were consider-ing moving from France to Berlin "to continue his aviation and other scientific studies in collaboration with German scientific circles." The medal again made an appearance in this article, reinforcing the growing perception that America's most famous aviator was growing dangerously close to the Nazi regime.[44]

Lindbergh assiduously recorded his thoughts about international affairs in a series of journals that provide an unmatched insight into his thoughts and activities during this critical period. As the medal episode suggests, one recur-rent theme is Lindbergh's naïveté about Nazi intentions and objectives. Reflect-ing on anti-Semitic violence of Kristallnacht that erupted shortly after his 1938 visit, Lindbergh remarked:

> *I do not understand these riots on the part of the Germans. It seems so contrary to their sense of order, and their intelligence in other ways. They undoubtedly had a difficult Jewish problem, but why is it so necessary to handle it unreasonably? My admiration for the Germans is constantly being dashed against some rock such as this. What is the object in this persecution of the Jews?*[45]

This was hardly the analysis of a man with a deep understanding of Nazi ideology. Lindbergh would continuously demonstrate a similar lack of under-standing toward his own actions as the decade proceeded.

Back in America, the damage continued to mount. In early December, TWA, the national airline which Lindbergh had helped establish after his 1927 flight, dropped its then-famous nickname of "The Lindbergh Line." Rumors spread that the change had been made because of the bad publicity his name was bringing. The airline president quickly issued the usual denials, but Lindbergh's reputation was clearly taking major damage.[46] More ominously, in late December, Secretary of the Interior Harold Ickes told a Jewish group meeting that anyone accepting a decoration from a dictator "automatically foreswears his American birthright." He then explicitly named Lindbergh and Ford as the men he had in mind.[47] The German embassy demanded an official apology, but the Roosevelt administration said nothing in reply.[48] Lindbergh sensibly decided to use this moment return to the United States and address the unfolding crisis. He arrived in April to face an inevitable media storm.

Docking in New York, Lindbergh was mobbed by reporters and photographers. He eventually slipped away into a waiting car. Over the coming days he accepted an active duty commission in the Army Air Corps and met with Roosevelt personally to discuss German aviation. Lindbergh, the president drily told the press, told him nothing that the US government had not already known.[49] Over the coming months, Lindbergh worked with the United States military on aviation-related issues. At the same time, however, his views about the need for America to stay out of the coming war hardened.[50] On September 1, 1939, this question became more than theoretical when the German military plunged into Poland.

Lindbergh now faced a decisive choice. He could easily have continued his defense work and quietly helped prepare the country for a war he hoped it would not join. Alternatively, he could use his fame to argue against the war, running the risk of further damage to his reputation. On September 15, he opted for the second route and accepted time on all three of the nation's radio networks. Speaking from a Washington hotel suite, he warned listeners that "If we enter fighting for democracy abroad, we may end up losing it at home." If the United States were to enter the war, he predicted, "a million men, possibly several million" would be killed, and the country would be "staggering under the burden of recovery during the rest of our lives." The better path was to remain neutral, with a strong army and navy to deter invasion. More sinisterly, he advised Americans to be skeptical of the news they were hearing from Europe and "ask who owns and who influences the newspaper, the news picture and radio."[51] This sentiment would soon take darker implications.

The response was immediate. Hundreds of messages, most of them supportive, flooded the Lindbergh residence. The press was less sympathetic, with left-
wing columnist Dorothy Thompson denouncing Lindbergh as a Nazi sympathizer
who had, after all, accepted a medal from Göring.[52] The FBI began collecting
mail from outraged citizens who denounced him as a possible threat to national security.[53] The Mutual radio network was forced to defend its decision to
make the initial arrangements for the speech (the other networks had simply
joined Mutual's plans and set up their own microphones). Lindbergh's views
were "entirely his own" and had not been "sponsored by a group or organization,"
Mutual's president assured the public.[54]

A month later, Lindbergh addressed the nation over the airwaves again. This
time he laid out a series of policy measures to ensure American neutrality. Specifically, he proposed a complete embargo on the sale of "offensive" weapons to
the belligerent nations while allowing them to buy "defensive" weapons. American shipping to the war zone would be immediately cut off, and US credit would
be withheld from all "warring nations or their agents." He concluded by arguing that if Canada—part of the British Empire and at war with Germany
already—was directly attacked the United States would come to its aid, but
Americans should not be drawn into the conflict simply because its northern
neighbor was already involved. "Have they the right to draw this hemisphere
into a European war simply because they prefer the Crown of England to American independence?" he asked the audience.[55]

This second radio address set off an even greater furor. Letters again poured
into the Lindbergh residence and the press had a field day. The US Senate, then
in the midst of a fractious debate over the Neutrality Act, jumped on the bandwagon. Democratic senator Key Pittman of Nevada, the powerful chairman of
the Foreign Relations Committee, denounced Lindbergh and argued the speech
"encourages the ideology of totalitarian governments and is subject to the construction that he approves of their brutal conquest of democratic countries
through war or threat of destruction through war."[56] The British response was
even more furious. The *Sunday Express* ran the salacious headline "Hitler's Medal
Goes to Lindbergh's Head" and alleged that the "honored and decorated
visitor of Hitler's, fervent admirer of Nazi strength, is now apparently developing the Hitler mind." His references to Canada, the paper went on, were
tantamount to saying that "Canada has no right to go to war unless with the
permission of the United States."[57] A week later, British politician and former
diplomat Harold Nicolson—from whom Lindbergh had rented his house in

England—published an article in British magazine *The Spectator* defending the aviator's right to say what he liked about Canada, but arguing that his world-view had fundamentally been warped by "fame and tragedy." Lindbergh was, he continued, "a fine boy from the Middle West . . . He is and always will be not merely a schoolboy hero but also a schoolboy."[58]

The two radio addresses rapidly catapulted Lindbergh into becoming "the nation's symbol of neutrality," as one of his biographers has put it.[59] The British ambassador to the United States, Lord Lothian, summarized the debate astutely in July 1940, telling Conservative MP Victor Cazalet, "The defeatists ask 'What is the good of our helping Great Britain which cannot now win? . . . Underlying the whole is the natural instinct of every democracy to avoid war if it possibly can, which is the ultimate explanation why Hitler has been able to take them one by one without any of them learning experience from the rest."[60] He might well have had Lindbergh in mind while writing these lines. American opinion was rapidly splitting on the issue of intervention, and Lindbergh was at the center of the debate. A poll in August 1940 found that an astonishing 51 percent of Americans had heard or read about Lindbergh's most recent radio address calling for nonintervention. Of those, 24 percent agreed with his sentiments while 56 percent disagreed.[61]

The Roosevelt administration now turned up the heat. Attorney General Robert H. Jackson denounced the aviator as a "modern protestor against democracy" and publicly alleged that his statements only served to weaken American resolve and help the country's enemies.[62] These criticisms were at least somewhat unfair to Lucky Lindy. While he certainly believed that the Nazis were likely to win the war, in large part because of the air power he had seen, he never explicitly said he *hoped* that this would be the case. An unnamed friend of the Lindbergh family told the *New York Times* in 1939 that his views were based in his "pacifist's horror at the mere fact of war" in addition to his belief in German air superiority. Lindbergh therefore hoped to "see the war end at once, avoiding the dreadful waste of a long struggle against a fait accompli which could not be reversed."[63]

Yet the wider political context of late 1940 must not be forgotten. Lindbergh was one of the country's most famous celebrities, and his radio speeches commanded great attention. Debates over neutrality were not the only political show in town: Roosevelt was also running for his unprecedented third term, in part explaining the sharp rebukes leveled from the White House toward the aviator. Lindbergh himself had been seen as a potential rival to the president, though only 9 percent of Americans reported wanting him to run in an August 1939 poll (of that small minority, 72 percent thought he would make a good president).[64] Later that year, 26 percent of Americans told *Fortune* magazine pollsters they wanted Lindbergh to be appointed to a high public office such as secretary of war.[65] These results were hardly overwhelming endorsements of Lindbergh's political potential, but they did indicate that he was taken seriously by a sizable constituency. Lindbergh's name had been mentioned as early as 1937 as a potential GOP steering committee member by a group of young Republicans who were concerned that the party had become "hopelessly reactionary and an incubator of Fascism." His association with Republican politics was clear, and for Roosevelt his speeches had to be viewed through a partisan lens.[66] There is no doubt the Nazis used Lindbergh's remarks for their own purposes as well. In Costa Rica, for instance, the head of a local Nazi organization printed leaflets quoting Lindbergh's speeches and distributed them around the country. It was difficult for the Nazis to get their propaganda printed in the Costa Rican press, the *Times* noted, but Lindbergh's speeches gave them an easy means to spread seemingly credible antiwar sentiment.[67]

In October 1940, less than a month before the election, Lindbergh accepted a fateful invitation to speak at Yale University under the auspices of the America First Committee. Nearly three thousand people packed a lecture hall for the event. He quickly launched into his usual themes, warning that intervention in the European war would mean long-term commitment to European affairs and denouncing the Roosevelt administration for "deliberately and ineffectively" antagonizing Germany by encouraging Britain and France to continue fighting. The speech ended with a standing ovation and made the papers the next day, with left-wing writers pillorying his remarks.[68] The speech was a major turning point, however, not because of what was said, but because it marked the beginning of Lindbergh's direct collaboration with America First. If his previous views had been even somewhat abstracted from the organization's official activities, this would no longer be the case.

Lindbergh had by now reached the stature of almost godlike proportions among Americans in the noninterventionist camp. He was flooded with letters from average citizens praising his radio addresses and public appearances. Many referred to him as an agent of destiny. "The future of this Nation depends on Men as you," a letter writer from the Bronx told Lindbergh in October 1940, "so do not let any one discourage you, but keep up the addresses till the White House makes it impossible for you to get Radio Time [*sic*] as they have Father

Coughlin."[69] A correspondent in Los Angeles was even more gushing: "You are meant by Destiny as another link in the chain of America's great. . . . The odds which you confront may be greater than the ones which stood before other American leaders; greater also is the prize to be won. . . . Not *you* are lacking in any way, but *we*, the people, who must rally to your support and give you the moral encouragement which is essential to the growth of any leader as well as artist."[70]

In November, Roosevelt cruised to reelection despite the attempted interference of William Rhodes Davis and John L. Lewis. The Republicans had admittedly run a reluctant interventionist (and former Democrat) in Wendell Willkie rather than an outspoken isolationist, but it was still indisputable that much of the country had endorsed the president's policies. Within days of starting his third term, Roosevelt asked Congress to pass a Lend-Lease bill that would allow him to directly "lend" weapons and other supplies to any country, without the need for payment. This was a clear attempt to send weapons to the British and the French, and the response from Congress was predictably virulent. Congressman Hamilton Fish—soon to be embroiled in the George Sylvester Viereck congressional franking scandal—sent a cable to Lindbergh asking him to testify before the Committee on Foreign Affairs, which the aviator duly did. The questioning turned nasty at points, with Lindbergh admitting he believed both England and Germany were to blame for the outbreak of war. He was interrupted by applause from the audience at times, but the press reaction was predictably split. Lindbergh subsequently crossed the Capitol to testify before a Senate committee, with similar results. Neither appearance had any effect on the Lend-Lease legislation, which passed the House by nearly 100 votes and the Senate by 29.[71]

In April 1941, Lindbergh was officially named to the national committee of America First, formalizing his direct involvement in the group. Membership numbers immediately exploded across the country. Throughout the spring, Lindbergh spoke at standing-room-only venues, attacking Roosevelt and urging full American neutrality. The president himself soon became convinced that Lindbergh was a fascist with dictatorial designs, and in late April Roosevelt launched a direct attack by comparing him to Southern-sympathizing Copperheads during the Civil War, and defeatists in George Washington's army at Valley Forge. Lindbergh, outraged, resigned his commission in the Army Air Corps Reserve.[72] Crowds at his rallies continued to grow, and in late May he packed Madison Square Garden with more than twenty thousand people. Thousands more listened on loudspeakers in the streets.[73] The presence of Bund members, various anti-Semites, and other extremists was widely reported in the press, as were scuffles between participants and protestors. Organizers deemed the event a success, but the publicity was far from completely positive. *Life* magazine observed that the audience had burst into deafening cheers for even the smallest aspects of Lindbergh's speech, including when he mopped his brow with a handkerchief. An unnamed Lindbergh associate was quoted referring to the phenomenon as "Führer-worship."[74]

As the summer of 1941 unfolded, America First chapters across the country began to feel serious political heat. Cities began denying organizers permits for their events. The president of the Brooklyn Dodgers refused to grant permission for a rally at Ebbets Field. Streets named for Lindbergh were renamed, and some libraries even removed books about his storied career.[75] Reverend Leon Birkhead, the antifascist campaigner who had helped end Gerald Winrod's political hopes in Kansas, published a pamphlet branding America First as "The Nazi Transmission Belt." "The America First Committee, whether its members know it or not and whether they like it or not, is a Nazi front!" the first page proclaimed. "It is a transmission belt by means of which the apostles of Nazism are spreading their anti-democratic ideas into millions of American homes!" It went on to note that in January 1941 a Nazi propaganda broadcast had hailed the organization as representing "true Americanism and true patriotism," and claimed German propaganda was being distributed at meetings.[76]

America First's leaders understandably resented these claims. They consistently tried to present themselves as patriotic Americans only concerned with their country's future and the lives of its young men. With isolationist sentiment still running high, arguments for caution in the face of the United States entering a faraway war still seemed plausible to many Americans. Open Nazi sympathies and anti-Semitism were becoming far less popular, however. A September 1941 poll found 74 percent of Americans agreeing with the statement that "if the United States is to be a free and democratic country, the Nazi government in Germany must be destroyed."[77] An overwhelming majority of Americans consistently told pollsters they would oppose a campaign of oppression against Jewish Americans.[78] Being too closely associated with the Nazis or racial prejudice was effectively the worst trap the America First Committee could fall into, and yet it would prove unavoidable. In the meantime, though, there were some hopeful public opinion indicators for its leaders. In August 1941, one month before the most disastrous speech of Lindbergh's life, Gallup polled Americans on their voting intentions in the 1942 midterm elections, with the addition of a hypothetical third party called "Keep Out of War" led by "Lindbergh, Wheeler, Nye and others." The results were telling: 40 percent of respondents said they would vote Democrat, 26 percent Republican, and 18 percent "Keep Out Of War." Depending on how this vote broke down nationally, this hypothetical party might have been expected to pick up a fair number of seats in Congress, especially in the America First stronghold of the Midwest.[79]

Yet the reality was that by 1941 the America First Committee had become the last political refuge for Hitler's American friends. Extremists swelled the organization's ranks as the war grew nearer. Lindbergh had long been iconic in these groups, and his presence in America First meant it now seemingly became the vehicle for the revolution the far right thought he would bring. Years before Lindbergh had even returned to the United States, a German American Bund leader told the undercover John C. Metcalfe that Lucky Lindy would return and become the leader of a far-right, pro-Nazi coalition that would sweep into power "at the right moment." "You know he would carry the public with him very easily. The Americans like him," Metcalfe was told. "You may not know it, but there is someone behind Lindbergh. . . . He was sent there for a specific purpose—to study conditions in Europe, to learn how dictators run their countries." When he returned, the Bundist predicted, Americans would "call on him to lead them. . . . Yes, there are a lot of things being planned that the public knows nothing about as yet."[80] Lindbergh was thus seen as the savior that Hitler's American friends had been waiting for. He was now the only man who could unite the far right, from uniform-wearing Bundists to Coughlinite brawlers and Nazi-sympathizing students. Lindbergh had the last, and best, shot at becoming the American Führer.

Accordingly, no matter how much America First and Lindbergh may have hated and denied it, extremists kept flocking to their banner. In Los Angeles, the local Bund encouraged its members to buy bumper stickers reading "Keep U.S. Neutral" and, "if you have the courage," told them to place them alongside ones reading "Buy and vote Gentile."[81] Advocating for neutrality had always been an important part of the political cover Nazi sympathizers used to make their activities seem respectable. Lindbergh did not seek to become the titular leader of the American far right, yet he had already been accorded that status whether he was aware of it or not. His affiliation with America First inadvertently made the organization a natural successor to the Bund and other extremist groups, and their former members were flooding into what they believed would become the "third party" to bring about fascist revolution. The fact that America First was fond of holding mass rallies reminiscent of their own organization's uniformed rallies in the same venues only increased its appeal for the Nazi-minded. Lindbergh himself recognized the odd ideological makeup of the movement he was heading. "It is a heterogeneous mass of Americans who have banded together in this anti-war movement," Lindbergh recorded in 1941. "We would break up in an instant on almost any other issue."[82]

The Nazis themselves recognized America First's potential importance in keeping the United States neutral in the unfolding conflict. Famed aviator Laura Ingalls, once as renowned as Amelia Earhart before her political involvement turned celebrity into notoriety, flew over the White House in September 1939 and scattered antiwar pamphlets across the lawns. She soon became a fixture on the America First lecture circuit. Less known was the fact that she was receiving payments from the German consulate to act as a Nazi propagandist. Her handler, German embassy second secretary Ulrich von Gienanth, instructed her to support America First and speak at its events because it was "the best thing you can do for our cause."[83] At his behest, she traveled the country giving speeches at America First meetings attacking Roosevelt while collecting payments from the German embassy for her troubles. She would eventually be imprisoned for failing to register as a foreign agent.[84]

It was Lindbergh himself, however, who ultimately made America First the final refuge of Hitler's increasingly demoralized American friends. On September 11, 1941, Lucky Lindy took to the stage in Des Moines to deliver the most infamous speech ever given by a twentieth-century isolationist. The timing could hardly have been worse. Public opinion was already beginning to move against America First's isolationist positions generally, and the increasing publicity given to the presence of former Bund members and other radicals at its meetings was doing little to help. Anti-Semitism was not gaining popularity, and polling confirmed that the overwhelming majority of Americans disagreed with the German treatment of Jews.[85] Lindbergh walked straight into a controversy he might have had the foresight to sidestep had he possessed a deeper understanding of American public opinion, and better-honed political instincts. As it turned out, he had neither. Before a crowd of thousands, he denounced "the British, the Jewish and the Roosevelt Administration" for pushing the country toward war. "We cannot allow the natural passions and prejudices of other people to lead our country to destruction," he concluded. If America were to enter the war, he warned darkly, Jews would "be among the first to feel its consequences."[86]

The maelstrom began immediately. Lindbergh himself was on a train to New York the following day and only became aware of the unfolding controversy when he arrived home. Since leaving Iowa, he had already been denounced by voices across the political spectrum and by most of the country's newspapers.[87] America First's headquarters was feeling the pressure as well. Several sponsoring members of its powerful New York chapter resigned immediately. Senator Burton K. Wheeler publicly clarified that he was not actually a member of the organization, though he spoke at its events and his wife was a leader in its Washington, DC, chapter.[88] The organization's most respectable voices were running for cover. Chicago lawyer and national America First leader Clay Judson urged his colleagues to make a public statement about the speech. In his view, they could not fully repudiate Lindbergh because doing so would "play directly into the hands of the war mongers which have been attacking him bitterly." At the same time, "Any statement must make clear that the question of religious tolerance or intolerance is not involved. . . . It must bring the discussion back to the principal issue . . . the big question of War or Peace."[89]

One of the few major politicians to defend Lindbergh was Senator Gerald P. Nye of North Dakota, the isolationist Republican who had rebuffed George Sylvester Viereck's overtures the year before but now showed far worse judgment. Nye insisted that Lindbergh was not an anti-Semite, and that the interventionist side was using a "red herring" to distract Americans from the real issue at hand. The senator was widely denounced in the press as a result. Pro-interventionist groups inserted ads in North Dakota newspapers accusing the senator of bigotry and of injecting "the racial issue" into American politics.[90] Nye's days as a senator were numbered.

Why did Lindbergh deliver such an inflammatory address? Surely it would have been far safer to stick to his usual themes and avoid courting unnecessary controversy. There are no conclusive answers, but Lindbergh's journals suggest an answer based on the company he kept after returning to the United States. In August 1939, Lindbergh had dinner with right-wing Mutual Broadcasting System radio personality Fulton Lewis Jr., who regaled him with stories about "Jewish influence on our press, radio and motion pictures. It has become very serious." Lindbergh's conclusion was that "Whenever the Jewish percentage of total population becomes too high, a reaction seems to inevitably occur. . . . If an anti-Semitic movement starts in the United States, it may go far. . . . When such a movement starts, moderation ends."[91] He then struck up a friendship with the openly fascist Lawrence Dennis, whom he referred to as "a striking man—large, dark complexioned, strong and self assured . . . he has a brilliant and original mind—determined to the point of aggressiveness. I like his strength of character but I am not yet sure how far I agree with him."[92] This was a bold statement about a man who was on the record predicting imminent fascist revolution in the United States. "He is brilliant, radical, and extremely interesting," Lindbergh wrote of Dennis in November 1940. "He told me that he was anxious to help in any way possible to build opposition to our involvement in the war." Given that Dennis was a paid German agent, this offer was hardly surprising.[93]

Just weeks before the Des Moines speech, Lindbergh spent the afternoon with Dennis again.[94] Lucky Lindy was effectively submerging himself in the intellectual milieu of Hitler's American friends. "We feel that the Jews are among the most active of the war agitators, and among the most influential," Lindbergh recorded in his journal exactly two months before Des Moines. "We feel that, on the one hand, it is essential to avoid anything approaching a pogrom; and that, on the other hand, it is just as essential to combat the pressure the Jews are bringing on this country to enter the war. This Jewish influence is subtle, dangerous, and very difficult to expose." As "a race," he continued, "they seem to invariably cause trouble." The only solution was "frank and open discussion" about "the Jewish problem" and "Jewish war activities."[95] Lindbergh's address was therefore no fluke: It was an expression of the anti-Semitic views he had been developing in conjunction with Hitler's American friends since his return to the country.

Given how deeply he had been drinking in the atmosphere of the American far right, it is perhaps unsurprising that Lindbergh was shocked by the response to the Des Moines speech. "I felt that I had worded my Des Moines address carefully and moderately," he reflected in his journal. "It seems that almost anything can be discussed today in American except the Jewish problem."[96] Days later, he bemoaned that "The Jewish press, and Jewish organizations are still striking at my Des Moines address."[97] The America First national committee soon made this situation worse by issuing a tone-deaf statement echoing Nye's sentiments and accusing Lindbergh's detractors of trying to conceal "the real issues."[98]

This was not the reassuring message most Americans needed to hear at this moment, but it was the one America First's members wanted. In the days after the speech, around 90 percent of the letters delivered to its Chicago headquarters praised the speech, often using anti-Semitic language.[99] "We wish to express our approval of Col. Lindbergh's speeches; all of them," one Minneapolis couple wrote to America First headquarters. "He speaks the truth. In regard to his last speech exposing the war agitators, he only said what everyone knows—that every Jew you talk to wants to [go to] war on Hitler for purely revengeful purposes. . . . They did wrong in Germany and Germany got rid of them because of it."[100] Given that America First's anti-Semitic orientation had only increased with the influx of former Bund members and other less-than-reputable elements in the previous year, the appearance of these views was hardly surprising. As historian Wayne Cole has written, after Des Moines "many anti-Semites within America First ranks and on its fringes interpreted the address as an invitation to use the Committee as a vehicle for spreading their anti-Semitic ideas."[101] Lindbergh himself was unapologetic for the controversy. "I feel: (1.) that the people of this country should know what Jewish influence is doing; and, (2.) that the Jews should be warned of the result they will bring onto their shoulders if they continue their current course," he reflected a week after the Des Moines address.[102]

America First's membership may have overwhelmingly supported Lindbergh's sentiments, but most other Americans did not. Theologian Reinhold Niebuhr, an advocate of American intervention, cabled America First headquarters to ask its leaders to repudiate Lindbergh. "It is clear by now that fascist devices are being used fight the Administration and we sincerely hope you will join all decent Americans regardless of your war stand in denouncing such tactics and their authors," he telegrammed. "Will you demand that the America First Committee divorce itself from the stand taken by Lindbergh and clean its ranks of those who would incite to racial and religious strife in this country[?]"[103] In Los Angeles, a heartland of both the Bund and America First, anonymous posters appeared bearing the text "Adolf loves Lindy" inside a heart with an arrow piercing it.[104] Alarmed by the growing controversy and the popularity of America First in the state, California's government took action on its own. Earlier in the year the state legislature had formed its own version of the Dies Committee, run by state senator Jack Tenney, to investigate subversion. Like its national counterpart, the Tenney Committee mostly focused on communism, but, unlike Martin Dies, Tenney quickly put America First on his radar. Traveling around the state, he summoned America First leaders to testify, humiliatingly often back-to-back with Bund leaders.

A month after the Des Moines speech, Tenney's committee summoned several Southern California America First leaders to testify about the objectives of their organization. The America Firsters retaliated by bringing a recording apparatus to the hearing, which the Committee forbade from use, and packing the venue with its supporters, including John L. Wheeler, son of the isolationist senator and head of the local chapter.[105] The tenor of the hearing was confrontational from the start. One witness, America First attorney Frank J. Barry, unsuccessfully demanded to cross-examine the Committee's witnesses and then turned the hearing into a spectacle:

> **MR. BARRY:** I would like to say at this time that America First Committee has no objection whatsoever in so far as I am concerned as a member of its Executive Committee, to any honest investigation of its affairs and we challenge anybody to show that the America First Committee is lacking in true Americanism or patriotism or [sic] in any subversive, it is truly American.

> **CHAIRMAN TENNEY:** We make no accusations of that kind, Mr. Barry. We feel that many fine, honest people are very definitely opposed to war. I think we are all opposed to war. But we are interested only in whether or not the pro-Germans, the pro-Nazis—might be using any organization for their own purposes.

> **MR. BARRY:** How about pro–Imperialistic British?

> (Applause from audience.)

> **CHAIRMAN TENNEY:** We are interested in democracy. I have repeatedly warned this audience about demonstrating. Officers, clear the Auditorium.[106]

Outside the hearing, two hundred demonstrators sang the national anthem, "God Bless America," and other tunes.[107] This had become a circus, no doubt, but the Tenney Committee's persistent questioning, and the fact that it was calling America Firsters to testify immediately before and after communists and Bund members, spoke volumes.

In the remaining months before Pearl Harbor, Lindbergh tried to salvage his reputation, telling a crowd in October that he had not spoken out of hatred for "any individuals or any people." He continued to draw large crowds, and held a final rally at Madison Square Garden at the end of the month. Attendance was again estimated above twenty thousand people.[108] The CBS radio network refused to carry the event live, telling organizers "We know of no reason why Lindbergh should have a nation-wide network every time he speaks."[109] Leon Birkhead used the opportunity to ask a group of motion picture industry bigwigs for $10,000 in donations to launch a publicity campaign branding Lindbergh as a Nazi and "the perfect type of American Hitler."[110] The man who had helped derail Gerald B. Winrod's changes in the Kansas Senate race was turning his sights on Lucky Lindy.

There would be no time for such a campaign to get underway. On Sunday, December 7, 1941, Lindbergh took his son Jon to a Massachusetts beach. On the way home, he let Jon sit on his lap and drive the car. They were quickly pulled over by a Massachusetts state trooper, who let the nine-year-old off with a warning. This charming morning was interrupted by the news from Pearl Harbor. "How did the Japs get close enough, and where is our navy?" Lindbergh wondered in his journal, before musing that perhaps the navy had been sent to aid Britain rather than protect Hawaii.[111] The following day, he phoned America First head Robert Wood, who remarked simply, "Well, he [Roosevelt] got us in through the back door."[112] Lindbergh himself now saw no option but war. "We have brought it on our own shoulders," he wrote, "but I can see nothing to do under these circumstances except to fight."[113]

America First was finished. "Our principles were right. Had they been followed war could have been avoided," the organization's last official statement read.[114] Leading members of the national organization, including Wood, entered war work immediately. Lindbergh attempted to rejoin the Army Air Corps but was rejected at the Roosevelt administration's behest. While Lindbergh's assessments of German air power had been valuable, Secretary of War Henry L. Stimson told him, he would not put American airmen under the command of a man "who had such a lack of faith in our cause as he had shown in his speeches."[115] America's most famous aviator would be denied the opportunity to lead his country in the greatest air war ever fought.

America First had not set out to represent the views and interests of Hitler's American friends, but by early 1941 it was effectively doing so. Just days before Pearl Harbor, a British intelligence official concluded it was "the most effective weapon at the disposal of the enemy for the purpose of keeping the United States out of the war." Pro-intervention groups were "unable to counteract the growing propaganda of this powerful isolationist body."[116] British agents conducted extensive studies of individual chapters and concluded that in some areas of the upper Midwest, "management and membership of AFC is of German Americans of more or less pronounced Nazi sympathies. In Indiana, we estimate it at one-third; in Michigan, at least one-half." In the West, "personal links between the Bund Headquarters and America First are strong." Its goal, British agents concluded, was nothing less than "the capture of the machinery of government."[117]

These conclusions reflected the reality of how America First functioned in American political discourse at the time. As the most respectable anti-intervention group in the country it was able to command press attention and substantial donations. It had no shortage of prominent supporters even before Lindbergh joined its ranks. A combination of government investigations and self-immolation among more openly pro-German groups left it as, effectively, the last organization standing to represent those who opposed entry in the European War. America First thus became the last refuge of those who sought to help the Nazi cause in the United States. This was far from the objectives of the organization's leaders, but it was increasingly the reality as war approached.

America First was ultimately discredited by a combination of events and Lindbergh's own missteps. Even the most sympathetic historians have found it difficult to conclude that the Des Moines speech was anything other than a catastrophe for America First generally and Lindbergh personally. There is little doubt that if Lindbergh had died prematurely in the mid-1930s he would be widely admired today. After 1941 his reputation would be permanently tarred with the stain of anti-Semitism and Nazi sympathies. The fact that he had long been a figure of fascination on the American far right—the ideal figure to serve as a future American Führer—only served to magnify the danger his actions posed. It was fortunate for the United States that Lindbergh was not yet ready to run for president in the 1940 election when he might well have been able to do better than Wendell Willkie and possibly even defeat Roosevelt. He also would have almost certainly received the backing, and money, of William Rhodes Davis and John L. Lewis. The nightmare scenario for Roosevelt and the Democrats would have been Lindbergh obtaining the GOP nomination and tapping into the support of Hitler's American friends and the corporate establishment. Even if Roosevelt had prevailed, such a vicious campaign would have left deep scars on the country at a key moment in American history. Such an opportunity for Lindbergh to seek the nation's highest office would never come around again.

Seventy-five years later, Americans would again hear the slogan "America First" from candidate and president Donald J. Trump. Whether Trump himself was personally aware of the slogan's history has never been sufficiently answered, but undoubtedly some in his campaign must have been. As then-candidate Trump said at the time, for him America First primarily meant putting his own country's interests above those of others. "Under a Trump administration, no American citizen will ever again feel that their needs come second to the citizens of a foreign country," the future president told an audience in April 2016. "I will view as president the world through the clear lens of American interests. I will be America's greatest defender and most loyal champion."[118]

This was a generally Lindbergh-esque argument, but lacked many of the undertones present in its 1940s equivalent. The original America First was not merely interested in protecting US interests or staying out of the war. As Lawrence Dennis's quote earlier in this chapter makes clear, America First was as much about opposing Roosevelt and the New Deal than it was nonintervention. These goals also aligned with those of Hitler's American friends, making a de facto alliance inevitable. Similarly, Trump's version of America First certainly signified more than foreign policy considerations for many supporters. Like Lindbergh, however, Trump's message was far larger than himself. Extremists inevitably flocked into both men's political camps. Lindbergh himself proved unable to control his own impulses and ended up discrediting himself to most Americans on a stage in Des Moines. It must be remembered, however, that his sentiments that night were greeted with overwhelming praise by his most vocal supporters. This served to only convince him further that his views were right, despite growing criticism. Lindbergh's personal echo chamber proved to be his downfall. Whether Trump was deliberately trying to evoke the darker aspects of America First's legacy is uncertain, but certainly some in his orbit must have been aware of the parallels the slogan would invite.

The original America First had never been just about nonintervention in the European war. It had always been an organization based in visceral opposition to internationalism, Roosevelt, and the New Deal. Its members overwhelmingly saw Lindbergh as their collective political voice, even when he digressed into crude anti-Semitism. The first verse of a 1941 America First campaign song summed up the organization's views:

The skies are bright, and we're all right,
In our Yankee Doodle way,

But it's up to us,
ev'ry one of us,
To stand right up and say:
AMERICA FIRST! AMERICA FIRST! AMERICA FIRST,
LAST AND ALWAYS![119]

Over the course of its short existence, America First became the collective political voice of Americans who believed their government had lost its way and was ignoring their concerns. The fact that its aims also aligned with those of Hitler's American friends made it extraordinarily threatening to the country's national security.

THE SPIES

I n early March 1939, Captain Fritz Wiedemann of the Third Reich
arrived in San Francisco to take up the position of consul general.
The captain was "tall, dark and immaculate," according to *Life* magazine, dressed "informally but well," and wore a monocle when he read. American
reporters expecting a scheming "Machiavelli" were disappointed. The captain,
they quickly decided at the San Francisco Press Club, was "not worth much
copy."[1] He did little to dispel this impression. "Politics are attended to by the
Embassy in Washington," he told reporters. His task would merely be building
"friendly relations between our two peoples," primarily "in the development of
trade and travel."[2] *Life*'s flashy profile of the captain, published a month after
his arrival, was replete with humanizing photos, including one of Wiedemann
in his dressing gown listening to the radio in the evening.[3] This was hardly the
image of a hardened German army officer–turned-spy that Americans were
anticipating.

Not everyone was as dismissive, however. There were a number of facts that
made Wiedemann's presence on the West Coast appear suspicious, if not outright sinister. For one, the captain's credentials in the Nazi Party appeared impeccable. Astonishingly, he had been Hitler's commander in the First World
War, sending the future Führer to carry dispatches under perilous conditions.
The shoe was now very much on the other foot. After the war, Wiedemann
reentered civilian life while Hitler went to Munich to ultimately pursue politics. After Hitler became chancellor in 1933, Wiedemann joined the Nazi Party

at his former subordinate's personal insistence. Following the brutal Night of the Long Knives purge, Hitler made Wiedemann his personal adjutant and secretary. "Every important decision made in the Chancellery crossed the Captain's desk and was handled by him with the efficiency and dispassion of a machine," *Life* reported. During the Munich crisis of 1938, it was claimed, Hitler relied heavily on Wiedemann's political instincts.[4]

What was this ultimate party insider doing in San Francisco? The answer was not hard to guess: Hitler had sent his trusted right-hand man to engage in some kind of intrigue, probably involving espionage. Aware of the potential danger, FBI director J. Edgar Hoover dispatched FBI agents to monitor Wiedemann from the moment he set foot on American soil.[5] The director was right to be skeptical of Wiedemann's intentions, but what he did not know was that the captain was carrying not one but two secrets. Hoover had already guessed the first. Wiedemann's mission did indeed include more than encouraging German-American "trade and travel." In reality, he would soon become a key player in the Nazi intelligence apparatus in the entire Western Hemisphere, overseeing operations in not just the United States but Latin America as well. As the California Un-American Activities committee described him, with some exaggeration, in its card catalog of subversives, Wiedemann was "alleged to be the most important Nazi agent in the Western Hemisphere . . . reportedly placed here as clearinghouse for espionage and intrigue that extends from the Pampas of the Argentine up to Washington."[6]

Wiedemann had a more important second secret too, however. Not only was he nowhere near as personally close to Hitler as the press claimed, he had actually become disenfranchised from the Führer. The stories about his intervention in the Munich crisis were greatly exaggerated and bordered on falsehood. Wiedemann's arrival in San Francisco was not just to take over a Nazi spy network but also because he had been sent from the Führer's inner circle with a cloud hanging over him. The Captain's frustration with his own government would soon lead him to make an audacious proposal to British intelligence. It was a betrayal so brash and outlandish that neither American nor British intelligence would be able to decide what to make of it.

The German intelligence network Wiedemann inherited in San Francisco was in a fairly disastrous state already. Most North American operations were subsumed under the authority of military intelligence in Berlin (the Abwehr) headed by Admiral Wilhelm Canaris. There were three main divisions of his operation: espionage, sabotage and counterespionage. Canaris was a true spy-master and had agents all over the world returning reports and operating at his behest. From 1939 onward, however, the Admiral had significantly fewer agents than he himself believed. That year, British intelligence enacted the Double Cross System that began turning his agents for their own purposes. Not only did his requests and orders end up in the hands of British officials, but in re-turn the British fed him false, misleading or unimportant information through his own intelligence network. It was one of the greatest intelligence coups of all time and Canaris would never know he was being played.[7]

The German intelligence network in the United States was not turned against Canaris in the same way, but its accomplishments were modest at best. Intelli-gence historian Ladislas Farago has estimated that by the late 1930s there were around fifty spies operating in the United States. This number may seem small, but the fact that some of these agents worked in the defense industry made them potentially dangerous. There is no doubt that some military secrets were passed to the Germans, including one major technical secret: the Norden bombsight. As Thomas H. Etzold has written, the German spy network acquired "plans for, or samples of, gyroscopes, bombsights, retractable landing gear, flight in-struments, improved propellers and fuels, designs of new planes and naval ships, specifications of various developmental aircraft, classified maps, infor-mation about American industrial capacity, and confidential communica-tions."[8] These were major intelligence coups, though how far they actually helped the Nazi war effort is less clear. Many of the technical secrets stolen were never put into practical use given the difficult wartime conditions in Germany, and others were simply filed away for potential future use.[9]

Despite these successes, there were real operational difficulties with spying in the United States. Unlike the film *Confessions of a Nazi Spy,* there was no organization that could easily conceal a real-life Nazi intelligence network. The Bund was under far too close surveillance and, as it turned out, had been infil-trated at its highest levels by John C. Metcalfe. After the war, Hermann Göring complained to his American interrogators that "the FBI was too observant in detecting invading spies and as a result the Nazis were never able to develop a spy network in the United States." The Germans received more information, he claimed, from "newspapers, magazines and radio speeches."[10] This failure was not through lack of trying, however.

In early 1940, Hoover secretly met with a British informant and updated him on American efforts to disrupt German intelligence activities in the United States. Some of these plots bordered on the comical, including one plan that called on a male German agent to acquire information about a new American rifle by seducing two privates in San Francisco when the same information could have been obtained openly and without subterfuge. (The only result was that the soldiers were thrown into jail, presumably for their sexual inclinations rather than cavorting with a German agent.) At the end of the day, Hoover concluded, German propaganda was "clumsy" and its agents "waste a lot of time, and money." Regardless, nearly all the German agents in the United States were under surveillance by the FBI already, he claimed. British propaganda methods, he concluded, were "better and subtler than those of the Germans," and there was little sympathy for the German cause except for in a few parts of the Midwest.[11]

Hoover's bluster was overly confident, as events would show. German spies had a number of methods they used to effectively gather information and communicate it to the fatherland, several of which the FBI would only discover relatively late in the game. Some of these were seemingly ripped from the scripts of Hollywood spy thrillers. Photographed documents were printed on microfilm that could be spooled and easily hidden any number of places. Small pieces of film could even placed under the tongue or even swallowed for later retrieval. Normal-looking matches could double as pencils writing in invisible ink. German spies could communicate with the fatherland by sending letters to prearranged Abwehr addresses in neutral countries like Portugal, much as George Sylvester Viereck had done. Seemingly innocuous letters could conceal either a coded message or information written in invisible ink that became perceptible when heated. British censorship officials in Bermuda became adept at identifying such messages and passed information about German agents to the FBI, just as they had done in the Viereck case. The most technically sophisticated spy technique was known as the microdot. This ingenious invention used a special camera and microscope to reduce an entire document to the size of a period or the dot on a lowercase *i*. The dots were printed and could be affixed to anything, including a letter or even the outside of an envelope. A spy knowing where to look would use a microscope to magnify the concealed document and read it.[12]

Unsurprisingly, the first major Nazi spy network in the United States centered around Friends of the New Germany, precursor of the Bund. In 1934, a former leader of the organization, Friedrich Karl Kruppa, testified before Congress that "Nazi propaganda was being smuggled into this country" and that there were "Nazi cells" on all German ships docking in the United States. Even more sensationally, he claimed that Heinz Spanknöbel, the first leader of the organization, had not left the United States voluntarily, but had been abducted at gunpoint from the home of a doctor named Ignatz T. Griebl and forced to board a ship to the Reich. "He was abducted because he did not obey orders from abroad," Kruppa concluded darkly.[13]

True or not, this story was interesting because it mentioned Griebl. A decidedly shady character, Griebl was born in Germany and moved to the United States in the 1920s after serving in World War I. He became an American citizen shortly thereafter. In 1933 Griebl was serving as president of Friends of the New Germany and, as it turned out, also volunteering his services as a spy at the same time.[14]

Over the coming years, Griebl provided the Abwehr with various pieces of information he obtained from a range of contacts. In return, he received $300 a month. He cultivated a wide network of informants, some of whom managed to obtain military secrets from their places of employment. One such informant, Otto Voss, worked in a defense plant and passed along blueprints of military hardware.[15] In 1937 Griebl traveled to Germany and met Canaris, who offered his personal thanks. Back in the United States, Griebl expanded his network and continued passing information to his German handlers. The scheme worked fairly well until a new actor entered the scene. He was Günther Gustav Rumrich, an Austrian American who had been born in Chicago and raised in prewar Austria-Hungary. In 1929 he moved back to America, just in time for the stock market crash. Floating between jobs, Rumrich joined the US Army, managed a promotion to sergeant, but deserted after embezzling funds. Desperate for money, in 1936 he wrote directly to the former head of German intelligence, Colonel Walter Nicolai, and offered to spy on the United States in return for cash.[16]

Nicolai forwarded the offer and, bizarrely, German intelligence accepted Rumrich's services. Rumrich began passing military information he managed to obtain by posing as a current soldier and from his friends who were still in the military.[17] Both the Abwehr and Rumrich quickly bungled this arrangement. His handlers demanded information that was increasingly difficult to obtain, including the plans to the aircraft carriers USS *Yorktown* and USS

Lexington. This would have been nearly impossible to obtain without somehow infiltrating the Department of the Navy itself, or managing to convince someone to give up the plans.

In 1938, the Rumrich's Abwehr handler demanded he obtain thirty-five blank passports, presumably to assist the insertion of future agents. Rumrich simply phoned the New York Passport Division, claimed he was a high-ranking State Department official (some accounts say even Secretary of State Cordell Hull) and demanded to be sent the blanks at a hotel address.[18] The passport official was understandably suspicious about this request and called the police. A trap was set, and Rumrich was arrested as he tried to collect the package from a boy he paid to pick it up on his behalf.[19]

Rumrich was interrogated by FBI agent Leon G. Turrou, who would eventually write a sensationalist book about the case. Hoping to save himself, Rumrich began to give up everything he knew about Nazi intelligence operations. The trail eventually led to Griebl, who was called before Turrou and also "sang like a canary." He even helped the FBI arrest several associates in his own plot.[20] In May 1938 Griebl manage to escape the United States on a German ocean liner, much to Turrou's frustration. Regardless, a grand jury delivered eight indictments against the Nazi spies. Most of the accused had already managed to make their own getaways to Germany, but the indictments and subsequent trial were a press sensation. The incompetent Rumrich ended up receiving two years behind bars.[21] In 1939, Turrou published *Nazi Spies in America*, a fanciful account of the case which would become partial source material for *Confessions of a Nazi Spy*. J. Edgar Hoover was incensed, partially because Turrou's public handling of the case had arguably tipped off the defendants and allowed them to escape.[22]

The Griebl case was disturbing to the US government for a number of reasons. First, the FBI had no idea the spy network existed until Rumrich inadvertently blew the entire operation open through his own ineptitude. It was too much to hope that future spies would give themselves away by foolishly calling up government officials and demanding paperwork be sent to them. Second, unraveling the extent of the conspiracy had only been possible because Griebl and Rumrich had given up their associates. If they had remained silent—or themselves been compartmentalized to only one part of the operation, as was preferred tradecraft—it would have been difficult or impossible to find their coconspirators. As historian Francis MacDonnell has written, "The unraveling of the New York spy network left Americans with the unsettling possibility that this episode exposed only the tip of a Fifth Column iceberg."[23]

Arriving less than a year after the Griebl case, Fritz Wiedemann must have known he was facing an uphill struggle. The shenanigans of the German American Bund and the Silver Legion were attracting press attention and being discussed by the Dies Committee and other government investigators. American perceptions of Nazi Germany were being quickly damaged by Hitler's American friends. Hitler appointed Wiedemann to the San Francisco post in January 1939, replacing the aptly named Baron Manfred von Killinger, a brutal former storm trooper who had been convicted of killing a clergyman in Germany but served no time in prison for the crime. Evidently this fact made him unpopular with San Franciscans, as did his open support for the Bund.[24] Wiedemann arrived in New York by ship in New York in early March, quietly disembarking and telling reporters that he would be making a visit to Washington before heading to replace Killinger.[25]

The guessing game around why Wiedemann was being sent to the West Coast started immediately. In London, the Foreign Office received a troubling report from a Dutch correspondent suggesting that Wiedemann's task would be to "unite the German Americans, collect big sums from them and start a campaign in favour of American neutrality in the case of war at the same time a strong anti-Jewish campaign." The main vehicle for this would be "prominent Industrialists in the U.S.A. who are in favour of fascism and they hope to get strong INDIRECT support from them." (Foreign Office officials were unsurprised, with one remarking darkly, "At one time they [the Nazis] were basing great hopes on Mr. Ford.")[26] *Life* magazine interpreted his mission similarly, imagining how he must have pitched his Bay Area move to Hitler. San Francisco was "a quiet post from which he could organize isolationist propaganda and resistance to Franklin Roosevelt's foreign policies among the powerful anti–New Deal elements of the West Coast," it had Wiedemann telling the Führer. "The German American Bund with its crazy firebrands must be recognized and muzzled, American sensibilities catered to."[27]

Wiedemann's real mission was not far from what the Foreign Office assumed. As consul general, he was afforded a broad range of diplomatic protections that allowed him to operate on the outer margins of the law. His staff was increased from eight to nearly thirty members, and his personal duties were extended to cover all Nazi diplomats in Central and South America. This was far beyond the normal portfolio for a consul general.[28] In addition, Wiedemann was placed in charge of the Orient Gruppe, an intelligence network that extended into Asia. He also became the regional head of the Foreign Organization (an organization of Germans abroad), another intelligence network sponsored by German industrial giant I.G. Farben that encouraged Germans to return to the fatherland. It was also a key recruiting tool for German intelligence. To link American businessmen to the Reich, Wiedemann created the German American Business League, an organization of a thousand small businesses that agreed to boycott Jewish companies. He made numerous trips to Mexico to keep an eye on the German intelligence network there.[29] Author Charles Higham has claimed Wiedemann oversaw as many as five thousand German agents operating throughout the Americas and elsewhere.[30] If true, this made him one of the key sources of German intelligence anywhere in the world. Both British and American intelligence feared that his ultimate mission was to serve as a liaison with Japanese intelligence.[31]

Overseeing Germany's spy apparatus was one thing, but Wiedemann's more pressing task was recruiting agents of his own in the United States. The FBI eventually identified more than a dozen Americans Wiedemann had apparently cultivated including a naval officer who purportedly wanted to talk about "lighter than air activity" with the consul general.[32] According to the FBI, Wiedemann "from all indications is presently the focal point of German espionage and propaganda activities in that section and possibly throughout the United States."[33] The propaganda campaign supposedly included a plan to "purchase newspaper firms, especially in the industrial towns and cities in the United States" and presumably turn them into pro-Nazi organs. Rumors circulated that his first unsuccessful target had been the *San Francisco Chronicle*.[34] In June 1940, the FBI learned that Wiedemann was preparing for the arrival of fifteen "German espionage agents" in San Francisco from elsewhere in the country. The agents were supposed to report to Wiedemann, and then depart by ship for Asia. The FBI soon ascertained from "a high German official" that the departing agents would be replaced with "harder, tougher and more violent groups" who were less known to American law enforcement. Later that month, fifty-three Germans arrived in San Francisco on a Japanese steamship. Most were technicians bound for Latin America, but three were allegedly potential agents in whom the consul general "was reported to be particularly interested."[35] At the same time, Wiedemann's vocal dislike for the German American Bund made him seem potentially even more scheming and nefarious to the FBI. "I don't like the Bund," he was quoted as saying in December 1939. "I told them in Washington we could only have trouble with the Bund because the people of the Bund are American citizens. With their stupid speeches they can only give us trouble."[36]

Wiedemann's intrigues quickly encountered major difficulties. As one of the most high-profile German officials in the country, he was dogged by the press and the public wherever he went. Communist protestors followed him constantly, and respectable Bay Area hostesses canceled parties scheduled in his honor when threatening letters arrived. "What would you *do*, my dear, if you found Captain Wiedemann sitting next to you at dinner?" became a common conversation among "social dowagers," *Life* reported.[37] The captain's social situation was about to change, however. On May 29, 1940, his erstwhile mistress, the glamorous Princess Stephanie von Hohenlohe, joined him on the West Coast. The princess was a mysterious and beguiling figure, and remains so to historians today.

Born Stephanie Richter in Vienna, the princess acquired her title by marrying Prince Franz Friedrich Hohenlohe-Waldenburg-Schillingsfürst, a lesser member of one of Europe's most prominent aristocratic families. There was always much gossip surrounding the princess. Two rumors were certainly true. First, she was at least half Jewish and possibly fully Jewish, though the identity of her biological father was never fully established. Second, by the time of her marriage she had acquired a lengthy retinue of male companions. This would become a recurring theme throughout her life. A US government report presented to Roosevelt uncharitably referred to her as a "gold digger."[38] How she managed to convince Franz Friedrich to marry her remains a mystery, but historian Karina Urbach has suggested that she had become pregnant by one of her husband's more prominent relatives and he was simply ordered to marry her to save face and make the child legitimate. Either way, it was a short-lived union. After the First World War, the Austro-Hungarian empire was broken up and Franz Friedrich was faced with the decision of adopting either Austrian or Hungarian citizenship. Unlike many of his relatives, he chose to become Hungarian, compelling his wife to do the same. In 1920 the couple divorced, but she kept both her noble title and her Hungarian passport.[39]

Princess Stephanie now embarked on a strange career heavy in international intrigue. In 1927, she met Lord Rothermere, the owner of the British tabloid the *Daily Mail*, and managed to interest him in Hungarian politics. The *Daily Mail* suddenly began heavily covering the affairs of a country that had not even existed a few years earlier. Rothermere started to trust Stephanie's judgment on the issues and leaders he should be covering, and began paying her a salary. In the 1930s, this assignment led to Stephanie meeting Hitler, who became personally and probably romantically infatuated with the princess despite her non-Aryan appearance (and, indeed, her at-least-partially Jewish parentage). The Führer's wider circle naturally included Wiedemann, who essentially controlled access to Hitler at this point.[40] Throughout the 1930s, Stephanie thus became the conduit for communication between Rothermere and Hitler. She also became a curiosity in upper-class British social circles, answering questions about Hitler's regime during her visits and acting "as a link between Nazi leaders in Germany and Society circles in this country," as MI5 (domestic intelligence) put it. Her affair with Wiedemann began around the same time.[41]

In the summer of 1938, Princess Stephanie and Wiedemann became mutually involved in a strange plot that would only be fully revealed decades later. While it was widely reported that Wiedemann had somehow been involved in resolving the Munich crisis that year, the true nature of his involvement was concealed. In fact, he and the princess set up a plan with Hermann Göring's backing to travel secretly to London and make back-channel contact with the British government. The goal was to secure Göring himself an invitation to undertake direct negotiations.

Wiedemann arrived in London and met with Lord Halifax, the foreign secretary, and assured the British government that "in present circumstances the German Government were planning no kind of forcible action" against Czechoslovakia. In other words, Hitler was not intending to start a war.[42] The British reciprocated the sentiment, which Wiedemann reported to Berlin. This back-channel information was well received by Hitler, but less so by Foreign Minister (and former ambassador to the United Kingdom) Joachim von Ribbentrop, who felt sidelined and became an implacable opponent of Wiedemann. The mercurial Göring soon turned against Wiedemann as well and ordered a wiretap of his office. Hitler thus became aware of his affair with Princess Stephanie and flew into a rage. Wiedemann was abruptly fired, and effectively exiled to San Francisco. The American press believed he had been sent there to act as a sinister Nazi spymaster, but instead he had simply been sent away to one of the most distant places Hitler could find.[43]

Princess Stephanie was in trouble too. Just as Wiedemann had fallen quickly, Rothermere abruptly fired Stephanie for reasons that remain unknown. In retaliation, she sued him for unpaid future wages and then tried to blackmail him by threatening to release his fawning letters to Hitler if he refused to pay her off. Rothermere declined, and the trial became a sensation when the correspondence were introduced in court. Stephanie eventually lost the case and fled to the United States in late 1939, where she would soon be reunited with Wiedemann. Unsurprisingly, she too was placed under FBI surveillance immediately after arriving in the United States.[44] She waited months before risking a personal reunion with Wiedemann, and even then they decided to have their first meeting in the small city of Fresno, California, rather than San Francisco. The ploy failed to fool the FBI agents who tailed both of them not only to Fresno, but also the cabin in nearby Sequoia National Park where they subsequently spent the night.[45]

Wiedemann and Stephanie both had a few more tricks up their sleeves, however. The captain had already tried to pull one of his own before Stephanie's arrival. It was a complicated plan, but one that might have carried huge ramifications. In 1939, Wiedemann had reunited with Felicitas von Reznicek, a German baroness and newspaper reporter whom he had known in Berlin. Reznicek was ostensibly in the United States to write a series of travel articles for German newspapers, but American authorities suspected she had ties to German intelligence. She and Wiedemann rekindled their friendship and, it was believed, became lovers shortly after.[46]

While staying in San Francisco, Reznicek met a British subject named Gerald O. Wootten over a game of bridge. They became fast friends, and Reznicek either took Wootten into her confidence or began telling him a series of tall tales, depending on the interpretation. Not only had she known Wiedemann very well in Berlin, she claimed, but she too had once been part of Hitler's inner circle. She had been so well-informed about the inner workings of the regime, Reznicek claimed, that she had been the one to warn Wiedemann about Ribbentrop's wiretapping. Reznicek even supposedly predicted the date of Hitler's invasion of Poland to Wootten the summer before it took place.[47] As the strange friendship grew, Wootten met Wiedemann socially as well.

Sometime in March 1940, Wiedemann erroneously received word from Berlin that he was going to be imminently recalled. According to Wootten, Wiedemann feared for his life if he returned to the country. Through Reznicek, he allegedly asked to be put in touch with the British ambassador, with the hope "that he might be permitted to come to England in the event of his dismissal." In exchange, Wiedemann offered to undertake "political action with a view to the replacement of Hitler's administration by one of more moderate policies." In other words, Wiedemann was offering to defect to the British and join the war effort against Hitler.[48]

Wootten conveyed this strange story to the British consul general in San Francisco, P. D. Butler, who in turn contacted the British ambassador in Washington and the Foreign Office. Questioned a second time, Wootten verified that the offer had come from Wiedemann personally. As a gesture of his displeasure with his former boss, Wiedemann had even refused to transmit a required birthday greeting to the Führer.[49] If Wiedemann was being genuine, this was a startling offer. US military intelligence believed everyone involved, including Wootten, was suspicious and could not be trusted. The skepticism was understandable. On the other hand, the possible payoff from Wiedemann's defection would assuredly have been large, especially given the key role he was suspected to play in the German intelligence network.

Remarkably, the Foreign Office seems to have given this offer almost no consideration before rejecting it. "We do not think the Baroness's messages need to be taken seriously," the Foreign Office told its Washington embassy. If Wiedemann were truly in danger, it continued, "he can surely stay in America. There is no reason why we should take him here. He has neither the qualities nor the prestige to be of any use against the present regime, even assuming that this account of his political sympathies is correct."[50] One official was even more blunt, scrawling on an official minutes sheet, "This looks to me like a rather transparent attempt to get Wiedemann into this country. I see no earthly reason why we should give him asylum."[51] P. D. Butler was ordered to do nothing, but he seems to have refused to give up so easily. Sending a transcript of a Wiedemann speech to the Washington embassy later in the year, Butler remarked pointedly, "This speech, I think, removed any doubts which may have existed as to Captain Wiedemann's outstanding abilities. A man who could make such a speech . . . evidently has diplomatic gifts which could profitably employed in a sphere far wider than that afforded by San Francisco."[52] The Foreign Office still took little notice.

Why were the British so reluctant to offer Wiedemann asylum? The Foreign Office's suspicions of him were certainly justified, but the potential payoff from such a high-profile defection might be huge. For one, Wiedemann would have known extensive details about Nazi espionage throughout the Western Hemisphere. Even if his importance as a spymaster was exaggerated, he presumably would have had significant information to offer in exchange for protection.

Indeed, after being arrested by American authorities in 1945 he willingly provided lists of German agents in the United States and elsewhere.[53] At a minimum, he would have been able to offer sophisticated psychological portraits of Hitler's inner circle. As the Führer's former commanding officer he might even hold propaganda value.

There are no clear answers, but surviving Foreign Office files offer some hints. Generally speaking, the British seem to have underestimated Wiedemann's role in German intelligence and viewed him more as a propagandist rather than a spymaster. Even if Wiedemann did have knowledge of the Nazi spy network in Latin America and the United States, the British had more pressing concerns at hand in April 1940. They also undoubtedly feared Wiedemann's potential as a double agent if allowed into wartime Britain. Finally, the Foreign Office may well have worried that if he were allowed into the country, Princess Stephanie might try to follow, and they had only recently rid themselves of her. It is telling that during his first interview with Wootten, the British consul general specifically asked whether he had met Stephanie (the answer was negative). Perhaps the British also simply didn't believe Wootten, who seems to have been a shady figure, though Butler thought he was telling the truth.[54] There may have even been a feeling that offering Wiedemann asylum in Britain would protect him from the consequences of his past actions. Regardless of the exact reason, the Foreign Office gave up the opportunity to crack open Hitler's intelligence network in the United States.

It seems unlikely Wiedemann informed Princess Stephanie of his defection plan, especially since it integrally involved another woman who may have been a romantic rival. In October 1940, Stephanie enlisted Wiedemann in an outlandish scheme of her own. Hoping to broker some kind of peace deal between Britain and the Third Reich, the pair contacted Sir William Wiseman, a former British intelligence agent who had maintained his government ties. Meeting covertly with Wiseman, Wiedemann and Stephanie told him there were opposition figures in Germany who would be willing to negotiate with the British, and even offered some names. Wiedemann told Wiseman that his instructions from Berlin were to "separate 'decent Americans' from Roosevelt," but that Hitler was "ignorant and contemptuous of America" and "under-estimates their military importance." He closed on a plaintive note. "We are in a most difficult position," he told Wiseman. "We are loyal to our country but we know that this will end in the worst disaster that will ever come to the German people."[55]

Wiseman relayed the messages to London, but was quickly warned off further discussions with the pair. Wiedemann and Stephanie's final attempt at recreating their success in 1938 was not to be, and neither was their relationship. In December 1940 they split up for good. In March 1941, Stephanie was detained by the Immigration and Naturalization Service (INS) for overstaying her visa. Remarkably, she then managed to seduce the commissioner of the INS, Lemuel B. Schofield, and the two began a torrid, booze-soaked affair that was carefully monitored by the FBI.[56]

Wiedemann found himself in increasingly hot water as well. The same month as Stephanie's arrest, Alice Crockett, a former actress and the ex-wife of an army colonel, sued the consul general in federal court. Crockett bizarrely claimed Wiedemann had asked her to take a $5,000 trip to Germany to meet Hitler, Göring, and propaganda minister Joseph Goebbels and quietly gauge their opinions on Wiedemann's job performance. She told the court she had taken the trip but was never paid, and now demanded $8,000 in expenses and salary. The captain had access to a purse of more than $5 million available for "espionage activity," she went on, and employed many agents for this purpose. Wiedemann had also allegedly bragged to her about working closely with Henry Ford and Charles Lindbergh, and talked about stockpiling ammunition in New Jersey for future use by the Bund. It was all explosive, if implausible, testimony. Wiedemann admitted to knowing Crockett "slightly" but called her allegations "bunk." A spokesman for Ford dismissed it as a "publicity stunt."[57] The case was soon thrown out by the judge, who noted that Crockett was admitting to espionage if her claims were true. Any contract between her and Wiedemann was therefore "tainted with illegality."[58]

Wiedemann's strange charade came to an abrupt end in June 1941. Tired of the obvious espionage being carried out his nose, Roosevelt ordered all German consulates in the United States closed, and all consul generals expelled. Wiedemann had until July 10 to leave the country. He hastily burned many of the consulate's papers and left for Berlin. Before he left, however, the future head of OSS, "Wild Bill" Donovan, asked President Roosevelt whether it might be desirable to try to cultivate Wiedemann as an American agent if he had indeed changed his views toward Hitler. After further discussion it was decided that nothing should be done on the matter.[59] The chance to bring Wiedemann over to the Allied side was lost a second time. From Berlin, Wiedemann was sent to Argentina, Brazil, and Japan. He ended up as consul general in Tientsin, China, where he sat out the war at the center of the German regional intelligence network.[60]

While Wiedemann had been busy intriguing against his former associates in Berlin, Hitler's American friends continued to their own schemes on behalf of the Führer. In the summer of 1941, FBI director Hoover made a stunning announcement. For more than a year, he reported, an FBI double agent had infiltrated a major German spy ring on the East Coast. The agent, William Sebold, had been born in Germany and moved to the United States in 1921. For the next decade he worked in a variety of manufacturing facilities connected with the defense industry. During a visit to his German mother in 1939, he was approached by the Gestapo and prevented from returning home until he agreed to become a German agent. If he refused, the Gestapo warned him, nothing good would happen to his family members in the Reich. Sebold agreed, but managed to tip off the American consulate about the plan. After attending espionage training in Germany, Sebold sailed for the United States under the alias Harry Sawyer. He arrived in New York and made contact with a network of German spies being run by Frederick Duquesne, a South African who had worked as a German saboteur during World War I.[61]

As it turned out, Duquesne had assembled an impressive operation. His network of more than thirty agents, at least one of whom was a former Bund member, provided information about defense technology, ship movements, and cargo leaving New York docks. This intelligence was transmitted to Germany via shortwave radio. Most of the spies were immigrants from Germany and naturalized American citizens. The most impressive feat was the theft of the sophisticated Norden bombsight by Herman W. Lang, an employee of the manufacturer who copied secret blueprints and passed them on to his handler for smuggling to the Reich. He later traveled to Germany himself and helped reconstruct the device for the Luftwaffe before returning to his job as if nothing had happened. It was a remarkable intelligence feat that demonstrated huge blind spots in American counterintelligence, but it proved to be of limited short-term utility to the Germans. The sight allowed bombs to be dropped with much greater precision than before but, ironically, Lang's subterfuge turned it over too late to be of use to the Luftwaffe during the bombing campaign of the Battle of Britain.[62] No doubt Allied lives were lost because of its acquisition, but the impact of this intelligence coup was relatively limited in the short term.

From the day of Sebold's early 1940 arrival in New York, the FBI had Duquesne right where they wanted him. FBI agents set up Sebold in an office that was completely bugged and allowed them to see every meeting he attended with the spies. In May, the FBI built a shortwave radio station in Long Island according to instructions Sebold received from Germany. Agents quickly established shortwave radio contact with the German radio station on the other side and began feeding disinformation directly to the Reich.[63] Sebold also passed much of the information he received from Duquesne to the FBI before it was transmitted to Germany so the most sensitive aspects could be removed. With the Duquesne network essentially at his mercy, Hoover simply bided his time and waited to discover the extent of its tentacles. In late June, the FBI moved in. Agents arrested thirty-three spies from his network and a less effective ring based in the Bronx. In the ensuing espionage trial, nineteen agents pleaded guilty and the remaining fourteen were convicted a few days after Pearl Harbor. Duquesne and Lang both received eighteen years in prison.[64] It was a major disaster for the Abwehr. Foreign Minister Joachim von Ribbentrop darkly warned Admiral Canaris that he would be held personally responsible if the United States entered the war because of the fiasco.[65]

The FBI quickly announced another major coup. In March 1941, a German intelligence captain named Ulrich von der Osten had been hit by a cab in Times Square. He died in the hospital the next day. Von der Osten was using the assumed identity of "Julio Lopez Lido" and had arrived in the country on a Spanish passport to make contact with Kurt Friedrich Ludwig, an American-born German spy who was passing on information about American convoys heading for Europe. Ludwig was walking with "Lido" when he was struck by the car, and foolishly aroused suspicion by picking up the injured man's briefcase, which was full of intelligence material, and shouting something about "the Jews" as he fled the scene.[66] This strange behavior was followed by a series of cryptic phone calls to the hotel where "Lido" had been staying, asking whether his luggage could be collected. The hotel called the police, who in turn called the FBI. Further detective work led to Ludwig, who fled New York for the West Coast after the breakup of the Duquesne ring. The FBI picked him up in Washington State and quickly rounded up his accomplices.[67] Ludwig received twenty years behind bars. His "pretty blonde" seventeen-year-old secretary, Lucy Boehmler, was brought to trial for her own role in the plot, which included touring army bases and passing along information for a reward of $25 a week (about $400 in 2018).[68] Her other duties involved riding around in a car with Ludwig and enticing hitchhiking soldiers to get in so he could question them "about Army posts, equipment, training, for the benefit of his own bosses in Germany."[69] She told the court she knew what Ludwig was up to and "found espionage lots of fun." Her testimony helped convict the rest of the spy ring, but she still received five years behind bars.[70]

This heavy pressure from the FBI was pushing the German spy network to its breaking point. With its consulates shut and diplomats like Wiedemann no longer in the country, it was difficult to conduct large-scale operations or pay off agents. Hitler was outraged when Admiral Canaris informed him that there were no longer functional intelligence networks in the United States following the FBI roundups. Ranting and raving at the Abwehr chief and the head of its sabotage division, Erwin Von Lahousen de Vivremont, Hitler demanded dramatic action.

Canaris and Lahousen had one more card to play against the United States, and it integrally involved the Führer's American friends. Operation Pastorius, as it was code-named, was an outrageous scheme to take the war directly to the United States through a series of violent terrorist attacks on dams, power stations, manufacturing facilities, train stations, and bridges. Agents would arrive on U-boats and land on the American coastline armed with explosives. After melting into American society, they would scout their targets and eventually blow them up in a way that would maximize disruption and casualties. It was a bold and bloody plot. Planning began in late 1941 and was run on the German side by Werner Kappe, a German-American former newspaper reporter and a onetime Bund member. Kappe recruited ten fellow German Americans to take part in the scheme, at least one of whom had also been in the Bund. Some were naturalized American citizens, and had spent significant time in the United States. Several had been convinced to return to Germany by the Foreign Organization that Wiedemann once helped run.[71]

Kappe eventually reduced the team to eight conspirators who would operate in two teams. They would be delivered to American shores by U-boat, deposited on beaches with their explosives, and later make their way to the appointed targets. One of the two team leaders was George John Dasch, a former New York City cook who had decided to return to Germany at the outbreak of war. He would later claim to have been anti-Nazi and opposed to the Bund during his time in America.[72] The saboteurs attended a training school in Brandenburg, near Berlin, where they learned about explosives, fuses, timing devices, and basic methods to conceal their identities. In the event of the mission's failure, the agents were given German marine uniforms so they would be treated as prisoners of war rather than spies. If they could manage to escape they were told to head for Argentina or Chile.[73] All these instructions would turn out to be unnecessary.

The eight men were given false names and identity papers. To enhance their credibility, their civilian clothing had been made in America and had labels indicating such. The Abwehr provided nearly $200,000 in cash ($3.2 million in 2018) for expenses (oddly, much of the money could not be used because the bills were an older out-of-circulation version of the currency, while others had a red Japanese marking on them, indicating how the Abwehr had obtained them).[74] Explosives were packaged in chests for easy delivery on the American shoreline. In late May, Dasch's team boarded *U-202* and headed for New Jersey. They were rowed to shore by sailors from the U-boat and landed on the night of June 12–13, 1942. Things immediately went wrong from there. On the beach, the four men encountered a young Coast Guardsman who began asking questions about why they were there in the middle of the night. Thinking quickly, Dasch told him they were lost fishermen and offered him $260 in cash to leave. The Coast Guardsman took the money, but immediately told his compatriots the strange story when he got back to his station. Meanwhile, the German sailors had slipped back to their U-boat without taking away the German marine uniforms and other incriminating items. Fearing detection, the saboteurs buried their chests of explosives and other items for later retrieval and slunk into the night. They caught a train to New York a few hours later and split into two teams from there.[75] A few hours later, the Coast Guardsman led his colleagues to the spot of his strange encounter. They soon discovered where the chests of explosives were buried, along with the German uniforms. Their next call was to the FBI. Agents knew they had a serious case on their hands, and a large-scale manhunt began.[76]

By this point, Dasch was sweating bullets in New York. His partner there was a former Nazi storm trooper named Ernest Peter Burger—a one-time Michigan National Guardsman before moving back to Germany—who was also skeptical about the plot's chances for success. Coming clean with the FBI was their best chance of survival, Dasch calculated. He told Burger to stay put and called the New York FBI office to turn himself in as a German saboteur. He was laughed off the line by the agent who answered the phone. Hours later, the bureau became aware of the explosives discovered on the beach alongside German uniforms and realized that perhaps the caller had not been a jokester after all. Meanwhile, events elsewhere were moving quickly. On June 17, the second team of saboteurs landed in Florida from *U-107* and, unlike Dasch's group, successfully buried their explosives and proceeded to melt into the civilian population.

Knowing he was running out of time, Dasch headed to Washington and took a room in the famous Mayflower Hotel. On June 19, he called FBI headquarters again and asked to speak directly to J. Edgar Hoover. He was not put through to the director, but convinced the FBI to send agents to his hotel room.[77] He was then taken to FBI headquarters, where he eventually met Hoover in person as he told his story. Dasch eventually produced more than $80,000 in cash from a suitcase in his hotel closet, convincing any remaining skeptics in the bureau that he was telling the truth. Over the next few days Dasch cooperated with the FBI. Within days, his entire sabotage team was in custody.[78] The Florida team was picked up after Dasch managed to identify the conspirators from his recollections about them from training, linked to records about their pasts in the FBI archives.[79] Dasch understandably expected to be rewarded for his help, but instead the FBI arrested him too. It later emerged that FBI agents insinuated that he would eventually be given a presidential pardon in exchange for ongoing cooperation and for pleading guilty to the ensuing charges.[80]

Hitler's final scheme using his American friends had been foiled without a single explosion or drop of American blood being shed. The Führer was incensed when he learned of the arrests, weeping and ranting about the loss of such fine young Nazis. "Next time," he told Admiral Canaris and Lahousen, "you can send Jews and criminals."[81] As everyone realized, the fate of the captured saboteurs would be grim. Roosevelt and Hoover, eager to dissuade the Germans from undertaking similar plots, threw the book at the captured agents. They also threw an unexpected one. Rather than try the conspirators in a normal courtroom, Roosevelt appointed a military tribunal on the grounds that the saboteurs had violated the rules of war. This was a highly unusual legal step that had not been used since the trial of the conspirators involved in Abraham Lincoln's assassination. Four of them, including a woman, had been hanged as a result.[82]

The Nazi saboteurs now faced a courtroom of military officers and were given military rather than civilian legal counsel. The only defense offered was that the men had supposedly only joined the plot as a way to get out of Germany and back to the United States. No one was convinced. All eight men were convicted and sentenced to death. The appeals process proceeded rapidly and, in late July, the US Supreme Court took up the case, called *Ex parte Quirin* after one of the defendants' last names. On July 31, 1942, just a month and a half after the saboteurs landed on American shores, the court ruled that the military tribunal had possessed the legal authority to try the men because they were non-uniformed "enemy combatants" and offenders of the laws of war.[83] The death sentence was upheld. Days later, all but Dasch and Burger went to the electric chair and were buried in unmarked graves.[84] The surviving plotters were informed that the president had reduced their sentences on the grounds that Dasch had helped the FBI unravel the plot and Burger had not stood in his way. Dasch would now face thirty years in prison and Burger a life sentence.[85] Hitler's last plot involving his American friends had come to an end.

Throughout the 1930s and early years of the war, Hitler's supporters in the United States passed a huge number of secrets to their handlers in the Third Reich. While many of the technical secrets probably had little impact on the war itself, lives were undoubtedly lost because they had been revealed. An unknown but assuredly substantial number of Allied sailors went to their graves thanks to the information that slipped from American ports and ended up with U-boat commanders in the Atlantic. The famous American propaganda poster reading "Loose lips might sink ships" was hardly exaggerating. Hitler's spies were motivated in their dastardly work by a variety of factors. Some felt an affinity for the fatherland and were undoubtedly radicalized by their past association with the Bund and other groups. It was no accident that at least one spy network was more or less based in the Bund and run by one of its leaders. Some who had immigrated to the United States had retained their loyalty to Germany. Others were motivated by money and some, like the teenaged Lucy Boehmler, were probably just bored and excited by the opportunity to do something seemingly glamorous. Regardless of their motivations, the damage they did to the war effort will never be fully known.

Yet it could have been far worse. Hitler's spy network was severely hindered in its mission by the diligence of local law enforcement and the FBI. Once Hoover became fully aware of the danger, his G-men did extraordinary work breaking up the Nazi intelligence network. Several times they simply got lucky, as when von der Osten was mowed down by a cab in the middle of New York, but this does not detract from the agency's overall accomplishments. There was another factor at play as well: Fritz Wiedemann's own position as a reluctant spy living in forced exile likely reduced the effectiveness of the Nazi network on the West Coast, where it might have been able to do significant damage by coordinating with the Japanese. Instead of serving the fatherland, the captain seemed to have been more concerned about trying to arrange his safe passage into an Allied country. With the United States not yet in the war he could not expect this treatment from Roosevelt, and therefore the only option was the British embassy. Ironically, his overtures were rebuffed, missing an opportunity to gain major insights into the inner workings of the Third Reich and the Abwehr's network. He and Princess Stephanie Hohenlohe serve as fascinating illustrations of the complexity of the period. While the FBI and the American press believed they were intended to become Hitler's key American friends, in fact they appear to have conspired against the Führer as much if not more than they conspired against the United States. As with many of Hitler's other spies, their full stories remain opaque even decades later.

The legacy of Hitler's spy network was grim. Pain, suffering, and death were visited upon both the spies themselves and their victims. The outrageous sabotage plot of 1942 compelled Roosevelt to make an example of the captured agents and push the boundaries of the law to make sure they were executed swiftly. It worked, and the Nazis never again attempted such a violent and brutal terrorist plot. Hitler's American friends had finally been shut down completely, but the consequences of their actions would persist far beyond the end of the war.

AFTERWORD

One of the most remarkable facets of post–World War II American life was the sheer number of people with something they wanted to hide. The Pearl Harbor attack of December 7, 1941, changed the country's political scene overnight, ending the debate over isolationism versus intervention for good. America was now at war, and even those who had opposed its entry rallied around the flag. Hitler's American friends slunk into the darkness or had to face the music for their past actions. As will be seen, some had no choice in the matter. Others managed to successfully disappear from postwar history and, presumably, lived out their lives in some form of blissful obscurity.

After 1945, many Americans tried to simply forget the recent past's more troubling aspects. With postwar economic prosperity, the baby boom, and the "American dream" arriving for many white, middle-class Americans, the late 1940s and early 1950s were seen as a time to focus on family and the future. Occasionally the veil of the past was lifted and the scarred face of the 1930s would briefly be revealed for public scrutiny once more. This could carry major consequences. The most prominent example was during the Red Scare of the early 1950s, when suddenly the clubs and associations one had belonged to, and the company one had kept, were under intense public scrutiny and could destroy present-day livelihood. Following the example of Representative Martin Dies Jr., Senator Joseph McCarthy was obsessed with tracking down communists wherever they could be found, instilling fear among those who had once cavorted with the left. But what if McCarthy's interest had been hunting former Nazi sympathizers rather than communist fellow travelers and party members? What if the former members of America First and the German American Bund had faced the same consequences and social approbation that former communists and socialists encountered?

These are unanswerable questions, but they highlight the fact that millions of Americans supported causes and groups before the war that would have, at a minimum, not reflected well on them later. For much of the twentieth century—and even the early twenty-first—average Americans were unwittingly next-door neighbors with former German American Bund members, America Firsters, and Silver Legion fanatics. American students who studied and traveled in the Third Reich returned home to raise families and pursue successful careers. How many of them ever discussed their experiences in any depth will never be known, but it likely depended on how far their Nazi sympathies had led them. The US National Archives contains an unknown but assuredly huge number of FBI files opened on Hitler's American friends before and during the war. Many of them remain classified and can only become available after a lengthy Freedom of Information Act review. We may realistically never know how many Americans were suspected of being Nazi sympathizers or made contributions to pro-German cause. What it known, however, is that only the most prominent of Hitler's friends faced legal sanctions for their activities. The rest, presumably, tried to simply keep their heads down and move on with life.

The German American Bund always maintained that it was a patriotic, cultural heritage organization, but the truth about its ideological orientation was not hard to uncover. It had always been essentially a one-man show built around the dynamic Fritz Kuhn and his flair for the dramatic. With Kuhn sitting in prison and the government keeping a close eye on its activities, the Bund quickly withered. His successors did little to save the organization he had built. Notorious West Coast leader Herman Schwinn was forcibly de-naturalized in November 1940, and Kuhn's national successor, Gerhard Kunze, resigned as Bund leader in 1941. As seen, he then fled to Mexico with the help of contacts in the Abwehr. He was eventually sent back to the United States where he was convicted of a range of offenses and ended up spending more than a decade behind bars.[1] His successor as Bund leader, George Froboese, committed suicide on the railroad tracks in 1942 rather than face a grand jury subpoena.[2]

Kuhn himself remained in prison and, in 1943, had his naturalization revoked on the grounds that he had maintained allegiance to a foreign power in violation of his oath to the United States. After the war, he was deported to

Germany and returned to Munich, initially as a free man. A year later he was arrested for questioning as a potential war criminal and held in the Dachau concentration camp. Dramatically, he managed to escape from the camp and went on the run. He was eventually recaptured and imprisoned until 1950. He died in late 1951.[3] Even this fate was less grim than that of his predecessor in Friends of the New Germany. Heinz Spanknöbel had fled to Germany in the early 1930s to avoid potential prosecution in the United States and returned to a life of obscurity. During the war he ended up in the German army, was captured by the Soviets, and died of starvation in 1947.[4] There were no happy endings for Hitler's most prominent American friends.

The man who had done so much to crack open the Bund's inner workings for both the government and the American public, John C. Metcalfe, returned to his career in journalism. During the war he worked as a diplomatic correspondent for *Time* and other publications. In 1948, he founded a lecture bureau and represented prominent political clients including Truman administration vice president Alben W. Barkley. In the late 1960s he returned to government service as part of the State Department's Agency for International Development. He died in 1971.[5]

While the Bund never achieved the widespread popularity for which its leaders hoped and critics feared, German Americans nationwide did demonstrably become increasingly disenfranchised from the Roosevelt administration. In the election of 1940, which Roosevelt won handily, there were only twenty counties where he lost by more than 35 percent of the vote. Nineteen of those twenty were majority German-speaking, indicating a large percentage of recent immigrants or those who closely guarded their cultural heritage. Dozens of other heavily anti-Roosevelt counties also reported high numbers of German-origin residents. Four years later, entire midwestern states with high German populations, including Kansas and Iowa, flipped to vote Republican.[6] While the vast majority of German Americans did not join the Bund and were demonstrably loyal to the United States, they were also not fans of their adopted country entering a second war against the fatherland.

As it turned out, Metcalfe was not the only journalist who had gone undercover among Hitler's American friends. In 1943, Armenian-American author Arthur Derounian published a sensational book entitled *Under Cover* under the pen name John Roy Carlson.[7] In 1939, Derounian infiltrated the New York City Bund and went on from there to join groups associated with Father Coughlin and other, lesser-known extremist organizations. His first-person account of conversations with far-right plotters hoping to eventually overthrow the US government were shocking to many and immediately made his book a best seller. Carlson showed no reluctance in naming the leaders of Hitler's American friends, subjecting them to public attention and ridicule. Notably, he reserved special ire for the isolationist senators and representatives who became involved in America First. Among the most upset was Senator Burton K. Wheeler, who inserted attacks on the book and its author into the *Congressional Record* and called for an investigation.[8] His outrage would have little effect. The book was heavily touted by anti-Nazi columnist and radio commentator Walter Winchell, who encouraged his listeners to pick up a copy.[9] As will be seen, *Under Cover* was not the last exposé published about Hitler's American friends, but it did much to make the public aware of the danger posed by groups many had never heard of previously. Wheeler's fears about the book's potential political impact would also prove well-founded.

Through publications like *Under Cover*, the extent of Hitler's American network was gradually revealed to the public after Pearl Harbor. Yet by that time the most effective German plot had already been shut down with significant help from the British. George Sylvester Viereck's successful propaganda and intelligence operation on Capitol Hill was the most direct assault on the US government by German agents, and while he had never been able to use his network to the maximum extent that might have been possible, it was still a serious threat to national security. Viereck himself had been arrested in October 1941, putting his operation out of business. He was convicted in March 1942 of failing to reveal the full extent of his activities as a foreign agent. The witnesses presenting evidence against him included one of the British censorship examiners who had helped intercept his letters to Germany.[10] George Hill, the aide who had given him access to the congressional franking service, had already been convicted of perjury and testified against Viereck as well.[11]

This was not the end of Viereck's legal battles, however. He appealed his sentence, and the case eventually ended up in the US Supreme Court. Viereck's attorneys argued that because the Foreign Agents Registration Act had been passed when he was already working as a German agent, it could not by applied to activities undertaken before the law was passed. The Supreme Court agreed, and Viereck's conviction was overturned in March 1943.[12] This itself proved to be only the prelude to a bigger legal fight. In December 1942, a federal grand jury indicted Viereck and more than two dozen other Americans with sedition and violations of the Espionage Act of 1917. The resulting Sedition Trial, as it became known, ensnared nearly all the big names of 1930s anti-Semitism. Gerald B. Winrod was among the first to be indicted, along with fascist intellectual Lawrence Dennis, Silver Legion "Chief" William Dudley Pelley, Paul Reveres founder and red-baiter Elizabeth Dilling, Bund leaders Gerhard Wilhelm Kunze and Herman Max Schwinn, and a host of lesser names. Notably, Father Charles E. Coughlin was not indicted.[13] The federal prosecutor in charge of the case was O. John Rogge, the Justice Department rising star who had been brought in to investigate Coughlin's Christian Front in Brooklyn.

The legal basis of the trial was questionable from the start. Rogge recounted later that his primary concern was the case's potential First Amendment implications. "Did not this amendment protect all manner of advocacy, even that which was part of a conspiracy to cause a violation of the law?" he reflected.[14] It was a good question. Making anti-Semitic statements was not against the law, and the Espionage Act required proof of an actual plot to be applicable.[15] A more applicable piece of legislation, called the Smith Act, had been passed in 1940 to combat subversion by communists and had a lower evidentiary standard. This was the path Rogge chose, arguing that the defendants intended to harm the morale of the US military because they had "unlawfully, willfully, feloniously and knowingly conspired with officials of the Government of the German Reich and leaders and members of the said Nazi Party".[16]

To prove this case, however, Rogge would have to show that the defendants were all part of the *same* conspiracy, even if they did not know one another directly or coordinate their actions. There was, of course, no evidence to support either of these claims. As critics of the trial wrote afterward, Rogge was left to argue that "the defendants were like the Nazis because both were anti-Semitic, hence the defendants were part of a Nazi world movement to cause insubordination in the armed forces."[17] This was outlandish at best. No one was arguing that the defendants were upstanding citizens, but there was no evidence to support the idea that they were all part of an actual conspiracy to undermine military morale. There was also a distinct political risk in all this. Viereck's operation had included some of Washington's most powerful politicians, and the evidence against him would inevitably lead to their names being revealed in court. This was considered to be such a sensitive matter that British Security Coordination declined to make its evidence available to the court and refused to let its personnel testify at the trial, "because it would be likely to implicate a number of distinguished Congressmen and national figures."[18]

The Sedition Trial finally began in April 1944. The judge was former congressman Edward C. Eicher, a Roosevelt ally and a liberal. Rogge was left to prove an almost impossible case. There was no question that the defendants had made anti-Semitic and pro-Nazi statements. Many of them were even willing to repeat those statements in court. The problem was that it was not illegal to hold and express those views, especially before the United States entered the war. To overcome this, the prosecution presented the theory that the accused seditionists had all echoed the same themes as Nazi propaganda. Using the work of propaganda expert Harold Lasswell, fourteen common Nazi propaganda themes were identified. The central ones were anti-Semitism and anti-communism. The prosecution then compared the writings and statements of the defendants to Lasswell's fourteen themes to argue that they were all part of a pro-Nazi conspiracy even if they weren't aware of it.[19] This was outlandish and held very little legal weight. The trial itself became a circus as the defendants openly mocked the court. Some wore signs to court reading "I am a Spy" to annoy prosecutors and the judge. The entire process was quickly descending into farce.[20] Yet the Roosevelt administration was convinced the alleged seditionists must be punished, and so it continued. More than eighteen thousand pages of testimony were generated and dozens of witnesses were called.[21]

On November 29, 1944, a former employee of Gerald B. Winrod took the stand to testify against the Kansas evangelist. As he spoke, Winrod claimed to have a prophetic vision:

> *While the young man was testifying, I glanced once in the direction of the Judge. . . . Suddenly, a heavy black shadow, like a thick cloud, a dark veil, covered his face. It seemed to drop down and envelop him. The hand of death was evidently upon him at that moment.*[22]

Winrod's "prophesy" was correct. Later that night, Judge Eicher died of a heart attack in his sleep. The government's case was now in serious trouble. The defendants themselves had to be asked whether they were willing to continue under a new presiding judge. Nearly all refused to go on. A week after Eicher's death, there was no choice but to declare a mistrial. It was an ignominious end to a quixotic legal effort. As the *Chicago Daily Tribune* put it bluntly, "Thus ended . . . the pending effort of the department of justice to prove that the defendants, including a collection of obscure anti-war, anti-semitic [*sic*], and anti-communist propagandists, all opponents of the Roosevelt administration, had conspired to undermine the loyalty and morale of the army and navy and set up a Nazi form of government in United States."[23] Various attempts to revive the case went nowhere, but it would take until 1947 for the government to formally abandon the case for good.

The accused seditionists felt vindicated. Fascist intellectual Lawrence Dennis coauthored a massive account of the case attacking the prosecution's case in excruciating detail. It was published in 1946.[24] Despite being legally off the hook, however, Dennis's best days were already behind him. He never fully disavowed his views on fascism, though in the 1950s he opposed the red-baiting of McCarthyism and the arms buildup of the Cold War on isolationist grounds.[25] After the war he published a new political newsletter that had some powerful subscribers in Washington, but his past associations with fascism made him politically untouchable to nearly all mainstream politicians. In 1964 he became vaguely involved in Barry Goldwater's ill-fated presidential campaign, but the connection went nowhere. He died in 1977, never publicly embracing his African American heritage and unable to overcome the perception that he was an unrepentant Nazi sympathizer.[26]

William Dudley Pelley, the colorful leader of the Silver Legion, had the most successful—and strange—postwar career of the accused seditionists. Despite the 1944 mistrial, the Chief still had a substantial sentence to serve for his other convictions. He remained in prison until 1950, continuing to write and becoming a figure of sympathy for the far right. A "Justice for Pelley Committee" argued that the Chief was the victim of a communist conspiracy and called for his release. After finally getting out of prison, Pelley remained on parole until 1957 and resumed his career as a spiritualist. He again issued prophesies related to world events and published two dozen books laying out a new spiritual system he called "Soulcraft." This was essentially a revised version of his previous mystical teachings, with added complexity that made the overall philosophy almost incomprehensible to all but the most dedicated students. He also became interested in UFOs and alleged alien abductions.

Toward the end of his life, Pelley claimed to have used his spiritualist techniques to contact the spirit of sixteenth-century French prognosticator Michel Nostradamus during a séance. Nostradamus then supposedly put Pelley in touch with the souls of famous historical figures including George Washington and Mark Twain. Accounts of these "conversations" were published in a new Soulcraft journal, and devotees were even offered the chance to buy audiotapes of the alleged discussions. It was a strange end to the even stranger career of a man who once saw himself as the American Hitler and convinced thousands of armed followers he was right. The Chief died in 1965. Soulcraft survived his death, and Pelley's writings on extraterrestrials have been integrated into aspects of the ufology movement. His anti-Semitic writings are periodically cited on far-right websites to the present day.[27]

For his part, Gerald B. Winrod went back to Kansas to resume his career as a firebrand preacher. He quickly found, however, that "practically of Winrod's friends had forsaken him," as a sympathetic biographer put it. The sedition controversy left him with only a small but dedicated following.[28] He now adopted a new and bizarre personal crusade. Winrod somehow became aware of Harry Hoxsey, a former insurance salesman who claimed to have discovered an herbal "cure" for cancer. Hoxsey had been marketing the "Hoxsey Therapy" for years and had naturally attracted the scrutiny and criticism of both the government and the mainstream medical profession. For reasons that remain opaque, Winrod now adopted alternative cancer treatments as his new cause and began touting a range of nontraditional remedies. To further the effort, he established a group called the Christian Medical Research League and began raising money to battle the mainstream medical establishment. The Food and Drug Administration was not amused, nor was the American Medical Association. The operation soon went bust. His biographer offers no explanation for the bizarre episode other than Winrod's "deep-seated empathy for every underdog in the world" and burning distrust of the government.[29]

By 1948 Winrod was physically ailing but, in line with his personal views, refused to seek medical treatment. Instead he relied on one of the alternative remedies he had been pushing to the public. It would be of little help. As it turned out, Winrod was suffering from multiple sclerosis. He concealed the illness from all but his closest friends and refused any semblance of medical care until the bitter end. He died in 1957. Remarkably, the organization he had founded decades before to battle the forces of modernism and the theory of evolution, Defenders of the Christian Faith, survives to the present day and has no association with the questionable views of its founder.[30]

Similarly, Father Charles E. Coughlin's reputation never recovered from his flirtation with Nazism. Silenced by his church superiors in 1942, he remained on the government's radar for years. In late 1941 the FBI received a tip that Coughlin was in communication with far-right groups seeking to overthrow the Mexican government with the help of Nazi agents. Naval Intelligence and the FBI investigated the troubling claims. Agents were soon visiting the Shrine of the Little Flower and listening in on his sermons to find out whether he was making subversive statements. Meanwhile, Christian Front groups continued to cause trouble across the country. Nothing concrete was ever found linking Coughlin to the Mexican plot or the remaining Christian Front, but both journalists and government investigators kept digging into Coughlin's affairs for years in the hope of finding a smoking gun linking him to money from the German embassy or other malfeasance.[31]

Even if there was no smoking gun to be found, the reality was that Coughlin had become rich through his rabble-rousing. In 1942, government investigators discovered a British bank account linked to Coughlin that contained a substantial $900,000 (about $14 million today). After the war, Coughlin became involved in real estate speculation and bought homes in Arizona and Florida.[32] He also purchased a house in Michigan near the home of Governor George Romney.[33] As his obituary in the *Detroit Free Press* drily noted, "Since he was not a member of a religious order, Father Coughlin was not bound by the vow of poverty."[34]

For all his wealth, however, Coughlin's political days were long behind him. He remained silent on the major issues of the day, building his personal fortune and ostensibly living the life of a parish priest. He was pushed into retirement by his church superiors in 1966 and began publishing tracts attacking the liberalizing reforms of the Second Ecumenical Council of the Vatican (Vatican II). Toward the end of his life he told an interviewer that he stood by his writings in *Social Justice* and still believed the United States should have stayed out of World War II. "If we had stayed out of the war we could have conquered the conqueror in Europe," he said. The war, he went on, was "the greatest faux pas in the whole history of civilization, from the days of Adam and Eve down to the present."[35]

Coughlin died in October 1979 at the age of eighty-eight. His obituary was carried on the front page of the *Detroit Free Press*, indicating his enduring local fame. The church he built, the Shrine of the Little Flower, stands to the present day in Royal Oak, Michigan. A writer in the 1970s found the basement where his staff processed incoming donations had been converted into a nursery school. The imposing tower of the church, from which the priest made most of his broadcasts, had fallen into disarray, and his former office was covered with pigeon droppings and feathers.[36] It was a physical metaphor for his career: The edifice Coughlin built through his demagoguery still stood, but its interior was rotten.

Gerald L. K. Smith was more vocal than Winrod or Coughlin in his continuing devotion to the extremist cause. During the Sedition Trial he raised money to support the defendants. His biographer has suggested this was part of a ploy to attract their followers for himself in the postwar world.[37] After the war, Smith became a Holocaust denier and claimed Hitler's memory was being defamed by the "Jewish press." He continued to rabble-rouse across the country, opposing the United Nations and maintaining his economic populism. The FBI kept close tabs on him throughout.[38] Unsurprisingly, he became a supporter of Senator Joseph McCarthy's red-baiting in the 1950s and supported segregation in the South, even attempting to run for president on the breakaway Dixiecrat ticket in 1948. Senator Strom Thurmond torpedoed his chances with the Dixiecrats by securing the nomination himself. Smith subsequently ran as the Christian Nationalist Party's nominee but the campaign was a miserable failure.[39] Smith ended up as an embittered and reluctant supporter of President Richard Nixon, despite the fact that Nixon had denounced Smith and his band of supporters as extremists in the past. He died in 1976, a prejudiced relic of an earlier time.[40] Despite his undeniable oratorical gifts and the political skills he had honed with Huey Long, Smith's career ultimately came to nothing. He was consumed by hatred and racism. After the war he was little more than a throwback to an earlier time, who maintained a following by appealing to the darkest instincts and traditions in American society. In the end, a biographer has written, "his true legacy is bigotry."[41]

Hitler's most important agent in the United States, George Sylvester Viereck, was similarly ruined. During the postwar Nuremberg Trials the US government gained huge amounts of information about the extent of his operations. He was eventually released from prison in 1947, following the final collapse of the Sedition Trial, and attempted to revive his career as a novelist and poet. Nothing landed well in the market until he published his memoirs, entitled *Men Into Beasts*, in 1952. The book became notorious for its portrayal of male rape Viereck had witnessed in prison, and eventually sold about half a million copies.[42] Viereck died in 1962, never able to escape his reputation as a dangerous Nazi sympathizer.[43]

Viereck's main ally at the German embassy had been First Secretary Heribert von Strempel. In December 1941, Strempel accompanied German Chargé d'Affaires Hans Thomsen to personally deliver the Third Reich's declaration of war to Franklin Roosevelt. Strempel's work as a diplomat was temporarily finished with the declaration of war, and he sat in Washington until arrangements could be made to return him in a formal diplomatic exchange. From there, he returned to the Lisbon branch of the Foreign Ministry press department. After the war, he was quickly declared denazified and took a job with the newspaper *Die Zeit*.[44]

This would have been the end of Strempel's story, except for the existence of recently declassified CIA files. As it turns out, the agency recruited Strempel in November 1947 to act as a spy against the Soviets. Strempel, whose CIA code name was Hiawatha, was recruited as part of an operation called Alcatraz that was designed to obtain economic and political data about organizations in the Soviet sector. Strempel was chosen because "subject is strongly inclined toward the Anglo-Saxon powers" and "has innumerable good friends in the US, he still has considerable property which, although blocked now, he hopes to see again some day."[45] Strempel's job as a journalist also meant that he required no cover or backstory.[46] However, it appears that while Strempel was successfully recruited he was never actually used as an agent, and was quietly dismissed of in 1948 when his handler returned to America. The exact reason is unclear, though his agent record states he was "Too marginal a case—never used."[47] It appears he was in touch with the CIA again in 1966, but the available files are again unclear why.[48] Whether the release of further information in the future will shed further light on Strempel's postwar career remains to be seen. No trace of him can be found in American newspapers after a few mentions in 1947. He appears to have died in West Germany in 1981.

Viereck and Strempel's connections in Congress were completely destroyed by a combination of the franking scandal and their outspoken isolationist views. Senator Ernest Lundeen was of course long dead, but his collaborators were still in office for the time being. In 1942, journalists Michael Sayers and Albert E. Kahn published a sensationalist exposé entitled *Sabotage! The Secret War Against America*. As with *Under Cover*, Walter Winchell praised the book, and it sold more than 150,000 copies in just three days.[49] Among other startling revelations, it demonstrated the extent of Viereck's Capitol Hill machinations and named twenty politicians who had their franks used in the scheme. "These members of Congress were the political heroes of the America First Committee," the book devastatingly concluded.[50] America First had now been directly linked to the work of a Nazi agent. The key player in the Viereck-Fish scheme, Congressman Hamilton Fish III, was narrowly reelected in 1942, but the damage only got worse from there. In 1944, direct mail advertising expert Henry Hoke penned a pamphlet entitled *Black Mail* that focused on Fish's involvement with Viereck. Images showing Fish speeches being directly quoted in Nazi propaganda newspapers added insult to injury.[51]

The political opportunity was now too great to pass up. Fish's opponent in the 1944 election flooded the district with thousands of copies of publications highlighting the Viereck affair. Fish was duly defeated, ending his twenty-five-year tenure in Congress. As the official history of British Security Coordination noted, he blamed "Reds and Communists" for the defeat, but "might—with more accuracy—have blamed BSC" for uncovering and revealing the Viereck plot.[52] Fish never ran for public office again and died at the age of 102 in 1991. He defended his isolationist views to the end, telling an audience at the age of 101, "I have always opposed war, and sometimes it has made trouble for me. . . . I often feel I am a voice in the wilderness. But what can one man do?"[53] A similar fate befell isolationist Republican senator Gerald P. Nye. Following extensive criticism of his foreign policy views and his vocal defense of Charles Lindbergh, Nye lost his seat in 1944. His political career was over, and he died in 1971.

The same was true of Senator Burton K. Wheeler. Outraged by his defiance of Roosevelt, links to Viereck, and the devastating portrayal of him as a pro-Nazi appeaser in *Under Cover*, the Montana Democratic Party ousted him in the 1946 primaries. The Republicans then picked up his seat handily in November. Wheeler was convinced that Jews and communists were responsible for the defeat. "Every day that goes by proves to me more conclusively than ever that Communists are using a lot of these Jewish people as pawns to stir up racial intolerance in this country," he told newspaper columnist and radio broadcaster George Sokolsky in 1944. "The amazing thing to me is that they would not have sense enough to realize that they were being used. You have to give the Communists credit—they know what they want and where they are going."[54] Wheeler's reputation never recovered and he died in 1975. Both he and Nye were remembered in their obituaries as leaders of the isolationist movement. "I think I was right then and I still do," Wheeler told a reporter two years before his death. "I said that if we got into war we'll make the world safe for the Communists and that's what we're doing."[55]

Hitler's friends in the business community would soon be looking for ways to escape the consequences of their own involvement with the Reich. The key player was, once again, O. John Rogge, the prosecutor in the unsuccessful Sedition Trial. As Rogge was preparing for a potential revival of the case in 1946, he suddenly received word from a US Army captain that there was dramatic evidence being uncovered in Germany about the network of Nazi sympathizers in North America. Realizing the possible implications, Rogge traveled to

Germany with a small staff and started investigating.[56] What he uncovered was shocking. Obtaining interviews with the most prominent Nazis still alive, including Hermann Göring, Rogge was able to put direct questions to the people who had personally plotted to undermine US politics. Poring over captured files from various government ministries, he determined that the Nazis had a far-reaching network of sympathizers, spies, and supporters in the United States who were far more dangerous than the defendants he was currently prosecuting.

The most insidious threat, he claimed, came from the "German and American industrialists" who had conspired to undermine the country. William Rhodes Davis was on the list, but it had many other names as well. Rogge produced an extensive report outlining these findings and citing huge amounts of evidence for submission to his boss, Attorney General Tom Clark.[57] The nation's chief law enforcement officer was shocked, but not for the reasons Rogge had hoped. Rather than insist on a far-reaching investigation, Clark was appalled that his friend Burton K. Wheeler was mentioned specifically in the draft document. Clark decreed that the report would remain secret, but Rogge convinced him that it should at least be completed. When it was done, Clark asked Rogge to redact the names of the prominent Americans included in its pages. Rogge refused, and an awkward standoff between the men resulted.[58]

The time-honored Washington tradition of leaking to the press now came into play. Within days of the report's completion, excerpts were mysteriously passed to political columnist Drew Pearson and published in his nationally syndicated column "Washington Merry-Go-Round." Rogge publicly confirmed the veracity of the text, but denied leaking it to Pearson. Within days, however, he began speaking out in public and revealed some of the report's further findings, mentioning Wheeler and others by name. Shortly after, he was approached by an FBI agent in an airport and handed an envelope. Inside was a letter from Clark firing him immediately. As it turned out, Wheeler was longtime friends with another former senator who had recently found new employment— President Harry Truman. Appalled by the appearance of Wheeler's name in the press, the president summoned Clark to the White House and ordered him to fire Rogge. The excuse given was that Rogge had quoted publicly from his own report, which was officially considered secret.[59]

Rogge would not be silenced so easily, however. To Clark's dismay, Rogge kept traveling the country and began writing articles to discuss his findings. He alleged publicly that the report was being withheld because "it names Americans who collaborated with the Nazis." The former assistant attorney general also explosively charged that the army had shut down the FBI's investigations into the Nazi espionage network, leading to the possibility that it might survive in the United States and fall into the wrong hands.[60] FBI agents closely monitored his public statements and investigated whether Rogge might have become a Soviet agent.[61] Nothing conclusive was ever found, though agents claimed to have found evidence of Rogge praising communist leaders.[62]

Regardless, Rogge went on to become a private practice attorney and wrote a book criticizing the FBI for violating the civil liberties of investigation targets. He later became involved in the ACLU and took on a range of First Amendment cases.[63] After much lobbying, Rogge was finally allowed in 1961 to publish his report on Nazi infiltration of the United States, long after many of the key players named in it were either dead or out of office. It was the first time the American public had heard anything close to the full story of what he had discovered about Hitler's American friends. "Where in the U.S. there was a Fritz Kuhn there is now a George Lincoln Rockwell [the head of the American Nazi Party]," a *Philadelphia Inquirer* reviewer reflected after reading Rogge's book. "And, unfortunately, the merchants of hate always seem to have someone to listen to them."[64] Rogge kept up the fight against political extremism until the end of his life. He died in 1981 and was remembered as the man who had helped bring down both Huey Long's political machine and Hitler's American friends.[65]

Despite Rogge's investigative activities, America's corporate leaders continued to reap the rewards of their German investments throughout the war and after. Coca-Cola's German division continued producing Fanta and amassing profits even as its trademark beverage became unavailable due to the British embargo. Coca-Cola's American wing cleverly positioned itself with the advancing US Army, providing a taste of home to weary soldiers. As the Reich began to collapse, the Nazi state targeted Coca-Cola GmbH as a subversive company that was harming morale by reminding war-weary Germans of happier times. Its chief, Max Keith, courageously refused to change the company name despite the threat of being sent to a concentration camp. At the end of the war, Keith wired corporate American headquarters to announce the company's survival. For his efforts, Keith was initially hailed as a hero by Coca-Cola but was soon sidelined as American managers took over his operation. He eventually managed to locate a large stock of Coke concentrate and reestablish his position in the company. Coca-Cola had successfully weathered the storm to remain the world's favorite soft drink. In the process, it had also invented a new soda—Fanta—that remains popular to the present day.[66]

Ford and General Motors also paid little price for their liaison with the Nazis. The Ford-Werke plant in Cologne continued operations and received its first batch of French prisoner-of-war laborers in 1940.[67] From there, the situation only got worse. In 1942, Ford produced 120,000 trucks for the German army in comparison to Opel/GM's 50,000.[68] In October 1944, the US Air Force attempted to bomb the Ford factory but hit the laborer barracks instead. By then the Allies were closing in on Cologne, and a general evacuation was soon ordered.[69] The factory itself would not be occupied until March 1945. Liberating American soldiers would find freezing slave laborers from the Soviet Union and elsewhere confined by barbed wire to the facility.[70]

The US government predictably began exploring the connections between the Ford family and their corporate interests in both Germany and occupied countries in Europe. In 1943, an investigation concluded that Ford's operations in France were being used "for the benefit of Germany," and that this had been approved by Henry Ford himself.[71] Despite the damning verdict, no action was taken by the US government. One reason was undoubtedly that Ford's leadership in the United States was undergoing abrupt transition. Edsel Ford, Henry Ford's son and heir apparent, died gruesomely of gastric cancer in May 1943 at the age of just forty-nine. Edsel's son Benson blamed his father's early death on the immense pressure placed on him by the family patriarch, reportedly proclaiming, "Grandfather is responsible for Father's sickness." Henry Ford's wife, Clara, seems to have agreed, and distanced herself from her husband for two months after Edsel's funeral.[72] The death created the potential for a dangerous power vacuum at the top of one of America's most powerful corporations. Two years after Edsel's death, the aged Henry Ford recommended his grandson, Henry Ford II, be given the role of company president at the age of twenty-eight. The younger Ford quickly denounced the anti-Semitism of his grandfather and reached out to the Jewish community to begin repairing the damage incurred in the 1930s.[73]

Henry Ford himself died in 1947 at the age of eighty-three, his name irrevocably sullied by his association with anti-Semitism and Hitler. Neither he nor his son would face the consequences of their flirtation with the Nazis and the material support they had provided the German war effort. In 1956, Henry Ford II took the extraordinary step of offering Ford stock in an initial public offering (IPO). This was a move his grandfather had always rejected because he feared that "Jew speculators" would get ahold of the company's shares. The Ford IPO was the largest issuance of stock in American history, and thousands of people stood in line for hours to buy shares. The biggest beneficiary was the charitable Ford Foundation, which made a sizable $640 million (around $6 billion today) from the IPO.[74]

One group that did not profit from Ford's postwar prosperity were the former forced laborers who had worked the Cologne plant's machines during the darkest days of the war. Starting in 1995, groups of former laborers began meeting, and visited the plant at the invitation of the mayor. In 1998 a former worker, Elsa Iwanowa, filed a class action lawsuit on behalf of her fellow forced laborers in New Jersey federal court.[75] Ford's lawyers argued that the court did not have jurisdiction over an international matter. At nearly the same time, German companies BMW and Siemens set up compensation programs for the victims of their own forced-labor activities during the war.[76] Both Ford and General Motors quickly joined a similar program and paid millions to compensate the victims of their forced-labor practices.[77] Iwanowa's suit, however, was dismissed on the grounds that the statute of limitations for court-ordered compensation had passed.[78] Ford remains one of the biggest automakers in Germany and Europe to the present day.

General Motors and Opel also fared well after the war, though many of their leaders did not. Former overseas president James D. Mooney never escaped the accusation of being a Nazi sympathizer. In 1947 he wrote a memoir recounting his rollicking experiences in the early days of the war, but was persuaded not to publish it by former colleagues who feared it would hurt GM's reputation.[79] He died in 1957 after pursuing a career as a management consultant. More dramatic controversy followed his former associate Graeme Howard. At the end of the war, Howard managed to get himself appointed as a colonel in the economics division investigating connections between German and American corporations. In April 1945, columnist Drew Pearson reported that Howard had once been in charge of GM's German operations and was now "busy as a hound dog around the State department wanting to get back to Germany," implying that his interests extended beyond military duty.[80]

Howard met his match with the arrival of James Stewart Martin, a Justice Department lawyer sent to join his investigation team. Martin was appalled that his superior officer had once enjoyed close connections with the Nazis and sent a copy of *America and the New World Order* to army headquarters. Howard was quietly dismissed by the army brass and sent home.[81] Martin eventually resigned his own position out of frustration at the obstruction he was encountering from American corporate interests who were eager to make profits in postwar Germany.[82] Among his most interesting coups was tracking down Gerhardt

Alois Westrick, the German lawyer Foreign Minister Joachim von Ribbentrop had sent to the United States to whip up business sentiment against the country entering the war. Westrick had stayed in Berlin to nearly the end of the war before fleeing to hide out in a castle. He was given a token jail sentence.[83]

Howard's career still had more twists in store, however. In 1948, he accepted the position of vice president and director of international operations at his old rival Ford, where he worked closely with Henry Ford II.[84] The appointment caused a brief controversy in Congress when Democratic representative George G. Sadowski of Michigan accused Howard of being "the man who 'fought most vigorously on behalf of German industrialists.'" His Republican colleague George A. Dondero, also from Michigan, leaped to Howard's defense and accused Sadowski of "slurring . . . one of America's foremost industrialists, a man of proven patriotism."[85] The war of words came to nothing, and Howard remained at Ford until his retirement in 1950. He died in 1962. Obituaries around the country highlighted his twenty-five years as a GM executive and his later work at Ford. *America and the New World Order* was nowhere to be found.[86]

General Motors itself ended up profiting modestly from its business interests in the Third Reich. US management lost touch with Opel around 1941, but its German leaders continued to cultivate connections with the Nazi regime. After losing control of the company, GM wrote off Opel as a tax loss in 1942.[87] However, the Opel plant continued to operate and built trucks for the German military and aircraft components for bombers. As with Ford-Werke, the labor supply was increasingly based on involuntary labor from POWs and transported civilians from occupied territories.[88] In 1944 the Opel factories were heavily bombed, and the main factory was occupied by Allied troops in March 1945. Technically, GM still owned the controlling stake in Opel and was therefore allowed to claim its property and the profits that had accumulated during the war. It emerged that these amounted to 22.4 million marks, including all the profits that had been locked in Germany throughout the 1930s. GM quietly repatriated these to the United States in 1951, but due to currency conversion rates the total amount brought back was only $261,000 (about $2.5 million in 2018).[89] Decades later, Opel and GM contributed $15 million to a fund used to compensate the forced laborers who had helped generate those profits.[90]

The American businessman who had been closest to the Reich, William Rhodes Davis, was dead by the time the United States entered the war. The controversy over his ill-gotten gains continued after the war's end, however. Within days of his death, the vice president of W.R. Davis, Inc. announced a gift of 5,000 barrels of oil to Great Britain that Davis had supposedly signed off on before his demise. Whether Davis had actually done so or whether the company's new leadership realized they needed to start repairing its reputation is unknown.[91] Two weeks later, executors estimated the Davis estate at between $5 million and $10 million, "or more."[92] No doubt part of the uncertainty concerned the value of Davis's German holdings. As the war continued, more information about the extent of his connections with the Reich began to emerge. Top Nazi leaders including Hermann Göring were questioned by Allied investigators and gave full details of their dealings with Davis and his associates, derailing the political career of his erstwhile associate Senator Joseph F. Guffey, who had helped with the Mexican oil scheme.[93]

The US government was not done with Davis yet, however. The FBI and Treasury Department had both been keeping an eye on Davis's finances for years and after his death filed a massive $38 million suit against his estate and corporate holdings. After years of legal wrangling, the government agreed to settle the case for a mere $850,000, or 3 percent of the original value. The settlement itself was not reported to the public until mid-1952. The turning point apparently came when the Davis estate hired the former chairman of the Democratic National Committee (and President Harry Truman's former secretary) as their legal counsel.[94] The Davis family's connections to the Democratic establishment apparently survived even the revelation of his involvement with the Third Reich.

Ironically, the Democratic Party itself was not done with the Davis family either. In 1952, Davis's son, Joseph Graham Davis, moved to California with his wife and son of the same name. Joseph Graham Davis Jr. entered state politics in 1974 by unsuccessfully running for state treasurer.[95] Universally known by his nickname Gray, he became chief of staff to Governor Jerry Brown and was elected to the State Assembly in 1982. From there he became state controller, lieutenant governor and, in 1998, was elected governor with 58 percent of the vote. A controversial governor, Gray Davis was recalled by voters in 2003 and replaced by former actor Arnold Schwarzenegger who, in another twist of fate, was originally from Austria.[96] The younger Davis never knew his controversial grandfather, who had died before he was born, and was estranged from the alcoholic father who had abandoned the family in the early 1960s.[97]

William Rhodes Davis's most important political partner in 1940 had been labor leader John L. Lewis. By siding with Republican Wendell Willkie against FDR, Lewis not only harmed his credibility with the labor movement rank and file but had also been forced to resign as head of the CIO. Yet he still remained the head of the powerful United Mine Workers (UMW), which severed its ties with the CIO in 1942. Still, Lewis was increasingly isolated and his political clout steadily decreased.[98] After Pearl Harbor he pledged his loyalty to the war effort but by 1943 was leading a series of controversial mining strikes that irked the White House.[99] Legal battles resulted, culminating with Lewis and his associates being convicted of contempt of court and fined.[100] National opinion had turned against the UMW, which was seen as unpatriotic and obstructionist by holding strikes during the war and afterward. Lewis held on as the controversial head of the UMW until 1960, and died in 1969.[101]

Lewis was always extremely private if not outright secretive. Even his cause of death was never publicly revealed, and there was no public funeral despite his larger-than-life image and continuing fame.[102] He refused to meet with reporters and historians during his last years and kept a low profile.[103] As a result, historians have had difficulty piecing together the exact nature of his relationship with Davis and the Nazis. Did Lewis know that Davis was setting him up to run for president, and did he know that the scheme was supported by the German embassy? How much did he know about Davis's dealings with the Germans? Why did he so dramatically break with Roosevelt when he must have known that the decidedly antilabor Nazis would benefit from the president being unseated? No doubt the personal differences between Roosevelt and Lewis played a major role, but this still fails to explain Lewis's willing association with Davis and his continued involvement after it should have been clear that the oilman was up to no good. The full story will probably never be known, but Lewis's reputation never recovered from the fiasco.

Charles Lindbergh's reputation would never recover from his actions before the war either. After Pearl Harbor, the aviator tried to volunteer for the Army Air Corps but was blocked by the Roosevelt administration as a defeatist. "I'll clip that young man's wings," President Roosevelt reportedly told senators.[104] Lindbergh ended up working for his old friend Henry Ford on aircraft engine improvements. In early 1944 he was finally permitted to fly test planes in the Pacific theater and, eventually, took part in combat missions against the Japanese.[105] By this time, however, the American public was in no mood to revive Lindbergh's reputation or even hear from him further. A 1942 poll found that just 10 percent of voters had a favorable view of Lindbergh, and 81 percent unfavorable.[106]

After the war, Lindbergh's old plane, the *Spirit of St. Louis*, ended up on display in the new National Air Museum (now the National Air and Space Museum) in Washington, DC. The man who had flown it in 1927 would be much less publicly venerated. Lindbergh spent many of his later years writing relatively successful memoirs and other books documenting his experiences in the heady days of the 1920s.[107] In the 1950s and 1960s he worked as a government consultant on a variety of projects, including environmental policy issues for the Nixon administration.[108] Toward the end of his life he became involved in a variety of conservationist causes, including the World Wildlife Fund, and spent most of his time in Hawaii. He died in 1974 and was buried near his home on the island of Maui.[109] The man who had come closest to uniting the American far right never overcame the consequences of becoming Hitler's key American friend, whether he intended to or not. Yet as the scars of those years have faded, Lindbergh's reputation has undergone a sort of renaissance. Two decades after his death, a poll found that 54 percent of Americans regarded Lindbergh as "a hero" while 36 percent disagreed.[110] This was a result Lindbergh could never have expected to see in his lifetime. The appeal and charm of Lucky Lindy's story has never lost its appeal for the American public, despite the ignominious chapters of his career.

Many of America First's—and Lindbergh's—most vocal supporters had been found at American universities. As already seen, the organization's original founder was Yale law student Robert Douglas Stuart Jr., who moved on to become its national director. Students at universities across the country formed their own local chapters of the group, particularly in its midwestern stronghold. University of Nebraska students, for instance, formed a campus chapter in October 1941, less than two months before Pearl Harbor. The group's faculty adviser described its aims as "keeping out of foreign wars, preserving and defending democracy at home, keeping American ships out of war zone [sic], building an impregnable defense and supplying the peoples of occupied countries with food and clothing."[111]

The question of war and peace was more than just political for the country's university students and young people generally. In the event of war, there would be little choice but to either face combat or join the war effort in other capacities. It is impossible to know how many of the American students who studied in the Third Reich, joined America First, or harbored sympathies for Germany ended up dead in the war they had opposed. It is, however, possible to trace the fate of some.

For his part, Stuart entered the army after Pearl Harbor as a field artillery officer. He survived the war and embarked on a sterling corporate career befitting his family background. His first employer was Quaker Oats, the company his father had helped found. Now the son followed in his father's footsteps and eventually rose to become company president in the mid-1960s and, later, CEO. Even in the midst of his high-flying corporate career, Stuart remained interested in the legacy of America First. In 1963 he corresponded with former America First chairman Robert E. Wood and publisher Henry Regnery, the son of a leading America First member, about the prospect of commissioning an official history of the organization. Stuart's primary concern was that the author of such a book not "be one of those who were instinctively critical of our efforts."[112] Nothing seems to have come of the plan, though books about America First began showing up regardless. (Ironically, Regnery had declined the opportunity to publish one of the first and most famous books on the subject back in 1951, claiming it would not be financially viable.)[113]

Stuart remained a diehard Republican throughout his life and eventually served as Ronald Reagan's Illinois campaign finance chair. Reagan rewarded him with an appointment as US ambassador to Norway in 1984. After returning to the United States in 1989 he obtained appointments from Presidents George H. W. Bush and Bill Clinton to serve on the Defense Base Realignment and Closure Commission tasked with evaluating post–Cold War military facility closures. Stuart died in 2014 at the age of 98. His creation of America First featured in many obituaries, but only as a minor part of his lengthy career.[114] At the time of his death, he appears to have been one of the last surviving leaders of America First. His much older colleague, America First chairman Robert E. Wood, died in 1969.

Successful, though far less high-profile, careers awaited several of the students who had been so adamant in their praise of the Third Reich during their time at Columbia University. Henry Miller Madden, the PhD student who turned his affinity for Germany into anti-Semitism and embarked on an extended European trip before the war, ended up in the US Navy. As already seen, he had attempted to convince the military that he was a conscientious objector, evidently to no avail. After a series of training assignments, he was sent to join the staff of Vice Admiral Robert L. Ghormley in occupied Berlin. His task there was to help negotiate a tripartite agreement with British and Soviet representatives and determine the fate of the surviving German navy. As a lifelong Germanophile, Madden must have recognized the irony in the fact that he was now part of a foreign military occupying his beloved Berlin.[115]

After the war, Madden returned to his academic career and finished his PhD but struggled to find employment as a professor. In 1949, he changed careers and accepted a job as a librarian at Fresno State College. In a twist of fate, he was relocating to same small California city where Fritz Wiedemann had covertly reunited with Princess Stephanie a few years earlier. Madden remained in the post for nearly the rest of his life. Unexpectedly, he appears to have abandoned many of his earlier views to become an outspoken supporter of academic freedom. In 1957 he was elected president of the California Library Association. "Books contain our record, both good and bad," he told a student group in 1964. Perhaps with his own example in mind, he concluded, "Books look in silence from their shelves at our antics and our follies, at our acts of creation and our acts of destruction. . . . Books are mirrors of the age in which they were written, and it is only through them that one can develop a sense of the appropriate."[116] Madden remained in his post until 1979 and dramatically extended his library's collections, in part by traveling to his old stomping grounds in Europe and purchasing rare books using the linguistic skills he honed decades earlier. He died in 1980, and the library was named in his honor the following year. The Henry Madden Library remains one of the largest public libraries in California to the present day and serves as an unexpected legacy for a man who once considered himself one of Hitler's American friends, however briefly.

Madden was not the only onetime Nazi-sympathizing student to find success in later years. His onetime correspondent at Columbia, William Oswald Shanahan, went on to an academic career of his own. Completing his PhD in history, Shanahan worked as a professor at Notre Dame, Cornell, the University of Oregon, and Hunter College. In 1963 he was invited to West Germany to report on the status of history instruction in the country, indicating the level of prestige he obtained in the field. He died in 1990 and was remembered as a well-respected historian and teacher.[117]

Neither Madden nor Shanahan seem to have been significantly impacted in their careers by their onetime views toward Hitler. Whether these views could be attributed to youthful indiscretion, or reflected deep-held prejudice that became unacceptable to express in public later, remains unclear. These were, after all, private opinions that undoubtedly influenced personal conduct, but never seem to have become a wider issue even at the time. Perhaps both men's views were changed by the war and the passage of time. Alternatively, it is possible they became caught up in the tenuous political atmosphere at Columbia and fed off the views they heard around them. If so, their example serves as a strong indictment of the university administrators and faculty members who cultivated a Nazi-friendly atmosphere at Columbia and other universities at a critical moment. Perhaps they were even taken advantage of by Hitler's propaganda network in the United States, just as John C. Metcalfe had warned the Dies Committee was taking place. Regardless, Shanahan and Madden followed the example of so many Americans and seem to have simply moved on with life and changing times after the war. Much the same was undoubtedly true for most of the young people who became temporarily enmeshed with Hitler's American friends.

Hitler's spy network in the United States was almost completely shut down well before the war's end. The failure of the 1942 Nazi sabotage operation was humiliating for Hitler, and ended with the execution of six saboteurs and the imprisonment of the other two. The Nazis would never again attempt such a bold and foolish plot in the United States. The two saboteurs who were spared, George John Dasch and Ernest Peter Burger, had their sentences commuted but still faced decades behind bars. In 1948, however, President Harry Truman abruptly ordered both men released from prison and deported to West Germany. By showing clemency, Truman hoped he could convince other plotters against the United States to turn themselves in and cooperate with authorities.[118]

Burger soon adopted a new identity and embarked on a career as a businessman. Dasch could not escape his past so easily, however. He wandered the country facing harassment and death threats from former Nazis when his past became known. At one point he contacted the German Communist Party in the hope of setting up a new life in the East. Party officials suspected that Dasch might be an American spy, and he was warned to return to the West while he could.[119] In 1959 he published a memoir of his experiences but was still denied the presidential pardon he had allegedly been promised decades before.[120] Throughout the 1950s and 1960s he requested admittance to the United States but was consistently denied at the personal request of J. Edgar Hoover, who resented the idea of anyone but the FBI getting credit for breaking up the sabotage plot. However, the end of Dasch's story remains somewhat uncertain. A 1980 investigation by the *Atlanta Constitution* discovered that Dasch's voluminous FBI file cut off abruptly in 1966, but there was no record of his death. No recent trace of him could be found in official documents, and an obituary search turned up nothing. Family members and former associates claimed they had no idea what had become of the missing man. A former FBI agent suggested it was possible that Dasch had been quietly allowed to enter the United States and was living under an assumed name. Some authors have claimed that Dasch remained in Germany—presumably living under an assumed identity—and died around 1992. No conclusive proof either way has seemingly ever been revealed. For all intents and purposes, Dasch simply disappeared from history.[121]

The same was true for many of the agents who served the Third Reich. The FBI has publicly identified around a hundred Nazi agents who were convicted of various offenses during the World War II period. Most were American citizens and many had been born in the United States.[122] While lengthy sentences were given to the most prominent spies and ringleaders, most convicted agents received modest sentences of a few years to a decade behind bars, and were presumably released from prison at some point after the war. Many appear to have changed their names and tried to start new lives. High school student Lucy Boehmler, for instance, was just nineteen when she was sent to prison for five years for her involvement in the Kurt Friedrich Ludwig spy ring. She would have only been in her early twenties when released, yet a newspaper archive search shows no trace of her in the postwar world.[123] Presumably she chose to disappear into obscurity and as much normalcy as could be managed. While it is unlikely that any of Hitler's agents are still alive at the time of writing, many probably went on to live normal and full lives after the war's end.

A grimmer and more abrupt end met their Abwehr boss in Berlin. As it turned out, Admiral Wilhelm Canaris and his sabotage chief, Erwin von Lahousen, were secretly leading double lives throughout the Third Reich. While ostensibly doing the Führer's bidding, both men were opposed to the regime and became members of the resistance. On July 20, 1944, German officer Claus von Stauffenberg planted a suitcase bomb in a room in Hitler's Wolf's Lair headquarters in East Prussia. The blast was intended to kill Hitler and decapitate the regime, but instead only wounded him. Believing the Führer was dead, Stauffenberg and his fellow conspirators tried to take control of the government but were overpowered. In the wake of the assassination plot, thousands of army officers and political leaders of the Reich were arrested. Lahousen was already fighting on the Eastern Front and had been involved in the plot, possibly by helping supply the bomb itself, but managed to conceal his involvement. He would survive the war and go on to testify against his former associates in the Third Reich in the Nuremberg Trials. He quietly lived out his days in his native Austria and died in 1955.[124]

Canaris was less lucky. He had already been under Gestapo surveillance for months before the Stauffenberg plot and was swiftly arrested.[125] The admiral was imprisoned for months and in April 1945, with the Reich collapsing, was convicted of treason in a summary trial. Facing certain death, Canaris requested the honor of death in combat against advancing Soviet troops. The request was denied, and hours later he was brutally hanged with piano wire on a meat hook. It took half an hour for the Abwehr chief to die.[126] Three weeks later, Abwehr agents blew up the Overseas Message Center that had been used to communicate by shortwave radio with its agents in the United States, to prevent it falling into Allied hands.

The two people who had once called themselves Hitler's friends and then changed their minds fared somewhat better. After being detained for overstaying her visa, Princess Stephanie von Hohenlohe started a relationship with the married commissioner of the Immigration and Naturalization Service, Lemuel B. Schofield. Its days were numbered, however. Princess Stephanie was arrested immediately after Pearl Harbor as a potential threat to national security. Ironically, she was held in a prison block full of avowed Nazis who regarded her as suspicious because of her Jewish appearance. Her usual machinations failed to gain her release, and she remained behind bars until May 1945. Remarkably, she then reunited with Schofield and spent the next decade living the high life off his income. He died in 1955.[127]

Princess Stephanie then reinvented herself yet again. As it turned out, she had a distant connection to the wife of political columnist Drew Pearson, who had broken many of the stories related to the Viereck propaganda operation. The pair had met decades before, and now Pearson offered to help her enter the Washington political scene. Over the next twenty years Stephanie wrote articles for German magazines and newspapers using Pearson's access and network of contacts. Remarkably, she even scored an interview with President John F. Kennedy in 1963 and several with President Lyndon B. Johnson. She died in 1972, colorful as ever in her old age and with her name still showing up in the papers.[128]

Her onetime lover and coconspirator, Fritz Wiedemann, was arrested by the Allies in Tientsin, China, at the end of the war. He was interrogated by OSS officers who found him helpful and willing to answer their questions about German intelligence operations. He was soon taken to Washington for further questioning, and cooperated again. Asked what should happen to his former associates in the Third Reich, he told interrogators that the worst war criminals deserved the death penalty. He later served as an official witness at the Nuremberg Trials and was officially denazified by paying a 2,000 deutschmark (about

$6,000 in 2018) fine in 1948.[129] He and Stephanie eventually reconnected, and she helped him write and publish his memoirs. Wiedemann lived out his days as a "Bavarian gentleman farmer dressed in lederhosen," as a 1968 newspaper article put it.[130] He died in 1970. The opulent mansion that served as his consular headquarters in San Francisco—and the center of his international spy network—still stands at the corner of Laguna and Jackson Streets. After the war, it served as the first permanent headquarters of the California Historical Society.[131]

There was another aspect to Wiedemann's story that only emerged later, however. During the Nuremberg Trials, a German-American woman living in New York named Kate Eva Hoerlin provided a startling deposition. In 1934, she recounted, she and her first husband, a well-known newspaper music critic, were living in Munich. One evening, four men in SS uniform arrived to take her husband to Dachau, mistaking him for a local SA leader they were intending to shoot as part of the Night of the Long Knives purge. After desperately seeking information about his fate for days, Hoerlin was told he had been shot "by accident" in Dachau. Hoerlin and the prominent owner of her husband's newspaper both contacted the Gestapo to ask why her husband had been killed. Remarkably, the Gestapo admitted that the shooting had been a mistake and offered Hoerlin money to drop the matter, which she refused. As the Gestapo became more persistent, Hoerlin went to Nazi Party headquarters, where she encountered Wiedemann.

Hearing her terrible story, Wiedemann arranged for a personal apology from Reich Deputy Führer Rudolf Hess, along with a formal letter stating her husband had not been guilty of any crime. He also managed to secure her a pension equivalent to her late husband's salary. In 1937, Hoerlin and her children moved to New York, and became American citizens in 1944. She never forgot the unexpected kindness she received, telling investigators, "In fairness I should state that Captain Wiedemann, formerly an influential member of the NSDAP, was at all times genuinely sympathetic with my case; and I feel that I owe more to him for having protected me from the Gestapo than to any other individual."[132] This turned out to not be the only compassionate act Wiedemann had undertaken in the Reich. In 2010, historian Thomas Weber revealed that the captain personally helped several Jewish former members of his (and Hitler's) First World War unit survive the Holocaust.[133] Despite his history as one of the führer's closest confidants, in some instances he had more compassion than anyone at the time could have imagined.

The failure of Hitler's friends ultimately stands as a testimony to the resilience of the American political system. President Roosevelt repeatedly showed great foresight in pushing the FBI to investigate right-wing subversives when J. Edgar Hoover himself wanted to focus on other priorities. The president's backdoor cooperation with British Security Coordination allowed the disruption of major German intelligence and propaganda efforts, including Viereck's Capitol Hill operation. Without British intelligence assistance, particularly in the key 1940–1941 period, German success in subverting the United States would have been much more likely. Prime Minister Winston Churchill and William Stephenson both deserve credit for allowing politically risky intelligence operations to be undertaken at this critical moment. Given the dire military situation, the British had little choice but to take risks, and in this case it paid off handsomely. American public opinion did not immediately swing toward intervention in the European war, but it did progressively allow Roosevelt a freer hand to aid the British.

Despite his Committee's questionable techniques, even Martin Dies Jr. deserves credit for helping bring down the Bund and the Silver Legion. "When we began our work, the Bund and a score of Nazi-minded American groups were laying plans for an impressive united front federation—a federation which would be able to launch a first-rate Nazi movement in the United States," Dies told Americans in a December 1940 radio address. "By our exposure of these plans, we smashed that Nazi movement even before it was able to get under way."[134] There was an element of truth to this. Dies would go on to a controversial postwar career and become associated with the excesses of McCarthyism, but for a few critical years he was a major thorn in the side of Hitler's American friends.

Finally, credit must be given to America's two political parties for their own discipline in this critical period. The Republican Party nominated the interventionist Wendell Willkie in 1940 rather than an isolationist. Neither party's leaders seriously considered nominating Charles Lindbergh, the only man who would have been able to unite the far-right factions under the banner of America First. Kansas Republicans disavowed Gerald B. Winrod at the key moment he might have become Hitler's most powerful political friend in the country. Both parties kept their distance from the likes of Gerald L. K. Smith and Father Coughlin. After the war, most of the isolationists who had been involved in Viereck's propaganda scheme saw their political careers end abruptly.

These were undoubtedly difficult calls for politicians to make. Attacking members of one's own party and alienating current or potential supporters is never easy. Lindbergh might well have been able to capture the White House for the Republicans in 1940, especially if he had been backed with the millions of dollars supposedly stashed in the German embassy for William Rhodes Davis to dispense. The prospect of a charismatic celebrity taking an isolationist foreign policy platform all the way to the White House was by no means impossible.

But at what cost? Twentieth-century American history would have pivoted in a completely different and unknowable direction, with vast consequences for millions of people around the globe. For whatever their flaws then and now, America's political parties and leaders rose to the challenge presented by this moment in history. In many cases, politicians made the difficult decision to act on principle and patriotism rather than out of political expediency and the pursuit of victory at any price. The far right could never find its American Führer, and the country's political parties ensured that none of the leading candidates, ranging from outlandish options like Fritz Kuhn or William Dudley Pelley to more plausible options like Father Coughlin or Charles Lindbergh, would ever get the chance to make a bid for the position. The American political system survived a series of major existential threats at a moment when the fate of the free world hung in the balance. In the face of such courageous stands by America's leaders, Hitler's friends never stood much of a chance.

ACKNOWLEDGMENTS

It is only appropriate to acknowledge the wide range of people who contributed to the writing of this book. The archival research required was extensive and only made possible by the outstanding archivists and archival assistants who not only made collections readily available but also lent their own expertise to my many queries. Namely, the staffs of the Hoover Institution; the Sam Houston Regional Library & Research Center in Liberty, Texas; the Wichita State University Library, Kansas; the Churchill Archives Centre, Cambridge; the UK National Archives, and the National Archives of Scotland deserve special thanks.

A wide range of friends generously offered their time and knowledge to point me in the right direction at a number of points. Thomas Dunne and his team at Thomas Dunne Books did a wonderful job with the manuscript and offered many helpful suggestions along the way. My fantastic agent, Andy Ross, deserves thanks for making this project possible. Richard Carr took the time to read drafts and offer his subject matter expertise over an extraordinary number of coffees. Julia Boyd generously offered guidance and direction in a variety of areas even as she was finishing her own book. Allen Packwood, director of the Churchill Archives Centre, extended his own expertise and pointed me in a number of profitable directions. My former PhD supervisor, Richard J. Evans, offered his encouragement from the early stages of the project onward. Finally, Sidney Sussex College and Churchill College, Cambridge, were both generous in allowing me to stay in college accommodations during much of the research and writing process.

I am grateful to all who contributed to this effort. They are of course absolved from any errors that may remain.

APPENDIX: HITLER'S AMERICAN FRIENDS IN NUMBERS

GROUP/CLASSIFICATION	APPROXIMATE MEMBERSHIP
Executed German Saboteurs	6
Convicted Nazi Spies in the United States	100
Friends of the New Germany	5,000 [at peak]
German American Bund Ordnungsdienst (OD)	5,000 [at peak]
Silver Legion Members	15,000 [at peak]
German American Bund Members	20,000 [at peak]
Votes for Gerald B. Winrod in Kansas GOP Primary [1938]	53,000
German American Bund Sympathizers	100,000 [at peak]
Silver Legion Sympathizers	100,000 [at peak]
Subscribers to the *Defender* (Gerald B. Winrod)	100,000
Subscribers to *Social Justice* (Father Coughlin)	200,000 [minimum—up to 1 million]
America First Members	800,000
Nationwide Votes for Coughlin-Backed Presidential Candidate William Lemke (1936 election)	892,000
Americans Agreeing Jews Should Be Deported "To Some New Homeland as Fast as It Can Be Done without Inhumanity" (1939 *Fortune* poll)	13 million
Semiweekly or More Frequent Father Coughlin Listeners (1938)	15 million
Monthly Father Coughlin Listeners (1938)	29 million

NOTES

Introduction

1. Wayne S. Cole, *America First: The Battle against Intervention* (New York: Octagon Books, 1971), 97–102.
2. "Lindbergh Sees a 'Plot' for War," *New York Times*, September 12, 1941, 2.
3. "Lindbergh Sees a 'Plot' for War," 2; "3 Groups Press U.S. to War, Lindbergh Says," *Washington Post*, September 12, 1941, 13.
4. "Lindbergh Address Condemned by Mayor," *New York Times*, September 19, 1941, 12.
5. "Assail Lindbergh for Iowa Speech," *New York Times*, September 13, 1941, 1.
6. "Senate Movie Probe to Call Charlie Chaplin," *Washington Post*, September 14, 1941, 7.
7. "Dewey Denounces Lindbergh's Talk," *New York Times*, September 15, 1941, 2.
8. Cole, *America First*, 152.
9. "The Un-American Way," *New York Times*, September 26, 1941, 22.
10. Cole, *America First*, 119.
11. Cole, *America First*, 121.
12. Gallup Organization, Gallup Poll (AIPO), June 1938 [survey question]. USGALLUP.38-126.QB05. Gallup Organization [producer]. Cornell University, Ithaca, NY: Roper Center for Public Opinion Research, iPOLL [distributor]; Gallup Organization. Gallup Poll (AIPO), January 1939 [survey question]. USGALLUP.39-145.QAB11. Gallup Organization [producer]. Cornell University, Ithaca, NY: Roper Center for Public Opinion Research, iPOLL [distributor].
13. Gallup Organization, Gallup Poll (AIPO), March 1937 [survey question]. USGALLUP.37-75.Q04B. Gallup Organization [producer]. Cornell University, Ithaca, NY: Roper Center for Public Opinion Research, iPOLL [distributor].
14. Gallup Organization, Gallup Poll, August 1940 [survey question]. USGALLUP.091540.RK03A. Gallup Organization [producer]. Cornell University, Ithaca, NY: Roper Center for Public Opinion Research, iPOLL [distributor].

15. Letter from Lothian to Sir Edward Peacock, April 5, 1940, GD 40/17/404/146-7, 11th Marquess of Lothian Papers, National Archives of Scotland, Edinburgh.

16. Roper Organization. Roper Commercial Survey, December 1940 [survey question]. USROPER.RCOM40-011.Q10A. Roper Organization [producer]. Cornell University, Ithaca, NY: Roper Center for Public Opinion Research, iPOLL [distributor].

17. Gallup Organization, Gallup Poll (AIPO), January 1941 [survey question]. USGALLUP .41-228.QT07. Gallup Organization [producer]. Cornell University, Ithaca, NY: Roper Center for Public Opinion Research, iPOLL [distributor].

18. Letter from Lothian to Leo Amery, January 9, 1940, GD 40/17/398, 11th Marquess of Lothian Papers.

19. *Fortune*: Roper/*Fortune* Survey, February 1941 [survey question]. USROPER.41-025 .Q09. Roper Organization [producer]. Cornell University, Ithaca, NY: Roper Center for Public Opinion Research, iPOLL [distributor].

20. Lord Lloyd to Dolobran to Lady Colefax regarding the possibility of meeting influential columnist Walter Lippmann, June 7, 1939, GLLD 19/10, Lord Lloyd of Dolobran Papers, Churchill Archives Centre, Cambridge.

21. Letter from Lothian to R. H. Brand, June 25, 1940, p. 1, GD 40/17/399, 11th Marquess of Lothian Papers.

22. Letter from Lothian to R. H. Brand, June 25, 1940, p. 3.

23. David Lawrence, *Diary of a Washington Correspondent* (New York: H.C. Kinsey & Company, Inc., 1942), 20.

24. Lawrence, 21.

25. "Refu-Jews Go Back" song sheet, box 15, file 21, Martin Dies Papers, Sam Houston Regional Library and Research Center, Liberty, Texas.

26. Letter from Lothian to R. H. Brand, June 25, 1940, p. 3.

27. "Wallace Defines 'American Fascism,'" *New York Times*, April 9, 1944, SM34.

28. Ernst Hanfstaengl, *Hitler: The Missing Years* (London: Eyre & Spottiswoode, 1957), 23–26.

29. Hanfstaengl, *Hitler*, 40–41.

30. Adolf Hitler, *Hitler's Table Talk 1941–1944: His Private Conversations*, translated by Norman Cameron and R. H. Stevens, 3d ed. (London: Phoenix, 2000), 188.

31. Memorandum to Saint, Amzon for AB/24; subject: Heribert von Strempel; References: AMZO 25267, January 23, 1946, file 9, pp. 1–2, Strempel, Heribert von, CIA CREST database.

32. Jeffery, 255, 438.

33. Gabler, 291; Jeffery, 438–41. See also Walter Winchell files, FBI Vault.

34. Francis MacDonnell, *Insidious Foes: The Axis Fifth Column and the American Home Front* (New York: Oxford University Press, 1995), 163–64.

35. Jeffery, 439.

36. MacDonnell, 171–72.

37. Cf. Lynne Olson, *Those Angry Days: Roosevelt, Lindbergh, and America's Fight over World War II, 1939–1941*, 1st ed. (New York: Random House, 2013), 339–40.

38. Olson, 338.

39. Olson, 339–40; Jeffery, 450–51.

40. Cf. Olson, 339.

41. William Gellermann, *Martin Dies* (New York: John Day Company, 1944), 3.

42. Letter from Dies to A. J. Sabath, September 26, 1938, box 15, HUAC Official Correspondence 1938–1940, Martin Dies Jr. Papers.

43. Letter from Dies to A. D. Covin, September 7, 1938, box 15, file 6, Martin Dies Papers.

44. Gallup Organization, Gallup Poll (AIPO), February 1939 [survey question]. USGALLUP .39-148. QB05B. Gallup Organization [producer]. Cornell University, Ithaca, NY: Roper Center for Public Opinion Research, iPOLL [distributor].

45. Dies speech on "We the People" program, August 22, 1939, box 90, file 7, Martin Dies Papers.

46. Robbie Gramer, "Why Mike Flynn Could Be in Trouble—Again," *Foreign Policy*, March 9, 2017, http://foreignpolicy.com/2017/03/09/why-mike-flynn-could-be-in-trouble -again-lobbying-disclosure-turkey-government-trump-struggling-to-drain-the -swamp/; "Paul Manafort to Register as a Foreign Agent over Past Lobbying Work," *Guardian*, April 12, 2017, https://www.theguardian.com/us-news/2017/apr/12/paul -manafort-foreign-agent-trump-russia.

47. Rosie Gray, "How the Manafort Indictment Gave Bite to a Toothless Law," *Atlantic*, October 30, 2017, https://www.theatlantic.com/politics/archive/2017/10/how-the -manafort-indictment-gave-bite-to-a-toothless-law/544448/.

48. Anthony Badger, *New Deal/New South: An Anthony J. Badger Reader* (Fayetteville: University of Arkansas Press, 2007), 1–3, 24–25.

49. Bruce M. Russett, *No Clear and Present Danger: A Skeptical View of the United States Entry into World War II*, Harper Torchbooks (New York: Harper & Row, 1972), 42–43.

1. The Bund

1. Account derived from undercover report of John C. Metcalfe, July 4, 1937, "Daily Notations of Undercover Work," 1937, John C. Metcalfe Papers, Hoover Institution.

2. "Hitler Rules Bund, Says Dies Witness," *New York Times*, September 29, 1938, 5.

3. Howard Hurtig Metcalfe, *Die Familie Oberwinder: Genealogical Encyclopedia of the Family Connections of Richard Maria Wilhe[l]m Oberwinder* (Decorah, Iowa: Anundsen Pub., 1999), 40.

4. Susan Canedy, *America's Nazis: A Democratic Dilemma: A History of the German American Bund* (Menlo Park, CA: Markgraf Publications Group, 1990), 3–4.

5. Canedy, 8–12.

6. Sander A. Diamond, *The Nazi Movement in the United States, 1924–1941* (Ithaca, NY: Cornell University Press, 1974), 86.

7. Henry W. Levy, "Germany's Big Question Mark," *Cincinnati Enquirer*, April 23, 1933, 80.

8. "Turn Verein Scores Hitler," *Brooklyn Daily Eagle*, June 5, 1933, 1.

9. "Hitler Cheered by German Americans," *Lincoln Star*, December 7, 1933, 7.

10. Diamond, 92–96.

11. Diamond, 99–102.

12. Diamond, 112–14; Canedy, 50–51.

13. Diamond, 117, 129 n.2.

14. Diamond, 121–27; Canedy, 51–65.

15. Diamond, 203–212; Canedy, 77. Diamond does not mention Kuhn winning the Iron Cross, perhaps suggesting that this was another inflated aspect of Kuhn's résumé.

16. Keith Sward, *The Legend of Henry Ford* (New York: Rinehart & Company, 1948), 457–58.

17. Diamond, 212; Canedy, 78.

18. Canedy, 81.

19. Diamond, 205, 209.

20. Wilhelm, 160–61; Canedy, 82–83.

21. "Pro American Rally and George Washington Birthday Exercises," pamphlet photocopies, German American Bund propaganda materials, 1939 folder, German American Bund Records, Hoover Institution.

22. Canedy, 92–97.

23. Canedy, 86.

24. Bund sympathizer registration form and sympathizer card, German American Bund membership forms, German American Bund Records.

25. Arnie Bernstein, *Swastika Nation: Fritz Kuhn and the Rise and Fall of the German-American Bund*, 1st ed. (New York: St. Martin's Press, 2013), 53.

26. The 10,000 or fewer figure is in Canedy, 86; Diamond suggests a figure of 17,000–25,000 (222). Cornelia Wilhelm estimated membership of around 30,000, which puts it in line with the Communist Party's membership in the 1930s.

27. Kershaw, *Hitler: 1889–1936: Hubris* (London: Allen Lane, 1998), 179.

28. Diamond, 242; Embargoed transcript of testimony, John C. Metcalfe Papers; Bund Dies Committee Hearings, vol. 6, p. 3384. The figure of twenty-four camps comes from Canedy, 97. Kuhn himself stated that there were approximately twenty camps, while Metcalfe listed the locations of fifteen in his testimony.

29. Embargoed transcript of testimony concerning Bund Youth Division, German American Bund, Dies Committee Hearings, John C. Metcalfe Papers.

30. Canedy, 97.

31. Dies Committee Hearings, vol. 14, p. 8367.

32. Dies Committee Hearings, vol. 6, p. 3758.

33. Dies Committee Hearings, vol. 6, p. 3758.

34. Dies Committee Hearings, vol. 14, pp. 8340–342, 8367–369.

35. "Nazi Past of Long Island Hamlet Persists in a Rule for Home Buyers," *New York Times*, October 19, 2015; "New York Enclave Finally Ends Nazi-Era Policies," *New York Post*, May 20, 2017, http://nypost.com/2017/05/20/new-york-enclave-finally-ends -nazi-era-policies/.

36. Oetje John Rogge, *The Official German Report: Nazi Penetration, 1924–1942* (New York: T. Yoseloff, 1961), 119–120.

37. See Bradley W. Hart, *George Pitt-Rivers and the Nazis* (London, New York: Bloomsbury Academic, 2015), 126.

38. Rogge, 119; Canedy, 116.

39. Diamond, 266–7.

40. Bund Command 2, October 29, 1936, German American Bund Command No. 1-50, 1936–1941, German American Bund Records.

41. Bund Command 3, October 30, 1936, Command No. 1-50, 1936–1941, German American Bund Records.

42. Bund Commands 4-13, German American Bund Command No. 1-50, 1936–1941, German American Bund Records.

43. Office of United States Chief of Counsel for Prosecution of Axis Criminality, United States Department of State, United States War Department and International Military Tribunal, *Nazi Conspiracy and Aggression*, 8 vols. (Washington: United States Government Printing Office, 1946), Appendix A, 552–54.

44. For instance, Bund Command 11, July 28, 1937; Bund Command No. 1-50, 1936–1941, German American Bund Records.

45. For instance, Bund Command 17, February 17, 1938, and subsequent orders insisting on fulfillment of orders from national HQ, German American Bund Command No. 1-50, 1936–1941, German American Bund Records.

46. Canedy, 150.

47. Canedy, 142, 149.

48. Metcalfe, 40.

49. Thomas Patrick Doherty, *Hollywood and Hitler, 1933–1939* (New York: Columbia University Press, 2015), 101–3; Larry Ceplair and Steven Englund, *The Inquisition in Hollywood: Politics in the Film Community 1930–1960* (Berkeley, CA.: University of California Press, 1983), 104–5.

50. See lists of car license plates and owners, German American Bund (1 of 3), box 3, folder 2, Hollywood Anti-Nazi League Papers (Collection 185), Charles E. Young Research Library, Special Collections, University of California, Los Angeles.

51. Account of Deutsches Haus meeting, German American Bund (1 of 3), box 3, folder 2, UCLA. Letters between League officials and Major Julius Hochfelder, 1937 German American Bund (2 of 3), box 3, folder 2, Hollywood Anti-Nazi League Papers.

52. Account of Deutsches Haus meeting, May 10, German American Bund (1 of 3), box 3, folder 2, Hollywood Anti-Nazi League Papers.

53. Account of Deutsches Haus youth meeting, March 11, 1939, German American Bund (2 of 3), box 3, folder 2, Hollywood Anti-Nazi League Papers.

54. Telegram from Schwinn to Dies, August 20, 1938, Dies Committee Hearings—Metcalfe's Reports/Correspondence, John C. Metcalfe Papers; Ceplair and Englund, 109.

55. Metcalfe, 40.

56. Accounts of Metcalfe travels in Los Angeles, July–August 1937, "Daily Notations of Undercover Work," box 1, John C. Metcalfe Papers; John W. Sherman, *The Mexican Right: The End of Revolutionary Reform, 1929–1940* (Westport, CT; London: Praeger, 1997), 63–64; Stanley G. Payne, *A History of Fascism 1914–1945* (London: UCL Press, 1995), 342.

57. Accounts of Metcalfe travels in San Antonio, August 11, 1937, p. 4, box 1, "Daily Notations of Undercover Work," John C. Metcalfe Papers.

58. Accounts of Metcalfe travels in St. Louis, Cleveland, and Washington, DC, box 1, "Daily Notations of Undercover Work," box 1, John C. Metcalfe Papers.

59. Account of Metcalfe meeting with Kuhn, 1937, "Daily Notations of Undercover Work," box 1, John C. Metcalfe Papers.

60. "Nazi Putsch Here Is Quickly Denied," *New York Times*, September 10, 1937.

61. Diamond, 297–99.

62. March 9, 1939, report: "The Activities of Mr. Fritz Kuhn and the German-American 'Bund,'" pp. 3–4, C 3299/94/18, FO 371/23035, National Archives, London.

63. Diamond, 326–27; "Many Injured in Bund Riots," *Los Angeles Times*, February 21, 1939, 1.
64. "Many Injured in Bund Riots," *Los Angeles Times*.
65. Diamond, 331–33.
66. Embargoed transcript of testimony, p. 3, German American Bund Dies Committee Hearings, John C. Metcalfe Papers; Luther Huston, "Bund Activities Widespread," *New York Times*, February 26, 1939, 70.
67. MacDonnell, 65.
68. MacDonnell, 62.
69. MacDonnell, 69; Olson, 365.
70. MacDonnell, 68.
71. MacDonnell, 69–70; Mark Glancy, *When Hollywood Loved Britain: The Hollywood "British" Film 1939–1945*, 54.
72. Rogge, 128–29.
73. Diamond, 345.
74. "National Leader of Bund Suicides in This County," *Garrett Clipper* [Garrett, Indiana], June 18, 1942, 1.
75. Rogge, 129.

2. The Silver Legion and the Chief

1. Account of Silver Shirts meeting, box 1, folder 8, California Surveillance files 1934–40, San Francisco State University Labor Archives and Research Center.
2. Eckard V. Toy, "Silver Shirts in the Northwest: Politics, Prophecies, and Personalities in the 1930s," *Pacific Northwest Quarterly* 80 (4) (1989) 141.
3. Rogge, 187–91.
4. Cf. Gustavus Myers, *History of Bigotry in the United States* (New York: Random House, 1943), 401.
5. Leo P. Ribuffo, *The Old Christian Right: The Protestant Far Right from the Great Depression to the Cold War* (Philadelphia: Temple University Press, 1983), 25–31.
6. Ribuffo, 43–46; Myers, 402.
7. Ribuffo, 48–50.
8. Ribuffo, 54; Myers, 402; Scott Beekman, *William Dudley Pelley: A Life in Right-Wing Extremism and the Occult*, 1st ed., Religion and Politics (Syracuse, NY: Syracuse University Press, 2005), 54–55.
9. Ribuffo, 53–54.
10. Report on Pelley, 1939, American Jewish Committee, p. 5, http://www.ajcarchives.org /AJC_DATA/Files/THR-SS2.PDF.
11. Ribuffo, 64.
12. Beekman, 83; Ribuffo, 64; Myers, 403.
13. Report on Pelley, 1939, American Jewish Committee, p. 2, http://www.ajcarchives.org /AJC_DATA/Files/THR-SS2.PDF.
14. Beekman, 85–87.
15. Silver Legion of America, *The Reds Are Upon Us: The First Council*, 1938, 8.
16. Silver Legion of America, 4–11.

17. Report on Pelley, 1939, American Jewish Committee, p. 5, http://www.ajcarchives.org /AJC_DATA/Files/THR-SS2.PDF.
18. This estimate appears to come from the work of John Werly, which has been accepted by virtually all other historians: see Ribuffo, 64; Beekman, 100–101.
19. Beekman, 101; Ribuffo, 65.
20. Johnpeter Horst Grill and Robert L. Jenkins, "The Nazis and the American South in the 1930s: A Mirror Image?" *Journal of Southern History* 58 (4) (1992), 670.
21. Toy, 142.
22. Ribuffo, 71–72; Beekman, 107–9.
23. Report on Pelley, 1939, American Jewish Committee, p. 5, http://www.ajcarchives.org /AJC_DATA/Files/THR-SS2.PDF.
24. Beekman, 113–15; Toy, 141.
25. Meyers, 409.
26. Beekman, 123; Toy, 142–44.
27. Dies Committee Hearings, vol. 6, p. 3766.
28. Dies Committee Hearings, vol. 6, p. 3786.
29. Report on Pelley, 1939, American Jewish Committee, p. 6, http://www.ajcarchives.org /AJC_DATA/Files/THR-SS2.PDF.
30. Metcalfe surveillance diaries, early August, John C. Metcalfe Papers.
31. Ribuffo, 73.
32. "Portrait and Brief Biographical Information on Elwood A. Towner, 'Chief Red Cloud,'" *Scribner's*, 1937; Lecture by Towner, Spokane, Washington, August 4, 1937, Silver Legion of America, Washington State Division Records, University of Washington Libraries, Special Collections, Seattle, Washington.
33. Accounts of German-American Bund meeting, July 4 and undated (likely 1939), box 3, folder 2, Hollywood Anti-Nazi League Papers.
34. *Nazi Conspiracy and Aggression*, Appendix A, p. 577.
35. Letter from Pelley to Orville Roundtree, December 11, 1937, Silver Legion of America, Washington State Division Records.
36. Letter from Pelley to state leaders, April 30, 1938, Silver Legion of America, Washington State Division Records.
37. Letter from Orville Roundtree to W. E. Monbeck, July 16, 1938, Silver Legion of America, Washington State Division Records.
38. Beekman, 125.
39. "Nazi Leader Run Out of Sharon," *News-Herald* (Franklin, Pennsylvania), November 18, 1938, 1.
40. Undated report on Christian Party, folder 2-17, Nathan Krems Papers, University of Washington Libraries, Special Collections, Seattle, Washington.
41. "Organized Bigotry," *Mason City Globe-Gazette*, August 19, 1938, 4.
42. "Dies Asks Action to Indict Witness: Challenges F. S. Gardner as Seeking Job with Committee to 'Sabotage' Its Work," *New York Times*, August 24, 1939, 16; Beekman, 127–28.
43. "Dies Asks Action to Indict Witness"; "Perjury Charge Asked Against Dies Witness: Committee Accuses Silver Shirt Aide of Sabotage Attempt," *Washington Post*, August 24, 1939, 3.

44. Myers, 412.
45. "Pelley Sues House Members," *New York Times*, September 10, 1939, 59; Beekman, 127.
46. Beekman, 133–34; "Silver Shirt's Chief Is Called to Court: Pelley Is Accused of Violating Suspended Sentences," *New York Times*, October 20, 1939, 15.
47. "Charge Against Dies Denied by Committee: Witness Said to Admit Forging Letters Linking Him to Pelley," *New York Times*, January 31, 1940, 10.
48. "House Embroiled by Mayne Letters: Hook's Failure to Expunge Alleged Forgeries Fans Tilt Over Pelley and Dies," *New York Times*, February 2, 1940, 2.
49. "Hook Takes Dies Charge from Record: Pelley Surrenders to House Group, Brands Mayne's Letters Forgeries," *New York Times*, February 7, 1940, 1.
50. Beekman, 135.
51. "Girl Secret Agent Tells Pelley 'Plot': Joins Dickstein at Dies Hearing in Linking Silver Shirt Chief to Plans for Uprising," *New York Times*, April 3, 1940, 4.
52. Address from Pelley to Washington State Silver Legion members, 1941(?), Silver Legion of America, Washington State Division Records.
53. Beekman, 135.
54. "Pelley in North Carolina Jail," *New York Times*, October 23, 1941, 19; "Pelley Is Ordered to Serve 2 to 3 Years," *New York Times*, January 21, 1942, 11.
55. Cf. Beekman, 137.
56. "U.S. Fascists: Several Arrests Made," *Manchester Guardian*, April 6, 1942, 6.
57. Report on Pelley, 1939, American Jewish Committee, pp. 5–6, http://www.ajcarchives.org/AJC_DATA/Files/THR-SS2.PDF.

3. The Religious Right

1. Charles J. Tull, *Father Coughlin and the New Deal*, Men and Movements (Syracuse, NY: Syracuse University Press, 1965), 197.
2. "Father Coughlin Given Rebuke," *Times Herald* [Port Huron, Michigan], November 21, 1938, 2.
3. "Coughlin Talks on Persecution: Says that Nazis Blame Jews for Ills," *Detroit Free Press*, November 21, 1938, 2.
4. "Father Coughlin Given Rebuke," *Times Herald* (Port Huron, Michigan), November 21, 1938, 1–2.
5. Tull, 202.
6. Sheldon Marcus, *Father Coughlin: The Tumultuous Life of the Priest of the Little Flower*, 1st ed. (Boston: Little, Brown, 1973), 182.
7. Conducted by Gallup Organization, December 18–23, 1938, and based on 1,500 personal interviews. Sample: National adult. Sample size is approximate. [USGALLUP.38-141 .Q01A]. Figures based on an estimated US population of 129.8 million in 1938.
8. Tull, 197.
9. David Harry Bennett, *Demagogues in the Depression: American Radicals and the Union Party, 1932–1936* (New Brunswick, NJ,: Rutgers University Press, 1969), 54.
10. "Is Rush Limbaugh in Trouble?" *Politico*, May 24, 2016, http://www.politico.com/magazine/story/2016/05/is-rush-limbaugh-in-trouble-talk-radio-213914.
11. Bennett, 57.
12. Bennett, 31.

13. Glen Jeansonne, *Gerald L. K. Smith, Minister of Hate* (New Haven, CT: Yale University Press, 1988), 55.
14. Bennett traces the 1936 attempt to combine these factions: see Bennett, 4–7.
15. Marcus, 14–23; Ruth Mugglebee, *Father Coughlin, the Radio Priest, of the Shrine of the Little Flower* (Garden City, NY: Garden City Publishing Co., 1933), 157–58.
16. "Shrine Service This Evening," *Detroit Free Press*, October 7, 1928, part 4, p. 8.
17. Mugglebee, 166.
18. Mugglebee, 169–71.
19. Marcus, 55.
20. Marcus, 29; Mugglebee, 178–79.
21. Mugglebee, 183.
22. Marcus, 35–36.
23. Marcus, 37; Mugglebee, 254–55.
24. Marcus, 45–48; "Roosevelt, Stimson Talk State Affairs," *Hartford Daily Courant*, January 10, 1933, 4.
25. Marcus, 46; Mugglebee, 325.
26. Gerald Horne, *The Color of Fascism: Lawrence Dennis, Racial Passing, and the Rise of Right-Wing Extremism in the United States* (New York: New York University Press, 2006), 54; Mugglebee, 324–25.
27. Marcus, 68–69.
28. Tull, 62–63, 69.
29. Tull, 72–73.
30. Richard J. Evans, *The Third Reich in Power, 1933–1939* (New York: Penguin Press, 2005), 341–42.
31. Cf. Mugglebee, 354.
32. Bennett, 72.
33. Conducted by Gallup Organization, June 29–July 3, 1936, and based on 1,500 personal interviews. Sample: National adult. Sample size is approximate. [USGALLUP .072636.R01].
34. Mugglebee, 357–58.
35. Tull, 86, 101.
36. Jeansonne, 21, 25.
37. Jeansonne, 36.
38. Report on Smith from Detroit office, May 20, 1941, p. 2, FBI file on Gerald L. K. Smith, pt. 1, FBI Vault.
39. Jeansonne, 48; Marcus, 102–3.
40. Marcus, 103.
41. Tull, 150.
42. See, for instance, "Landon's Manager Scores Injection of Racial Issue into Presidential Campaign," *Wisconsin Jewish Chronicle*, July 19, 1936, 1–2.
43. Bennett, 97–98; Tull, 125–26.
44. Bennett, 210.
45. Dorothy Thompson, "On the Record: The Lunatic Fringe," *Cincinnati Enquirer*, July 21, 1936, 4.
46. Letter from Coughlin to Dies, August 5, 1936, box 89, file 52, Martin Dies Papers.
47. Cf. Jeansonne, 55.

48. Jeansonne, 55; Donald I. Warren, *Radio Priest: Charles Coughlin, the Father of Hate Radio* (New York: Free Press, 1996), 89.

49. Dorothy Thompson, "On the Record: The Lunatic Fringe."

50. Bennett, 239.

51. Report on Smith from Detroit office, May 20, 1941, pp. 5–6, FBI file on Gerald L. K. Smith, pt. 1, FBI Vault.

52. Bennett, 263–64.

53. Jeansonne, 63.

54. Bennett, 279.

55. "From Other Papers: The Winrod Campaign," *Iola Register* [Kansas], June 17, 1938, 4.

56. G. H. Montgomery, *Gerald Burton Winrod: Defender of the Faith* (Wichita, KS: Mertmont Publishers, 1965), 10; Ribuffo, 80–81.

57. Montgomery, 12; Ribuffo, 81.

58. Montgomery, 14–16.

59. Montgomery, 21–23, Ribuffo, 88.

60. Ribuffo, 51–52, 103, 113.

61. Rogge, 213.

62. "Bible School Park Minister Defends Hitler," *Binghamton Press* [New York], July 26, 1935, 3; Memorandum on the Rev. Gerald B. Winrod, April 1947, Gerald B. Winrod; subject folder, John C. Metcalfe Papers.

63. Rogge, 215.

64. Strong, *Organized Anti-Semitism in America*, 75.

65. Rogge, 213, 215.

66. Kroeker to General H. S. Parks, US Army, August 13, 1945, subject box 1, Autobiographical—J, John Jakob Kroeker Papers, MS. 501, Mennonite Library and Archives, Bethel College, North Newton, Kansas.

67. Ribuffo, 119.

68. Letter from Winrod to Kroeker, August 22, 1938, Correspondence series, Corres. Winrod, Gerald, John Jakob Kroeker Papers, MS. 501, Mennonite Library and Archives.

69. Transcript of radio addresses by Winrod, March 3 and 17, 1938, Correspondence series, Corres. Winrod, Gerald, John Jakob Kroeker Papers, MS. 501, Mennonite Library and Archives.

70. *New York Times*, "Hamilton Assails Kansas Candidate," July 23, 1938.

71. Ribuffo, 122–23.

72. Ribuffo, 123.

73. Letter from Roosevelt to White, June 8, 1938, White, William Allen folder, box 173, President's Secretary file, Franklin D. Roosevelt Presidential Library & Museum, Hyde Park, New York.

74. Letter from White to Roosevelt, June 10, 1938, White, William Allen folder, box 173, President's Secretary file, Franklin D. Roosevelt Presidential Library & Museum.

75. "Progressives Target," *Kane Republican* [Kane, Pennsylvania], March 24, 1938, 7.

76. "Arch-Fascist seeks US Senate post," *Chicago Times*, July 5, 1938; Gerald B. Winrod file, John C. Metcalfe Papers.

77. *New York Times*, "Windrod of Wichita," July 23, 1938, 12.

78. *New York Times*, "Kansas Feud Helps Winrod," July 31, 1938, 59.

79. *New York Times*, "Hamilton Assails Kansas Candidate," July 23, 1938.

80. *New York Times*, "Kansas Sees Bigotry Beaten," August 7, 1938, 59.

81. Winrod "Prayer Circle" letter, October 14, 1939, box 1A, folder 1, Gerald B. Winrod Papers, Wichita State University Libraries, Special Collections.

82. *Los Angeles Times*, "Aimee's 'Sub' Protested," November 12, 1938, A1; "Aimee Temple Defies Protest," November 13, 1938, A7; "Temple Bomb Threat Fails," November 14, 1938, A1; "Winrod Drops Sermon Plans," November 17, 1938, A8.

83. Survey by *Fortune*. Methodology: Conducted by Roper Organization during August, 1938 and based on 5,157 personal interviews. Sample: National adult. [USROPER .38-002.Q09].

84. Methodology: Conducted by Gallup Organization, March 10–15, 1939, and based on 1,500 personal interviews. Sample: National adult. Sample size is approximate. [USGALLUP.39-151.QA08].

85. Survey by *Fortune*. Methodology: Conducted by Roper Organization during July, 1939 and based on 5,236 personal interviews. Sample: National adult. [USROPER .39-007.QB3].

86. Bennett, 279–80.

87. Tull, 207–8; Marcus, 156.

88. Albin Krebs, "Charles Coughlin, 30's 'Radio Priest,' Dies," *New York Times*, October 28, 1979, 44.

89. Cf. Bennett, 281.

90. Rogge, 303–4.

91. Walter W. Williamson, *Heil Roosevelt: An American Student in Nazi Germany* (Xlibris, 2000), 67.

92. *Nazi Conspiracy and Aggression*, Appendix A, p. 571.

93. Rogge, 306–7: Warren, 233.

94. Letter from Kroeker to Winrod, February 12, 1939, Correspondence series, Corres. Winrod, Gerald, John Jakob Kroeker Papers, MS. 501, Mennonite Library and Archives.

95. Letter from Kroeker to Winrod, April 19, 1939, Correspondence series, Corres. Winrod, Gerald, John Jakob Kroeker Papers, MS. 501, Mennonite Library and Archives.

96. Letter from Kroeker to Winrod, April 18, 1939, Correspondence series, Corres. Winrod, Gerald, John Jakob Kroeker Papers, MS. 501, Mennonite Library and Archives.

97. MacDonnell, 108.

98. Kroeker to General H. S. Parks, US Army, August 13, 1945, subject box 1, Autobiographical—J, Correspondence series, Corres. Winrod, Gerald, John Jakob Kroeker Papers, MS. 501, Mennonite Library and Archives.

99. Winrod "Prayer Circle" letter, October 14, 1939; undated letter headlined "The Defender asks for fair play," box 1A, folder 28, Gerald B. Winrod Papers.

100. Tull, 223.

101. Winrod "Prayer Circle" letter, November 20, 1941, box 1A, folder 42, Gerald B. Winrod Papers.

102. Gellerman, 230.

103. Reports filed by Dies Committee investigators, 1938, Gerald B. Winrod file, John C. Metcalfe Papers.

104. *New York Times*, "Fifth Columnists Active in America," September 1, 1940, BR5.

105. Cf. Tull, 213.

106. Rogge, 306.

107. Bennett, 281; Tull, 211.

108. "Coughlin Questions Democracy's Value: Priest Asks Whether It Might Be Worse Than Dictatorship," *New York Times*, January 8, 1940, 3.

109. "18 Seized in Plot to Overthrow U.S.; Arms Found Here: Some of the Prisoners and Weapons in Plot Disclosed by G-men," *New York Times*, January 15, 1940, 1.

110. "The Menace of the Christian Front," March 1940 speech, p. 9, folder 19, box 40, Joseph Hansen Papers, Hoover Institution.

111. "Coughlin Condemns Group: Expresses Hope for Conviction of Men Seized Here," *New York Times*, January 15, 1940, 3.

112. "'Front' Once Hailed by Father Coughlin," *New York Times*, January 17, 1940, 14.

113. "Attacks Involved Those on Both Sides of the Iron Curtain," *Los Angeles Times*, March 30, 1981, 34.

114. "Attorney General Sends Ace Aide Here to Assist Kennedy in Case," *Brooklyn Eagle*, January 22, 1940, 1.

115. Cf. Tull, 220.

116. "Wider Conspiracy Probe Promised," *Ithaca Journal*, January 22, 1940, 9.

117. Warren, 194.

118. Warren, 195–96; Tull, 223.

119. Warren, 218–19.

120. Warren, 222–25.

121. Tull, 230.

122. Winrod "Prayer Circle" letter, February 24, 1942, box 1A, folder 48, Gerald B. Winrod Papers.

123. Tull, 233.

124. Tull, 234–35; Warren, 248–49. 259.

125. Warren, 265–69.

126. *New York Times*, "Dethridge Post in Defense Studied," February 22, 1942, 22.

127. *New York Times*, "28 Are Indicted on Sedition Charge," July 24, 1942, 1; Rogge, 173.

128. Jeansonne, 75.

129. Jeansonne, 66–67; Report on Smith from Detroit office, May 23, 1942, p. 3, FBI file on Gerald L. K. Smith, pt. 1, FBI Vault.

130. Jeansonne, 77–78.

131. Strong, 63–64.

132. Strong, 76.

4. The Senators

1. Appendix to the *Congressional Record*, June 19, 1940, p. 4036.

2. "Strict Neutrality Urged by Lundeen," *New York Times*, March 21, 1940, 10; "Lundeen Issues Call for Anti-War Party to be Formed in Chicago by Farmers, Labor," *New York Times*, August 2, 1940, 5.

3. *PM*, "George Viereck (Benedict Arnold) is Germany's Paid Press Agent," August 12, 1940, 8; Dies Committee Hearings—Appendix—part 7, vol. 1, pp. 39–40.

4. Niel M. Johnson, *George Sylvester Viereck, German-American Propagandist* (Urbana: University of Illinois Press, 1972), 10–16; Phyllis Keller, *States of Belonging: German-American Intellectuals and the First World War* (Cambridge, MA; London: Harvard University Press, 1979), 121; George Sylvester Viereck, *Confessions of a Barbarian* (London: John Lane, Bodley Head, 1910).

5. Johnson, 29–38.

6. Johnson, 40–43.

7. Keller, 154.

8. Johnson, 69; Keller, 168–69.

9. Johnson, 81.

10. Cf. Keller, 176.

11. Derived from Foreign Office reports 1939–41, including: report on *Axis America*, April 1941, FO 371/26214; report on Nazi and Nazi-inspired propaganda in the United States, June 5, 1940, FO 371/24237.

12. *Nazi Conspiracy and Aggression*, Appendix A, 561.

13. Dies Committee Hearings—Appendix—part 7, vol. 1, pp. 39–40.

14. Keller places this number at closer to $200,000 (180).

15. "German War Declaration Handed U.S." *Daily Independent* [Murphysboro, Illinois], December 11, 1941, 1.

16. Geraldine Smith, "Revolt of the Major's Daughter," *Philadelphia Inquirer Everybody Weekly*, August 31, 1941, 3.

17. *Nazi Conspiracy and Aggression*, Appendix A, 551.

18. Preliminary interrogation report on Heribert von Strempel, December 14, 1945, Strempel, Heribert (von) file 6, Nazi War Crimes Disclosure Act, CIA CREST.

19. Memorandum from Saint to Amzon on von Strempel, file 9, p. 2, Nazi War Crimes Disclosure Act, CIA CREST.

20. Memorandum from Saint to Amzon on von Strempel, file 9, p. 2, Nazi War Crimes Disclosure Act, CIA CREST.

21. *Nazi Conspiracy and Aggression*, Appendix A, 563.

22. Memorandum from Saint to Amzon on von Strempel, file 9, p. 3, Nazi War Crimes Disclosure Act, CIA CREST.

23. "Lundeen to Replace Olson on the Ballot," *New York Times*, August 30, 1936, 3.

24. "Lundeen Noted as Isolationist," *New York Times*, September 1, 1940.

25. Letter from Viereck to Lundeen, April 23, 1937, folder 7, box 179, Ernest Lundeen Papers, Hoover Institution.

26. Letters between Viereck and Lundeen, April 1937, folder 7, box 179, Ernest Lundeen Papers.

27. "Viereck's Letter Barred at Trial," *New York Times*, March 3, 1941, 13.

28. Letter from Viereck to Lundeen, June 12, 1937, folder 7, box 179, Ernest Lundeen Papers.

29. Letter from Viereck to Lundeen, February 1, 1938, folder 7, box 179, Ernest Lundeen Papers. Lundeen himself marked this letter with the note "no reply."

30. Alton Frye, *Nazi Germany and the American Hemisphere, 1933–1941*, Yale Historical Publications Miscellany (New Haven: Yale University Press, 1967), 162.

31. Cf. Frye, 162.

32. Dies Committee Report, *Investigation of Un-American Propaganda Activities in the United States,* Vol. 14, p. 8188.
33. Letter from Viereck to Fish, August 4, 1938, folder 7, box 179, Ernest Lundeen Papers.
34. Viereck v. United States, 318 U.S. 236 (1943), *Justia,* https://supreme.justia.com/cases/federal/us/318/236/case.html.
35. Letters from Viereck to Lundeen, October 10–12, 1939, folder 7, box 179, Ernest Lundeen Papers.
36. *Nazi Conspiracy and Aggression,* Appendix A, 562.
37. Adolphus Werth, *It Happened Again: How the War Came,* A Flanders Hall Book-of-the-Hour (Scotch Plains, NJ: Flanders Hall, 1940).
38. Lothian, Philip Henry Kerr, *Lord Lothain vs. Lord Lothian: Excerpts from the Speeches and Writings of the Marquess of Lothian, British Ambassador to the United States* (Scotch Plains, NJ: Flanders Hall, 1940); *Nazi Conspiracy and Aggression,* Appendix A, 563.
39. *Nazi Conspiracy and Aggression,* Appendix A, 562.
40. *Nazi Conspiracy and Aggression,* Appendix A, 562.
41. Richard M. Langworth, "Tangling with the Media: The Curious Case of William Griffin," *Finest Hour,* Autumn 2011, https://www.winstonchurchill.org/publications/finest-hour/finest-hour-152/tangling-with-the-media-the-curious-case-of-of-william-griffin.
42. *Nazi Conspiracy and Aggression,* Appendix A, 565.
43. "Say Hill Ordered Mail Bags Moved," *New York Times,* January 13, 1942, 40.
44. Frye, 161.
45. FBI file, Lindbergh, report on the book *Sabotage,* September 17, 1942, p. 14.
46. "Say Hill Ordered Mail Bags Moved," *New York Times,* January 13, 1942, 40.
47. Undated letter from Fish to be included with copy of speech, box 179, Ernest Lundeen Papers.
48. *Nazi Conspiracy and Aggression,* Appendix A, 577–78; Rogge, 355.
49. November 21, 1941 report to FBI by Office of Naval Intelligence, San Diego, FBI Lindbergh file, FBI Vault.
50. Letter from Lundeen to Viereck, August 23, 1940; Letter from Viereck to Lundeen, August 22, 1940; Box 179, Folder 8, Ernest Lundeen Papers.
51. "25 Dead in Crash of Air Transport; Lundeen Is Killed," *New York Times,* September 1, 1940, 1; "Says Fatal Plane Struck Full Tilt: Wreckage and Two of Those Killed in Plane Crash," *New York Times,* September 2, 1940, 32.
52. Report on the book *Sabotage,* September 17, 1942, pp. 13–14, Lindbergh FBI file, FBI Vault.
53. Letter from Jackson to Lundeen, October 10, 1940, "Death of Ernest Lundeen Investigation," Ernest Lundeen Papers.
54. Report on the book *Sabotage,* September 17, 1942, p. 14, Lindbergh FBI file, FBI Vault.
55. Viereck to Lundeen, August 14, 1940, box 179, Ernest Lundeen Papers.
56. Letter from the Make Europe Pay War Debts Committee to Walter Winchell, October 12, 1940, box 179, Ernest Lundeen Papers.
57. Letters from Viereck to Mrs. Lundeen, September–November 1940, box 179, Ernest Lundeen Papers.
58. Letter to Norma Lundeen from Widow's Protective League, San Francisco, September 17, 1940, box 179, Ernest Lundeen Papers.

59. Address by Norma Lundeen, National Broadcasting Company, May 18, 1941, Death of Ernest Lundeen Posthumous Lawsuits file, Ernest Lundeen Papers. Underlining original.

60. "Memorandum for Mrs Lundeen," testimony of February 24, 1942, reporter's transcript, Death of Ernest Lundeen Posthumous Lawsuits file, Ernest Lundeen Papers.

61. File on Wirsing, Giselher, file 16, p. 47, Nazi War Crimes Disclosure Act, CIA CREST.

62. "The Congressional Frank and Nazi Propaganda" secret report, p. 2, FO 1093/167/1. Italics mine.

63. "The Congressional Frank and Nazi Propaganda" secret report, p. 4, FO 1093/167/1.

64. "The Congressional Frank and Nazi Propaganda" secret report, p. 9, 11–12, FO 1093/167/1.

65. "The Congressional Frank and Nazi Propaganda" secret report, p. 3, FO 1093/167/1.

66. Correspondence related to interception of mail at Bermuda, September 17–27, 1941, DEFE 1/205.

67. Johnson, 225–27.

68. Letter from George A. McNulty to Major H. Montgomery Hyde, July 19, 1943, DEFE 1/205. Also see letter from Viscount Halifax to Foreign Office, July 27, 1943, DEFE 1/205.

69. "Arrest Fish Secretary as Espionage Suspect," *Lansing State Journal*, October 25, 1941, 8.

70. "Aide to Fish Is Sentenced," *Oakland Tribune*, February 6, 1942, 24.

5. The Businessmen

1. Dale Harrington, *Mystery Man: William Rhodes Davis, Nazi Agent of Influence*, 1st ed. (Virginia: Brassey's, 1999), 16; Rogge, 239.

2. Rogge, 238.

3. Harrington, 1–10.

4. Harrington, ix, 17.

5. O. D. Tolischus, "American Autos Plan to Invade German Market," *New Castle News* [Pennsylvania], January 4, 1929, 9.

6. Edwin Black, *IBM and the Holocaust: The Strategic Alliance between Nazi Germany and America's Most Powerful Corporation*, 1st ed. (New York: Crown Publishers, 2001), 46.

7. John Gillingham, *Industry and Politics in the Third Reich: Ruhr Coal, Hitler, and Europe*, Veröffentlichungen des Instituts für Europäische Geschichte Mainz, Abteilung Universalgeschichte Beiheft (Stuttgart: F. Steiner Verlag Wiesbaden, 1985), 76.

8. J. Adam Tooze, *The Wages of Destruction: The Making and Breaking of the Nazi Economy* (London, New York: Allen Lane, 2006), 128.

9. "American Factories Help Hitler in War," *Arizona Republic*, November 14, 1939, 3.

10. Sally Denton, *The Plots against the President: FDR, a Nation in Crisis, and the Rise of the American Right*, 1st US ed. (New York: Bloomsbury Press, 2012), 136–37.

11. Denton, 178, 194–97.

12. Denton, 200–201.

13. "The Fascist Plot," *Daily Tribune* [Wisconsin Rapids, Wisconsin], November 22, 1934, 4.

14. "The National Whirligig," *Altoona Tribune*, November 25, 1934.

15. Cf. Denton, 207.

16. Denton, 211.
17. Denton, 193.
18. John P. Diggins, *Mussolini and Fascism: The View from America* (Princeton University Press, 1972), 146.
19. "Capitalism's Frontier," *Barron's*, September 14, 1936, 12.
20. Rogge, 288.
21. *Fortune.* Roper/*Fortune* Survey, July 1940 [survey question]. USROPER.40-019.R08. Roper Organization [producer]. Cornell University, Ithaca, NY: Roper Center for Public Opinion Research, iPOLL [distributor].
22. Henry Ashby Turner, *General Motors and the Nazis: The Struggle for Control of Opel, Europe's Biggest Carmaker* (New Haven: Yale University Press, 2005), 3; "General Motors and Ford Carry Fight to Germany," *Zanesville Signal* [*Times Recorder*], March 12, 1929, 1.
23. Turner, 5–7.
24. Reinhold Billstein, "1945. How the Americans Took Over Cologne—and Discovered Ford Werke's Role in the War," in Reinhold Billstein, Karola Fings, Anita Kugler, and Nicholas Levis, eds., *Working for the Enemy: Ford, General Motors, and Forced Labor in Germany During the Second World War* (New York: Berghahn Books, 2000), 110.
25. Mark Pendergrast, *For God, Country and Coca-Cola: The Definitive History of the Great American Soft Drink and the Company That Makes It*, 3d ed. (New York: Basic Books, 2013), 214–15.
26. Pendergrast, 215–16.
27. Turner, 9.
28. Pendergrast, 216.
29. Edwin Black, *Nazi Nexus: America's Corporate Connections to Hitler's Holocaust* (Washington, DC: Dialog Press, 2009), 129–30.
30. Turner, 10, 158.
31. Turner, 18–20.
32. Turner, 21–30.
33. Turner, 29.
34. Pendergrast, 218.
35. Pendergrast, 219–20.
36. "Popular Motor Car Planned in Germany," *Marshfield News-Herald* [Marshfield, Wisconsin], February 16, 1935, 13.
37. Turner, 3–6.
38. Billstein, 111.
39. Neil Baldwin, *Henry Ford and the Jews: The Mass Production of Hate* (New York: Public Affairs, 2001), 59–60.
40. Baldwin, 208–10, 277.
41. Cf. Baldwin, 149, 185.
42. Billstein, 111.
43. "Cantor Calls Ford Foolish for Accepting Hitler Medal," *Los Angeles Times*, August 4, 1938, 9.
44. "Appeal to Henry Ford: Ask Him to Give Back Hitler Decoration," *Town Talk* [Alexandria, Louisiana], August 6, 1938, 11.
45. Tooze, 133.
46. Harrington, 1–10.

47. Jane Mayer, *Dark Money: The Hidden History of the Billionaires Behind the Rise of the Radical Right*, 1st ed. (New York: Doubleday, 2016), 29–30; Harrington, 11–19.
48. Rogge, 239.
49. Harrington, 21, 23, 32.
50. Harrington, 42; "Secret $175,000 Contribution to Democrats Made by Oil Man Davis," *St. Louis Post-Dispatch*, April 7, 1940, 3A.
51. Harrington, 44–47.
52. Harrington, 46–48.
53. Harrington, 50, 57; Rogge, 240.
54. "American Gives Details of Oil Deal with Mexico," *St. Louis Post-Dispatch*, August 5, 1938, 7A.
55. "Secret $175,000 Contribution to Democrats Made by Oil Man Davis," *St. Louis Post-Dispatch*.
56. Harrington, 82.
57. *Handbook of Labor Statistics: 1950*, US Bureau of Labor Statistics, 139.
58. Saul David Alinsky, *John L. Lewis: An Unauthorized Biography* (New York: Putnam, 1949), 203.
59. Alinsky, 169–71.
60. Robert H. Zieger, *John L. Lewis: Labor Leader*, Twayne's Twentieth-Century American Biography Series (Boston: Twayne Publishers, 1988), 107; Melvyn Dubofsky and Warren R. Van Tine, *John L. Lewis: A Biography* (New York: Quadrangle/New York Times Book Co., 1977), 332.
61. William B. Breuer, *Hitler's Undercover War: The Nazi Espionage Invasion of the U.S.A.*, 1st ed. (New York: St. Martin's Press, 1989), 127.
62. Breuer, 127; Rogge, 242; Harrington, 89.
63. Harrington, 88.
64. Cf. Rogge, 245.
65. Cf. Breuer, 128.
66. Harrington, 93.
67. Cf. Harrington, 97–99; Rogge, 246–48.
68. Rogge, 250–51; Harrington, 105–7.
69. Breuer, 128; Harrington, 118–19. Harrington and Breuer disagree as to when Davis actually became an Abwehr agent, with Breuer suggesting he was already formally working for the Germans before his trip to Italy.
70. Harrington, 118–19.
71. Louise Overacker, "Campaign Finance in the Presidential Election of 1940," *American Political Science Review* 35 (4) (August 1941), 701–27.
72. Rogge, 248.
73. Rogge, 253.
74. Rogge, 249.
75. Billstein, 112.
76. Billstein, 115.
77. Turner, 88–89.
78. Turner, 91–98.
79. Turner, 98.
80. Turner, 102, 127–28.

81. "American Factories Help Hitler in War," *Arizona Republic*, November 14, 1939, 3.
82. Dubofsky and Van Tine, 333.
83. Cf. Turner, 111.
84. Turner, 120–24.
85. Drew Pearson and Robert S. Allen, "The Washington Merry-Go-Round," *Gazette and Daily* [York, Pennsylvania], March 11, 1941, 6.
86. James Stewart Martin, *All Honorable Men*, 1st ed. (Boston: Little, Brown, 1950), 24.
87. Graeme Keith Howard, *America and a New World Order* (New York: C. Scribner's Sons, 1940), 90–105.
88. Howard, 110–16.
89. Howard, 121.
90. Robert E. S. Thompson, "Three Facets of Our Battle for Freedom," *Philadelphia Inquirer*, October 9, 1940, 17.
91. Higham, *Trading with the Enemy: An Exposé of the Nazi-American Money Plot, 1933–1949* (New York: Delacorte Press, 1983), 166.
92. Testimony of Heribert von Strempel, February 15–18, 1946, *Nazi Conspiracy and Aggression*, Appendix A, 584.
93. *Nazi Conspiracy and Aggression*, Appendix A, 584.
94. Higham, 171–72.
95. *Nazi Conspiracy and Aggression*, Appendix A, 585.
96. "'G' Men on Nazi Agent's Trail in U.S.," *Des Moines Register*, August 2, 1940, 11; "Baroness Aids Nazi Envoy," *Pittsburgh Press*, August 2, 1940, 15.
97. *Nazi Conspiracy and Aggression*, Appendix A, 585.
98. Rogge, 296; Martin, 53.
99. Harrington, 142–3.
100. Gallup Organization, Gallup Poll (AIPO), March 1940 [survey question]. USGALLUP .40-188. QT04C. Gallup Organization [producer]. Cornell University, Ithaca, NY: Roper Center for Public Opinion Research, iPOLL [distributor].
101. *Fortune*. Roper/Fortune Survey, April 1940 [survey question]. USROPER.40-16C. Q03D. Roper Organization [producer]. Cornell University, Ithaca, NY: Roper Center for Public Opinion Research, iPOLL [distributor].
102. Harrington, 143–44.
103. Harrington, 147–48.
104. Dubofsky and Van Tine, 351–52.
105. Gallup Organization, Gallup Poll, October 1940 [survey question]. USGALLUP .110440.RK02A. Gallup Organization [producer]. Cornell University, Ithaca, NY: Roper Center for Public Opinion Research, iPOLL [distributor].
106. Harrington, 150–51.
107. Rogge, 256.
108. Dubofsky and Van Tine, 357; Alinsky, 191.
109. Rogge, 256.
110. Rogge, 257.
111. Appendix to the *Congressional Record*, January 21, 1941, p. A 179; Appendix to the *Congressional Record*, May 6, 1941, p. A 179;
112. Harrington, 178.
113. Turner, 124.

114. Martin, 24–25.

115. Turner, 158.

116. J. C. Louis and Harvey Yazijian, *The Cola Wars*, 1st ed. (New York: Everest House, 1980), 47.

117. Pendergrast, 221.

118. Pendergrast, 221–22.

119. Pendergrast, 213.

120. Higham, 157–59.

121. Billstein, 140–41.

122. Harrington, 190–91.

123. "W. R. Davis Dies; Oil Man, Reputed Nazi Peace Agent," *St. Louis Post-Dispatch*, August 1, 1941, 1, 3.

124. Cf. William Stevenson, *A Man Called Intrepid: The Secret War*, 1st ed. (New York: Harcourt Brace Jovanovich, 1976), 295.

125. Harrington, 194–97.

6. The Students

1. "Cottrell Upholds Books Censored by Germany," *Stanford Daily*, October 11, 1933, 1.

2. "Over-Zealous Nazi Students Attempt to Burn Cultural History," *Stanford Daily*, April 27, 1933, 2.

3. "German Plays to Be Presented," *Stanford Daily*, May 15, 1939, 2.

4. "Frost Views Germany: People Not Anxious to Fight," *Stanford Daily*, May 11, 1939, 4.

5. United States Congress, House Special Committee on Un-American Activities (1938–1944), *Investigation of Un-American Propaganda Activities in the United States* (Washington, DC: United States Government Printing Office), vol. 2, p. 1133.

6. Stephen Norwood, *The Third Reich in the Ivory Tower: Complicity and Conflict on American Campuses* (Cambridge: Cambridge University Press, 2009); Stephen Norwood, "The Expulsion of Robert Burke: Suppressing Campus Anti-Nazi Protest in the 1930s," *Journal for the Study of Antisemitism* 4 (1) (2012), 89–113.

7. Norwood, *Third Reich*, 99.

8. Norwood, "Expulsion," 89.

9. Albert Grzesinsky and Charles E. Hewitt Jr., "Hitler's Branch Offices, U.S.A.," *Jewish Veteran*, December 1940, 12.

10. "Goettingen Cites Three Americans," *New York Times*, June 28, 1937, 19; "Gauss-Johnson Engineering Building and Laboratory, 1941–," http://www.lib.uidaho.edu /digital/campus/locations/Gauss-JohnsonEngineeringBuildingandLaboratory.html.

11. "Faculty Member Discusses European Trip Impressions," *California Daily Bruin*, October 3, 1938, 1. After leaving UCLA, Hoffman moved to New York and practiced as a psychoanalyst. He was found dead alongside his wife in the burned-out vacation cabin of *Fortune* magazine editor John Knox Jessup in 1951. The police ruled the grisly case a murder-suicide, despite the subsequent discovery of a third body near the scene: "Fire-Swept House Yields New Bodies," *New York Times*, March 31, 1951, 19; "Third Body Found Near Burned Cabin," *New York Times*, April 2, 1951, 18; "Couple's Death Settled," *New York Times*, April 3, 1951, 18.

12. "Nazi Plot at UCLA Comes to Grief," *Long Beach Independent* [California], March 7, 1939, 8.

13. "Storm Boils over Asserted Nazi Influence at U.C.L.A.," *Los Angeles Times*, February 26, 1939, 3.

14. "Towards Academic Democracy," *California Daily Bruin*, February 27, 1939, 2.

15. "German Enrollment in American Institutions of Higher Learning," *German Quarterly* 7 (4) (November 1934), 129.

16. "German University Summer Schools," *Monatshefte für Deutschen Unterricht* 27 (4) (April 1935), 149.

17. W. H. Cowley and Willard Waller, "A Study of Student Life," *Journal of Higher Education*, 6 (3) (March 1935), 141.

18. Evans, 294.

19. Evans, 298.

20. "Fraulein, Co-Ed Compared: Conventions Don't Bother German Students," *Stanford Daily*, August 2, 1932, 1.

21. Evans, 291–92; Charles Beard, "Education under the Nazis," *Foreign Affairs*, April 1936, 440.

22. Evans, 293–94.

23. "Nazi Education," *School Life*, February 1934, 113; Evans, 295.

24. "Nazi Education," *School Life*, February 1934, 113; Evans, 298.

25. I. L. Kandel, "Education in Nazi Germany," *Annals of the American Academy of Political and Social Science* 182 (November 1935), 153–63.

26. Evans, 303–5.

27. Charles A. Beard, "Education under the Nazis," *Foreign Affairs*, April 1936, 452.

28. Bernhard Rust and Ernst Krieck, *Das nationalsozialistische Deutschland und die Wissenschaft; Heidelberger Reden von Reichsminister Rust und prof. Ernst Krieck* (*National Socialist Germany and the Pursuit of Learning*), Schriften des Reichsinstituts für Geschichte des Neuen Deutschlands (Hamburg: Hanseatische Verlagsanstalt), 11.

29. Rust and Krieck, 16.

30. Memo from Agent Edward J. Conway, point 7, p. 1: FBI interview of Cyrus Follmer, September 2, 1943 (Karl L. Falk FBI file, 65-HQ-25294, National Archives, College Park, Maryland).

31. Norwood, *Third Reich*, 124.

32. Norwood, *Third Reich*, 122.

33. Norwood, *Third Reich*, 126.

34. "German Camp Chooses Two," *Stanford Daily*, May 12, 1938, 4; "Exchange Student Speaks of Nazi Colonial Demands," *Stanford Daily*, October 25, 1938, 2.

35. Phyllis White, "German Instructor Heads Trip Abroad," *Stanford Daily*, October 25, 1937, 2.

36. Malcolm Letts, *Nazi Germany: "I Lived with the Brown Shirts"* (Los Angeles: M. Letts, 1933), foreword.

37. Letts, 6.

38. Letts, 7–8.

39. Letts, 16.

40. Letts, 16.

41. E. W. H. Cruickshank, "Impressions of Nazi Germany," *Dalhousie Review* 13 (4) (1934), 410–11.

42. John L. Spivak, *Plotting America's Pogroms: A Documented Exposé of Organized Anti-Semitism in the United States* (New York: New Masses, 1934), 73.

43. Spivak, 75–76.

44. Spivak, 76.

45. Spivak, 74.

46. "Col. Hadley, 80, Business Man and Writer, Dies," *Chicago Tribune*, February 17, 1953, 41.

47. Cf. Spivak, 74.

48. "Spivak Charges Dean Alexander and Student Conduct Anti-Semitic, Pro-Nazi Activities Here," *Columbia Daily Spectator*, November 19, 1934, 1, 4.

49. Norwood, *Third Reich*, 83; "Notable Events at Columbia in 1934," *Columbia Daily Spectator*, January 7, 1935, 4; "T.C., New College Will Make Trip to Berlin Games," *Columbia Daily Spectator*, February 7, 1936, 1.

50. Norwood, *Third Reich*, 36–37, 106–7.

51. "Exchange Student Speaks of Nazi Colonial Demands," *Stanford Daily*, October 26, 1938, 2.

52. "Nazi Party Member Accepts A.S.U. Debate Invitation," *Stanford Daily*, May 24, 1939; Andries Deinum, "Deinum Speaking," *Stanford Daily*, May 25, 1939, 4.

53. "Ex-Matean on List as Nazi," *San Mateo Times* [California], March 1, 1947, 2.

54. "E. Pluribus Unum," *Columbia Daily Spectator*, December 11, 1933, 2; "Dennis to Talk before Institute," *Columbia Daily Spectator*, January 14, 1935, 1;

55. Horne, 17–27.

56. Horne, 17–19.

57. Horne, 24–25.

58. Rogge, 174–76.

59. Horne, 61–66.

60. Rogge, 179–80.

61. Horne, 71–73, 85.

62. *Nazi Conspiracy and Aggression*, Appendix A, p. 567.

63. *Nazi Conspiracy and Aggression*, Appendix A, p. 567.

64. Lawrence Dennis, *The Coming American Fascism*, 1st ed. (New York: Harper, 1936), 308.

65. John R. Commons, "Review: *The Coming American Fascism* by Lawrence Dennis," *American Economic Review* 26 (2) (June 1936), 298–300.

66. "A Rose by Any Other Name," *Columbia Daily Spectator*, January 16, 1936, 2.

67. "Fife Recalls Arrested Nazi," *Columbia Daily Spectator*, October 3, 1940, 4.

68. "Fife Recalls Arrested Nazi," *Columbia Daily Spectator*.

69. *Nazi Conspiracy and Aggression*, Appendix A, 556.

70. Norwood, *Third Reich*, 83.

71. Norwood, *Third Reich*, 79–80.

72. Norwood, *Third Reich*, 85–99; Frank C. Hanighen, "Foreign Political Movements in the United States," *Foreign Affairs*, October 1937, 16.

73. Norwood, *Third Reich*, 101.

74. Letter from Madden to Heinz Rüdiger, April 24 [1930], Correspondence—1930, Henry Madden Papers, University Archives, Henry Madden Library, California State University, Fresno.

75. "Itch Powder Discourages Nudist Cult," *San Bernardino Daily Sun* [California], May 10, 1932, 1.

76. Letter from Madden to Heinz [Rüdiger], December 14, 1935, Correspondence—1935, University Archives, Henry Madden Library.

77. Letter from Madden to "Edward," February 12, 1935, folder 7 of 7, Correspondence—1935, University Archives, Henry Madden Library.

78. Letter from Madden to "Pontchen," April 3, 1935, Correspondence—1935, University Archives, Henry Madden Library.

79. Letter from Shanahan to Madden, January 2, 1936, Correspondence—1936, University Archives, Henry Madden Library.

80. Letter from Shanahan to Madden, October 9, 1936, Correspondence—1936, University Archives, Henry Madden Library.

81. Letter from Madden to his mother, June 30, 1936, Correspondence—1936, University Archives, Henry Madden Library.

82. Letter from Shanahan to Madden, updated [likely September 1936] on reverse of letter dated October 9, 1936, Correspondence—1936, University Archives, Henry Madden Library.

83. Letter to Madden from "Bissell," February 6, 1937, Correspondence—1937, University Archives, Henry Madden Library.

84. Williamson, 16.

85. Williamson, 42.

86. Williamson, 69–70.

87. Williamson, 250–59.

88. "Laney Wins Tarver Award: Frost Writes from Heidelberg," *Stanford Daily*, May 10, 1939, 2.

89. "Farm Soph Flees Nazi Air Attack," *Stanford Daily*, September 26, 1939, 1.

90. Letter from Shanahan to Madden, September 3, 1939, Correspondence—1939 University Archives, Henry Madden Library.

91. "Bowman, Rubinstein, Stout, Swope to Speak at Forum in McMillin at 11 A.M.," *Columbia Daily Spectator*, April 18, 1941, 1.

92. "Farm Hears Heated War Symposium," *Stanford Daily*, May 20, 1941, 1.

93. Letter from Madden to Col. Edgar Erskine Hume, June 20, 1942, Correspondence—1942, University Archives, Henry Madden Library.

94. Williamson, 258.

95. "America First and the Colleges" secret report, Appendix B, p. 1, FO 1093/167/1.

7. America First!

1. "500 Police Ready for Peace Rally," *New York Times*, May 23, 1941, 10; "60% at Garden Rally Pro-Nazi, Morris Says," *New York Times*, May 25, 1941, 3; "Lindbergh Joins in Wheeler Plea to U.S. to Shun War," *New York Times*, May 24, 2941, 1.

2. "Lindbergh Joins in Wheeler Plea to U.S. to Shun War," *New York Times*, 1, 6.

3. "Lindbergh Joins in Wheeler Plea to U.S. to Shun War," *New York Times*, 1, 6.

4. "Lindbergh Joins in Wheeler Plea to U.S. to Shun War," *New York Times*, 6.

5. Letter to P. N. Loxley, November 29, 1941, FO 1093/167/1.

6. Report on the America First Committee, 1941, p. 30, FO 1093/167/1.

7. Letter from Dennis to Justus Doenecke, March 30, 1970, folder 22, box 3, Lawrence Dennis Papers, Hoover Institution, Stanford University.

8. Report on the America First Committee, 1941, p. 3, FO 1093/167/1; Cole, *America First*, 10–11.

9. Report on the America First Committee, 1941, pp. 5–7, FO 1093/167/1; Cole, 12–13.

10. Report on the America First Committee, 1941, p. 5, FO 1093/167/1; Cole, 13.

11. September 16, 1940 journal entry, Box 2, Folder 12, Charles Augustus Lindbergh Papers, Missouri History Museum, St. Louis, Missouri.

12. Report on the America First Committee, 1941, p. 9, FO 1093/167/1; Cole, *America First*, 20–22.

13. Report on the America First Committee, 1941, p. 1, FO 1093/167/1.

14. Cole, *America First*, 30.

15. Cole, *America First*, 27–30.

16. Cole, *America First*, 31.

17. Cole, *America First*, 58, 119.

18. Report on the America First Committee, 1941, p. 10, FO 1093/167/1.

19. Cole, *America First*, 142; A. Scott Berg, *Lindbergh* (London: Macmillan, 1998), 410–12.

20. Report on the America First Committee, 1941, p. 29, FO 1093/167/1.

21. Berg, 276.

22. Berg, 355; Letter from Lindbergh to Smith, June 5, 1936, box 1; Draft of *My Life, Berlin August 1935–April 1939*, p. 91, box 6, Truman Smith Papers, Hoover Institution.

23. Letter from Lindbergh to Smith, June 5, 1936, p. 5, box 1, Truman Smith Papers.

24. "Amazing Aviation: In a Speech Delivered at a Luncheon of the German Air Ministry in Berlin." *New York Times*, July 26, 1936, Pg. E8, "Lindbergh in Reich Warns on Air War: Tells Germans the World Must Find Security from Peril of Bombing Planes. Civilization Held Stake Colonel's Speech Makes the 'Strongest Impression,'" *New York Times*, July 24, 1936, 1, 4.

25. Berg, 354–55, 361; Draft of *My Life, Berlin August 1935–April 1939*, 98–99, box 6, Truman Smith Papers.

26. Draft of *My Life, Berlin August 1935–April 1939*, p. 99, box 6, Truman Smith Papers.

27. "Lindbergh Studies Reich Air Center," July 26, 1936, *New York Times*, 25.

28. Draft of *My Life, Berlin August 1935–April 1939*, p. 113, box 6, Truman Smith Papers.

29. "Lindbergh Ends Stay in Germany: Leaves Without Seeing Hitler, Although Two Sat Close Together at Olympics," *New York Times*, August 3, 1936, 17.

30. Berg, 360.

31. "Lindbergh Ends Stay in Germany," *New York Times*.

32. Letter from Lindbergh to Smith, August 6, 1936, box 1, Truman Smith Papers.

33. Berg, 360–61.

34. Letter from Lindbergh to Smith, April 28, 1937, box 1, Truman Smith Papers.

35. Letter from Lindbergh to Smith, October 28, 1937, box 1, Truman Smith Papers.

36. Letter from Lindbergh to Smith, March 18, 1938, box 1, Truman Smith Papers.
37. Draft of *My Life, Berlin August 1935–April 1939*, p. 194, box 6, Truman Smith Papers.
38. Letter from Lindbergh to Smith, September 16, 1938, box 1, Truman Smith Papers.
39. September 21, 1938 journal entry, Box 1, folder 18, Charles Augustus Lindbergh Papers.
40. Berg, 378–79.
41. Draft of *My Life, Berlin August 1935–April 1939*, p. 237, box 6, Truman Smith Papers.
42. "Hitler Grants Lindbergh High Decoration after Bitter Attacks on Flier by Russians," *New York Times*, October 20, 1938, 1.
43. Cf. "Magazine Suggests Lindbergh Go Home: British Publication Refers to His Activities in Recent Crisis," *New York Times*, November 1, 1938, 25.
44. "Lindbergh Said to Plan to Move to Berlin Because of Reich's Aviation Research Fame," *New York Times*, November 16, 1938, p. 1.
45. November 13, 1938 journal entry, box 1, folder 20, Charles Augustus Lindbergh Papers.
46. "Airline Drops Lindbergh Slogan; Denies Nazi Activities Cause," *Los Angeles Times*, December 6, 1938, 1.
47. "Ickes Berates Americans Who Accept Medals from Dictators," *Los Angeles Times*, December 19, 1938, 1.
48. "The News of the Week in Review," *New York Times*, December 25, 1938, E1.
49. Berg, 387–88.
50. Berg, 395.
51. "Lindbergh Urges We Shun the War," *New York Times*, September 16, 1939, 1, 9.
52. Berg, 397.
53. Lindbergh file 1A, FBI Vault.
54. "Asserts Lindbergh Spoke Own Views," *New York Times*, September 17, 1939, 22.
55. "Lindbergh Favors a Split Arms Ban," *New York Times*, October 14, 1939, 1.
56. Cf. "Lindbergh Speech Assailed in Senate," *New York Times*, October 15, 1939, 1.
57. "Lindbergh Scored by Press in London," *New York Times*, October 16, 1939, 8.
58. "British Host Gives Lindbergh Excuse," *New York Times*, October 22, 1939, 29.
59. Berg, 399.
60. Letter from Lothian to Victor Cazalet, July 1, 1940, GD 240/17/399/508, 11th Marquess of Lothian Papers.
61. Gallup Organization, Gallup Poll (AIPO), August 1940 [survey question]. USGALLUP .40-205.QKT03B. Gallup Organization [producer]. Cornell University, Ithaca, NY: Roper Center for Public Opinion Research, iPOLL [distributor].
62. "Lindbergh Called Foe of Democracy," *PM*, October 17, 1940, 7.
63. "Lindbergh Speeches Attributed to Horror of a Stalemated War," *New York Times*, October 27, 1939, 5.
64. Conducted by Gallup Organization, August 18–24, 1939, and based on 1,500 personal interviews. Sample: National adult. Sample size is approximate. [USGALLUP .39-167.QA07C]; conducted by Gallup Organization, August 18–24, 1939 and based on 1,500 personal interviews. Sample: National adult. Sample size is approximate. [USGALLUP.39-167.QA07D].
65. Survey by *Fortune*. Methodology: Conducted by Roper Organization during Novem-

ber 1939 and based on 5,244 personal interviews. Sample: National adult. [USROPER .39-012.Q05A].

66. "New Blood Asked in G.O.P. Lindbergh's Name Tops List," *New York Times*, December 13, 1937, 4.

67. "Nazis Quote Lindbergh," *New York Times*, October 25, 1939, 12.

68. "U.S. Antagonizing Powers," *PM*, October 31, 1940, 9; Berg, 412–13.

69. Letter to Lindbergh from Mrs. John W. Pendleton, October 18, 1940, box 25, folder 16, Campaign for Non-Intervention in WWII Letters—October 1940 radio speech, October 19–24, 1940, Charles Augustus Lindbergh Papers.

70. Letter to Lindbergh from Karl Draxler, October 20, 1940, box 25, folder 16, Campaign for Non-Intervention in WWII Letters—October 1940 radio speech, October 19–24, 1940, Charles Augustus Lindbergh Papers.

71. Berg, 414–15.

72. Olson, 313; Berg, 417–19.

73. Berg, 419.

74. Robert Butterfield, "Lindbergh: A Stubborn Young Man of Strange Ideas Becomes a Leader of Wartime Opposition," *Life*, August 11, 1941, 67.

75. Olson, 325.

76. "The Nazi Transmission Belt," pamphlet, box 2, folder 2, Hollywood Anti-Nazi League Papers.

77. Conducted by Gallup Organization, September 19–24, 1941, and based on 1,500 personal interviews. Sample: National adult. Sample size is approximate. [USGALLUP .41-248.QT11].

78. Conducted by Gallup Organization, September 4–9, 1939, and based on 1,500 personal interviews. Sample: National adult. Sample size is approximate. [USGALLUP .39-156.AQB08B]; Conducted by Gallup Organization, March 10–15, 1939 and based on 1,500 personal interviews. Sample: National adult. Sample size is approximate. [USGALLUP.39-151.QA08]

79. Gallup Organization, Gallup Poll (AIPO), August 1941 [survey question]. USGALLUP .41-245.QKT11B. Gallup Organization [producer]. Cornell University, Ithaca, NY: Roper Center for Public Opinion Research, iPOLL [distributor].

80. Account of meeting between Metcalfe and German American Bund leader Hermann Schwarzmann, Astoria, Queens, New York, July 19 [1937], Metcalfe surveillance diaries, "Daily Notations of Undercover Work," John C. Metcalfe Papers.

81. Account of Schwinn and Witmar speakers at Bund meeting, box 3, folder 2, Hollywood Anti-Nazi League Papers.

82. August 12, 1941 journal entry, box 2, folder 19, Charles Augustus Lindbergh Papers.

83. Cf. Olson, 332; "Miss Ingalls Says FBI Rejected Her: Testifies in Defense of Nazi Links That She Aspired to Be a Spy," *New York Times*, February 13, 1942, 23.

84. Rogge, 307.

85. See, for instance, poll conducted by Gallup Organization, November 24–29, 1938, and based on 1,500 personal interviews. Sample: National adult. Sample size is approximate. [USGALLUP.120938.R01A].

86. "Lindbergh Sees a 'Plot' for War," *New York Times*, 2; Berg, 427.

87. Berg, 427.

88. Michele Stenehjem Gerber, *An American First: John T. Flynn and the America First Committee* (New Rochelle, NY: Arlington House Publishers, 1976), 136–37.
89. Letter from Judson to national committee members, September 18, 1941, Colonel Lindbergh's Des Moines speech, America First Committee Records, Hoover Institution.
90. Wayne S. Cole, *Senator Gerald P. Nye and American Foreign Relations* (Minneapolis: University of Minnesota Press, 1962), 190–92.
91. August 23, 1939 journal entry, box 2, folder 4, Charles Augustus Lindbergh Papers.
92. September 17, 1940 journal entry, box 2, folder 12, Charles Augustus Lindbergh Papers.
93. November 9, 1940 journal entry, box 2, folder 12, Charles Augustus Lindbergh Papers.
94. July 15, 1941 journal entry, box 2, folder 4, Charles Augustus Lindbergh Papers.
95. July 11, 1941 journal entry, box 2, folder 18, Charles Augustus Lindbergh Papers.
96. September 15, 1941 journal entry, box 2, folder 19, Charles Augustus Lindbergh Papers.
97. September 16, 1941 journal entry, box 2, folder 4, Charles Augustus Lindbergh Papers.
98. Cole, *Senator Gerald P. Nye*, 152.
99. September 17, 1941 journal entry, box 2, folder 4, Charles Augustus Lindbergh Papers.
100. Letter from Fred and Alana Peterson, Minneapolis, Minnesota, September 16, 1941, chapter reactions to C. A. Lindbergh's Des Moines speech, America First Committee Records.
101. Cole, *Senator Gerald P. Nye*, 150.
102. September 18, 1941 journal entry, box 2, folder 4, Charles Augustus Lindbergh Papers.
103. Telegram from Niebuhr to Judson, September 14, 1941, Colonel Lindbergh's Des Moines speech, box 5, America First Committee Records.
104. Letter to Page Hufty with accompanying photographs, September 23, 1941, Western Trip file, America First Committee Records.
105. Transcript of Assembly Fact-Finding Committee on Un-American Activities in California, October 14–17, 1941, vol. 3, pp. 780–86, California Un-American Activities Committees Records, California State Archives.
106. Transcript of Assembly Fact-Finding Committee on Un-American Activities in California, October 14–17, 1941, vol. 3, pp. 844–45. California Un-American Activities Committees Records.
107. "Spectators Ejected at 'Un-American' Hearing," *Santa Cruz Sentinel*, October 16, 1941, 1.
108. Cole, *Senator Gerald P. Nye*, 153; Berg, 430.
109. "CBS Is Firm in Row with America First," *New York Times*, October 26, 1941, 16.
110. "$10,000 to Combat Lindbergh Is Sought from Movie Unit of Friends of Democracy," *New York Times*, October 31, 1941, 3.
111. December 7, 1941 journal entry, box 3, folder 1, Charles Augustus Lindbergh Papers.
112. December 8, 1941 journal entry, box 3, folder 1, Charles Augustus Lindbergh Papers.

113. December 8, 1941 journal entry, box 3, folder 1, Charles Augustus Lindbergh Papers.
114. Cf. Cole, vii.
115. Cf. Berg, 437.
116. Letter from Perkins from P. N. Loxley, November 29, 1941, FO 1093/167/1.
117. Report on the America First Committee, 1941, p. 10, FO 1093/167/1.
118. "America First," address by Donald Trump, delivered at the Mayflower Hotel, Washington, DC, April 27, 2016, *Vital Speeches of the Day*.
119. Reidy Reid, "America First!" musical score and lyrics, Dixie Music Pub. Company, 1941.

8. The Spies

1. Frederic Sondern Jr. "Captain Fritz: Consul Wiedemann, Hitler's Old Superior Officer Runs into Trouble Selling Nazism to West," *Life*, June 26, 1939, 26, 28. See also memorandum for Mr. Justice Jackson regarding Wiedemann, October 11, 1945, Donovan Nuremberg Trials Collection, Cornell University Law School, http://lawcollections.library.cornell.edu/nuremberg/catalog/nur:01939.
2. "No Politics, Declares Hitler Diplomat in Bay Area," *Oakland Tribune*, March 8, 1939, 1.
3. Sondern, 28.
4. Sondern, 28.
5. Breuer, 113.
6. "Wiedemann, Captain Fritz," box 57, index cards, California Un-American Activities Committee Records.
7. J. C. Masterman, *The Double-Cross System in the War of 1939 to 1945* (Canberra: Australian National University Press, 1972), 36–38.
8. Thomas H. Etzold, "The (F)utility Factor: German Information Gathering in the United States, 1933–1941," *Military Affairs* 39 (2) (1975), 77–78.
9. Etzold, 78.
10. *History of the SIS Division*, vol. 2. FBI Vault.
11. Report from Sir F. White regarding conversation with Hoover, August 11, 1940, FO 371/24237.
12. Breuer, 116, 136.
13. "Bare Nazi Spy System in U.S. to House Quiz," *Chicago Tribune*, October 17, 1934, 10.
14. MacDonnell, 50–51.
15. MacDonnell, 50.
16. Leon G. Turrou and David G. Wittels, *The Nazi Spy Conspiracy in America* (London: G. G. Harrap, 1939), 35–36; MacDonnell, 52–53.
17. MacDonnell, 53.
18. Turrou and Wittels, 46–47; MacDonnell, 55.
19. Turrou and Wittels, 46–51; MacDonnell, 55.
20. Cf. MacDonnell, 56; Turrou and Wittels, 223–25.
21. MacDonnell, 61.
22. MacDonnell, 62–63.

23. MacDonnell, 71.
24. Sondern, 28; Breuer, 109. See also "Appointment of Captain Wiedemann as German Consul General in San Francsico," February 8, 1939, C 1614/1168/18, FO 371/23055.
25. "New German Counsel Greeted in N.Y.," *Oakland Tribune*, March 4, 1939, 1.
26. February 20, 1939, report: "German Activities in the United States," C 2138/94/18, FO 371/23035.
27. Sondern, 28.
28. Grzesinsky and Hewitt Jr., 12.
29. Jim Wilson, *Nazi Princess: Hitler, Lord Rothermere, and Princess Stephanie Von Hohenlohe* (Stroud: History Press, 2011), 156.
30. Higham, 133.
31. "Appointment of Captain Wiedemann as German Consul General in San Francisco," May 29, 1939, C 7562/1168/18, FO 371/23055.
32. Memorandum for Mr. Justice Jackson regarding Wiedemann, October 11, 1945, pp. 27–35, Donovan Nuremberg Trials Collection, http://lawcollections.library .cornell.edu/nuremberg/catalog/nur:01939.
33. Memorandum for Mr. Justice Jackson regarding Wiedemann, October 11, 1945, p. 31, Donovan Nuremberg Trials Collection, http://lawcollections.library.cornell.edu /nuremberg/catalog/nur:01939.
34. Memorandum for Mr. Justice Jackson regarding Wiedemann, October 11, 1945, pp. 6–7, Donovan Nuremberg Trials Collection, http://lawcollections.library.cornell .edu/nuremberg/catalog/nur:01939.
35. Memorandum for Mr. Justice Jackson regarding Wiedemann, October 11, 1945, p. 27, Donovan Nuremberg Trials Collection, http://lawcollections.library.cornell.edu /nuremberg/catalog/nur:01939.
36. "So They Say," *Bakersfield Californian*, December 12, 1939, 18.
37. Sondern, 28.
38. Report on Princess Stephanie von Hohenlohe, p. 1, box 3, safe files, President's Secretary file, Franklin D. Roosevelt Presidential Library & Museum.
39. Karina Urbach, *Go-Betweens for Hitler* (Oxford: Oxford University Press, 2015), 219–22.
40. Urbach, 234–38.
41. Cf. Urbach, 244.
42. July 20, 1938 Cabinet minutes, CAB 23/94/6 p. 194 UK National Archives, Urbach, 259–60.
43. Urbach, 267–68.
44. Urbach, 271.
45. Report on Princess Stephanie von Hohenlohe, p. 1, box 3, safe files, President's Secretary file, Franklin D. Roosevelt Presidential Library & Museum.
46. "Neutrals 'Jittery,' Baroness Reports," *Oakland Tribune*, November 17, 1939, 21.
47. Confidential memorandum on Gerald O. Wootten, April 9, 1940, Cypher from Lord Lothian to Foreign Office, April 13, 1940: Captain Wiedemann, C 5452/520/18, FO 371/24419.
48. Confidential memorandum on Gerald O. Wootten, April 9, 1940, Cypher from Lord Lothian to Foreign Office, April 13, 1940: Captain Wiedemann, C 5452/520/18, FO 371/24419.
49. Message from Butler, San Francisco, to Lord Lothian, April 26, 1940, April 9, 1940,

Cypher from Lord Lothian to Foreign Office, April 13, 1940: Captain Wiedemann, C 5452/520/18, FO 371/24419.

50. Letter from Foreign Office to Washington Chancery, April 18, 1940, Cypher from Lord Lothian to Foreign Office, April 13, 1940: Captain Wiedemann, C 5452/520/18, FO 371/24419.

51. Minutes cover page, Cypher from Lord Lothian to Foreign Office, April 13, 1940: Captain Wiedemann, C 5452/520/18, FO 371/24419.

52. Dispatch from Consul General Butler, San Francisco, to Foreign Office, October 29, 1940, C 11558/520/18, FO 371/24419.

53. The testimony of Fritz Wiedemann/Headquarters/Office of Strategic Services/China Theater, Donovan Nuremberg Trials Collection, http://lawcollections.library .cornell.edu/nuremberg/catalog/nur:01141.

54. Confidential memorandum on Gerald O. Wootten, April 9, 1940, p. 5, Cypher from Lord Lothian to Foreign Office, April 13, 1940: Captain Wiedemann, C 5452/520/18, FO 371/24419.

55. Secret letter C/5097, October 7, 1940, FO 371/24419.

56. Urbach, 277–78.

57. "Woman Cites German Agent as Spy Chief," *Democrat and Chronicle* [Rochester, New York], March 6, 1941, 6; "Ford and Lindbergh Linked with Nazi Consul in Suit," *Great Falls Tribune* [Montana], March 6, 1941, 2.

58. "Court Dismisses Wiedemann Suit," *Arizona Republic*, June 10, 1941, 8.

59. Weber, *Hitler's First War: Adolf Hitler, the Men of the List Regiment, and the First World War* (Oxford: Oxford University Press, 2010), 325.

60. Wilson, 162–63.

61. "Frederick Duquesne Interesting Case Write-Up," FBI Vault.

62. Etzold, 79.

63. "Counter-Espionage: U.S. Detectives Worked German Transmitter," *Manchester Guardian*, September 10, 1941, 8.

64. "Frederick Duquesne Interesting Case Write-Up," FBI Vault.

65. *History of the SIS Division*, vol. 2, p. 435, FBI Vault.

66. "Auto Death Started FBI on Spy Trail," *St. Louis Star-Times*, February 7, 1942, 3.

67. MacDonnell, 128–29.

68. Alice Hughes, "A Woman's New York," *Indianapolis Star*, March 31, 1942, 6; "Spy for Fun," *Daily Times-Tribune* [Alexandria, Indiana], March 27, 1942, 1.

69. Martha Strayer, "This War's Mata Haris a Sad, Stupid Lot," *Pittsburgh Press*, September 17, 1944, 1.

70. "Girl, 19, Who Found Spying 'Lots of Fun,' Gets 5 Years," *St. Louis Post-Dispatch*, March 20, 1942, 4C.

71. Charles Wighton and Günter Peis, *They Spied on England: Based on the German Secret Service War Diary of General von Lahousen* (London: Odhams Press, 1958), 199–202.

72. Louis Fisher, *Nazi Saboteurs on Trial: A Military Tribunal and American Law* (Lawrence, KS: University Press of Kansas, 2003), 6–9.

73. Memorandum on saboteurs, July 20, 1942, CIA-RDP13X00001R000100170004-2, CIA CREST Archive.

74. Wighton and Peis, 207.

75. Fisher, 28–29, Wighton and Peis, 212–14.

76. Fisher, 29–32.
77. Wighton and Peis, 221–23.
78. Wighton and Peis, 224–28.
79. Wighton and Peis, 228–29.
80. Fisher, 46.
81. Cf. Wighton and Peis, 234.
82. Fisher, 43.
83. *Ex parte Quirin* (1942), *FindLaw*, http://caselaw.findlaw.com/us-supreme-court/317/1
    .html.
84. Wighton and Peis, 235–36.
85. Wighton and Peis, 236–37; MacDonnell, 133.

Afterword

1. Diamond, 344.
2. Diamond, 345.
3. Diamond, 351.
4. Diamond, 350.
5. Metcalfe, 41.
6. La Vern J. Rippley, *The German-Americans, The Immigrant Heritage of America*
   (Boston: Twayne Publishers, 1976), 211.
7. John Roy Carlson, *Under Cover: My Four Years in the Nazi Underworld of America—
   The Amazing Revelation of How Axis Agents and Our Enemies within Are Now Plotting
   to Destroy the United States* (New York: E.P. Dutton, 1943), TK.
8. Memorandum for Mr. Ladd, January 2, 1944, file 5C, Walter Winchell FBI files, FBI
   Vault.
9. Memorandum for Mr. Ladd, October 17, 1943, file 5B, Walter Winchell FBI files, FBI
   Vault.
10. Cypher to Blanketing, London, from Charles des Graz, February 26, 1942; Letter
    from Hyde to Des Graz, February 23, 1942, DEFE 1/205.
11. William Samuel Stephenson, ed. *British Security Coordination: The Secret History of
    British Intelligence in the Americas, 1940–1945*, 1st Fromm international ed. (New
    York: Fromm International, 1999), 80.
12. Viereck v. United States, 318 U.S. 236 (1943), *Justia*, https://supreme.justia.com/cases
    /federal/us/318/236/case.html.
13. Maximilian St.-George, Lawrence Dennis, and National Civil Rights Committee. *A
    Trial on Trial: The Great Sedition Trial of 1944* (N.p.: National Civil Rights Commit-
    tee, 1946), 115.
14. Rogge, 173.
15. St.-George et al., 91.
16. St.-George et al., 116.
17. St.-George et al., 109.
18. Stephenson, 80.
19. Letter from Frederick L. Schuman to Lawrence Dennis, April 27, 1944, folder 8, box 5,
    Lawrence Dennis Papers; Richard Gid Powers, *Not Without Honor: The History of Amer-
    ican Anticommunism* (New Haven, CT; London: Yale University Press, 1998), 186–87.

20. Johnson, 248.
21. Johnson, 248.
22. Winrod "Prayer Circle" letter, December 13, 1944, box 1A, folder 81, Gerald B. Winrod Papers.
23. "Sedition Trial Ends; New One Is Up to Biddle," *Chicago Tribune*, December 8, 1944, 9.
24. St.-George et al.
25. Horne, 149–50.
26. Horne, 175–77.
27. Beekman, 142–23, 146–47, 154–55, 160–61.
28. Montgomery, 91.
29. Montgomery, 92–93.
30. Montgomery, 98–101.
31. Warren, 276–90.
32. Warren, 291–92.
33. Marcus, 222.
34. Harry Cook, "Fiery '30s Radio Priest Father Coughlin Dies," *Detroit Free Press*, October 28, 1979, 9A.
35. Cf. Marcus, 224.
36. Marcus, 232.
37. Jeansonne, 84.
38. Jeansonne, 89, 95; Gerald L. K. Smith FBI files, FBI Vault.
39. Bennett, 285; Jeansonne, 120, 138, 159.
40. Jeansonne, 165–67.
41. Jeansonne, 217.
42. Johnson, 252.
43. "George Sylvester Viereck Dies; Poet, Propagandist," *St. Louis Post-Dispatch* March 20, 1962, 18.
44. Classified 1966 message on von Strempel, file 26, von Strempel files, Nazi War Crimes Disclosure Act, CIA CREST.
45. Memorandum von Strempel, file 15, p. 2; Memo to Chief, Foreign Branch "M," April 2, 1948, file 22, von Strempel files, Nazi War Crimes Disclosure Act, CIA CREST.
46. Dispatch MGH-A-2573, file 18, von Strempel files, Nazi War Crimes Disclosure Act, CIA CREST.
47. Agent service record, file 24, von Strempel files, Nazi War Crimes Disclosure Act, CIA CREST.
48. Classified 1966 message on von Strempel, file 27, von Strempel files, Nazi War Crimes Disclosure Act, CIA CREST.
49. Memorandum for Mr. Ladd, December 26, 1943, p. 2, file 5C, Walter Winchell FBI file, FBI Vault.
50. Michael Sayers and Albert E. Kahn, *Sabotage: The Secret War Against America* (New York, London: Harper and Brothers: 1942), 195.
51. Henry Reed Hoke, *Black Mail* (New York: Reader's Book Service, 1944), 35–37; "Henry Hoke, Author and Trade Editor," *New York Times*, November 23, 1970, 40.
52. Stephenson, 80.

53. "Hamilton Fish; Feisty Critic of FDR," *Los Angeles Times*, January 20, 1991, A42.

54. Letter from Wheeler to Sokolsky, February 29, 1944, folder 1, box 122, George E. Sokolsky Papers, Hoover Institution.

55. "Burton K. Wheeler, Former Senator, 92," *Times Record* [Troy, New York], January 7, 1975, 178; "Gerald P. Nye Dies; Former U.S. Senator," *Hartford Courant* [Connecticut], July 19, 1971, 10.

56. Harrington, 205.

57. Harrington, 206.

58. Harrington, 206–7.

59. Harrington, 207–8.

60. Office memorandum on O. John Rogge, January 2, 1947, O. John Rogge FBI file, file 1, FBI Vault.

61. Office memorandum on O. John Rogge, March 25, 1947, April 28, 1947, O. John Rogge FBI file, file 1, FBI Vault.

62. Office memorandum on O. John Rogge, January 22, 1951, O. John Rogge FBI file, file 1, FBI Vault.

63. Letter from J. Edgar Hoover to Rogge, June 12, 1957, O. John Rogge FBI file, file 1, FBI Vault.

64. Harold J. Wiegand, "Old Nazi Moves in U.S. and Neo-Nazis of Today," *Philadelphia Inquirer*, September 20, 1961, 20.

65. "Attacks Involved Those on Both Sides of the Iron Curtain," *Los Angeles Times*, March 30, 1981, 34.

66. Pendergrast, 222–26.

67. Billstein, 141–42.

68. Billstein, 142.

69. Billstein, 157.

70. Baldwin, 315.

71. Higham, 160–61.

72. Baldwin, 316; Richard Bak, *Henry and Edsel: The Creation of the Ford Empire* (Hoboken, NJ: John Wiley & Sons, 2003), 257–58.

73. Baldwin, 316–17.

74. "Henry Ford Never Wanted His Company to Go Public," *Automotive News*, June 16, 2003, http://www.autonews.com/article/20030616/SUB/306160730/henry -ford-never-wanted-his-company-to-go-public.

75. Iwanowa v. Ford Motor Co., 67 F. Supp. 2d 424 (D.N.J. 1999), October 28, 1999, *Justia*, http://law.justia.com/cases/federal/district-courts/FSupp2/67/424/2375384/.

76. Billstein, 239–40.

77. Billstein, 244–45.

78. "Conclusion," Iwanowa v. Ford Motor Co., 67 F. Supp. 2d 424 (D.N.J. 1999), October 28, 1999, *Justia*, http://law.justia.com/cases/federal/district-courts/FSupp2/67 /424/2375384/.

79. Turner, 125.

80. Drew Pearson, "U.S. Attitude Feeds Distrust," *Emporia Daily Gazette* [Kansas], April 26, 1945, 4.

81. Higham, 215; Martin, 24. Martin does not mention that he was the one to send Army HQ the book.

82. Higham, 222.
83. Higham, 215–16; Martin, 52–53.
84. "Ford Motor Company: Satisfactory Achievements," *Manchester Guardian*, May 10, 1950, 8.
85. Esther van Wagoner Tufty, "Michigan in Washington," *Port Huron Times Herald*, March 4, 1949, 9.
86. "Obituaries," *Chicago Daily Tribune*, December 8, 1962, 85; "G. K. Howard, Retired Ford VP, Dies," *Detroit Free Press*, December 8, 1962, 15.
87. Turner, 141.
88. Turner, 142–45.
89. Turner, 148–49.
90. Turner, 158.
91. "Peace Envoy's Oil Helps British in War," *Salt Lake Tribune*, August 17, 1941, 6A.
92. "Oil Man Davis' Estate Put at Five to 10 Million," *St. Louis Post-Dispatch*, September 6, 1941, 5.
93. "Guffey Is Uncovered as Figure in Oil Deal Made by Nazi Agent," *Pittsburgh Press*, October 22, 1946, 1.
94. "Bares Boyle Aid to Settle Tax Claim for 3 Pct," *Chicago Daily Tribune*, June 27, 1952, 9.
95. Bill Boyarsky, "Bradley Campaign Leader to Seek State Treasurer's Post," *Los Angeles Times*, January 3, 1974, 6.
96. Patt Morrison, "There Was Much to Love About the Inauguration," *Los Angeles Times*, November 18, 2003; Valerie J. Nelson, "Doris Meyer Morell, 83; Mother of Gray Davis Helped in His Campaigns," *Los Angeles Times*, October 4, 2006, B9; "Obituary: Armand Martin Morell," *Palm Beach Post*, September 29, 2007, 6B.
97. Nelson, "Doris Meyer Morell"; David Ferrell, "Davis' Friends Fall Away, Ambition Endures," *Los Angeles Times*, October 10, 2002, http://articles.latimes.com/2002/oct /10/local/me-davis10.
98. Zieger, 119–25.
99. Zieger, 132–34; Dubofsky and Van Tine, 404–5.
100. Dubofsky and Van Tine, 467–69.
101. Dubofsky and Van Tine, 528.
102. Dubofsky and Van Tine, 528.
103. Zieger, 181.
104. Cf. Berg, 437.
105. Berg, 449–53.
106. Gallup Organization, Gallup Poll (AIPO), April 1942 [survey question]. USGALLUP .42-265.QT08C. Gallup Organization [producer]. Cornell University, Ithaca, NY: Roper Center for Public Opinion Research, iPOLL [distributor].
107. Berg, 485, 490, 501.
108. Berg, 537.
109. Berg, 560.
110. Scripps Howard News Service/Ohio University. Scripps Howard News Service/Ohio University Poll, July 1994 [survey question]. USSCRIPP.94SH08.R09K. Scripps Howard News Service/Ohio University [producer]. Cornell University, Ithaca, NY: Roper Center for Public Opinion Research, iPOLL [distributor].

111. "Student America First Organization Here Is Approved," *Evening Star Journal* [Lincoln, Nebraska], October 24, 1941, 9.
112. Letter from Stuart to Wood, copying Regnery, February 14, 1963, folder 18, box 2, Henry Regnery Papers, Hoover Institution.
113. Letter from Regnery to Wayne S. Cole, June 25, 1951, folder 18, box 2, Henry Regnery Papers.
114. "Robert D. Stuart Jr. 1916–2014: Ex-CEO of Quaker Oats, U.S. Ambassador," *Chicago Tribune*, May 14, 2014, sec. 2, p. 6.
115. Copy of Madden CV, sent to "Mr. Robinson," June 25, 1946, Correspondence—1946, Henry Madden Papers, University Archives, Henry Madden Library.
116. "Record Number of Grads Is Shadow of Future," *Fresno Bee*, June 2, 1964, 41.
117. "Passages," *Democrat and Chronicle* [Rochester, NY], December 21, 1990, 4; "U of O Historian to Evaluate Teaching Abroad," *Eugene Register-Guard* [Oregon], June 27, 1963, 20.
118. Fisher, 175.
119. Wighton and Peis, 237.
120. George J. Dasch, *Eight Spies against America* (New York: Robert M. McBride Company, 1959).
121. Seth Kantor, "He Expected Reward, But Was Delivered to Enemies," *Philadelphia Inquirer*, July 8, 1980, 6A [from p. 1A]; David Johnson, *Betrayal: The True Story of J. Edgar Hoover and the Nazi Saboteurs Captured During WWII*, (New York: Hippocrene Books, 2007), 258.
122. Breuer, 321–24.
123. A search of the database Newspapers.com reveals no hits for "Lucy Boehmler" after October 1946.
124. Wighton and Peis, 320.
125. Wighton and Peis, 318.
126. Breuer, 318–19.
127. Urbach, 277–78.
128. Urbach, 314.
129. "Wiedemann, Former Adjutant of Hitler, Fined as Minor Nazi," *Chicago Tribune*, November 18, 1948, 26; Weber, 341.
130. Clay Gowran, "TV Today: ABC Presents Unique Story of Third Reich," *Chicago Tribune*, March 3, 1968, sec. 10.
131. "State's Historical Society in Expansion," *San Bernardino Daily Sun* [California], May 15, 1956, 18.
132. "Deposition of Kate Eva Hoerlin," *Nazi Conspiracy and Aggression*, vol. 7, pp. 883–88.
133. "Intelligence Papers Reveal How Hitler's Close Ally Sought the Help of the British," August 17, 2012, Aberdeen University, https://www.abdn.ac.uk/news/4447/.
134. Speech by Dies on NBC Radio, December 2, 1940, box 157, file 51, Martin Dies Papers. Capitalization of "Nazi" has been changed from original for consistency.

BIBLIOGRAPHY

ARCHIVAL MATERIAL

American Jewish Committee Archive [available online]
Report on William Dudley Pelley [available online]

California State Archives, Sacramento, California
California Un-American Activities Committee Records

Central Intelligence Agency Freedom of Information Act Electronic Reading Room
Nazi War Crimes Disclosure Act Files [available online]

Charles E. Young Research Library, Special Collections, University of California, Los Angeles
Hollywood Anti-Nazi League Papers

Churchill Archives Centre, Cambridge
Lord Lloyd of Dolobran (George Lloyd) Papers

Law Library, Cornell University Law School
Donovan Nuremberg Trials Collection, Cornell University Law School [available online]

Federal Bureau of Investigation FOIA Vault [available online]
Charles Lindbergh
German American Federation/Bund
Rosenberg Case: O. John Rogge
History of the SIS Division
Walter Winchell
Gerald L.K. Smith

Franklin Delano Roosevelt Presidential Library & Museum, Hyde Park, New York
The President's Secretary's File (PSF), 1933–1945

Henry Madden Library, Special Collections, Research Center, California State University, Fresno
Henry Madden Papers

Hoover Institution, Library & Archives Stanford University
America First Committee Records
Joseph Hansen Papers
Lawrence Dennis Papers
George E. Sokolsky Papers
German American Bund Records
Ernest Lundeen Papers
Henry Regnery Papers
John C. Metcalfe Papers
Truman Smith Papers
Walter Winchell Miscellaneous Papers

Labor Archives and Research Center, J. Paul Leonard Library, San Francisco State University
California Surveillance Papers

Mennonite Library and Archives, Bethel College, North Newton, Kansas
John Jakob Kroeker Papers

Missouri History Museum, St. Louis, Missouri
Charles Augustus Lindbergh Papers

National Archives, London
Cabinet Papers (CAB)
Foreign Office Papers (FO)
Ministry of Defence Papers (DEFE)

National Archives of Scotland, Edinburgh
Phillip Kerr, 11th Marquess of Lothian Papers

National Archives [US], College Park, Maryland
FBI Files (Record Group 65)

Roper Center for Public Opinion Research, Cornell University
iPoll Databank [available online]

Sam Houston Regional Library and Research Center, Texas State Library and Archives Commission, Liberty, Texas
Martin Dies Jr. Papers

University of Washington Libraries, Special Collections, Seattle, Washington
Silver Legion of America, Washington State Division Records
Nathan Krems Papers

Wichita State University Libraries Special Collections, Kansas
Reverend Dr. Gerald Burton Winrod Papers

NEWSPAPER AND PERIODICAL SOURCES
*denotes papers available online in Newspapers.com database

Altoona Tribune [Pennsylvania]*
*Arizona Republic**
*Automotive News**
*The Bakersfield Californian**
Barron's
Binghamton Press [New York]*
*Brooklyn Eagle**
California Daily Bruin
*Chicago Daily Tribune**
Chicago *Times**
*The Cincinnati Enquirer**
Columbia Daily Spectator
Congressional Record
The Daily Independent [Murphysboro, Illinois]*
Daily Times [Chicago]
The Daily Times-Tribune [Alexandria, Indiana]
Democrat and Chronicle [Rochester, New York]*
*The Des Moines Register**
*The Detroit Free Press**
The Emporia Daily Gazette [Kansas]*
Evening Star Journal [Lincoln, Nebraska]*
Eugene Register-Guard [Oregon]
Foreign Policy
*The Fresno Bee**
Garrett Clipper [Garrett, Indiana]*
The Gazette and Daily [York, Pennsylvania]*
Great Falls Tribune [Montana]*
The Hartford Courant [Connecticut]*
*The Indianapolis Star**
The Iola Register [Kansas]*
*The Ithaca Journal**
The Jewish Veteran
The Kane Republican [Pennsylvania]*
Life
The Lincoln Star [Nebraska]*

Long Beach Independent [California]*
*Los Angeles Times**
*The Manchester Guardian**
Marshfield News-Herald [Wisconsin]*
Mason City Globe-Gazette [Iowa]*
New Castle News [Pennsylvania]*
New York Enquirer
The New York Times
The News-Herald [Franklin, Pennsylvania]*
*Oakland Tribune**
*The Palm Beach Post**
The Palm Beach Post-Times [Florida]*
*The Philadelphia Inquirer**
*The Pittsburgh Press**
PM [New York]
Politico
Port Huron Times Herald [Michigan]*
*The Salt Lake Tribune**
San Bernardino Daily Sun [California]*
San Mateo Times [California]*
*Santa Cruz Sentinel**
Scribner's
*St. Louis Post-Dispatch**
St. Louis Star-Times
The Stanford Daily
The State Journal [Lansing, Michigan]*
The Times [London]
The Times Record [Troy, New York]*
The Washington Post
Weekly Town Talk [Alexandria, Louisiana]*
*The Wisconsin Jewish Chronicle**
*Wisconsin Rapids Daily Tribune**
World [New York]
The Zanesville Signal [Ohio]*

PRINTED SOURCES

"German Enrollment in American Institutions of Higher Learning." *German Quarterly* 7, no. 4 (1934): 129–44.

"German University Summer Schools." *Monatshefte für Deutschen Unterricht* 27, no. 4 (1935): 149–50.

"Iwanowa v. Ford Motor Co., 67 F. Supp. 2d 424 (D.N.J. 1999)," Justia, http://law.justia .com/cases/federal/district-courts/FSupp2/67/424/2375384/.

"Nazi Education." *School Life* (1934): 113.

"Viereck v. United States 318 U.S. 236," Justia, https://supreme.justia.com/cases/federal/us/318/236/.

Alinsky, Saul David. *John L. Lewis: An Unauthorized Biography.* New York: Putnam, 1949.

Badger, Anthony J. *New Deal/New South: An Anthony J. Badger Reader.* Fayetteville: University of Arkansas Press, 2007.

Bak, Richard. *Henry and Edsel: The Creation of the Ford Empire.* Hoboken, NJ: John Wiley & Sons, 2003.

Baldwin, Neil. *Henry Ford and the Jews: the Mass Production of Hate.* New York, NY: Public Affairs, 2001.

Beard, Charles A. "Education under the Nazis." *Foreign Affairs* 14, no. 3 (1936): 437–52.

Beekman, Scott. *William Dudley Pelley: A Life in Right-Wing Extremism and the Occult.* 1st ed. Religion and Politics. Syracuse, NY: Syracuse University Press, 2005.

Bennett, David Harry. *Demagogues in the Depression: American Radicals and the Union Party, 1932–1936.* New Brunswick, NJ: Rutgers University Press, 1969.

Berg, A. Scott. *Lindbergh.* London: Macmillan, 1998.

Bernstein, Arnie. *Swastika Nation: Fritz Kuhn and the Rise and Fall of the German-American Bund.* 1st ed. ed. New York: St. Martin's Press, 2013.

Billstein, Reinhold. "How the Americans Took Over Cologne—and Discovered Ford Werke's Role in the War." In Billstein, Reinhold, Karola Fings, Anita Kugler, and Nicholas Levis, eds. *Working for the Enemy: Ford, General Motors, and Forced Labor in Germany During the Second World War.* New York: Berghahn Books, 2000.

Black, Edwin. *IBM and the Holocaust: The Strategic Alliance between Nazi Germany and America's Most Powerful Corporation.* 1st ed. New York: Crown Publishers, 2001.

———. *Nazi Nexus: America's Corporate Connections to Hitler's Holocaust.* Washington, DC: Dialog Press, 2009.

Breuer, William B. *Hitler's Undercover War: The Nazi Espionage Invasion of the U.S.A.* 1st ed. New York: St. Martin's Press, 1989.

Canedy, Susan. *America's Nazis: A Democratic Dilemma: A History of the German American Bund.* Menlo Park, CA: Markgraf Publications Group, 1990.

Carlson, John Roy. *Under Cover: My Four Years in the Nazi Underworld of America—The Amazing Revelation of How Axis Agents and Our Enemies within Are Now Plotting to Destroy the United States.* New York: E.P. Dutton, 1943.

Carpenter, Ronald H. *Father Charles E. Coughlin: Surrogate Spokesman for the Disaffected.* Great American Orators. Westport, CT: Greenwood Press, 1998.

Ceplair, Larry, and Steven Englund. *The Inquisition in Hollywood: Politics in the Film Community 1930–1960.* Berkeley, CA.: University of California Press, 1983.

Cole, Wayne S. *Senator Gerald P. Nye and American Foreign Relations.* Minneapolis: University of Minnesota Press, 1962.

———. *America First: The Battle against Intervention, 1940–1941.* New York: Octagon Books, 1971.

Commons, John R. "Review: *The Coming American Fascism* by Lawrence Dennis." *American Economic Review* 26, no. 2 (1936): 298–300.

Coughlin, Charles E. *A Series of Lectures on Social Justice, 1935–1936, Broadcast.* Royal Oak, MI,: The Radio League of the Little Flower, 1936.

Cowley, W. H., and Willard Waller. "A Study of Student Life." *Journal of Higher Education* 6, no. 3 (1935): 132–42.

Cruickshank, E. W. H. "Impressions of Nazi Germany." *Dalhousie Review* 13, no. 4 (1934): 410–11.

Dasch, G. J. *Eight Spies against America*. New York: Robert M. McBride, 1959.

Dennis, Lawrence. *The Coming American Fascism*. 1st ed. New York: Harper, 1936.

Denton, Sally. *The Plots against the President: FDR, a Nation in Crisis, and the Rise of the American Right*. 1st US ed. New York: Bloomsbury Press, 2012.

Diamond, Sander A. *The Nazi Movement in the United States, 1924–1941*. Film and Culture. Ithaca, NY: Cornell University Press, 1974.

Diggins, John P. *Mussolini and Fascism: The View from America*. Princeton University Press, 1972.

Doherty, Thomas Patrick. *Hollywood and Hitler, 1933–1939*. Film and Culture. New York: Columbia University Press, 2015.

Dubofsky, Melvyn, and Warren R. Van Tine. *John L. Lewis: A Biography*. New York: Quadrangle/New York Times Book Co., 1977.

Dunn, Susan. *1940: FDR, Willkie, Lindbergh, Hitler: The Election Amid the Storm*. New Haven, CT: Yale University Press, 2013.

Etzold, Thomas H. "The (F)utility Factor: German Information Gathering in the United States, 1933–1941." *Military Affairs* 39, no. 2 (1975): 77–82.

Evans, Richard J. *The Third Reich in Power, 1933–1939*. New York: Penguin Press, 2005.

Fisher, Louis. *Nazi Saboteurs on Trial: A Military Tribunal and American Law*. Lawrence, KS.: University Press of Kansas, 2003.

Frye, Alton. *Nazi Germany and the American Hemisphere, 1933–1941*. Yale Historical Publications Miscellany. New Haven, CT: Yale University Press, 1967.

Gabler, Neal. *Winchell: Gossip, Power, and the Culture of Celebrity*. 1st ed. New York: Knopf, 1994.

Gellermann, William. *Martin Dies*. New York: John Day Company, 1944.

Gerber, Michele Stenehjem. *An American First: John T. Flynn and the America First Committee*. New Rochelle, NY: Arlington House Publishers, 1976.

Gillingham, John. *Industry and Politics in the Third Reich: Ruhr Coal, Hitler, and Europe*. New York: Columbia University Press, 1985.

Glancy, Mark. *When Hollywood Loved Britain: The Hollywood "British" Film 1939–45*. Manchester: Manchester University Press, 1999.

Grill, Johnpeter Horst, and Robert L. Jenkins. "The Nazis and the American South in the 1930s: A Mirror Image?" *Journal of Southern History* 58 (4) (1992): 667–94.

Hanfstaengl, Ernst. *Hitler: The Missing Years*. London: Eyre & Spottiswoode, 1957.

Harrington, Dale. *Mystery Man: William Rhodes Davis, Nazi Agent of Influence*. 1st ed. Dulles, VA: Brassey's, 1999.

Hart, Bradley W. *George Pitt-Rivers and the Nazis*. London, New York: Bloomsbury Academic, 2015.

Higham, Charles. *Trading with the Enemy: An Exposé of the Nazi-American Money Plot, 1933–1949*. New York: Delacorte Press, 1983.

Hitler, Adolf. *Hitler's Table Talk, 1941–1944: His Private Conversations*. Translated by Norman Cameron and R. H. Stevens. 3d ed. London: Phoenix, 2000.

Hoke, Henry Reed. *Black Mail*. New York: Reader's Book Service, 1944.

Horne, Gerald. *The Color of Fascism: Lawrence Dennis, Racial Passing, and the Rise of Right-Wing Extremism in the United States.* New York: New York University Press, 2006.

Howard, Graeme Keith. *America and a New World Order.* New York: C. Scribner's Sons, 1940.

Jeansonne, Glen. *Gerald L. K. Smith, Minister of Hate.* New Haven, CT: Yale University Press, 1988.

Johnson, Niel M. *George Sylvester Viereck, German-American Propagandist.* Urbana: University of Illinois Press, 1972.

Juhnke, James C. *A People of Two Kingdoms: The Political Acculturation of the Kansas Mennonites.* Mennonite Historical Series. Newton, KS.: Faith and Life Press, 1975.

Kandel, I. L. "Education in Nazi Germany." *Annals of the American Academy of Political and Social Science* 182 (1935): 153–63.

Keller, Phyllis. *States of Belonging: German-American Intellectuals and the First World War.* Cambridge, MA; London: Harvard University Press, 1979.

Kershaw, Ian. *Hitler: 1889–1936: Hubris.* London: Allen Lane, 1998.

Langworth, Richard M. "Tangling with the Media: The Curious Case of William Griffin." *Finest Hour* 152 (Autumn 2011).

Lawrence, David. *Diary of a Washington Correspondent.* New York: H.C. Kinsey & Company, 1942.

Letts, Malcolm. *Nazi Germany: "I Lived with the Brown Shirts."* Los Angeles: M. Letts, 1933.

Lothian, Philip Henry Kerr. *Lord Lothian vs. Lord Lothian: Excerpts from the Speeches and Writings of the Marquess of Lothian, British Ambassador to the United States.* Scotch Plains, NJ,: Flanders Hall, 1940.

Louis, J. C., and Harvey Yazijian. *The Cola Wars.* 1st ed. New York: Everest House, 1980.

MacDonnell, Francis. *Insidious Foes: The Axis Fifth Column and the American Home Front.* New York: Oxford University Press, 1995.

Marcus, Sheldon. *Father Coughlin: The Tumultuous Life of the Priest of the Little Flower.* 1st ed. Boston: Little, Brown, 1973.

Martin, James Stewart. *All Honorable Men.* 1st ed. Boston: Little, Brown, 1950.

Masterman, J. C. *The Double-Cross System in the War of 1939 to 1945.* Canberra: Australian National University Press, 1972.

Mayer, Jane. *Dark Money: The Hidden History of the Billionaires Behind the Rise of the Radical Right.* 1st ed. New York: Doubleday, 2016.

Metcalfe, Howard Hurtig. *Die Familie Oberwinder: Genealogical Encyclopedia of the Family Connections of Richard Maria Wilhe[l]m Oberwinder.* Decorah, Iowa: Anundsen Pub., 1999.

Montgomery, G. H. *Gerald Burton Winrod: Defender of the Faith.* Wichita, KS: Mertmont Publishers, 1965.

Mugglebee, Ruth. *Father Coughlin, the Radio Priest, of the Shrine of the Little Flower.* Garden City, NY: Garden City Publishing Co., 1933.

Myers, Gustavus. *History of Bigotry in the United States.* New York: Random House, 1943.

Norwood, Stephen H. *The Third Reich in the Ivory Tower: Complicity and Conflict on American Campuses.* Cambridge: Cambridge University Press, 2009.

Office of United States Chief of Counsel for Prosecution of Axis Criminality. United States Department of State, United States War Department, and International Military Tribunal. *Nazi Conspiracy and Aggression.* 8 vols. Washington, DC: United States Government Printing Office, 1946.

Olson, Lynne. *Those Angry Days: Roosevelt, Lindbergh, and America's Fight over World War II, 1939–1941*. 1st ed. New York: Random House, 2013.

Overacker, Louise. "Campaign Finance in the Presidential Election of 1940." *American Political Science Review* 35, no. 4 (1941): 701–27.

Payne, Stanley G. *A History of Fascism, 1914–1945*. London: UCL Press, 1995.

Pendergrast, Mark. *For God, Country and Coca-Cola: The Definitive History of the Great American Soft Drink and the Company That Makes It*. 3d ed. New York: Basic Books, 2013.

Powers, Richard Gid. *Not without Honor: The History of American Anticommunism*. New Haven, CT; London: Yale University Press, 1998.

Ribuffo, Leo P. *The Old Christian Right: The Protestant Far Right from the Great Depression to the Cold War*. Philadelphia: Temple University Press, 1983.

Rippley, La Vern J. *The German-Americans*. The Immigrant Heritage of America. Boston: Twayne Publishers, 1976.

Rogge, Oetje John. *The Official German Report: Nazi Penetration, 1924–1942*. New York: T. Yoseloff, 1961.

Russett, Bruce M. *No Clear and Present Danger: A Skeptical View of the United States Entry into World War II*. Harper Torchbooks. New York: Harper & Row, 1972.

Rust, Bernhard, and Ernst Krieck. *Das nationalsozialistische Deutschland und die Wissenschaft; Heidelberger Reden von Reichsminister Rust und prof. Ernst Krieck (National Socialist Germany and the Pursuit of Learning)*. Schriften des Reichsinstituts für Geschichte des Neuen Deutschlands. Hamburg: Hanseatische Verlagsanstalt, 1936.

Sherman, John W. *The Mexican Right: The End of Revolutionary Reform, 1929–1940*. Westport, CT; London: Praeger, 1997.

Silver Legion of America. *The Reds Are Upon Us: The First Council*, 1938.

Spivak, John L. *Plotting America's Pogroms: A Documented Exposé of Organized Anti-Semitism in the United States*. New York: New Masses, 1934.

St.-George, Maximilian, Lawrence Dennis, and National Civil Rights Committee. *A Trial on Trial: The Great Sedition Trial of 1944*. N.p.: National Civil Rights Committee, 1946.

Stephenson, William Samuel, ed. *British Security Coordination: The Secret History of British Intelligence in the Americas, 1940–1945*. 1st Fromm international ed. New York: Fromm International, 1999.

Stevenson, William. *A Man Called Intrepid: The Secret War*. 1st ed. New York: Harcourt Brace Jovanovich, 1976.

Sward, Keith. *The Legend of Henry Ford*. New York: Rinehart & Company, 1948.

Tooze, J. Adam. *The Wages of Destruction: The Making and Breaking of the Nazi Economy*. London, New York: Allen Lane, 2006.

Toy, Eckard V. "Silver Shirts in the Northwest: Politics, Prophecies, and Personalities in the 1930s." *Pacific Northwest Quarterly* 80(4) (1989): 139–46.

Tull, Charles J. *Father Coughlin and the New Deal*. Men and Movements. Syracuse, NY: Syracuse University Press, 1965.

Turner, Henry Ashby. *General Motors and the Nazis: The Struggle for Control of Opel, Europe's Biggest Carmaker*. New Haven, CT: Yale University Press, 2005.

Turrou, Leon G., and David G. Wittels. *The Nazi Spy Conspiracy in America*. London: G. G. Harrap, 1939.

United States Congress, House Special Committee on Un-American Activities (1938–1944). *Investigation of Un-American Propaganda Activities in the United States.* 17 vols. Washington, DC: United States Government Printing Office, 1938.

Urbach, Karina. *Go-Betweens for Hitler.* 1st ed. Oxford: Oxford University Press, 2015.

Urwand, Ben. *The Collaboration: Hollywood's Pact with Hitler.* Cambridge, MA: Belknap Press, 2013.

Viereck, George Sylvester. *Confessions of a Barbarian.* London: John Lane, Bodley Head, 1910.

Ward, Louis B. *Father Charles E. Coughlin: An Authorized Biography.* Detroit: Tower Publications, 1933.

Warren, Donald I. *Radio Priest: Charles Coughlin, the Father of Hate Radio.* New York: Free Press, 1996.

Weber, Thomas. *Hitler's First War: Adolf Hitler, the Men of the List Regiment, and the First World War.* Oxford: Oxford University Press, 2010.

Werth, Adolphus van. *It Happened Again: How the War Came.* Flanders Hall Book-of-the-Hour. Scotch Plains, NJ: Flanders Hall, 1940.

Wighton, Charles, and Gèunter Peis. *They Spied on England: Based on the German Secret Service War Diary of General von Lahousen.* London: Odhams Press, 1958.

Williamson, Walter W. *Heil Roosevelt: An American Student in Nazi Germany.* Philadelphia, PA: Xlibris, 2000.

Wilhelm, Cornelia. *Bewegung Oder Verein? Nationalsozialistische Volkstumspolitik in den USA.* Transatlantische Historische Studien. Stuttgart: F. Steiner, 1998.

Wilson, Jim. *Nazi Princess: Hitler, Lord Rothermere and Princess Stephanie von Hohenlohe.* Stroud: History Press, 2011.

Winrod, Gerald Burton. *Mussolini's Place in Prophecy.* Wichita, KS: Defender Publishers, 1933.

Zieger, Robert H. *John L. Lewis: Labor Leader.* Twayne's Twentieth-Century American Biography Series. Boston: Twayne Publishers, 1988.

INDEX